MW01003924

Titanic

ANATOMY OF A BLOCKBUSTER

EDITED BY

KEVIN S. SANDLER

GAYLYN STUDLAR

Rutgers University Press

New Brunswick, New Jersey, and London

Library of Congress Cataloging-in-Publication Data

Titanic : anatomy of a blockbuster / Kevin S. Sandler, Gaylyn Studlar, editors.
    p. cm.
    Includes bibliographical references and index.
    ISBN 0–8135–2668–X (cloth : alk. paper). — ISBN 0–8135–2669–8
(pbk. : alk. paper)
    1. Titanic (Motion picture : 1997)   I. Sandler, Kevin S., 1969– .
    II. Studlar, Gaylyn.
PN1997.T54T58 1999
791.43'72—dc21   98-55317
                                                                       CIP

British Cataloging-in-Publication data for this book is available from the British Library

This collection copyright © 1999 by Rutgers, The State University
Individual chapters copyright © 1999 in the names of their authors
"Women First: *Titanic*, Action-Adventure Films, and Hollywood's Female Audience," by Peter
Krämer, first appeared, in slightly different form, in the *Historical Journal of Film, Radio, and
Television* 18, no. 4 (1998). Reprinted with permission.

Manufactured in the United States of America

CONTENTS

ACKNOWLEDGMENTS

This volume would not have been possible without the incredible efforts of our contributors, who came through in fine fashion and responded with grace under pressure to impossible deadlines. Special gratitude is extended to David Culbert for allowing us to reprint Peter Krämer's article in *Historical Journal of Film, Radio, and Television* 18, no. 4 (1998); Emily Nussbaum of *Lingua Franca* for getting the word out; and Bill Paul and Evan Kirchhoff for their manly emotional support. We also thank Carl Derrick, Sue Kirby, and Steve Townsend for creating a welcoming work environment for us. Carol Henry, at Lightstorm Entertainment, and Twentieth Century Fox have our thanks for permitting us to reproduce a still from *Titanic* on the book cover. We wish to express our gratitude to Leslie Mitchner, Marilyn Campbell, Lisa Gillard, Victoria Haire, and the rest of the Rutgers University Press staff. Finally, we thank our families, killer pets, and the good people of the La Grange, Texas, post office for putting up with us.

Titanic

Introduction

THE SEDUCTIVE WATERS OF JAMES CAMERON'S FILM PHENOMENON

GAYLYN STUDLAR AND KEVIN S. SANDLER

On 14 April 1912, White Star's new liner, the *Titanic*, struck an iceberg off Newfoundland. Taking over 1,500 souls with it, the *Titanic* sank on what was intended to be the glorious maiden voyage of the biggest, most expensive, and most technologically advanced ship ever built. In 1997, James Cameron's *Titanic*, the most expensive (and most technologically advanced) movie ever made, hit movie theaters; in thirteen short weeks, it became the highest-grossing film in North America, and shortly thereafter, the first motion picture to earn $1 billion worldwide, finally taking in over $1.8 billion.

The film's unprecedented theatrical success quickly overflowed into lucrative ancillary markets. From the soundtrack album to couture fashions, from recycled film props in the upscale J. Peterman catalog to jewelry and lifeboat replicas, sales of *Titanic*-related merchandise matched the intense discursive interest in all things "*Titanic*" evidenced in Internet chat rooms, television documentaries, and publishing trends. As Michael Klein noted, the film "has had a stunning effect on popular culture, dazzling trend-spotters and confounding market experts amazed at the public's desire to buy into a disaster."[1]

It is logical that the box office and cultural impact of *Titanic* leads us to ask why this film, which is only one among the many fictionalized accounts of the *Titanic*'s sinking produced in the eighty-plus years since the event, should have such appeal with the public.[2] Before the release of the film, many wags and pundits were understandably skeptical of the film's potential for success. This view seemed to be shared by *Titanic*'s home studio, Twentieth Century Fox, which sold off some rights to Paramount in exchange for cash to soothe the unprecedented overruns of the film's escalating production costs. The studio's fears did not appear unfounded, for its $200–plus-million film-in-the-making was an Edwardian period piece, a costume film, a romance, a story whose ending was known—and

Titanic-related merchandise: Lipstick shades by Max Factor

roducing six romantic shades inspired by the epic blockbuster, TITANIC.

the

Tina Earnshaw
collection

Tina Earnshaw Oscar® nominated
makeup artist TITANIC

Exhilarated

Rebellious

Heartbroken

Passionate

Independent

Rebellious

Exhilarated

Independent

a "downer" so to speak. To many, these qualities seemed to constitute an unlikely formula for film success in Hollywood of the 1990s.

So we are led to ask: Why has *Titanic* become so popular? Why has this film become a cultural and film phenomenon? What makes it so fascinating to the film-going public? Answering these related questions is the goal of this volume. Our strategy is to offer not one answer or one perspective but many, and we have gathered thirteen articles (somehow, an appropriately unlucky number for a book intimately bound up with the most unlikely and "unlucky" maritime disaster in public memory). These essays are the work of film and cultural studies scholars from the United States and Great Britain. In a sense, their interest in the film and its impact on audiences mirrors the apparent desires evidenced in public discussions of the film as well as in *Titanic*-generated habits of consumption, and of a broad cross section of international moviegoers, to give greater meaning to their experience of *Titanic*. Therefore this book speaks directly to the desire of those readers who want to explore more seriously *Titanic* as a personal film-going experience as well as a global film phenomenon.

However, we need to remind ourselves that even though the meaning of *Titanic* may be taken for granted as obvious, since the film is the most popular of popular cinema, we should not be so quick to jump to conclusions. There may be those among us who believe that this film has become so popular because it is expensive, because it is a romance, or because it is about a disaster; but meaning is not a given, as Steven Biel reminds us in his remarks about the original sinking.

> The *Titanic* disaster was historically not intrinsically meaningful. While we like to think that the disaster's resonance is timeless—that it has to do with universal themes of humans against nature, hubris, false confidence, the mystery of the sea, hydrophobia, heroism, and cowardice—the *Titanic* seared itself into American memory not because it was timeless but because it was timely. Americans in 1912 made it speak to concerns of contemporary politics, society, and culture.[3]

So, too, the meanings to be derived from Cameron's *Titanic* are also neither as singular nor as self-evident as we might suppose. Although the poignancy of the original *Titanic* disaster is at the heart of many discussions of the film's appeal, in terms of human disaster, the loss of life on the *Titanic* pales beside other catastrophes in modern times. Consequently, the much repeated sentiment that "the sinking of the *Titanic* remains one of the most momentous events of the twentieth century" rings hollow as an explanation of the film's success, even as it falls into the trap of ascribing an unchanging meaning to the disaster's representation.[4]

Yet the revived interest in the historical facts of the *Titanic* sinking that has come about in conjunction with the release of Cameron's film seems significant. That significance relates to the need to understand the dynamics of film and of the film-going experience across the spectrum of production, exhibition practice, and consumption. On the one hand, interest in the original disaster seems to be predicated on the predictable exploitation of the event as fodder for extratextual material (publicity, promotion, etc.), but it also has depended upon the less pre-

Cloudy and cooler Wednes-
day. Thursday probably fair;
moderate northerly winds.

Average temperature yesterday 94
Average temperature for corresponding date last year .. 45
Average temperature for corresponding date last thirty-
three years 66

New York American
THE TWENTIETH CENTURY NEWSPAPER

Sunday American
WANT ADS.   READ BY
A MILLION
THE GREAT CIRCULATING MARKET PLACE OF
NEW YORK AMERICA—Published by Star Company,

EDITION FOR   GREATER NEW YORK.

No. 10,500.   Copyright, 1912, by the Star Company.   WEDNESDAY, APRIL 17, 1912—24 PAGES   PRICE ONE CENT In Greater New York | Elsewhere
and Jersey City.   TWO CENTS

ALL TITANIC SAVED ON CARPATHIA
NO HOPE LEFT; 1,535 DEAD

BERGS AND ICE-FIELD PHOTOGRAPHED LAST FRIDAY FROM STEAMSHIP NIAGARA IN LATITUDE 41.50, NEAR TITANIC'S GRAVE

The French liner Niagara, which arrived yesterday, hit two small nearly submerged icebergs last Friday night, which crushed her starboard bow. She called for aid by wireless. Cunarder Carmania responded and stood by until the
Niagara's captain found his ship able to proceed unassisted. The photograph above was taken at daylight after the accident.

REVISED LIST OF THE TITANIC'S RESCUED AND MISSING PASSENGERS

The following list of survivors
of first-class passengers was
issued by Vice-President Franklin at the office of the White Star
Line yesterday. In making it
public Mr. Franklin said that the
list had been gone over and
checked up by cable with the
London office of the company.
These survivors are among those
known to be aboard the incoming
Cunarder Carpathia:

Anderson, Harry.
Appleton, Mrs. E. W.
Abbott, Mrs. Rose.
Allison, Master, and nurse.
Andrews, Miss Cornelia.
Allen, Miss E. W.
Astor, Mrs. John Jacob Astor
and maid.
Behr, Karl B.
Bessette, Miss.
Bucknell, Mrs. William.
Barkworth, Mr. A. H.
Bowerman, Miss E.
Brown, Mrs. J. J.
Burns, Miss C. M.

Bishop, Mr. and Mrs. D.
Blank, H.
Bassina, Miss A.
Baxter, Mrs. James.
Bayton, George A.
Bonnell, Miss C.
Brown, Mrs. J. M.
Bowen, Miss G. C.
Beckwith, Mr. and Mrs. R. L.
Cambers, Miss D. D.
Clarke, Mrs. W. M.
Chibinaco, Mrs. B.
Crosbie, Mrs. E. G.
Carter, Miss Lucile.
Carter, Master William.
Cardell, Mrs. Churchill.
Calderhead, N. P.
Chandanson, Miss Victorine.
Cavendish, Mrs. Turrell, and
maid.
Chaffee, Mrs. H. L.
Cardeza, Thomas and Mrs.
Cummings, Mrs. John B.
Chevre, Mr. Paul.
Cherry, Miss Gladys.
Chambers Mr. and Mrs. B. C.
Carter, Mr. and Mrs. W. E.

Douglass, Mrs. Fred.
De Villiers, Mr. B.
Daniel, Mr. Robert W.
Davidson, Mrs. Thornton.
Douglass, Mrs. Walter.
Dodge, Miss Sarah.
Dodge, Mrs. Washington and
son.
Dick, Mr. and Mrs.
Daniell, Mr. H. Haren.
Emmock, Mr. Phillip.
Endres, Miss Caroline.
Ellis, Miss.
Earnshaw, Mrs. Boulton.
Flegheim, Miss Antoinette.
Francatelli, Miss.
Flynn, J. J.
Fortune, Miss Alice.
Fortune, Miss.
Fortune, Mr. Mark.
Fortune, Miss Mabel.
Frauenthal, Mr. and Mrs. Henry
W.
Frauenthal, Mr. and Mrs. J. G.
Frolicher, Miss Margaret.
Futrelle, Mrs. Jacques.
Gracie, Col. Archibald.
Graham, Mr. and Mrs. William.
Graham, Miss.
Gordon, Sir Cosmo Duff.
Gordon, Lady.

Gibson, Miss Dorothy.
Goldenberg, Mrs. Samuel.
Goldenberg, Miss Ella.
Greenfield, Mr. G. B.
Greenfield, Mr. Wm.
Gibson, Mrs. Leonard.
Goognl, James.
Hippach, Miss Jean.
Harris, Mrs. Henry.
Halverson, Miss Alex.
Hogiboom, Mrs. J. C.
Hawksford, Mr. W. J.
Harper, Mr. Henry, and man-
servant.
Harper, Mrs. H. S.
Hoyt, Mr. and Mrs. Fred.
Horner, Mr. Henry E.
Harder, Mr. and Mrs. G. C.
Hays, Mrs. Chas. M.
Hippach, Mrs. Ida S.
Hays, Miss Margaret.
Imlay, J. Bruce.
Kimball, Mr. and Mrs. E. N.
Kenyon, Mr. F. A.
Kenchen, Miss Emile.
Longley, Miss G. F.
Leader, Mrs. A. F.
Lavory, Miss Bertha.

Lines, Mrs. Mary.
Lindstrom, Mrs. Singird.
Lesneur, Mr. Gustave, Jr.
Madill, Miss Georgette A.
Melinard, Madame.
Marvin, Miss Roberta.
Marvin, Mrs. D. W.
Marochall, Mr. Pierre.
Minahan, Mrs. Daisy.
Minahan, Mrs.
Newell, Miss Alice.
Newell, Miss Madeline.
Newell, Mr. Washington.
Newsoh, Miss Helen.
O'Connell, Miss R.
Ostby, Mr. and Mrs.
Ostby, Miss Helen.
Olivia, Miss.
Omond, Mr. Fleuman.
Panhart, Miss Ninette.
Potter, Mrs. Thos., Jr.
Pondran, Major Arthur.
Rogerson, John.
Rehago, Mrs. Maman.
Ranelt, Miss Appie.
Rothchild, Mrs. Lord Martin.
Rosenbaum, Miss Edith.
Rheims, Mrs. George.
Rosibie, Miss H.

Continued on Page 4

GREAT BEAR SPRING WATER
50c, yet one of 8 glass-stoppered bottles—Adv.

St. Johns, N. F., April 16.—The report is current,
said to have emanated from the Bruce, en route to Sydney,
giving a version of the disaster to the Titanic obtained
from other ships. It is to the effect that when the Titanic
struck the iceberg she was going eighteen knots.

The impact almost rent the ship asunder. It cut
decks, sides and bulkheads from bow nearly to amidships.
It smashed boats and upper works to pieces.

The Titanic struck partially bow-on, listing to port
side and almost turning turtle.

Passing over the submerged portion of the iceberg,
it is supposed to have torn the bottom out of the liner as
the compartments from amidships forward were quickly
flooded and the ship rapidly settled by the head with a
port list, rolling heavily in the trough of the sea.

The force of the impact was so terrific that it practically rent the ship from stem to stern.

For a short while sufficient order was maintained to
launch safely most of the boats and embark about six hundred persons. Then the cry went up that the ship was
sinking and a frenzied crowd rushed madly for the boats.

As the ship settled into the sea, it is said that many
of the boats were smashed to pieces in the davits. Some

Post-disaster newspaper for contemporary consumption

dictable and therefore more intriguing vagaries of public response that flow across the representational conundrum that must deal with the paradoxes of popular film as history and as fiction. If audiences were intrigued only by the cross-class romance that fuels *Titanic*'s narrative, why are folks calling travel agents so that they can visit the graves of the *Titanic*'s victims in Halifax, Nova Scotia, or willing to spend $30,000 or more to board a submersible and be dropped into the depths of the Atlantic to view the liner's rustile-draped wreckage?

As the articles in this volume demonstrate, the possible meanings to be read across *Titanic* suggest the richness of this film as an "open text," no matter what individual critic-scholars may think of the film's aesthetic or narrative shortcomings or strengths. Here is the common ground for all the articles in this volume: *Titanic* is significant because of its popularity, and that popularity is a very complicated matter. It appears dependent on contemporary culture, on perceptions of history, on patterns of consumerism and globalization, as well as on those elements experienced filmgoers conventionally expect of juggernaut film events in the 1990s—awesome screen spectacle, expansive action, and, more rarely seen, engaging characters and epic drama.

Titanic cannot be approached without an appreciation of the need to make sense of this film, and film in general as an important aspect of contemporary culture. The structure and organization of this volume reflect our belief that the best way to understand a film phenomenon like *Titanic* is through a number of theoretical and critical avenues, with none privileged over another. The essays included here represent a wide range of methodologies familiar in film and cultural studies, but perhaps less so to the general reader. However sophisticated the approach used, all the authors have minimized jargon to make their observations about the film readable (in addition to insightful). Authors have addressed everything from the nostalgia evoked by the film to the semiotic meaningfulness created around the Heart of the Ocean diamond that figures so prominently in the film symbolization. They address questions of the representation of class, of sexuality, and of gender, which readers familiar with cultural studies will recognize as the modern sine qua non of the field. Other authors provide cross-cultural analysis of the reception of the film in nationally specific contexts, as well as analyses of the impact of strategies for marketing the film through music and a discourse of finance. Finally, other contributors address the film's multifaceted relationship to genre, to history, to stardom, and to contemporary social and economic concerns.

By using a well-known and much-viewed example of contemporary cinema as our focus, we hope that this volume can make the critical and theoretical means of current film and cultural studies accessible and relevant to students of film as well as to general readers. Certainly, one of the aims of contemporary film scholarship should be to make its methods more transparent to a broader constituency of readers, who can bring their own film experience and cultural expertise into play with the "interpretive" skills of the authors. Therefore, we hope this volume will be helpful for understanding not only an unprecedented film phenomenon but also current scholarly approaches to the subject of popular cinema.

Nevertheless, the reader will observe a certain overlap between the articles.

That overlap emerges, we hope, as a kind of comforting validation that the approaches employed here are not entirely arbitrary, reliant only on the ivory tower musings of the individual authors. The contributors all see *Titanic* differently, but they see it collectively too. And the meanings they find in *Titanic*, and the reasons they discern regarding the hows and whys of its popularity, are probably not much different from those recognized consciously, half-consciously, and unconsciously by the film's millions of fans.

As an embarkation of our search for *Titanic*'s meaning, Matthew Bernstein provides a map for the waters navigated within this anthology in "'Floating Triumphantly': The American Critics on *Titanic*." By examining fifty-four American newspaper and magazine reviews, Bernstein demonstrates how critical evaluations of *Titanic* articulate possible viewer, and thus popular, response to the film. Reflecting, as he says, "the same diverse concerns, values, ideals, and assumptions that the film played upon" in achieving international success, these reviews confirm that *Titanic*'s popularity lies in offering "diverse pleasures for diverse audiences." In summarizing critical reaction to the film into five primary but interrelated factors, Bernstein isolates many of reasons the contributors that follow give in deciphering the *Titanic* phenomenon. He focuses on the narrative framing device linking the past and present, the interpenetration of a cross-class romance in a disaster picture, the star appeal of Leonardo DiCaprio, James Cameron's visual style, and the nostalgic appeal of the film's evocation of classic Hollywood. Placing all of these factors within the cultural context of the dawn of the millennium helps to provide the cultural context for *Titanic*'s unprecedented success.

In "The Drama of Recoupment: On the Mass Media Negotiation of *Titanic*," Justin Wyatt and Katherine Vlesmas indicate that *Titanic* first entered the public sphere through discourses on its budget in the industry trade papers and popular media. The budget, initially presented in conjunction with the film's production problems, Cameron's obsessiveness, and the unlikeliness of recouping its cost, negatively positioned *Titanic* as a disaster waiting to happen (again). Yet after its world premiere in Tokyo, the budget functioned as a constant reminder of the film's quality and popularity; the press refocused its attention on the film's record-breaking gross, and the studios employed the budget as a marketing tool. By resituating the high budget of *Titanic* as a reflection of Cameron's status as a "fiscally sound auteur" and his preoccupation with historical authenticity, Twentieth Century Fox posited a link between the film's high cost with a higher-quality cinematic product. The press interest in and public appetite for discourse on data (between quality and budget, cost and gross), argue Wyatt and Vlesmas, became a key component of *Titanic*'s popularity in the age of "enfotainment." Tapping into a consumerist culture inundated with and hungry for industry and entertainment gossip, *Titanic* became the quintessential property for an enfotainment story. Playing the budget against "Hollywood spectacle [and] larger-than-life personalities" provided ready-made copy for newsworthiness. Subsequently, the extraordinary commercial success of *Titanic*, conclude Wyatt and Vlesmas, is due, in part, to the media exploitation and proliferation of its extratextual economic drama.

Like the budget, the exposure of Celine Dion's song "My Heart Will Go On" prior to *Titanic*'s stateside premiere also generated a positive buzz for the film. In "Selling My Heart: Music and Cross-Promotion in *Titanic*," Jeff Smith examines how the soundtrack to *Titanic*—its "combination of canny marketing and dramatic effectiveness"—was "instrumental" to *Titanic*'s popularity. First examining *Titanic* within its larger economic context, Smith traces the strategies of the marketing campaign of its soundtrack and its reliance on proven industry formulas and synergy: the hiring of a big-name composer (James Horner) for the album; the hiring of a well-established lyricist (Will Jennings) and romantic balladeer (Celine Dion) for "My Heart Will Go On," and an impeccably timed release pattern for the song to garner airplay and recognition before the film's opening. While the commercial fortunes of the soundtrack can in part be tied to its campaign, Smith notes that *Titanic*'s phenomenon is directly attributable to the film itself and Horner's score. Through the complexity and "thematic integration" of four musical leitmotifs, Horner "provide[s] an aural correlative of the film's synthesis of historical spectacle, class politics, and romantic sacrifice." By linking these musical themes to concepts rather than characters or settings, the film communicated a sense of emotional drama and romantic passion that made *Titanic* seem less like a disaster film than a love story, and as a result, it coaxed audiences to buy the soundtrack as a "take-home souvenir of the[ir] cinematic experience."

The largest segment of the audience to purchase the *Titanic* soundtrack, however, was girls fourteen and under, and it is with them, claim Melanie Nash and Martti Lahti, that *Titanic*'s popularity rests. In "'Almost Ashamed to Say I Am One of Those Girls': *Titanic,* Leonardo DiCaprio, and the Paradoxes of Girls' Fandom," the authors argue that the star presence of DiCaprio drew heavily on a preexisting Web fan base of young girls who were "already 'psyched to see' *Titanic* long before its release" and whose valorization and desire for DiCaprio fueled repeat viewings of the film. Through girl-related periodicals and Internet fan sites, *Titanic* was already discursively marked as a DiCaprio vehicle and, most important, as another context for teenage girls' fantasies of him which surfaced during *William Shakespeare's Romeo + Juliet* (1996), a similar tale of arranged marriages, fate, forbidden love, and death. In serving as, what Nash and Lahti call, a "mise-en-scène for their desires," DiCaprio fandom fulfilled teenage girls' spectatorial fantasies despite contradictory and often scathing discursive attacks by the popular press and DiCaprio himself. The blame placed on his heartthrob status in devaluing his merits as a "great actor" might at first appear to conflict with and endanger the pleasure of fan viewing experience. Yet by employing a "wide variety of compensatory, defensive, and evasive strategies" to combat negative critical evaluations and mainstream marginalization of their fandom, girl fans were able to reconstruct, normalize, and take pleasure in their fervent consumption and repeat viewings of *Titanic*.

What became irrelevant in the Internet communities of these teenage girls was the *Titanic*'s collision with the iceberg itself; their fan fiction and Web chatter mainly focused on the love story of the two leads. Yet the mere prioritizing of the love story, argues Peter Lehman and Susan Hunt, bypasses any analysis of the nature of that love story in explaining *Titanic*'s universal popularity. In "'Something and Someone Else': The Mind, the Body, and Sexuality in *Titanic*," Lehman and Hunt situate *Titanic*'s ability to appeal to young girls. While not alienating the male audience in the process, this appeal draws upon and deviates from two divergent literary and cinematic praxes: the love story wherein a working-class man awakens the sexuality of an upper-class woman, and the male action-adventure films of the 1980s and 1990s. Consistent with a mind/body duality deeply embedded in twentieth-century Western culture, particularly D. H. Lawrence's *Lady Chatterley's Lover*, *Titanic* recapitulates the triumph of a body-oriented laborer over a rich intellectual elitist in fulfilling a woman's desire through his sexual expertise. However, DiCaprio's adolescent body type is dramatically opposed to other mind/body narratives as well as to the pumped-up Arnold Schwarzeneggers and Bruce Willises of the action-adventure vehicles. Lehman and Hunt reveal that *Titanic*'s generic and textual mockery of "masculinity" and size reestablishes its conventional self in the lovemaking scene in the car, as DiCaprio is "suddenly empowered with the qualities he seems to lack"—awesome phallic power. Displaced also onto the promotional discourses of the film, *Titanic* can strike a responsive coming-of-age chord with teenage girls while remaining true to the male-approved formula of the all-endowed action hero.

For a contemporary blockbuster film even to foreground the romantic couple at all, argues Peter Krämer in "Women First: *Titanic*, Action-Adventure Films, and Hollywood's Female Audience," marks Hollywood's "long overdue return to the big-budget romantic epics of [its] past." In latching onto the recent, but far from new, production trend of female-centered action-adventure films, *Titanic* represents the zenith of a self-conscious industrial attempt to woo female cinemagoers without simultaneously alienating its key male demographic in the process. Like the main female protagonists in James Cameron's *Aliens* (1986), *The Abyss* (1989), and *Terminator 2: Judgment Day* (1991), to the strong woman heroes in *Speed* (1994), *Twister* (1996), and *Contact* (1997), *Titanic* perfectly balanced female issues of "romantic and mother love" as an emotional counterpoint to male desires of "thrill and spectacle." Through an examination of *Titanic*'s marketing campaign and a close analysis of the film itself, Krämer reveals how the tale of love and loss, amid the backdrop of a horrifying real-life tragedy, replicated the publicity discourse surrounding it, enabling the viewing audience to "[translate] the disaster into human terms." By being "a different kind of action movie" concerned with female subjectivity and empowerment, *Titanic* met the demands of a female market often marginalized and neglected by Hollywood.

Yet the film nevertheless appealed to all five demographic quadrants: under age twenty-five, over age twenty-five, male, female, and "ethnic." The popularity of *Titanic*, as a "*product* for everyone," argues Alexandra Keller, "is endemic to, and reflective of, postmodern conditions," where consumable commodities of spectacle and nostalgia replace and erase issues of history, class, and gender. In "'Size Does Matter': Notes on *Titanic* and James Cameron as Blockbuster Auteur," Keller links the hybridization of culture and capital to the hybridization of "blockbuster" and "auteur" in a postmodern economy—James Cameron being its prime example. The success of Cameron's films resides in his consistency of "vision" in a blockbuster culture—his ideological and narrative concerns, an aesthetic and visual style, the sheer size and expenditure of his projects—but these auteurist markings are ultimately unthreatening and apolitical as the filmic event and its spectacle overwhelm any notions of critique. *Titanic*'s conflation of historical recognition and emotional response—a postmodern entity that Keller identifies as "virtual history"—presents a past event with so much accurate detail enhanced by emotional catharsis that the cultural event passes as the historical event itself, but without the "historical anxiety." As the world's most successful blockbuster, *Titanic* allows viewers to float with ease, "leaving them," says Keller, "with the impression that they have participated in something of vital importance" and global significance through the very act of consumption.

If everything in Titanic functions as spectacle, as gratification for its audience, the diamond necklace (the Heart of the Ocean or Le Coeur de la mer), claim Adrienne Munich and Maura Spiegel in "Heart of the Ocean: Diamonds and Democratic Desire in *Titanic*," provides the entry into the film's ideological system and unlocks the secrets of *Titanic*'s popularity. As the diamond's commodity and symbolic value shifts between classes, genders, and histories, it serves to gratify and legitimize the American Dream, appealing to both the attraction of wealth and "higher American values," while "exposing the poverty of riches and honoring the *important* fulfillments" accessible to the middle class. At first a symbol of capitalist patriarchy, the diamond travels a path—what Munich and Spiegel call "democratic desire"—from Cal Hockley to Rose Bukater, becoming an emblem of feminist and American democratic awakening. What was once a symbol of monarchy, possession, and subjugation turns into an object of personal empowerment, liberty, and rebellion. Yet the irony of a film that preaches emotion above profit, and real experience over technological simulation, is lost when one considers *Titanic*'s cost overruns, computer graphic manipulation, and commodification of the Heart of the Ocean and other *Titanic* memorabilia. In the collapse of *Titanic*'s status as both fictional and authentic—as "real make-believe"—the diamond blurs the boundaries between rich and poor, reality and film, past and present. What emerges from this postmodern pastiche is the "democratic desire" of all to both own and relinquish luxury.

By simultaneously enjoying and rejecting the special privileges of wealth and stature, *Titanic*, says Laurie Ouellette, also "mystifies" the causes and continuities of class inequalities. In "Ship of Dreams: Cross-Class Romance and the Cultural Reception of *Titanic*," Ouellette links the *Titanic*'s phenomenon to the film's textual and extratexual reaffirmation of the United States as a classless society at a point in history when socioeconomic trends and policies undermine that very illusion. *Titanic* soothes the prospect of class polarization by promoting what Benjamin DeMott calls "the myth of the imperial middle"—a newer American class mythology that, unlike the Horatio Alger stories of the early twentieth century, centers on the contemporary "erroneous assumption that the United States is now a vast middle class that encompasses all but the outer fringes of society." Any class differences are smoothed over or renunciated in these myths by presenting class privilege as "attainable but unenviable." As a prime example of this new mobility fantasy, *Titanic*, argues Ouellette, shows class as fluid, transcendable, and superficial; ultimately nothing more than a temporary order easily moldable by romantic love. In promoting an "us versus them" opposition, the coding of class hierarchy as un-American, narrow-minded, and selfish becomes reframed as apolitical, antediluvian, and accessible. Classless love, says Ouellette, not class critique, overcomes all inequalities. *Titanic*'s popularity is dependent on such an eclipse of class-related tensions in favor of romantic hurdles and victories; nothing works better than a great love story to align "working-, middle-, and 'humbled' upper-class viewers against class hierarchy without prompting a reassessment of capitalism."

Such over-the-top melodrama is inextricably linked to the film's emotional impact on a majority of its viewers. This "deeply felt cinematic experience," or the "it" as Vivian Sobchack claims in "Bathos and the Bathysphere: On Submersion, Longing, and History in *Titanic*," refers to the film's narrative structure and poetic mode that enable viewers to submerge themselves into a factitious and historical past without getting ideologically wet. Focusing on *Titanic*'s framing story and poetic imagery, Sobchack argues that these devices function narratively and figuratively as a "bathysphere," a hermetically safe and sheltering device to the issues of capitalist greed, class disparity, and gender inequality of present Western civilization. By providing viewers an "authentic experience" of history without the pathos, while at the same time evoking imagery and spectacle to an "intimate immensity," *Titanic* creates a visceral paradox that "keeps real trauma, but not real emotion, at bay." As a result, *Titanic*'s narrative structure and poeticism provide audiences with "'authentic emotion' felt as 'historic experience,'" generating a "nostalgic utopia" for what Sobchack calls a "past-perfect" and a "future-perfect." Not only does *Titanic* enable viewers to descend into an impossibly purified past, but it also enables a "very present and contemporary *search* for this 'place of origin'"; its popularity emerges from a contemporary culture "longing to feel (rather than understand)." Operating within and alongside a consumer culture dampened with irony and impermanence yet tied up in an exchange economy, the film satisfies the viewers' desire to reconnect with some "pure context of experience"—the collection of *Titanic* souvenirs, the pilgrimages to gravesites, and multiple viewings of the film commodify and transform this lost authenticity with gestures of reenactment. By conflating truth and fiction, and replacing authenticity with the "material things that bear its 'trace,'" *Titanic* can fulfill contemporary desires through a "sea of tears and false historical consciousness."

In "'The China Had Never Been Used!': On the Patina of Perfect Images in *Titanic*," Julian Stringer also recognizes material culture's role as a "'bridge' to the feelings and sentiments we choose to unload onto the past." He compares contemporary culture's fusion of nostalgia and consumerism to Cameron's synthesis of two contemporary film genres—the high-concept film and the heritage film— to explain *Titanic*'s international success. By combining the awe of technological spectacle characteristic of high-concept filmmaking with invocations of nostalgia, conspicuous consumption, and fetishistic objectification that mark the heritage aesthetic, *Titanic* enables diverse spectators to play out the spectacular epic of death and destruction alongside their own intimate epic of national identity. Such is the case, argues Stringer, because the intermediary presence in *Titanic* of patina—the cultural status attached to aged goods or objects—resonates uniquely in distinct cultural arenas. Historically specific images of nostalgia associated with Rose and dramatized in Cameron's double dicgesis (what Sobchack calls the frame story) mediate responses of loss, authenticity, and adversity symbolic of national fantasies and sentiments. As the "antiquarian" sensibility encouraged by *Titanic* ahistoricizes history, similarly, viewers enamored with patina "miss the things they have never actually been denied," a sentiment, like antiquarianism, that knows no national boundary.

Building bridges to a past that never existed through the patina of objects parallels another contemporary preoccupation, this one about the future, or the nonexistence of one. The film's success, argues Diane Negra in "*Titanic*, Survivalism, and the Millennial Myth," can be understood in conjunction with the popularization of narratives of annihilation and survivalism that have proliferated across film (*Armageddon*, 1998), television (*Avalanche*, 1994), and other media forms as the world approaches the year 2000. Negra shows how the film's capitalizes on and appropriates the doomsday ideology of survivalist rhetoric—self-sufficiency and self-reliance, the presupposition of imminent disaster and its preparedness—as narrative tropes leading to postapocalyptic utopia and recovery. By making endurance itself heroic, *Titanic* "restores a sense of autonomy and agency" seen as largely disabled in the late twentieth century by an overly technology-reliant culture and unpredictable weather patterns. *Titanic*'s survivalist text also resonates with its production and promotion history, for the film's shoot and Cameron's endless dedication to the project are framed as survival and endurance narratives themselves. Intersecting with the immediacy of live television news disaster coverage, and the circulation of disaster and recovery-themed programs on the Discovery Channel, PBS, and *The Oprah Winfrey Show*, *Titanic* activates the fears and pleasure of contemporary culture, while camouflaging the profit-seeking enterprise of the film itself and its appropriation of a real-life disaster with real-life victims.

The displacement of urgent survivalism in Cameron's *Titanic* for self-sacrifice that characterized earlier *Titanic* cinematic treatments as well as popular memory in Britain was one of the many criticisms leveled against the film by the British press. Witnessed as a triumph of American cultural imperialism over British national history and character, *Titanic*, claim Anne Massey and Mike Hammond, was nevertheless a major success in England, enjoying tremendous popularity in, of all places, Southampton—the city of *Titanic*'s embarkation and home of many of the ship's victims. In "'It Was True! How Can You Laugh?': History and Memory in the Reception of *Titanic* in Britain and Southampton," Massey and Hammond show that despite the fact that *Titanic* fails to personalize the disaster in Southampton terms, the film still offered the community a rich ground for exploring issues of national identity and personal and public memory. Using Barbara Klinger's model of "cinematic digressions"—the various forms of mass media intertexts that fragment rather than assemble a text—the authors demonstrate how the critical perspectives addressed in this anthology may have been articulated in one specific local site of reception. From critical reviews and studio publicity to Celine

Dion and Leonardo DiCaprio, the personal accounts of Southampton residents reveal the multiple public and private forms of intertextual frameworks that led to the mass consumption of *Titanic*.

If James Cameron's "King of the World" speech operates as a memorial to hubris and perseverance, postmodernism and self-reflexivity, the thirteen essays in this anthology address the same issues as they apply to the phenomenon of the blockbuster exemplified by *Titanic*. In addition, they show us the value in considering *Titanic* not only as one of a type but also as a film unique in its impact in many respects. This collection allow viewers "to go back to *Titanic*" to discover what Jeff Smith calls "the goosebump factor," what Vivian Sobchack terms the powerful "it," or what Peter Lehman and Susan Hunt refer to as the ever elusive "something" of *Titanic*'s visual and emotional impact on audiences around the world. That impact is a significant phenomenon that deserves critical inquiry. *Titanic*'s popularity opens up intriguing questions about contemporary culture as a global (as well as local) phenomenon and the role of mass media in culture. But it also forces us, rather as if we were Rose, to recall and remember. For the essays in this volume not only suggest the relationship of a film-as-blockbuster to the present and even to the future, but also suggest *Titanic*'s relationship to earlier traditions in popular filmmaking shared by other generations. They also experienced the romance, the spectacle, the star power, and "elusive . . . something" that continues to draw us to the box office even as we move into the new millennium and the second century of Hollywood cinema.

Notes

1. Michael Klein, "As Anniversary Nears, No Escaping *Titanic*," *Detroit News*, clipping, n.d., n.p.
2. The first film version, *Saved from the Titanic* (1912), was produced by Eclair Film Company of Fort Lee, New Jersey, and starred an actual Titanic sinking survivor, Dorothy Gibson. Other versions have included a pro-German account, *In Nacht und Eis* (1943), *Titanic* (1953) directed by Jean Negulesco, and the Rank production *A Night to Remember* (1958) directed by Roy Ward Baker. Numerous other film references exist, including a *Titanic*-like sinking in Frank Borzage's *History Is Made at Night* (1937), the film adaptation of the Broadway musical *The Unsinkable Molly Brown* (1964) directed by Charles Walters, the French-made *The Chambermaid on the Titanic* (1997) directed by J. J. Bigas Luna, as well as figuring as the key plot motivation of the TV miniseries *No Greater Love* (1996). Made-for-television versions of the sinking include *S.O.S. Titanic* (1979).
3. Steven Biel, *Down with the Old Canoe: A Cultural History of the Titanic Disaster* (New York: Norton, 1996), 132.
4. This version of the truism is repeated in David E. Williams, "All Hands on Deck," *American Cinematographer*, December 1997, 30.

"Floating Triumphantly"

THE AMERICAN CRITICS ON *TITANIC*

MATTHEW BERNSTEIN

$\mathcal{T}$he Saturday following the 1998 Academy Awards ceremony, readers of the *Los Angeles Times* opened their Calendar section to discover a front-page diatribe from *Titanic* director James Cameron against the taste and competence of film critic Kenneth Turan.[1] Turan, writing in a "company town," was one of the few reviewers in the entire country who found *Titanic* to be a cinematic disaster, and probably the only one who repeatedly attacked the film and Cameron himself.

Although *Titanic* won eleven Oscars and Cameron collected three personally (for editing, directing, and producing), the filmmaker was still perturbed by Turan's critiques. He responded in writing: "Turan sees himself as the high priest of some arcane art form that is far too refined for the average individual to possibly appreciate." Cameron accused Turan of "the worst kind of ego-driven elitism," of condescending to his readers, and of abusing his position. His concluding paragraph was blunt: "Forget about Clinton—how do we impeach Kenneth Turan?"

Cameron's reasoning was that Turan had "lost touch with the joys of film viewing as most people would define it. He has lost touch, therefore, with his readership, and no longer serves a useful purpose." Cameron could point to the record-breaking popularity of the film for support, as well as to the many "letters to the editor" that followed Turan's initial review. These letters praised the film by a ratio of five-to-one; one person swore never to read Turan again after viewing Turan's own best-picture-of-the-year choice, the "boring, depressing" *The Sweet Hereafter* (1997).[2] Turan and Cameron's exchanges and the readers' responses made theirs the dominant critical controversy after the film premiered.

Unlike Turan, most American newspaper and newsweekly film critics acclaimed *Titanic* in their reviews; they were, in Cameron's terms, "in touch" with what viewers enjoy. Their responses, and Turan's, are worth considering when pondering *Titanic*'s popularity. Although critics usually have a deeper knowledge of movie traditions and current trends than their readers, their charge is to gear their reviews to the average Joe in the back row, not the cultural studies major. In the critics' reviews we can see possible responses of individual audience members, articulating how the film achieved its powerful effects and its popularity, the ways in which *Titanic* solicited its viewers' fascination.[3]

Moreover, though movie critics reputedly have limited effect on the box office of mainstream films, let alone "cultural events" like *Titanic*,[4] their reviews, as Barbara Klinger has observed, are "types of social discourse which, like film advertisements, can aid the researcher in ascertaining the material conditions informing the relation between film and spectator at given moments."[5] In fact, one could argue that because *Titanic*'s enormous popularity has made it an American cultural event, the critics' reviews reflected the same diverse concerns, values, ideals, and assumptions that the film played upon in achieving that popularity.

When one reads the critics' reviews, it becomes clear that *Titanic*'s popularity arose not from its aesthetic coherence but, in part, from the sheer diversity of its various elements. "*Titanic* is no masterpiece," wrote David Sterritt of the *Christian Science Monitor*, "but it's an absorbing entertainment with enough different moves, moods, and ideas to keep everyone happy at least part of the time."[6] Perhaps we could describe all the most popular films (*Gone With the Wind*, 1939; *Casablanca*, 1943; etc.) of American movie history in these terms. But the "moves, moods, and ideas" that seem to have been most resonant for *Titanic*'s audiences range from its romantic story and the charisma of star Leonardo DiCaprio to its nostalgic framing and rewriting of two kinds of history. One is the tragic story of the doomed liner itself, which Cameron's script reworked as the exhilarating setting for a youthful romance. This reworking elicited the applause of the film's most enthusiastic supporters and makes the plight of the fictional young lovers of even greater moment than their two-thousand-plus fellow passengers. History also refers to the traditions of grand, intimate epic moviemaking that Cameron himself invoked in publicity pieces—*Titanic* was to be his *Doctor Zhivago* (1965).[7] *Titanic*, in this light, arguably lacks the aesthetic coherence of such traditional entertainments (themselves acclaimed as cinematic art when they first appeared) and instead welds spectacle and special effects to retrograde melodrama. As a pastiche of moviemaking modes that revises history, one might argue that *Titanic* revamps the movie epic in a postmodern fashion.

This essay examines forty-two newspaper reviews from around the United States that were published in December 1997 and twelve national newsweekly reviews of that same time.[8] Of the forty-two daily reviews, more than half (twenty-three) could be described as extremely positive and only four (Turan—*Los Angeles Times*, the *Boston Herald*, the Durham, North Carolina, *Herald-Sun*, and the *San Francisco Chronicle*) were wholly negative about *Titanic*. The rest had to juggle the film's flaws against its merits in weighing their final dicta, and regardless of their region or readership, most of them still recommended that readers buy a ticket. The newsweeklies I consulted told a similar story: out of twelve, five were extremely favorable, two were negative, and five were balanced.[9] In a list of sixteen ten-best film lists for 1997, *Titanic* appeared only on eight, and it ranked as one of the year's three best films on only five lists.[10] One concludes that the film was not necessarily a critics' picture even though it became an unprecedented audience favorite.

In other words, few reviewers hailed *Titanic* as an unqualified success; most often, the film was deemed to have a flawed romantic melodrama plot, remarkably authentic production values, and an astonishing final hour. Although the precise analysis used in a particular publication might have varied as much as the personalities of each critic, there was surprising unanimity across regions and city demographics; most reviewers felt the film floated "triumphantly," and that its strengths outweighed its weaknesses. That those weaknesses were firmly and directly discussed supports the view that *Titanic* was "no masterpiece," which in turn reflects the diminished expectations that audiences and critics maintain for contemporary Hollywood movies. Rather, *Titanic* was as good as grand, sweeping filmmaking could get in contemporary Hollywood, and that the best audiences could hope for were throwbacks to Hollywood's grander, earlier era.

For purposes of convenience, I will summarize critical reaction to several features of the film that contributors to this volume have isolated as primary and often overlapping factors in the film's popularity, proceeding in roughly chronological order through the film: (1) *Titanic*'s evocative frame device of a survivor's recollections; (2) Rose Bukater and Jack Dawson's conventional but vividly realized courtship and infatuation; (3) the charismatic and dynamic performance of heartthrob Leonardo DiCaprio in the role of Jack; (4) the aesthetic of astonishment achieved in the spectacle of the ship itself and its sinking; and most generally (5) the film's nostalgic appeal to history, both that of the *Titanic* itself and of Hollywood moviemaking. In various critics' comments, we can see how these elements combined to give the film that mixture of moods and moves—something for everyone—that boosted its extraordinary box office success.

Memory and Inspiration

The frame tale whereby treasure hunters search the ship's wreck for cash and jewelry was one of Cameron's most striking choices in scripting the film, since Cameron could have set the entire story in the past. Some critics (e.g., *USA Today* and *The Wall Street Journal*) neglected to mention the present-tense frame. Two or three critics dismissed it as unnecessarily lengthening the film's duration; the *Washington Post* felt "the whole framing story is a cartoon, so much so that it seems another element of doomed hubris: Cameron is a guy who thinks he can improve the story of the *Titanic*!"

Yet most reviewers applauded the frame for several reasons. From a purely informational level, search leader Brock Lovett's explanation of the ship's sinking via computer graphics was judged a shrewd move, making the actual event more comprehensible to viewers, and allowing them to focus on the characters' plight rather than the mechanics of the disaster. From an auteurist standpoint, the *New Yorker* pointed out that *Titanic* thus shared the *Terminator* films' obsession with "the bending and shaping of time. It is only in retrospect, appropriately, that we can see how serious that obsession was, how swiftly it went beyond a technical trick, and how thoroughly it has crept into every cranny of *Titanic*."

In fact, for many critics, Rose's flashback and narration (by actress Gloria Stuart) gave the entire film a literally haunting dimension. Allowing Stuart's voice-over to intervene at various points was an effective device for ensuring that the human drama of the film remained in the forefront (*Baltimore Sun*). Her tale, coming after viewing the wreckage through the deep-level submarine, the *Rocky Mountain News* noted, made *Titanic* a ghost story; it gave the film a "spooky quality that may surpass the emotional eloquence of the plot," while rooting the action in historical actuality. Rose's loss becomes our loss, and yet the entire film can be recast as a tribute to the power of memory. The *Christian Science Monitor* found that the frame tale "makes a haunting framework for the main body of the film, setting up *Titanic* as a tale of time and memory as well as drama, danger, and disaster." In this connection, the dissolve from Brock's video monitor image of the wreck to its recreated vital self dockside in April 1912 was the film's most dazzling effect; to the *New Yorker*, it evoked the magic of Jean Cocteau's *Beauty and the Beast* (1946), perhaps "the most beautiful special effect ever seen."

Finally, the frame tale and the cynical, treasure-hunting "scientist-cowboys," as Janet Maslin of the *New York Times* called them, were seen as crucial to the thematics of the film. In Maslin's view, they are "big 90's hotshots" who are gradually humbled by Rose's tales. The film's "early brashness gives way to near-religious humility when the moments of reckoning arrive." As such, they are, in the words of the *Sacramento Bee*, onscreen surrogates for the audience, who "come expecting one thing [of the film]—obvious and expensive—but end up with something much richer." While one review (*Detroit News*) suggested the Heart of the Ocean mystery was a waste of time, the *New York Daily News*, like the *New York Times* and others, found the entire frame tale a metaphor for the film itself: "At first a symbol of commercial profit, the diamond becomes an image of the place the past occupies in the present, as memory and as inspiration. That's the same ennobling route that *Titanic* takes as it leaves the port of enterprise and arrives on the far shore of art."

In short, in most critics' views, the frame tale of a present-day treasure hunt (itself asserting the historical reality of the ship's wreck) interrupted by a frail survivor enabled *Titanic* to transcend the disaster action formula, providing a moving and fateful recounting of unexpected events beyond anyone's control. One might argue that this device resonated with viewers because the mixed emotions it elicited entailed the vague sensibility that Janet Maslin characterized as "millennium-ready unease."

Frivolous Unconsciousness

The rueful, fateful separation of young lovers with the ship's sinking also gave *Titanic* considerable appeal, of course; Cameron was reported to have described his project as "*Romeo and Juliet* on the Titanic." Rather than focus entirely on actual passengers, even though the latter—Molly Brown, the ship's captain, officers, and others—appear throughout the film,[11] Cameron elected to use the romance to convey the human drama and stakes of the ship's sinking; and this decision has been widely acknowledged to account for much of the film's extraordinary box office.

Many reviewers singled out the romantic story line as a weak element, because its star-crossed, cross-class dynamic was too conventional; because Rose's fiancé, the evil Cal Hockley, was so one-dimensional and lacked moral ambiguity; and/or because the characters' dialogue was simply too unbelievable. The *Herald-Sun* described *Titanic* as "a $200 million movie with a $2 story." The *Washington Post* dwelled on this point at length. Cameron had replaced "the actual" with "a thin, nearly inane melodrama that at least feels appropriate to the era. It's as if the film were written by a scriptwriter in 1912 fresh from reading stories in *Woman's Home Companion*—but completely unversed in the psychological complexities of Mr. James and Mr. Dreiser. The dialogue is so primitive it would play as well on title cards." Several other critics made this comparison to 1912 one- or two-reelers shown in nickelodeons (*New York Daily News*), and the *New York Times* thought Cal's "odiousness" played like "Edith Wharton Lite." Still another complaint came from the film's many anachronisms: Rose giving the finger to a ship steward; that, as the *Columbus Dispatch* observed, Jack's "philosophy (roughly, 'Go for it!') could be cribbed from any athletic shoe commercial"; and that Jack quotes Bob Dylan during the poker game—"When ya got nothin, ya got nothin' to lose."

If most critics did not complain of anachronistic dialogue, many found Jack and Rose's lines as clichéd as the romance itself. For the *Boston Herald*, Rose and Jack's spitting scenes were "almost unbearably silly"; the *Denver Post* found their dialogue "stale and obvious," and the *Detroit News* decried the entire romance as "silly beyond belief." The *Buffalo News* found the "upper-class verbal badminton of the first hour . . . amateurish and sometimes painful to listen to. [Cameron] has about as much chance of getting away with Noel Coward chitchat as he would quarterbacking the Packers."[12] Indeed, the overwhelming majority of critics noted the heavy-handedness with which Cameron contrasted the uptight, power-mad upper class and the unpretentious, fun-loving, and expressive passengers in steerage, and its deadly consequences.

The degree to which critics denounced the story line and dialogue correlated with their overall assessment of *Titanic*. Those critics most offended by the script tended to denigrate the entire film. Here was Kenneth Turan at his most vehement: "What audiences end up with word-wise is a hackneyed, completely derivative copy of old Hollywood romances, a movie that reeks of phoniness and lacks even minimal originality. Worse than that, many of the characters . . . are cliches of such purity they ought to be exhibited in film schools as examples of how not to write for the screen." Richard Corliss of *Time* magazine completely agreed: "In the 90 or so minutes before the iceberg slices open the starboard side, some compelling romantic fiction is in order. Here the film fails utterly. . . . the narrative events that should add emotional heft are substandard action tropes: kids in jeopardy, bad guys menacing pretty women, Jack manacled to a water pipe."

Many critics admitted, albeit less vehemently, that such flaws existed in the romantic story line, yet they argued that it was perfectly serviceable for this kind of film. The *Boston Globe* found the love story "a representation of a love story rather than the heat and primal chemistry of the love story itself." Yet even this critic had found that it served a worthwhile purpose: "If the romance is hokey, it keeps the film from being solely about the technical side of rendering the legendary disaster." Stanley Kauffmann of the *New Republic* agreed: "The dialogue and characters of the main story are completely predictable, presented with an air that we would want a predictable story because our interest is elsewhere—as it certainly is." For *USA Today*, if a "crank" viewer did not find Rose's predicament of imminent marriage to Cal involving, s/he was to be pitied: "Stay home and sink a plastic boat in the bathtub, OK?"

One variation on this view was to acknowledge the romantic plot's flaws but to argue that it became more affecting as the film progressed. The *New York Daily News* asserted that the characters "grow in stature and sensibility as Cameron brings them into his grand design." Similarly, Roger Ebert of the *Chicago Sun-Times* commented, "The setup of the love story is fairly routine, but the payoff—how everyone behaves as the ship is sinking—is wonderfully written, as passengers are forced to make impossible choices." The *Sacramento Bee* alone suggested ingeniously that the clichéd script and dialogue were meant to be perceived as such: the romance initially seems "incredibly weak and clichéd" but its "corny and old-fashioned" qualities were deliberately achieved, a "thoughtful idea and absolutely crucial to the film." Or in another variant, the melodramatic aspects of the love story were realistic: "What young love isn't [melodramatic]?" the *St. Louis Dispatch* critic wrote. "An older, less idealistic romance would not have captured the innocence of the time, or the heartbreak of its death."

The film's strongest supporters, based in New York and Chicago, felt there was nothing to apologize for in the *Titanic* story line, and that the movie was extremely romantic. For Maslin, the Rose-Jack affair was "a sweet, life-changing courtship," thanks in part to "splendid chemistry between the stars, along with much color from the supporting cast." David Denby (*New York*), finding the entire film "a celebration of youthful reckless gaiety," observed: "Indeed, what's most endearing about this movie is the two kids running around the ship looking for a place to make love. Highly preoccupied, they don't know that they're in an epic. . . . Their frivolous unconsciousness is charming."

Similarly, Michael Wilmington (*Chicago Tribune*) praised Cameron's decision to focus on the young couple because it made the film one of the most romantic epics ever produced by Hollywood, buoyed by "the idea that, in the midst of this tumult—the disaster that became the symbol of the 20th Century's shocks of upheaval—two lovers and their battle to stay together for one hour more are all that really matter." While making the strongest case for the film's dizzying appeal, Wilmington articulated a major characteristic of American popular culture in the 1990s, the context in which *Titanic* was viewed: a postmodern disregard for history, where what actually occurred could be happily replaced by fanciful narratives. This was best exemplified by commentary on the film's action where the ship's lookouts are distracted by Jack and Rose's adventures from observing the looming iceberg; Maslin and Anthony Lane (*New Yorker*) referred to this commingling of fiction and historical causality with approval. Wilmington acknowledged that the love story was "overblown, a travesty of the truth." "But," he retorted, "so what? Cameron is not really making a realistic film. . . . He gives us instead a wild romance and a supreme cliffhanging melodrama, laced with thrills, shocks and ecstasy. . . . It's easy to scoff at this movie. But how can you look at it for long, unmoved?" Style and sensibility are what mattered most.

Judging from critical comments, either viewers would "buy" *Titanic*'s romance or they wouldn't. One could see Jack and Rose's relationship as exhilarating or tiresome, naturalistic or clichéd, intentionally conventional or utterly incompetent. For reviewers, what one made of the film's romance dictated one's assessment of the entire film: undistinguished dialogue and action could even overwhelm the unmistakable power of the ship's sinking.

One Serious Dreamboat

For several critics, any flaws, worn-out conventions, or improbabilities in Cameron's script were mitigated by the lead performances. As the *St. Petersburg Times* put it: "Even the moldiest cliché can have freshness breathed back into it through creativity." Many of the secondary character actors were singled out for vivid performances, particularly Gloria Stuart, Kathy Bates, and Victor Garber; of the entire cast, Billy Zane received the most frequent condemnation for playing to the hilt his tintype villain Cal Hockley.

Many critics recognized how central Leonardo DiCaprio and Kate Winslet were to the film's success as entertainment. While some commented only on how they looked together ("She's 23 and looks 30. He's 23 and looks 14," the *San Francisco Chronicle* quipped), most attended to their successful performances. Winslet's was "luminous" (*USA Today*), and she was credited by some with saving the film: "The situation reeks of crude Victorian melodrama, but it works because Kate Winslet . . . is no ordinary young actress" (*New York*). Together they gave "such powerful performances that they compel belief in the most extreme situations: frantically racing down corridors filling up with torrents of water while gunshots crack, or clinging to the ship's upraised stern as the boat plunges into the ocean" (Wilmington—*Chicago Tribune*). They were "fresh-faced, unaffected and charismatic" (The *Advocate*—Baton Rouge).

Of course, DiCaprio's performance was a major source of the film's appeal. While no one could have anticipated the overwhelming enthusiasm he generated (though the *Hartford Courant* predicted that his "effortless style will win many hearts"), DiCaprio inspired some major flights of enthusiastic prose: he "makes Jack a vibrantly free spirit" (*Wall Street Journal*) and is "carelessly dashing" (*Hartford Courant*). *The Kansas City Star* felt "it's impossible to overemphasize how important DiCaprio is to the film's success." Gene Siskel (*Chicago Tribune*) found the film's "most delightful element" watching DiCaprio, "a 5-foot-9 actor steal the $200 millon epic from an 800-foot boat." Even a critic not overwhelmed with DiCaprio's performance could credit him with maintaining "focus and energy"

(*Baltimore Sun*). For the one or two critics who criticized his performance and persona as immature—The Fort Lauderdale *Sun Sentinel* thought Brad Pitt would have been much better, and Kauffmann called DiCaprio "insubstantial, lightweight in every regard"—the *Sacramento Bee,* for one, felt this was part of the script's conscious design: "His Jack is supposed to be unformed. He's still a boy—a kid having his first fling at life and love."

Most enthusiastically, some critics saw DiCaprio's role and performance as a throwback to earlier filmmaking eras. Maslin felt he "successfully" met "the biggest challenge for an actor of his generation: a traditional role." Two critics saw fit to evoke explicitly classic Hollywood leading men: DiCaprio "has a captivating presence in a role that might have been written for young Clark Gable" (*Newsday*); he is "rakishly designed, boyishly commanding" and "unites elements of James Dean and James Cagney" (*San Diego Union-Tribune*).

In both character and performance, then, DiCaprio embodied the spirit of the film. The *St. Petersburg Times* critic thought him "incapable of making a wrong acting move, cementing his leading man image with a performance that exudes the same daredevil bravado that made an undertaking like the *Titanic*—the ship and this movie—possible in the first place." Dashing, gallant, earnest, almost pretty—his performance and his character's persona were intimately connected to the film's popularity.

The Sinking

Critics had unanimous praise for the production values of *Titanic*, with several seeing Cameron's treatment of the ship as emblematic of his admiration for the moviemaking apparatus itself and for futuristic technology (*Advocate*—Baton Rouge). For someone favorably disposed to the entire film, like Anthony Lane (*New Yorker*), even the use of computer-generated images, which seemed unrealistically graphic (like "one of those splendid, stylized liners from travel posters of the nineteen-twenties"), "was no shortcoming, for it drove home the *Titanic* as a dream—a fatal vision of efficient loveliness for those who sailed in her, and a kind of unreal, awesome trip for those of us watching her now." Downplaying the demand for cinematic realism enabled critics to celebrate Cameron's delirious visual style.

As a subject, the sinking of the *Titanic* gave the film considerable gravity. Nearly all of *Titanic*'s detractors and supporters saw the fact of the sinking as an indictment of the hubris and naive optimism of the Victorian era, undone by its worship of technology and its ability to both conquer nature and contribute to unrelenting progress. The *Boston Globe* summed up this view of the event well: it was "a colossal blunder that still stands as the metaphorical disaster of the century, a monument to arrogance and stupidity, and a forerunner of the death of the Victorian world, both overstuffed and cruel, made final a few years later by World War I."

The film's rendering of this event in its final ninety minutes was almost unanimously judged as James Cameron's true triumph (with just two of the forty-two newspaper critics finding the ship's sinking a bore or tiresome). As Jack Matthews of *Newsday* put it, none of the previously made films or documentaries on the subject had tackled Cameron's focus: "The only thing that has eluded our imagination is the sense of actually going down with the ship."[13] Here, Cameron's scripting, choreography, staging, and editing of the disaster itself was generally deemed flawless and astounding. Even Turan had to concur: the film's final hour "is jammed with the most stirring and impressive sights."

"The details of the disaster are enthralling," agreed the *Wall Street Journal*, and the lengthy sequence fulfills "its subject's vast potential." *New York* wrote evocatively: "As a piece of movie staging and directing, the sinking is lovely—detailed, agonizingly slow at first and then rushed and panicky and grandly gruesome at the end, a whirl of bodies hurling themselves at restricted lifeboats." The *Washington Post*, which had berated the scripted romance plot, summarized: "Cameron captures the majesty, the tragedy, the fury and the futility of the event in a way that supersedes his trivial attempts to melodramatize it." Critics praised in particular various details, such as the walls of water crashing through to the ballroom, the old couple embracing in their bed as the water floods the floor, the mother comforting her two children with a fairy tale as they wait to die, the rising of the deck as bodies fall and crash—all these and more were singled out as audacious, haunting, unforgettable.

The shots of floating, freezing survivors were the most powerful images of all. To the *Sun Sentinel* critic, among the "most vivid and bracing images ever seen on film" was "a rescue dinghy plying through frozen bodies bobbing on the dark frigid sea [which] looks like a Gustave Doré illustration of Dante's Inferno come to life." It inspired Maslin to flights of poetic prose: "Ultimately a haunting tale of human nature, with endless displays of callousness, gallantry or cowardice, [the film] offers an unforgettable vision of millennium-ready unease in the sight of passengers adrift in icy seas on that last, moonless night." Speaking of the sight of those bodies, the *Wall Street Journal* summarized, "At times like this, you know you're in the hands of a visionary filmmaker, and you gladly forget how imperfect his film has been."

In short, the sinking sequence, in its deliberate pacing, striking vignettes, and awesome spectacle, gave the film the profound meaning and gravity some had found lacking in its first half. This was where the film's claim to greatness, to *Doctor Zhivago* grandeur, rested most securely.

In the Grand Tradition

Movie critics always balance a film's flaws against its strengths before recommending that their readers go see it. As mentioned earlier, four newspaper critics and two newsweekly reviewers found *Titanic* wanting. The *Boston Herald* called it "just a disaster movie" and felt that turning the sinking into a "theme-park thrill ride" was "unseemly." The *San Francisco Chronicle* was similarly underwhelmed: "The good news is that it's a fairly decent movie. The bad news is that this is the extent of the good news." *Time*'s Richard Corliss was similarly unimpressed: "The regretful verdict here: Dead in the water."

Most reviewers, however, wrote some variation on the argument that even if the film featured what the *Wall Street Journal* characterized as "many lapses, large and small," its flaws paled next to its spectacular, breathtaking aspects. The subtext of such apologies for a film critics could otherwise rave about is a sensibility that finds little in contemporary movies that is similarly moving. Roger Ebert and Mike Clark (*USA Today*) provide two examples of the "compromised satisfaction" view of the film. Ebert reminded his readers, "Movies like this are not merely difficult to make at all, but almost impossible to make well. The technical difficulties are so daunting that it's a wonder when the filmmakers are also able to bring the drama and history into proportion." For him, *Titanic* was "flawlessly crafted, intelligently constructed, strongly acted and spellbinding. If its story stays well within the traditional formulas for such pictures, well, you don't choose the most expensive film ever made as your opportunity to reinvent the wheel." Similarly, Clark commented that the film "can be picked at, but unlike its subject, not broken apart. . . . [Cameron's] movie may not be perfect, but visually and viscerally, it pretty well is."

Perhaps the greatest surprise in the film's reception was that its strongest supporters were big-city critics who found the power of cinema reflected in *Titanic's* best qualities: its sense of panache, its heady romanticism, and its astounding sights. Wilmington wrote that the film "sweeps us away into a world of spectacle, beauty and excitement, a realm of fantasy unimaginable without the movies. . . . Everything we see depends on the special magic of the cinema, its technical tricks and wondrous mechanics and the way they reflect or magnify the worlds of reality and dreams." Wilmington, like a latter-day Dziga Vertov trumpeting the virtues of kino-eye, noted the camera's extraordinary range, from swooping movements over the ship as it sails to the elevated prow before it sinks to the ocean depths where the *Titanic* now rests. Characterizing its "vision of oceanic luxury, a glorious and desperate love story, a storm of humanity, a blood-freezing nightmare," Wilmington writes: "As you watch it, you may feel that this almost foolishly extravagant picture gets right to the core of what movies—and popular storytelling—are all about."

Both the critics who raved and those who panned the film took the great film epics of previous decades—*Gone With the Wind, Spartacus* (1960), *Lawrence of Arabia* (1962)—as their term of comparison, thereby appealing, like Cameron himself, to the nostalgia of great movies past. Turan wrote that Cameron "lacks the skills necessary to pull off his coup" of entering *Doctor Zhivago/Lawrence of Arabia* territory. The *Denver Post*, after mentioning Cameron's ambitions, explicitly declared that the contemporary film industry could not and would not cultivate visionary filmmaking with the profundity of past masters: "There aren't many David Leans (*Zhivago* director) out there in a Hollywood of *Batman* (1989) sequels and *Starship Troopers* (1997)," and that Cameron had succeeded enough to make *Titanic* "worth seeing despite its length and sluggish parts. But not enough to make it a great movie."

Not surprisingly, *Titanic's* supporters invoked the same kinds of films but with an entirely different spin. For Clark of *USA Today*, *Titanic* "nearly exclusively recalls the reserved-seat 'event' attractions of the mid-1950s to mid-1960s, that long-gone era when a thousand extras stood up and shouted, '*I* am Spartacus.'" Like Stanley Kubrick's epic, Clark continued, *Titanic* uses cutting-edge technology within a disaster tale focused on a love story. Though its emotional pull opposed *Titanic* to the more cerebral *Lawrence of Arabia*, Clark believed that the film integrated "haunting loss" with "sheer cinematic braggadocio" in a completely compelling way. The *Baltimore Sun* felt the film "beckons filmgoers into a bygone time—not 1912 . . . but a time when going to the movies meant being dazzled and seduced and awed by their sheer magnitude and meaning."

This invocation of a grand filmmaking tradition, invoked nostalgically, was the keynote of Maslin's assessment: the film's similarities, onscreen and off, to David O. Selznick's *Gone With the Wind*. Peppering her review with statistics on the film's making, Maslin proclaimed it a "gloriously retrograde new epic," and one that, like Selznick's film, draws its audience into a lost world. It was a film, in other words, that reconciled contemporary Hollywood with its golden age, providing "astonishing technological advances" in the service "of one spectacular illusion: that the ship is afloat again."

The *New Yorker* invoked Selznick's predecessor, the first director of American epic cinema.

> Cameron is pushing at cinema much as D. W. Griffith did at the start—raising the stakes of the spectacular, outwitting the intellect, and heading straight for the guts. He piles on the astonishment as if he owed it to the nature of his medium; there are sights here that no other director would have the nerve to design and stage—an old couple embracing on the double bed while the water flows beneath it like Lethe, or the ice-whitened bodies of passengers bobbing in the endless darkness, as if on a battlefield of water.

Even Cal's unrelieved villainy proved that "*Titanic* is, for all its narrative dexterity and the formidable modernity of its methods, an old-fashioned picture."

Indeed, as a welding of the old and traditional to the new technologies, *Titanic* was for many critics an encouraging sign about the state of contemporary Hollywood. The *Boston Globe* described it as a fulfillment of Hollywood's ideals: "it floats triumphantly, supplying the rationale Hollywood craves for its own perpetually titanic profligacy. It's the kind of movie Hollywood believes in, has bonded its soul to, wants to see validated, needs to believe can blow the competition out of the water."

Other critics found Cameron's film a refreshing return to character-centered epics. David Denby (*New York*) wrote of the relief he found in discovering that "*anyone* in Hollywood could put together, in this age of cynicism and ineptitude, a hearty, big entertainment in the manner of such broadly pleasing, Oscar-winning movies as, say *Ben-Hur* (1959)." For Dave Kehr (*New York Daily News*), "it is a magnificent object, a feat of engineering and an overwhelming visual, aural and emotional experience that alone justifies all the worrisome tendencies of recent American movies." David Sterritt summarized: "While this is hardly the $200 million art film some moviegoers had hoped for, it cares as much about its characters as about its visual effects and seems genuinely mournful about the human loss caused by the disaster. . . . And when a techie like Cameron starts cultivating human values, it bodes well for Hollywood's future." That Cameron, action director par excellence whose most tender scenes had previously been played by Arnold Schwarzenegger, had come up with a film with so much heart was an unanticipated surprise.

For similar reasons, Maslin was enthralled by the film's rebuke, on many levels, to cynicism in general. Just as the hubris of the ship builders, designers, and steamship officials is literally undercut by the iceberg, the present-day gold diggers led by Brock are unexpectedly moved by Rose's tale and faced with the futility of their quest. And a third parallel Maslin constructed was to the contemporary industry: "It's the rare Hollywood adventure film that brings mythic images of tragedy—the fall of Icarus, the ruin of Ozymandias—so easily to mind."

Such proclamations bring us back to the cultural context of *Titanic*'s appearance and its critical reception. The film sustains enough ambiguity to provide ammunition for the film's supporters and detractors. Enthusiastic viewers (like Maslin) might see Cameron's traditional story line as a rejection of the cult of postmodernist, senselessly thrilling, contemporary action films to which Cameron had contributed. *Titanic*'s box office success in this view implies that audiences crave such old-fashioned entertainments.

Meanwhile, the film's detractors could find *Titanic*'s juxtaposition of an unsatisfactory story line with the astonishing ship's sinking to be a vivid example of the film's lack of aesthetic coherence and an unwitting embodiment of Hollywood's postmodern aesthetic. This was the very argument Turan made in a think piece that appeared shortly before the Oscar ceremony. "The overall mandate of critics must be to point out the existence and importance of other criteria for judgment besides popularity." (He noted that restaurant critics "don't send couples seeking that special anniversary meal straight to McDonald's on the 'everybody goes there, it must be the best' theory.") *Titanic*'s success, from his viewpoint, showed that "deadened by exposure to non-stop trash . . . audiences have been sadly eager to embrace a film that . . . is a witless counterfeit of Hollywood's Golden Age, a compendium of clichés that add up to a reasonable facsimile of a film."[14] Far from rejecting contemporary Hollywood practice, *Titanic*, in this view, embodies it.

From a critical standpoint, this seems the most compelling explanation for *Titanic*'s unsurpassed popularity—that it offered diverse pleasures for diverse audiences, in an era of diminished expectations when films rarely overwhelm viewers any longer for all or part of their duration. We know that audiences found the film to be pleasurable and worthwhile. As most of the critics discussed here demonstrate, there were any number of rationales for doing so.

Notes

Thanks to Gaylyn Studlar and Kevin S. Sandler for editorial suggestions on this essay. Thanks also to Eleanor Ringel of the *Atlanta Journal-Constitution* for background on the framework of newspaper film reviewing.

1. James Cameron, "He's Mad as Hell at Turan," *Los Angeles Times*, 28 March 1998, F1.

2. "Critic Misses the Boat on Cameron's *Titanic*," *Los Angeles Times*, 27 December 1997, Calendar sec., F6.

3. It is worth noting as well that reviewers reached their assessments before any one else, influenced perhaps by their press kits, the reviews in the trade papers (*Variety*, the *Hollywood Reporter*), and the hype and publicity surrounding its troubled production. This fact gives a unique quality to their reactions to *Titanic*'s aesthetic and entertainment merits.

4. Bernard Weintraub, "*Titanic* Is Turning Out to Be a Success on the Scale of Its Doomed Subject," *New York Times*, 2 February 1998. Weintraub wrote that *Titanic* had quickly attained the status of "what Hollywood terms a cultural event, a movie so embedded in the culture that critical reviews are irrelevant."

5. Barbara Klinger, *Melodrama and Meaning: History, Culture, and the Films of Douglas Sirk* (Bloomington: Indiana University Press, 1994), 69.

6. David Sterritt, "*Titanic* Surfaces with Hefty Tab and Big Heart," *Christian Science Monitor*, 19 December 1997, Film sec., 12A.

7. See Nancy Griffin, "James Cameron Is the Scariest Man in Hollywood," *Esquire*, December 1997, 98+. Cameron is quoted as saying: "I think of it as an epic romance. I told the studio, 'This is going to be a three-hour *movie*. The films I'm trying to emulate are *Gone With the Wind* and *Dr. Zhivago*. It is imperative that this epic be intimate."

8. The newspaper reviews I consulted follow in alphabetical order by newspaper name (all appeared on 19 December 1997, unless otherwise noted): John Wirt, "*Titanic* Spectacular Tale of Doomed Love," *Advocate* (Baton Rouge, La.), Fun sec., 17; Bob Fenster, "See-Worthy: This *Titanic* Stays Course," *Arizona Republic*, Preview sec., D1; Steve Murray, "*Titanic*," *Atlanta Journal-Constitution*, Preview sec., 1P; Ann Hornaday, "Gigantic *Titanic*," *Baltimore Sun*, Features sec., 1E; Jay Carr, "This Titanic Floats," *Boston Globe*, Arts & Film sec., E1; James Verniere, "Rough Seas," *Boston Herald*, Scene sec., S3; Jeff Simon, "That Sinking Feeling," *Buffalo News*, Lifestyles sec., 1D; Roger Ebert, "Full Steam Ahead; The Master Epic *Titanic* Pulls into Port," *Chicago Sun-Times*; Gene Siskel, "DiCaprio Is the Ballast for *Titanic*," *Chicago Tribune*; Michael Wilmington, "See-Worthy: Romance and Catastrophe Make for a Highly Entertaining Mix in the Three-Hour-Plus Epic Thriller *Titanic*," *Chicago Tribune*, Friday sec. A; David Sterritt, "*Titanic* Surfaces with Hefty Tab and Big Heart," *Christian Science Monitor*, Features sec., 12; Joanna Connors, "*Titanic* Floats in a Sea of Hollywood Grandeur," *Cleveland Plain Dealer*, Friday sec., 4; Frank Gabrenya, *Columbus Dispatch*, Accent & Arts sec., 12H; Philip Wuntch, "*Titanic*: Cameron Helms Stunning, Involving Cruise," *Dallas Morning News*, Today sec., 1C; Steven Rosen, "Big-Budget *Titanic* Rises above the Swill," *Denver Post*, Weekend sec., F1; Susan Stark, "*Titanic* Hits Rough Water," *Detroit News*, Screens sec., D1; Malcolm Johnson, "Taking on Water: DiCaprio Dashing in Meticulous, Preposterous *Titanic*," *Hartford Courant*, Life sec., D1; Melanie Credle, "Expensive *Titanic* Has Cheap Story," *Herald-Sun* (Durham), 26 December 1997, Preview sec., 6; Jeff Millar, "*Titanic*: Sea Saga Delivers a Bang for Its 200 Million Bucks," *Houston Chronicle*, Weekend Preview sec., 1; Bonnie Britton, "A Dream & a Nightmare," *Indianapolis Star*, Weekend sec., F1; Robert W. Butler, "*Titanic* Is Truly Unsinkable," *Kansas City Star*, Preview sec., 4; Duane Dudek, "*Titanic*'s Vivid Detail Keeps It Afloat," *Milwaukee Journal*, Cue sec., 4; Dave Kehr, "*Titanic* a Fantastic Voyage, Book Passage Now," *New York Daily News*, New York Now sec., 59; Janet Maslin, "A Spectacle as Sweeping as the Sea," *New York Times*, sec. E, part 1, 1; Jack

Matthews, "A Sight to Remember: A Vivid Re-Creation of the Sinking of the Titanic Dominates an Epic," *Newsday*, Weekend sec., B3; Jim Delmont, "*Titanic* Offers Tech Marvels, Big Romance," *Omaha World-Herald*, 18 December 1997, Living Today sec., 49; Holly McClure, "*Titanic* Hugely Entertaining but Deserves a Tougher Rating," *Orange County Register*, Show sec., F28; Jay Boyar, "*Titanic* Presents an Entertaining Romantic Saga That Boasts Spectacular Special Visual Effects," *Orlando Sentinel*, Calendar sec., 19; Ron Weiskind, "The Love Boat: *Titanic* Is an Epic Romance in the Classic Tradition," *Pittsburgh Post-Gazette*, Arts & Entertainment sec., 15; Robert Denerstein, "A Sumptuous Sinking," *Rocky Mountain News* (Denver), Entertainment/Weekend/Spotlight sec., 8D; Joe Baltake, "First-Class Voyage," *Sacramento Bee*, Ticket sec., TK22; Joe Holleman, *St. Louis Post-Dispatch*, E3; Steve Persall, "*Titanic* a Waterproof Epic," *St. Petersburg Times*, Weekend sec., 18; David Wlliott, "No Iceberg Can Stop This *Titanic*," *San Diego Union-Tribune*, Entertainment sec., 35; Mick LaSalle, "That Sinking Feeling: *Titanic* Looks Great but Has Little Life to Buoy It," *San Francisco Chronicle*, Daily Datebook sec., C1; Jeff Strickler, "Love Boat," *Star Tribune* (Minneapolis), Variety sec., 1E; Rod Dreher, "Action, Emotion Fill Grand New *Titanic*," *Sun Sentinel* (Fort Lauderdale), Showtime sec., 5; Bob Ross, "Ship of Doom," *Tampa Tribune*, Friday Extra sec., 22; David Baron, *Times-Picayune* (New Orleans), Lagniappe sec., L26; Mike Clark, "Old-Fashioned Tale Strikes Unsinkable Balance," *USA Today*, 1D; Joe Morgenstern, "Film: *Titanic* Arrives; Bond Returns," *Wall Street Journal*; Stephen Hunter, "*Titanic*'s Unsinkable Saga," *Washington Post*, D1.

9. Richard Alleva, "Ships in the Night," *Commonweal*, 13 February 1998, 17–19; Owen Gleiberman, "Sunken Treasure," *Entertainment Weekly*, 19 December 1997, 49; Nancy Griffin, "James Cameron Is the Scariest Man in Hollywood," *Esquire*, December 1997, 98+; Manohla Dargis, "That Sinking Feeling," *L.A. Weekly*, 19 December 1997, 45+; Brian D. Johnson, "A Canadian Sails Hollywood's High Seas," *Maclean's*, 8 December 1997, 86; Stanley Kauffmann, *New Republic*, 5 and 15 January 1998; David Denby, "Stacked Deck," *New York*, 15 December 1997; Anthony Lane, "The Current Cinema: The Shipping News," *New Yorker*, 15 December 1997; Corie Brown and David Ansen, "Rough Waters," *Newsweek*, 15 December 1997, 64; Leah Rozen, Tom Gliatto, and Karen Brailsford, "Picks and Pans," *People*, 22 December 1997, 21; Peter Travers, "The Year in Movies," *Rolling Stone*, 25 December 1997–8 January 1998: 171–173; Richard Corliss, "Down to a Watery Grave," *Time*, 8 December 1997, 91.

10. "And Then There Were 10: A List of Critics' Favorites," *Star Tribune* (Minneapolis), 2 January 1998, 8E. The critics listed were: Bob Campbell, Mike Clark, Roger Ebert, Ann Hornaday, Janet Maslin, Owen Gleiberman, Chris Hewitt (*St. Paul Pioneer Press*), Eleanor Ringel (*Atlanta Journal-Constitution*), Gene Siskel, Kevin Thomas, Richard Corliss, Peter Travers, Kenneth Turan, and Sara Voorhees (*Albuquerque Times*).

11. This decision, in and of itself, drew one difference of opinion that illustrates how diverse critical sensibilities can be: the *Columbus Dispatch* critic faulted the film for not covering a wider variety of subplots, while *Newsday*'s critic found the focus on the two young lovers extremely effective and a praiseworthy departure from the disaster movie formula of *The Poseidon Adventure* (1972) and *The Towering Inferno* (1974).

12. Steve Murray of the *Atlanta Journal-Constitution* alone pointed out the unfortunate nature of Rose's dialogue, with her referring to the *Titanic* as a slave ship, particularly with Steven Spielberg's *Amistad* (1997) in the theaters.

13. Two critics saw Rose's heroics in saving Jack as an echo of Ripley's maternal heroine in *Aliens* (1986) or Linda Hamilton's courageous mother in *The Terminator* (1984) (*Columbus Dispatch* and *Denver Post*).

14. Turan's piece was reprinted as "*Titanic* Is Just the Tip of the Iceberg of Big Flicks with Weak Scripts," *Washington Post*, 24 March 1998, D2. It was this piece that specifically provoked Cameron's vehement response that Turan had lost touch with the audience and had taken to berating them for not sharing his taste.

Cameron faxed his manifesto to the *Los Angeles Times* on 26 March 1998, the Thursday after Oscar night; the paper cut it by one-third and ran it that Saturday. See "Fearless L.A. Times Critic Faces Down King Cameron," *Variety*, 6 April 1998. The continuing articles and reader responses appeared as follows: Joe Lucas, "Counterpunch: It's Unfair to Zero in on *Titanic*'s Isolated Clunkers," *Los Angeles Times*, 29 December 1997, Calendar sec., F3; Kenneth Turan, "The 70th Academy Award Nominations; Commentary; At Least One Place the Ship Didn't Dock," *Los Angeles Times*, 11 February 1998, Calendar sec., F1; Kenneth Turan, "Oscars '98; Surprise! Cameron Subdued; Analysis: *Titanic*'s Big Night Brought Out a Moment of Reflection in Its Oscar-Winning Director," *Los Angeles Times*, 24 March 1998, Calendar sec., F4. Cameron's reply predictably inspired condemnation from journalists around the country.

The Drama of Recoupment

ON THE MASS MEDIA NEGOTIATION OF *TITANIC*

JUSTIN WYATT AND KATHERINE VLESMAS

*W*idely heralded as the most expensive film ever produced, costing over $200 million, James Cameron's *Titanic* entered the public sphere first and foremost through its budget. The cost figure proved to be a resilient hook for journalists writing about the film, allowing for a large number of related concerns to be expressed: the possibility of a director out of control, the ethics of two studios spending such a large amount on a single motion picture, the likelihood of recoupment from a commercial standpoint, and the emphasis on the blockbuster as a form of contemporary media production. However, after the film's release, the budgetary issue became secondary to another commercial parameter: box office gross. Suddenly, the press became obsessed not with *Titanic's* cost but with its record-breaking potential.

The discourse of data—the media focus on *Titanic's* cost and gross—is key to assessing the film's popularity since in many ways, *Titanic* lacked the most conventional box office "insurance": stars. After all, *Titanic* no doubt cemented Leonardo DiCaprio's stardom and greatly facilitated Kate Winslet's career, but the pair could not "open" a film at the box office prior to *Titanic*. Instead, data replaced stardom as the film's primary asset; the industry and popular press, the studios, and the filmmakers themselves all capitalized on and exploited the "unique story" of *Titanic's* cost overruns and box office success. Reflecting the public's growing fascination over the past two decades with "enfotainment"—entertainment industry news and entertainment news—*Titanic* profited from a media environment inundated by and hungry for information on film production, particularly one as scandalous as *Titanic*. Taking advantage of this fascination, *Titanic's* marketing, advertising, and news coverage were elemental to the film's popularity, having a solid impact on its reception and commercial standing.

Considering the History of Negotiating the Big-Budget Spectacle

Since the 1920s, the Hollywood studios have been able to utilize budgets as part of the entire marketing package of their films. As with *Titanic*, the advertisements for most of these spectacles did not directly reference the budget. The advertisement for *Foolish Wives* (1922) is one exception, positioning the film's cost above the title in the ad campaign ("The First Real Million Dollar Picture").[1] Ads for other big-budget films—*Ben-Hur* (1925), *Gone With the Wind* (1939), *The Ten Commandments* (1956), *Spartacus* (1960), *Lawrence of Arabia* (1962), and *Apocalypse Now* (1979)—only allude to the budget in the advertising by referencing the scope and size of the film. These film ads instead concentrate mainly on other elements such as box office stars, special effects, the epic quality, and aspects of exhibition (e.g., technical considerations and roadshow presentations).

The issue of budget is presented more openly in the reviews of these big-budget spectacles, positioned as positive or negative, but always as a narrative facilitating public awareness of the film. The review for *Foolish Wives* in the *New York Times*, for example, foregrounds the cost before assessing the film's merits: "*Foolish Wives*, first of all, but not most importantly, is an expensive picture. It is said to have cost exactly $1,103,736.38, and although a good deal of this cost was probably due to delays and other misfortunes that beset the production of the film, no inconsiderable sum was actually spent in the things that show on the screen."[2] The review proceeds to discuss the cost at several points, including a description of the set, a replica of Monte Carlo, built in California.

As time progressed, cost continued to be a factor and common reference point in film reviews in three major ways. First, the budget is directly referenced in the opening of the reviews as was the case with *Foolish Wives*. The *New York Times* review for *Ben-Hur* also begins by mentioning the cost, but in more inflammatory terms: "The magnificent pictorial conception of *Ben-Hur*, on which no less than $3,000,000 has been lavished and which has taken nearly two years to produce, was presented last night."[3] Second, the budget becomes implicit in a discussion of the epic quality of the film: the cost of *The Ten Commandments* is indirectly cited through a discussion of the elaborate Egyptian set commissioned by Cecil B. DeMille, the large cast of characters, and the use of Technicolor.[4] A review of *Lawrence of Arabia* similarly references the budget's epic nature in a secondhand fashion, listing 1,500 camels and horses, 5,000 extras, fifteen months of filming, and a running time of four hours.[5] Third, the potential folly of a big budget is engaged by reviewers who become interested with the commercial success and failure of the big-budget spectacle. A review of *The Ten Commandments* follows this pattern: "DeMille has told the story of the Book of Exodus at a length of three hours and 39 minutes, and at a cost of $13.5 million. To break even, Producer DeMille may have to gross as much as $25 million. But shrewd old 'Mr. Movies,' the man who in forty years has lured more than 3 1/2 billion customers past the wicket, is calmly confident that he will do a great deal better than that; that he will, in fact, do something in the neighborhood of $100 million."[6]

While the reviews of *Titanic* make use of all three aspects, the budget discourse of *Titanic* recalls two particular traits from big-budget spectacles of the past: the creation of unparalleled size/scope and the vision of a commercial auteur. In this manner, the budget discourse of *Titanic* can be appreciated most in conjunction with two of the most notorious big-budget spectacles, *Cleopatra* (1963) and *Heaven's Gate* (1980).

At a budget close to $30 million, "about twice the budget of the most costly picture ever released," Twentieth Century Fox's *Cleopatra* was widely heralded as the most expensive film ever produced.[7] While star Elizabeth Taylor and her infamous affair with co-star Richard Burton garnered press for the film, the discourse revolved primarily around the budget. The guiding principle in the press's representation of the film was "bigger is better." Chief among the elements impacted by this philosophy was the film's "unprecedented" $20 million in advance guarantees from exhibitors.[8] The advance guarantees functioned as promotional material for the film: they were widely publicized in the press, and the level of guarantees was described as phenomenal. By implication, *Cleopatra* was valuable, a hit before even opening. The advance exhibitor interest was matched in the press by reports on the film's grandiose size, particularly in terms of production. Articles considered the elaborate sets and locations and the lengthy production schedule, hinting that *Cleopatra* would be the "event" of the year, parallel to a Broadway production rather than a run-of-the-mill studio picture. On release, the film received a mixed reaction but still managed to become the number one box office hit of 1963, grossing over $26 million. However, with the phenomenal negative cost, *Cleopatra* did not break even until 1966 when the television rights were sold for $5 million to ABC.

The connection between the $35–million epic western *Heaven's Gate* and *Titanic* exists primarily at the level of the auteur. Unlike Joseph L. Mankiewicz's *Cleopatra*, *Heaven's Gate* was constructed as a production from a "visionary" director, Michael Cimino, fresh off his Oscar-winning *The Deer Hunter* (1978). Originally budgeted at $7.5 million by United Artists, *Heaven's Gate* ballooned to a cost of around $35 million.[9] The film's production difficulties, narrative incoherence, and epic folly became synonomous with Cimino.[10] The budgetary excess and stylistic overabundance applauded and condemned for *Cleopatra*, was used as an entry point for a vendetta against the director. Critics lambasted Cimino for his "abuse" of the Hollywood system, for the waste of producing authentic wooden roller skates and for having his 1,200 extras attend bull-whipping and wagon-driving lessons, and for the film's almost four-hour running time.[11] *Heaven's Gate* was and still remains an epithet for the big-budget, director vanity project gone out of control.

Cleopatra and *Heaven's Gate* embody central aspects of the budget discourse that would be formed by *Titanic*. Both depend upon the element of scandal (albeit *Cleopatra* appears in a different form than the institutional scandal of *Heaven's Gate* and *Titanic*), and both films' size, scope, and spectacle are focused on through the press and through the trade papers. *Titanic* follows suit, playing out the scandal aspect and relying on the auteur working relatively separate from the studio's intervention. Matching both core elements—vastness and the auteur—*Titanic* is

The size, scope, and spectacle of the budget in *Cleopatra*

eventually coded as positive in terms of quality and entertainment value, suggesting that size, scope, spectacle, and vision can still be marketable commodities.

Titanic: The Budget as Marketing Force

Given the strong commercial qualities (presold property, genre allegiance, and target audience) of *Titanic*, some of the press were more open to Cameron's film, shifting from a mixed/negative reception during production to positive coverage that mirrored the strong public reaction to the film after its release. While *Titanic*'s $200–million budget was certainly a point of contention for the press and the two studios involved in its production, the publicity generated was filtered through the commercial track record of Cameron. The director received financial backing from both Twentieth Century Fox and Paramount, with Fox handling the bulk of the financing and retaining international distribution rights, while Paramount was given domestic distribution. Dual distribution deals were relatively uncommon at the time, yet the move was not unprecedented. Other high-profile releases—*Twister* (1996), *Air Force One* (1997), and *Saving Private Ryan* (1998)— also were coventures between two studios.[12] While Fox sought Paramount as a partner, the terms of the deal limited Paramount's investment to $65 million with an

Authentic roller skates in *Heaven's Gate*

additional $50 million in domestic marketing costs. Consequently, Fox was responsible for the ballooning budget. By release date, it was estimated that Fox's investment was approximately $100 million more than Paramount's expenditure. Revenue from box office was pooled until Paramount recouped $115 million, at which time the percentage shifted to Fox's advantage.[13]

The confidence evidenced by such an arrangement was no doubt based on the positive relationship between Cameron's budget and the commercial performance of his films. After the phenomenal success of *The Terminator* (1984), Cameron's budgets jumped considerably: $18 million for *Aliens* (1986), $80 million for *The Abyss* (1989), $106 million for *Terminator 2: Judgment Day* (1991), and over $135 million for *True Lies* (1994).[14] With the exception of *The Abyss*, as the budget increased with each project, so did the box office return. The big-budget stakes of these projects led critic Richard Corliss to rhapsodize about Cameron's daring: "*The Terminator, Aliens, The Abyss*, and *Terminator 2: Judgment Day* all took big risks, with film form and finance, that paid off. Cameron is a daredevil director: he goes skydiving without a chute and lands in clover."[15]

Despite this claim, Cameron's career actually illustrates a less imaginative trajectory: he could be described as the fiscally responsible auteur. An auteur can exist inside the current studio system only by working within a commercially viable genre and a marketing-oriented project. In Cameron's case, the science fiction and action-adventure films were the appropriate vehicles. Both forms feature extensive special effects and are generally star driven (Arnold Schwarzenegger for *The*

Terminator, *Terminator 2*, *True Lies*). In this manner, Cameron became a type of insurance—almost a brand name—for the high-tech, action movie. Cameron's commercial track record therefore suggests that his future grand, big-budget projects, including *Titanic*, could be "good bets" for a certain level of popularity and audience support.

But *Titanic* was also a "good bet" because of its rather unusual, yet powerful, presold quality. Instead of being based on a best-selling novel or stage play—although it remained visible in the public eye due to the unaffiliated $10–million Broadway musical—*Titanic* was a real-life historical event that achieved mythic dimensions since its sinking in 1912. Given the audience's familiarity with *Titanic*, the event, and its well-known disastrous results, the modicum of dramatic tension in the film would naturally appear to shift to the level of the love story. Even so, Cameron's framing story of Rose Bukater returning to the *Titanic* and the scientists' explanation of the physics of its demise primarily divides the audience's interest in the film between the lovers' tragedy and the external characteristics involved in re-creating the *Titanic*'s tragedy: the production design, its historical authenticity, and the sinking itself.

As another narrative through which viewers could filter their reception of the film, *Titanic*'s "secret" marketable aspect was its large-scale production or immense budget, a lure for audiences interested in attending the most expensive movie ever made. With previous Cameron films, the budget appeared in an ancillary manner as a marketing tool, mainly through mention in reviews. Typical of such a strategy is an article concerning *Terminator 2* from the *Washington Post* in which Joe Brown claimed, "Budgeted in excess of $90 million (*T1* cost a mere $6 million), *T2* is the most expensive movie ever made, and Cameron puts it all on screen—the make-up, special effects, and especially the harrowing chase scenes . . . redefine 'spectacular.'"[16] Similarly, critics such as Jim Byerley (HBO) and Richard Corliss (*Time*) remarked about the budget, and the strong potential for commercial returns, in reviews of *True Lies*.[17]

With *Titanic*, the budget became a more substantial issue from the inception of the project. In the industry press, the budget was initially positioned as a negative, mentioned in conjunction with *Titanic*'s production problems. Production reports varied from the curious (film crew on location in Nova Scotia rushed from the set to the hospital after eating clam chowder laced with PCP) to the more banal (complaints about dangerous working conditions, endless night shoots, and Cameron's inability to control his temper).[18] The press also concentrated on the rescheduling of *Titanic*'s release date from 2 July to 19 December 1997, and the alleged disagreements between the studios. Typically the connection was made between the release date shift and the budget; as one *Variety* report mentioned, "sources estimate that the postponement will add another $20 million to the already bloated budget."[19]

As a result of the intense press interest in the budget, Cameron attempted to use the hyberbolic quality of the film's cost to his advantage when asked to comment frequently in the trade papers on the size and expansion of the budget. At the film's world premiere in Tokyo, he defended the expenditure by claiming that "what you will lose as a result of a film like *Titanic* is maybe three Steven Seagal films."[20] While the press's attention to the budget was beyond Cameron's control, Cameron eventually responded by addressing the budget directly. He proclaimed, "I've decided to tell people how much it cost, otherwise they'll assume it's more."[21] By *Titanic*'s domestic release, Cameron even self-authored an article in *Time* entitled "Settling Accounts," designed to "help clarify rumors and exaggerations." Cameron begins with, "The movie cost $285 million. FALSE. The total cost is $200 million." The next two self-posed issues in Cameron's article also concern the budget: *Titanic* is the most expensive film ever made (unadjusted for inflation), and the film did go far over budget.[22] William Mechanic, chairman of Fox Filmed Entertainment, similarly reiterated the budget in interviews, and added to the drama by claiming that he was beleaguered by stories of the film's budgetary excesses prerelease. Some trade papers had rumored that Rupert Murdoch would put Mechanic's job "on the chopping block" if the film failed.[23] In effect, the budget became another marketing angle for Cameron and the studio—particularly given Cameron's foregrounding of the issue in his own article.

Articles concerning the commercial prospects of the film admitted the high break-even level, yet several hedged their bets about *Titanic*'s failure at the box office. In the summer preview section of *Premiere*, Cameron's film was predicted as ranking in second place by the end of the summer: *Titanic* would not "go down" with less than $190 million.[24] The mixed review suggested that the film would be extremely popular, at the same time implying that it would not recoup its costs. With similar apprehension, *Variety* editor Peter Bart's editorial offered an open memo to Cameron sardonically titled "Auteur as Terminator." Although chiding the director for the "nightmarish hours for the crew, extras having to stay in the water for 18–hour stretches, [and] your temper tantrums over mistakes and malfunctions," Bart also applauded Cameron's ability to leverage his previous box office success as negotiating power with the studios. Despite the positive buzz generated through the Internet, advanced screenings, and gossip, Bart wondered if the film would be as successful as the rumors indicated.[25]

Cameron's desire not to pursue *Terminator 3* as his next project also drew attention to *Titanic*'s budget. Representatives for Cameron and Fox announced in October 1997 that the project would be canceled to curtail "runaway costs" even before a script had been completed. Unsurprisingly, they wanted to avoid the intense media scrutiny over another big-budget project directly after *Titanic*.[26]

Amidst a *Heaven's Gate*–like buzz of criticism and derision, Paula Parisi's *Entertainment Weekly* article, published five weeks prior to *Titanic*'s North American release, prefigured the media's about-face positive spin on the budget. Acknowledging the press's negative reports on the film, Parisi chose to resituate the high budget in terms of Cameron's preoccupation with precision and historical accuracy. Cameron was represented as a perfectionist who pays extreme attention to detail and who was determined to represent an era and a historical event as accurately as possible—even if the project must go over budget and the film's release must be delayed.[27] The historical authenticity became a justification for the budget's price tag after this point. Whenever possible, Cameron stressed this issue in interviews: "Everything is accurate. The set is accurate, the model's accurate, and so it's like going back in a time machine and being able to walk the deck of the most famous ship in history. That's something that could not have been done without these techniques."[28] Historian Don Lynch supported Cameron's claims, appearing in a one-hour promotional film, *Breaking New Ground*, for Fox and on CNN. Lynch testified that every aspect of the film—from the sinking of the ship, to the "actual" footage of the *Titanic*, through the costuming and set design—was accurate.

Perhaps most illuminating are comments made by Tomas Jegeus, Fox's UK marketing manager, in equating the film's expenditure with higher quality production values. At a film advertising conference in July 1997, Jegeus stated the controversy over the budget would be used to convey a message that cost reflects quality, "like a Ferrari." Mentioning that "everyone knows the ship is going to sink," Jegeus proclaimed, "We know we have a great film and people will see that all of the money is up on the screen."[29] These explicit comments on the company's strategy—at least for the international campaign—parallel more oblique references on the budget by Cameron and Mechanic. Peter Travers's query to Cameron on the film being the most expensive ever made was met with a terse, "What do you care? It doesn't cost you or anybody else more than the price of a movie ticket."[30] The implication is that the audience member benefits from the higher budget through higher production values yet pays the same ticket price as for lower-budget films. Similarly, Mechanic's rather audacious claim that *Titanic* constitutes a "$200 million art film" implies that viewers will enjoy higher entertainment value through the match of strong artistic quality (the art film) and the enhanced production values from the budget.[31]

Indirectly, the advertising for *Titanic* also posits a link between the budget as represented by the spectacle (sets, costumes, period re-creation) of the film and entertainment value. While the budget is not mentioned overtly in the film's advertising, it certainly appears in a coded form throughout much of the visual advertising. The official *Titanic* Web site contains all of the traditional information from a printed press kit (star bios, stills, production stories and information, etc.).[32] In terms of the production information, the site emphasizes the scale and physical size of the sets and production. Evidence the site's headings: The Building and Sinking of the Ship Set, the Fox Baja Studios, and Design for Living: Stitch by Stitch and Motion by Motion. Both the print ad and the television commercial reinforce the physical significance and spectacle of the ship. The print ad offers a huge *Titanic* jutting upward through the embracing lovers in a design reminiscent of the *Jaws* shark threatening the vulnerable swimmer on the water's surface. Expressing the epic quality of the production, the commercial's beginning narration, "It's nothing you've ever seen," is juxtaposed to shots of the sinking ship, countless distraught passengers, and Kathy Bates (Molly Brown) exclaiming, "God almighty!"

The equation suggested by this publicity and advertising is that a higher budget correlates with a higher-quality cinematic product. Quality in this case reflects exacting attention to detail and craftsmanship, both of which presumably enhance the re-creation of the time past and the fictional drama at the heart of *Titanic*. Further, the historical accuracy is also valued in its own right. A peek into a time past—presumably an accurate and exacting presentation of the past given the budget—augments the dramatic representation, increasing the potential audience and heightening popular interest for the film.

By intentionally foregrounding the film's budget in the media, the studios could distinguish the quality of the *Titanic* viewing experience from other movies in an age of uniform ticket prices. Altered only slightly by time of day (i.e., bargain matinees), release date (second-run theaters), and geography (rural vs. urban), ticket price no longer corresponds to a film's budget. Whereas in previous decades, the marketplace sustained the quality/price difference through roadshow engagements—charging higher prices and printing hard tickets to epics and spectacles that became akin to legitimate theatrical experiences—the contemporary saturation release method cannot adequately signify the difference between a film's budget, production, or quality in a similar fashion. The roadshow form dictated that the film was of a "higher quality," thereby warranting special distribution and pricing. Unable to take advantage of the roadshow form, *Titanic* made it part of its marketing campaign, promoting the rich value and high caliber of *Titanic* like none other at the box office.

Nevertheless, regardless of the film's "quality," one question still pervaded the prerelease press discourse on *Titanic*: whether a single film, regardless of the subject, should ever cost $200 million? As Parisi describes this dilemma, "Even if it is a huge success, is *Titanic*'s $200 million cost—66% over budget and more than most filmmakers would have the imagination to spend—justified?"[33] As with *Heaven's Gate*, the press constructed a media scandal around the production of the film, complaining of the budget's excessiveness and wastefulness on the part of Cameron and the studios. Following James Lull and Stephen Hinerman's typology of media scandals, the controversy over the *Titanic* budget falls into the category of institutional scandals in which actions in a corporate or governmental setting disgrace or offend the public. Lull and Hinerman build a framework for institutional scandals involving the actions of a single individual not matching the accepted standards of the institution to which he or she belongs. As modern institutions often set moral examples through institutional advertising and public relations, the scandal destabilizes the image of the institution through highlighting the indiscretions of a single individual.[34] With *Titanic*, the newsworthy quality of the budget derives primarily from one individual, Cameron, operating beyond "accepted" guidelines for making the big-budget spectacle and secondarily from the studio executives, especially Mechanic, facilitating Cameron's behavior.

Justification for the enormous budget follows the quality/price correlation, although those associated with *Titanic* also offered other explanations why the budget overruns were neither excessive nor frivolous. Producer Jon Landau, for example, argued that the high budget was a boom for the economies in *Titanic*'s shooting locations such as Baja, Mexico, and Halifax, Canada.[35] Rob Legato, *Titanic*'s visual effects supervisor, stated plainly that the budget was always allocated for filmmaking and any speculation on its alternative uses was unrealistic.[36] The attempts to counter the impression of foolhardy expenditure either through economic explanation or quality arguments served to fuel the media scandal and the judgment that *Titanic* was newsworthy.

Fears of a critical backlash against the film, Cameron, and the budget dissipated shortly after *Titanic*'s world premiere in Tokyo, Japan, on 1 November 1997. Scheduling a premiere overseas prior to a domestic release date was a calculated gamble few studios attempted for a big-budget film: a negative reception could substantially harm the outcome of a North American opening. Nevertheless, Twentieth Century Fox's (the international distributor) majority stake in *Titanic*'s budget made it economically imperative to create strong international press and publicity for the film. A premiere outside the domestic market in Tokyo seemed appropriate since Japan was potentially the most lucrative foreign market and Leonardo DiCaprio was a major star in the country.[37] *Titanic* was a major hit, and glowing news of the film's international reception soon reached American audiences through trade publications, television programs, and popular magazines. Articles, such as one in *Variety* entitled "*Titanic* Deemed Seaworthy in Tokyo," and news segments in entertainment news, such as *E! News Daily*, just two days after the premiere, illustrate how quickly the American public was notified.[38] As a result, the positive word of mouth increased interest and demand domestically in the seven-week period leading up to its stateside release on 19 December and contributed to a shift in the media's reception to *Titanic*.

Now synonymous with *Titanic*'s quality, the budget became a central feature in American reviews of the film in spite of the *Hollywood Reporter*'s erroneous prediction that "*Titanic*'s turn at plate this weekend promises to switch the media focus from its extravagant $200 million production price tag to the merits of the movie and its positively princely performance."[39] While a few reviews, like Kenneth Turan's of the *Los Angeles Times*, simply stated that the $200 million behind *Titanic* had bought "not enough," most other opinions were more charitable in their assessment of *Titanic*'s quality and budget. Roger Ebert of the *Chicago Sun-Times* glowingly described *Titanic* as "value for money," and Andy Jones of *TNT Rough Cut Reviews* estimated that a ticket was worth $10 for *Titanic*, since "every cent of the $200 million plus spent in production flickers on screen."[40] Without a doubt, the most honest reaction to the budget issue came from José Arroyo in *Sight and Sound*: "It is hard to judge whether the budget is on the screen—who's seen a $200 million movie before?"[41]

Shortly after *Titanic*'s domestic release, it became clear that the film was a blockbuster, and the media discourse shifted to a different kind of data: the speed with which *Titanic* would break even and how many box office records it would set. Both the industry and the popular press watched the film's commercial progress closely, informing the public of each record *Titanic* broke. Among the most impressive of these records were *Titanic* grossing over $100 million in twelve days, $25 million across six consecutive weekends, and passing the $250–million mark in twenty-five days—breaking *Jurassic Park*'s (1993) record by a day. The Associated Press (AP) was one news agency that tracked *Titanic*'s box office success on a daily basis. On 23 February 1998, the AP reported that *Titanic* had passed *E.T.* (1982), becoming the second-highest domestic grosser ever. A week later, the

AP informed the public that *Titanic* had surpassed *Jurassic Park* as the highest-grossing international release. In the same article, the AP mentioned that *Titanic* was the first film to gross $1 billion.[42] Finally, on 24 March 1998, the AP reported that *Titanic* had topped *Star Wars* as the highest-grossing film of all time.

While the film's box office gross replaced the concerns over budget and production difficulties, data on *Titanic* continued to permeate the marketplace, especially through the soundtrack album, the Oscar nominations, and the phenomenal rise to (super)stardom of Leonardo DiCaprio. *Variety* tracked the soundtrack's success weekly and emphasized the uniqueness of a classical soundtrack ranking in first place on the album sales chart. *E! News Daily*, *Entertainment Weekly*, and the Associated Press all followed suit.[43] Solidifying a positive critical response, *Titanic* received fourteen Academy Award nominations, tying *All About Eve*'s (1950) record for the greatest number of nominations. As Oscar night approached, most of the trade papers and entertainment magazines agreed that *Titanic* would win for best direction and best film;[44] *USA Today* went so far as to predict that *Titanic* would "sweep" the Academy Awards, winning most of the categories in which it was nominated.[45] In fact, this prediction was validated shortly after: *Titanic* did win eleven awards, tying *Ben Hur*'s (1959) record. Data information even extended to the media audience for the Oscars broadcast. The awards show ranked the highest in history of the A. C. Nielsen ratings, and *Titanic*'s popularity was widely recognized as a key factor in its success.[46]

Prior to the Academy Awards, DiCaprio's escalating star power also fueled *Titanic*'s prominence in the marketplace. On 13 March 1998, another DiCaprio vehicle, *The Man in the Iron Mask*, was released, creating competition for Cameron's film. With articles titled "Leo vs. Leo in Dead Heat," the press fueled the notion that DiCaprio was competing with himself at the box office.[47] Paramount and MGM, distributors of *The Man in the Iron Mask*, both projected that each film would garner $17.5 million in the first weekend of direct competition. When these projections were released to the press, much interest was generated over the possibility of *Titanic* falling from the first place on the box office charts for the first time in thirteen weeks. Ultimately, *Titanic* remained at the top by generating $17 million, with *The Man in the Iron Mask* coming in a close second. Even at this point in the film's release, data served to create a hook for further stories about *Titanic* and for keeping the film in the public sphere.

The Discourse of *Titanic* in the Age of Enfotainment

The shift toward a positive representation of *Titanic* undoubtedly was facilitated by the strong public acceptance of the film. Nevertheless, the manner in which *Titanic* was presented to the public indicates an alteration in the journalistic negotiation of the big-budget spectacle. The specific components of the *Titanic* case allowed for a more positive reception by the press—in part due to the track record of Cameron and in part due to the public's strong appetite for enfotainment in the 1990s.

Suggesting that viewers are "sold" on the discourse of *Titanic*'s budget responds, in part, to the increasing significance of enfotainment as a means of marketing films. The term is defined by James Twitchell as a by-product of new technologies and the broader sense attributed to news: "Showbiz even has its mythology carried in the fastest growing sector of the entertainment industry: information and gossip about showbiz. Called 'enfotainment,' this grist is the result of the surge of delivery systems of entertainment in the 1980s: home video, cable, compact disks, and an audience eager to know not merely 'what's on' but 'what's in.'"[48]

Enfotainment can be traced to the introduction of entertainment news in the early 1980s, especially to the premiere of the syndicated television show *Entertainment Tonight* in 1981. Offering entertainment industry and celebrity information as news, the show pioneered the presentation of "soft news." All the trappings of a typical news show—the anchors, the feature segments, high-tech graphics—were marshaled for information about Hollywood, its inhabitants, and the industry. The result was wildly successful: *Entertainment Tonight* airs in 179 markets covering 95 percent of North America and in seventeen foreign countries as well.[49]

One of *Entertainment Tonight*'s innovations that had a long-lasting impact on media news was the weekly reporting of box office gross and television ratings. This information, previously the domain of trade papers, eventually was translated to daily papers. In many urban newspapers, the listing of the Top Twenty films at the box office became routine: every Tuesday the "winners" from the previous weekend were presented along with total box office receipts, per-screen average, and percentage change from the previous weekend.[50] News about Hollywood, such as production budgets, star salaries, and commercial trends, were reported at an accelerated rate in *Entertainment Tonight* and its descendants: *Entertainment Weekly* and *Premiere* magazines, Fox's *Entertainment Daily Journal*, and E! Entertainment Network. On the Internet, entertainment industry news, "scoops," and gossip are carried by a variety of sites, such as the official studio Web pages for a film, and, most notoriously, "Harry Knowles' Ain't-It-Cool News" that frequently reports on confidential studio market research screenings.[51] All of these sources operate to bolster awareness in upcoming films.

The tent pole strategy that lies at the core of contemporary studio production meshes perfectly with the rise of entertainment industry news in the past two decades: entertainment journalists are able to report on big-budget tent pole movies in production or in the planning stages to generate interest and gossip for a film. Tent pole films "hold up" the remainder of a studio's distribution slate through being extremely commercial and having a built-in audience for strong opening box office. In the past two decades, with the shift away from the 1970s auteur projects and toward high-concept, marketing-oriented films, the tent pole system has been crucial to the operation of several studios. As a result, a tent pole film can support less certain commercial endeavors.[52] Non-tent-pole pictures are subsequently unable to benefit from the kind of awareness and immediate viewer interest shaped by forms of enfotainment. In this manner, entertainment industry journalism bolsters the tent pole strategy by focusing on these films to a greater extent than on films more difficult to classify and describe.

Nevertheless, the strategy does embody at least one major danger: as studios seek to develop more "reliable" tent poles, the budgets increase with the size of production and number of stars. As costs for the tent poles dramatically rise, the number of other films being produced decreases, so a studio becomes even more dependent on the tent pole films. *Titanic* illustrates this syndrome in the extreme. Although there would exist a presold audience for *Titanic*, the movie, and *Titanic*, the event, due to the cost of the film, Twentieth Century Fox and Paramount had to partner to support this single tent pole project. Even after the success of *Titanic*, the dangers of the tent pole strategy still remain in place; as Peter Bart describes it, "The 'tent pole picture' is having a bumpy ride, *Titanic* notwithstanding."[53]

Therefore, enfotainment as a marketing tool must be considered as the result of the ubiquity of media delivery systems and the conglomerate ownership structure at their core. As conglomerates more tightly focused on media in the 1980s and 1990s, the synergy between the components of the conglomerate became a major concern. Part of the disappearance of the boundaries between "traditional" news and entertainment was due to many of these areas existing under the same conglomerate umbrella. The News Corporation, for instance, controls Twentieth Century Fox Films and Television, satellite broadcasting, books, newspapers, magazines, and computer services. *Titanic*'s other partner, Paramount, is under the ownership of Viacom, which also has interests in MTV, Showtime cable, Blockbuster video, book publishing, and sports franchises.[54] Enfotainment and the creation of media events fit perfectly with the overall goals of the contemporary media conglomerate structure.

Titanic contains some most attractive elements for potential enfotainment stories: Hollywood spectacle, larger-than-life personalities, and, of course, ridiculous sums of money. The specific "story" originally created within the press suggests the negatives of *Titanic*: a budget growing higher and higher, an auteur known for his dictatorial style given freedom due to his commercial track record, and a project that appears to be a tent pole for studio production but lacks some of the usual components, like stars and a bankable genre. All of these story points are set against spectacular visuals from the production and the true story of the *Titanic* sinking known to all.

The negative scenario envisioned by these initial enfotainment stories is largely undone by the eventual onslaught of positive story lines: the constant reminder of *Titanic*'s historical authenticity and accuracy, many strong reviews, and perhaps the strongest element, the public's resonant vote as evidenced through extraordinary box office levels. These positives respond to many of the queries initially posed within the press and offer a validation of the studio decision making for big-budget production. Conveniently, this system of production fits most comfortably with the media conglomerates sponsoring the tent pole movies and the enfotainment stories.

Titanic represents the perfect property to take advantage of the new marketing angles from enfotainment. Its budget discourse—the scandal over the size and cost of the film—plays into one of the key social developments identified by advertising firms in the mid-1990s: the match of political apathy and a fascination with extremes and margins in cultural expression. Instead of ignoring the extremes and margins, "liberation marketing" embraces both in advertising. Consumers are able to "live on the edge" without actually altering their own traditional lives. As Thomas Frank explains this advertising phenomenon, "Even the word 'extreme' itself is virtually everywhere, from Taco Bell's 'extreme combos' to Boston Market's 'extreme carvers' to Pontiac commercials in which the company announces that it is 'taking it to the extreme.'"[55] *Titanic*'s budget discourse taps fully into this trend to consider, appreciate, and consume the extreme. By breaking boundaries and limits, the extreme also connotes a degree of newsworthiness; the combination of *Titanic* and the extreme is therefore even more attractive to the producers of enfotainment. After learning about the film in myriad ways through enfotainment, audience members can "consume" the most extreme of motion pictures, the most expensive film ever produced.

In addition to the size factor, the press was able to create an alternative narrative for *Titanic*. Because the film's narrative was so well known (due to the public's familiarity with the sinking of the ship), the real drama was created extratextually through the journalistic representation of the film and its production. The tremendous cost and the grand scale became the focal points, with James Cameron cast simultaneously as hero and villain in the role of visionary and fiscally responsible auteur. A new drama of recoupment was created by the troubled production, the driven auteur, and the awe-inspiring budget. All these "challenges" were overcome through the mighty public response and the repeat-viewing phenomenon that ensured a satisfying denouement. As with any contemporary Hollywood film, the obligatory happy ending was supplied by the incredible commercial success of the film. The narrative trajectory of *Titanic*—the media discourse—thus serves to reinforce both the studio system committed to high-concept projects and the auteur who can work within the system to produce them.

Appropriately, in terms of the industry, the long-term impact of *Titanic* and its budget return once again to the obsession with size and data. Many industry representatives believe that the standard for budgets has been elevated considerably by *Titanic*'s success—perhaps not to the extent of $200 million, but certainly in the $100- to $125-million range.[56] A *Variety*-sponsored film panel on 31 March 1998, titled "The Movie Business: Dodging Icebergs in an Era of Megamovies," focused solely on the issue of *Titanic*'s impact. Panelists Peter Bart (*Variety*), Jonathan Dolgen (Viacom), Lynda Obst (producer), Michael Kuhn (Polygram), and Harvey Weinstein (Miramax) concurred that budgets would be bid up post-*Titanic*. Obst noted that medium- and low-budget pictures would not be impacted as greatly as high-budget studio films; she concluded, "The bar has been raised in physical production and in the power we give directors."[57]

While these claims may well be valid, the *Titanic* case illustrates just as clearly the complexity of contemporary film marketing for the studio tent pole film—a system in which the traditional routes of creative advertising, publicity, and promotion have been augmented by a public fascination with entertainment industry news, budgets, and box office. The extraordinary commercial success of *Titanic* is due, in part, to this dynamic mix of marketing forms and to the film's capacity, through its budget, commercial auteur, and impressive data, to tap directly into these routes for public awareness and interest.

Notes

The authors wish to thank Jeffrey Clarke and the editors, Kevin S. Sandler and Gaylyn Studlar, for comments on an earlier version of this essay.

1. Advertisement for *Foolish Wives*, *New York Times*, 12 January 1922.
2. *Foolish Wives* (review), *New York Times*, 12 January 1922, 15. For a discussion of the selling of *Foolish Wives* see Janet Staiger, "Announcing Wares, Winning Patrons, Voicing Ideals: Thinking about the History and Theory of Film Advertising," *Cinema Journal* 29, no. 3 (spring 1990): 21–22.
3. Mordaunt Hall, "A Stupendous Spectacle," *New York Times*, 31 December 1925, 10.
4. Bosley Crowther, "*The Ten Commandments* (review)," *New York Times*, 9 November 1956, 35.
5. "The Spirit of the Wind," *Time*, 4 January 1963, 58.
6. "*The Ten Commandments*" (review), *Time*, 12 November 1956, 120.
7. *New York Times*, 1 June 1962, 18.
8. *Look*, 7 May 1963, 42; *Life*, 19 April 1963, 72; *Fortune*, August 1963, 234; *Variety*, 5 June 1963, 1; *Variety*, 12 June 1963, 17; *Variety*, 19 June 1963, 4.
9. See Steven Bach, *Final Cut: Dreams and Disaster in the Making of Heaven's Gate* (New York: Morrow, 1985).
10. While Cimino was undoubtedly monomaniacal, the big-budget blunder must also be attributed to the structural problems of United Artists and the "sea change" of American cinema of this period, which saw auteur filmmaking being replaced by genre and marketing-driven projects like *Jaws* (1975), *Star Wars* (1977), *Saturday Night Fever* (1977), *Close Encounters of the Third Kind* (1977), and *Grease* (1978).
11. In "The System That Let *Heaven's Gate* Run Wild," Vincent Canby proclaimed that the studios routinely rewarded large-scale hits with a director's "vanity" project, which often became a resounding flop: Steven Spielberg following *Close Encounters of the Third Kind* with *1941* (1979), William Friedkin making *Sorcerer* (1977) after *The Exorcist* (1973), and Martin Scorsese bombing with *New York, New York* (1977), after *Taxi Driver* (1976). Canby framed his article as a cautionary tale, claiming that *Heaven's Gate*'s massive failure was inevitable in the Hollywood system, the result of a hit-driven film economy favoring those directors with a proven commercial record. See *New York Times*, 30 November 1980, sec. 2, p. 1.
12. Robert W. Welkos, "Sharing the Risk and Wealth; Studios Turn to Co-Financing, Other Deals for Big-Budget Films," *Los Angeles Times*, 8 April 1996, Calendar sec., p. 1.
13. Anne Thompson, "Cameron Is God," *Premiere* April 1998, 44.
14. Peter Bart, "Auteur as Terminator: The Curse of Cameron," *Variety*, 2 June 1997.
15. Richard Corliss, "*True Lies*," *Time*, 18 July 1994.
16. Joe Brown, "*Terminator 2: Judgment Day*," *Washington Post*, 5 July 1991.
17. Richard Corliss, "Lies, *True Lies*, and Ballistics," *Time*, 18 July 1994.
18. See, for example, David Robb, "SAG Probes Set of *Titanic*," *Hollywood Reporter,* 16 December 1996; David Robb, "SAG: *Titanic* Safely Ship Shape," *Hollywood Reporter,*

6 January 1997; Carl DiOrio, "*Titanic* a Wash for DD Fxers," *Hollywood Reporter*, 23 May 1997; Etan Vlessing, "Sinking Feeling: PCP on *Titanic*," *Hollywood Reporter*, 29 August 1996.

19. *Variety*, 19 May 1997.

20. Jon Herskovitz, "*Titanic* Clicks in Tokyo," *Variety*, 4 November 1997.

21. "Drowning by Numbers," *Empire* (England), February 1998, 92.

22. James Cameron, "Settling Accounts," *Time*, 8 December 1997, 92.

23. Bernard Weinraub, "*Titanic* Is Turning Out to be a Success on the Scale of Its Doomed Subject," *New York Times*, 2 February 1998.

24. "Summer Movie Preview," *Premiere*, June 1997, 50–51.

25. Bart, "Auteur as Terminator."

26. Chris Petrikin, "Fox, Cameron Opting out of *Terminator 3*," *Variety*, 6 October 1997.

27. Paula Parisi, "Man Overboard!" *Entertainment Weekly*, 7 November 1997, 26–37. Shortly after the film's release, Parisi authored a book on Cameron and the making of *Titanic*, so her unique and "unbiased" take on the production must be viewed in the context of marketing as much as "entertainment news." See *Titanic and the Making of James Cameron* (New York: Newmarket Press, 1998).

28. Quoted in Alex Gove, "*Titanic* Ambition," *Red Herring,* January 1998, 78.

29. Quoted in Erich Boehm, "*Titanic* Price a Selling Point," *Variety*, 11 July 1997.

30. Peter Travers, "A Night to Remember," *Us*, January 1998, 36.

31. Bernard Weinraub, "At the Movies," *New York Times*, 13 February 1998.

32. www.titanicmovie.com.

33. Paula Parisi, "Sink or Swim for Cameron," *Hollywood Reporter*, 22 December 1997.

34. James Lull and Stephen Hinerman, "The Search for Scandal," *Media Scandals: Morality and Desire in the Popular Culture Marketplace*, ed. Lull and Hinerman (New York: Columbia University Press, 1997), 20.

35. Herskovitz, "*Titanic* Clicks in Tokyo."

36. Michael Mallory, "Miracles for Sale (at $200 Million)," *Millimeter*, January 1998, 32.

37. Herskovitz, "*Titanic* Clicks in Tokyo."

38. Jon Herskovitz, "*Titanic* Deemed Seaworthy in Tokyo," *Variety*, 3 November 1997.

39. Roger Cels, "Boxoffice Preview," *Hollywood Reporter*, 19 December 1997.

40. Kenneth Turan, "*Titanic* Sinks Again (Spectacularly)," *Los Angeles Times*, 19 December 1997; Roger Ebert, "Special Effects Live up to Hype in *Titanic*," *Chicago Sun-Times*, 7 December 1997; Andy Jones, *TNT Rough Cut Reviews*.

41. José Arroyo, "Massive Attack," *Sight and Sound*, February 1998, 19.

42. Associated Press, 2 March 1998.

43. Adam Sandler, "*Titanic* Disc Sets a High Water Mark," *Variety*, 2 February 1998.

44. For example, *Miami Herald*, 22 March 1998; *Arizona Republic*, 23 March 1998; *TV Guide*, 21 March 1998; *Entertainment Weekly*, 20 March 1998; *USA Today*, 23 March 1998.

45. Jeannie Williams, *USA Today*, 23 March 1998.

46. Lynn Elber, Associated Press, 24 March 1998.

47. Andrew Hindes, "Leo vs. Leo in Dead Heat," *Variety*, 16 March 1998.

48. James Twitchell, *Carnival Culture: The Trashing of Taste in America* (New York: Columbia University Press, 1992), 9.

49. Steven D. Strak, *Glued to the Set* (New York: Free Press, 1997), 250.

50. Michael Lewis, "All Grossed Out," *New York Times Magazine*, 19 May 1996, 24.

51. www.aint-it-cool-news.com.

52. As an example, consider that Paramount's 1989 schedule was based around *Indiana Jones and the Last Crusade*, which was able to support such prestigious and relatively uncommercial pictures as Roland Joffe's study of the development of the atomic bomb, *Fat Man and Little Boy*.

53. Quoted in Dan Cox and Chris Petrikin, "Big Boat's Success Buoys Film Budgets," *Variety*, 6 April 1998, 20.

54. For an examination of the exchange between components of a single conglomerate, consult Ian Grey, *Sex, Stupidity, and Greed: Inside the American Movie Industry* (New York: Juno Books, 1997), 31.

55. Thomas Frank, "Liberation Marketing and the Culture Trust," in *Conglomerates and the Media*, ed. Erik Barnouw et al. (New York: New Press, 1997), 175.

56. Benjamin Svetkey, "In the Wake of *Titanic*," *Entertainment Weekly*, 6 February 1998, 21.

57. Cox and Petrikin, "Big Boat's Success Buoys Film Budgets," 20.

Selling My Heart

MUSIC AND CROSS-PROMOTION IN *TITANIC*

JEFF SMITH

*I*n a recent issue of the *Hollywood Reporter*, Elliot Lurie, a former music department head at Fox, described the process of selecting songs for films. While most music supervisors acknowledge that a number of factors enter into such decisions, ranging from the producer's desire for an exploitable soundtrack to the record label's interest in pushing new acts, Lurie suggests that the most important criterion is ultimately a simple one: "If you get goosebumps watching the scene, you've picked the right song."[1]

The idea of a "goose bump" factor seems doubly appropriate when discussing the music of *Titanic*. Not only was James Horner's score, especially the popular theme "My Heart Will Go On," a key element in the film's arousal of emotional responses, but it brilliantly underscored the film's final sequences during which hundreds of passengers are plunged into the frigid waters of the Atlantic. Audiences around the globe can attest to the goose bumps they felt as they watched Rose Bukater, floating amid a sea of frozen corpses, say good-bye to her beloved, Jack Dawson, before releasing his body to the sea. The combination of James Cameron's images of icy death and Horner's heartrending melodies sent chills up and down the audience's collective spine.

Yet the goose bumps experienced by audiences in theaters are only part of the story. As many composers and music supervisors point out, an audience's affective response to film music can be a key factor in a score's success in ancillary markets. According to Gary LeMel, president of Warner Bros. Music, "It's always better if you can marry the music to an emotional piece of film because that's what makes people react."[2] In such instances, the soundtrack functions as a take-home souvenir of the cinematic experience, one that can prompt whole vistas of emotional reflection with just a few notes of a popular theme. In this respect, the *Titanic* soundtrack is not unlike the books, replica jewelry, or other catalog consumer goods that were purchased by the thousands.

The combination of sentiment and melody in *Titanic* proved a potent weapon in garnering radio airplay and soundtrack sales. The soundtrack album set several records during its stay on the charts and sold some 10 million copies in the United States alone. Most significantly, it remained atop the album charts for sixteen weeks during the film's theatrical run, a feat that helped keep *Titanic* in the public eye and encouraged repeat viewings among devoted fans. No other instrumental score has ever sold as steadily or as much as Horner's music for *Titanic*.

Yet while the success of the soundtrack was unprecedented, the score's sales seem less surprising when one considers the growing market for film music. Annual sales of soundtrack albums have quadrupled in the last ten years, and during any given week, one can find between ten and twenty soundtracks perched on *Billboard*'s album charts.[3] Similarly, the increasing importance of music-licensing for films has greatly enhanced the value of publishers' and record labels' back catalogs. EMI-Capitol Music, for example, has seen its master licensing business nearly quintuple since 1989.[4] Licensing fees have also risen at a comparable rate. According to one label executive, the cost of using a particular recording over a film's opening credits is now five to ten times higher than it was ten years ago.[5]

It is within this larger economic context that the performance of *Titanic*'s soundtrack must be understood. In the first part of this essay, I will examine the cross-promotional campaign used to support the *Titanic* soundtrack in order to trace the ways in which it intersects with this larger matrix of historical precedents and industrial forces. In tapping into this growing market for film music, *Titanic* skillfully exploited a cross-promotional formula that can be traced back several decades. More specifically, while *Titanic* updates the strategies of the theme scores of the classical Hollywood studio era, it also takes advantage of more modern promotional techniques, such as the music trailer and the dance remix.

But clearly the present economic context for film music accounts for only one aspect of *Titanic*'s success. After all, there have been several recent score albums released for blockbuster films—*Jurassic Park* (1993) and *Independence Day* (1996) come to mind—but very few have had the kind of cultural impact of *Titanic*. Although several factors might be cited to account for this difference, perhaps the most important of these is the way in which Horner's music functions within the film. In the second half of this essay, I will look more specifically at the score itself in order to trace the development of several musical themes of the film, most significantly the love theme, "My Heart Will Go On." My contention here is that while the cross-promotional campaign enabled the soundtrack's success, it was the album's function as a musical memento that made it such a cultural phenomenon. Unlike soundtracks like *Batman and Robin* (1997), which sell independently of the film, *Titanic* realized its success through a prerequisite combination of canny marketing and dramatic effectiveness.

"Hearts" and Minds: Putting Together *Titanic*'s Musical Package

Throughout its history, Hollywood has long used music to sell films and vice versa.[6] During the silent era, for example, several exhibitors included song slides and singers as special attractions in their programs. The singers were frequently employed by music publishers for the express purpose of "plugging" a particular tune. In exchange for the plug, the exhibitor typically sold copies of sheet music in the theater and retained a small percentage of the monies from such sales.[7] This period also witnessed the rise of the "musical illustration" as a specific film genre. According to Charles Merrell Berg, these films were a variation of the song slide principle since they were created not only to accompany a specific song but also to illustrate that song dramatically. Interest in this genre culminated in the late teens with two series of song illustrations produced by Harry Cohn and Carl Laemmle respectively. By featuring song slides and filmed "illustrations" of music, movie theaters joined department stores, music shops, and vaudeville as important venues for song-plugging and as hubs of a multimillion-dollar industry.[8]

The practice of using song slides gradually died out in the 1920s when composers began writing specific theme songs for films. Although sheet music sales for film themes were generally modest in the early years of that decade, the music industry took note of the promotional possibilities proffered by a specially composed or compiled film score. Early sound films reversed this trend, however, with the estimable success of "Charmaine" from *What Price Glory?* (1926) and "Diane" from *Seventh Heaven* (1927). In the wake of these successful theme scores, which were typically organized around a single prominent tune, record companies advised their retailers that "each week the tune studded talking picture leaves customers of yours with impressively presented theme songs echoing in their ears."[9]

With the coming of sound, several studios began buying music publishing houses in order to gain copyright control of the songs that appeared in their films. Although Paramount and Loew's were the first to buy their own publishing houses, Warner Bros. proved to be the most aggressive in its acquisitions. In January of 1929, Warners purchased the original Tin Pan Alley house, M. Witmark & Sons, and shortly thereafter acquired interests in the Harms Music Publishing Company, the Remick Music Corporation, and a host of smaller music houses. By mid-1929, Warners' newly formed music division commanded a major share of the music publishers' vote in the American Society of Composers, Authors, and Publishers (ASCAP), the major performance rights organization in the United States.[10] By 1939, the thirteen music houses affiliated with Hollywood earned about two-thirds of the total monies distributed to publishers by ASCAP.[11]

When sheet music sales declined in the 1950s, due in part to competition from the burgeoning market for recorded music, Hollywood turned to new forms of cross-promotion, such as the soundtrack album and theme song single. Between 1957 and 1958, several film distributors, among them Paramount, Twentieth Century Fox, and United Artists, followed the lead of MGM and Universal by either buying or starting up their own record subsidiaries. Hollywood's sudden interest in recorded music was at least partly spurred by the resurgence of the theme score in the mid-1950s. The success of musical tie-ins for films like *High Noon* (1952), *Love Is a Many Splendored Thing* (1955), and *A Summer Place* (1959) led to a rash of imitators, and soon producers were commissioning pop songs to serve as the basis of theme scores.[12]

Generally speaking, however, Hollywood was less interested in the outright sale of records than it was in using records and radio as promotional vehicles for film scores and theme songs. Consequently, most studios approached their cross-promotional campaigns much as a publisher or song plugger would. Rather than seek sales and exposure of a particular version of a theme song, film companies simply sought as much repetition of the tune as possible and often commissioned several recordings of the song, each released by a different label. By authorizing multiple versions of the song, studios not only enhanced the tune's overall licensing revenues but also increased its chances for heavy radio play.[13]

When a film theme clicked, the benefits of this multiple exposure became obvious. During a single week in 1961, Ernest Gold's theme for *Exodus* (1960) was featured on four different albums in *Billboard*'s Top Fifty. In addition, *Exodus*'s soundtrack spent fourteen weeks at the top of the charts, a record for score albums that was only recently broken by *Titanic*. Similarly, Manos Hadjidakis's theme from *Never on Sunday* (1960) was recorded more than thirty times in the United States, and more than four hundred times worldwide. Together these different versions of the song accounted for sales of approximately 14 million singles. Through its sales and airplay, a hit song or album could easily supply as much as $1 million's worth of "cuffo promotion."[14]

Although the record industry's climate of "profitless prosperity" encouraged some studios to sell off their record interests during the 1970s, the soundtrack album remained a key component of film promotion, its position sustained by several notable hits, including *The Graduate* (1967), *Easy Rider* (1969), *American Graffiti* (1973), *Saturday Night Fever* (1977), and *Grease* (1978). By 1979, the role of film and music cross-promotions had become so standardized that there was a general industry awareness of what was necessary to create a hit soundtrack: "[C]ommercially viable music. Timing. Film cooperation on advance planning and tie-ins. Music that's integral to the movie. A hit movie. A hit single. A big-name recording star. A big-name composer."[15] While not all of these ingredients were absolutely essential, the absence of one or two could spell the difference between a soundtrack's overall success or failure. The 1980s saw minor changes in this formula following music video's emergence as an additional ancillary market for film music. By 1985, the typical film and music cross-promotion operated according to a concise formula that R. Serge Denisoff and George Plasketes express as "movie + soundtrack + video = $$$."[16]

Of these ingredients, timing is perhaps the most critical element. Since 1960, the conventional wisdom about soundtracks is that they should be released about four to six weeks before the film's general release in order to give the music an opportunity to work its way up the charts and circulate the film's title in radio and retail markets.[17] The same generally holds true for theme songs and music videos. In theory, a so-called scout single generates positive buzz for the film, which in turn creates consumer interest in the film's theme song and soundtrack album. As record executive Danny Goldberg explained in coining the term "synergy" to describe such cross-promotions, interest in one component synergistically feeds off interest in the other until both film and soundtrack album reign supreme over box offices and record charts.[18] To illustrate the effect of such tie-ins, industry analysts conservatively estimate that a successful theme song can add as much as $20 million to a film's box office take.

Yet most cross-promotional campaigns work better in theory than in actual practice. As Denisoff and Plasketes point out, several films succeed despite the lack of consumer interest in their music ancillaries.[19] Similarly, soundtrack albums like *Above the Rim* (1994) and *The Crow* (1994) sometimes outpace their counterparts by attracting record buyers who have never seen the films they accompany. In still other instances, both film and soundtrack fail in their respective markets. When problems occur, they can often be traced to difficulties coordinating the release schedules of album and film. After all, although film companies, music publishers, and record labels all exploit soundtracks through a kind of joint venture, one company's short-term economic interests may impinge on its cooperation with the other two points of the cross-promotional triangle. Because they are primarily interested in the soundtrack's promotional function, film companies generally want to coordinate the album's release with the film's release. Record labels, on the other hand, realize most of their profits in album sales and are thus more inclined to schedule releases that are favorable to the album itself or to the recording artists who participate in the soundtrack. (Executives often view soundtrack cuts as stopgap measures designed to keep artists in the public eye between major releases.) Publishers, however, derive their revenues from licensing fees. As such, they show comparatively greater interest in pushing the film's theme song in the hope that it will become an "evergreen," an oft-recorded standard like "Moon River" that will generate revenues for many years to come.

Not only did the *Titanic* soundtrack pose fewer scheduling problems than a multiartist pop compilation usually does, but it benefited from the careful coordination of music and film interests. Yet the success of *Titanic*'s soundtrack might never have occurred if composer James Horner had strictly adhered to the instructions given to him by director James Cameron. Horner and Cameron had previously collaborated on *Aliens* (1986), but their experience working together on that film was one of mutual frustration. According to Horner, "It was a very difficult experience for both of us, because there was so little time for such a mammoth job. I wasn't able to give him everything he wanted."[20] After receiving several Oscar nominations for such scores as *Apollo 13* (1995) and *Braveheart* (1995), Horner reunited with Cameron on *Titanic*. The two met in February 1997 during the final two months of filming, and Cameron reportedly gave Horner two simple instructions: no standard orchestration and no pop songs.[21]

After starting work on *Titanic*, however, Horner soon decided that the best way to capture Rose's feelings at film's end and the best way to give the film a timeless, yet contemporary appeal was to compose a song for the closing credits. To that end, Horner secretly hired lyricist Will Jennings to write words for the tune and got longtime friend Celine Dion to surreptitiously record a demo in May of 1997 at New York's Hit Factory. Knowing the problems with their previous collaboration, Horner withheld the tape from Cameron for about three weeks until he was sure he had established a good rapport with the director. Then after what

Horner describes as a "good long streak of positive vibes," the composer played the tape for Cameron in his study. After hearing it two or three times, the director was sold.[22]

Horner's decision to use Jennings and Dion proved wise from a commercial standpoint because each had well-established track records for film. In fact, all three of them had worked together once before on the song "Dreams to Dream" for the film *An American Tail: Fievel Goes West* (1991). More important, though, Jennings had penned lyrics for six previous chart-topping singles, most notably Joe Cocker and Jennifer Warnes's recording of "Up Where We Belong" for the film *An Officer and a Gentleman* (1982). Films had played an equally important role in Celine Dion's buildup as a recording artist. According to her husband and manager, Rene Angelil, her organization made a decision in 1991 to use movie work as "a way for her to get known quickly."[23] Dion's team then pursued several plum film assignments and succeeded in placing her on the soundtracks for *Beauty and the Beast* (1991), *Sleepless in Seattle* (1993), and *Up Close and Personal* (1996). After the latter spawned a huge hit with "Because You Loved Me," Dion became widely regarded as an artist who specialized in romantic movie themes. Not surprisingly, she is pitched to some twenty films each year.[24] More than that, however, Dion's soundtrack participation helped her become one of the top-five recording artists in the industry with sales of her 1995 album, *Falling Into You*, tallying more than 25 million units worldwide.

Even before Dion's involvement, however, Horner and Cameron began peddling the soundtrack rights to the *Titanic* score. Citing the soundtrack's estimated $1–million price tag, several labels turned them down, including Polygram, which had previously released Horner's score for *Braveheart* in 1995. The soundtrack finally found a home at Sony Classical, which bought the rights as part of a broader plan to use film scores as a way of sustaining the label's fortunes.[25] In October 1997, Sony Classical announced that *Titanic* would be released as part of a long-term, exclusive deal with Horner. Under the terms of this contract, Sony Classical secured the rights to several of Horner's future projects, including a ballet score as well as a symphonic work based on his themes for *Titanic*.[26]

Meanwhile, Horner frantically worked to ready his score for *Titanic*'s initial release date of 4 July. Although composers work under great duress in the best of circumstances, Horner's problems were exacerbated by *Titanic*'s three-hour running time and by the production's late reshoots, which threatened to cut even further into the composer's work schedule. When Cameron's rough cut was finally ready, Horner had approximately six weeks to write and record *Titanic*'s 138–minute score. Horner's furious work pace, however, suddenly slackened when *Titanic*'s release was pushed back to 19 December. The score continued to evolve throughout the fall of 1997 as Horner refined and polished his work to accommodate the various editing changes made by Cameron.[27]

On 1 November 1997, *Titanic* received its world premiere at the Tokyo International Film Festival. There were several reasons for choosing Tokyo as the site of the film's premiere, chief among them being the popularity of Cameron, Dion, and Leonardo DiCaprio within the Japanese entertainment market. The decision proved to be a shrewd one on the part of *Titanic*'s production and marketing team for the film's screening sold out within a matter of minutes. The clamor for tickets undoubtedly helped create a positive buzz for the film, as did reports that the festival's office was "inundated with requests from domestic and international media for press passes as well as from scores of U.S. movie execs."[28] The Tokyo premiere's combination of intense curiosity, high expectations, and a largely receptive local audience helped give *Titanic* the "must-see" aura it so desperately needed some six weeks before its U.S. release. Perhaps more important, the laudatory notices sent back by trade reviewers established a welcome precedent for the largely favorable critical reception *Titanic* received in the United States.

About two weeks after the film's premiere, Sony began its campaign on behalf of Horner's score. On 18 November, the company's music group issued two albums featuring *Titanic*'s theme song, "My Heart Will Go On." The first, of course, was the *Titanic* soundtrack, and the second was Dion's *Let's Talk About Love*, the much anticipated follow-up to *Falling Into You*. Noting the unusual nature of this simultaneous release, some industry observers questioned the wisdom of Sony's marketing strategy by arguing that the new Dion album could potentially siphon off prospective buyers of the soundtrack.

In retrospect, such fears proved to be quite unfounded. For one thing, it is rather unlikely that Sony saw these two albums as competing products in the first place. After all, the respective targets for each album—a small, largely male, niche market of film score connoisseurs for the *Titanic* soundtrack; a massive, largely female, adult contemporary audience for Dion—are rather different indeed, and the expectation of sales for each album would be calculated accordingly. Sony undoubtedly anticipated the multiplatinum success of Dion's album but probably only hoped to top about 100,000 in sales of the *Titanic* soundtrack. Moreover, Sony executives must have recognized that each album would have a rather different sales pattern. To use a film analogy, Dion's album is the record industry equivalent of a blockbuster receiving a saturation booking. Released for the crucial holiday sales period, *Let's Talk About Love* was virtually guaranteed a significant number of sales and extensive airplay. In contrast, the *Titanic* soundtrack is closer to a "sleeper" film that requires a platform release pattern in order to build strong word of mouth. As such, Sony executives would expect sales of the soundtrack to be sluggish until the film was released in theaters. Once the film was out, the album, which is almost entirely instrumental, would depend heavily on the film for whatever financial success it could muster.

Viewed from this perspective, the simultaneous release not only reveals the interdependent logics behind the *Titanic* campaign but also offers a textbook example of film and record industry synergies at work. On the one hand, the release of Dion's album in November accords with industry wisdom that the Christmas season is a peak period of buying. In fact, it has become axiomatic for record labels to hold back greatest hits packages or major new releases until the holidays in order to take advantage of those occasional consumers who purchase compact discs as gifts and stocking stuffers. In 1997, several companies hoped that new releases by Dion, Garth Brooks, and the Spice Girls would help boost overall sales figures and salvage a somewhat moribund year. On the other hand, both the soundtrack and the Dion album would help promote *Titanic* during the crucial month-long period before the film's release. The immediate hoopla surrounding Dion's album would help garner airplay for "My Heart Will Go On," while the use of the song in trailers would highlight the film's romantic story line by taking advantage of "Queen Celine's" previous track record with melodramatic ballads. The month-long window would also give Dion's album a chance to ascend to the Top Ten at the time *Titanic* was released to theaters. In return, *Titanic*'s opening weekend would help give Dion's album one final push in the week before Christmas and, at least in theory, would help sustain sales of both albums during the early part of 1998.

The plan's success is evident in the chart action achieved by both the two albums and the theme song. Although it did not reach number one on *Billboard*'s charts until January of 1998, *Let's Talk About Love* became the fastest-selling album of Dion's career. Within two months, it had sold more than 3 million copies domestically and more than 12 million worldwide. Attesting to her popularity abroad, the album achieved platinum status in twenty-four sales territories, including Norway, France, Hong Kong, and Japan.[29] According to its most recent tally, *Let's Talk About Love* showed sales of more than 8 million units in the United States. and a comparable number abroad.

If anything, the chart performance of the *Titanic* soundtrack was even more astonishing. As expected, sales of the soundtrack were slow at first, but before the year was out, the album debuted at number 154 on *Billboard*'s Top 200. The following week it leaped to 72, and the week after that it hit 31. By 17 January, some two months after the album's release, the soundtrack neared the Top Ten with overall sales in the neighborhood of 1 million units. Describing the soundtrack's initial sales pattern, Eric Vaughan, a major label buyer for the retailer Disc Jockey, said, "We really didn't see anything happening with the album until the movie opened. Then it just snowballed."[30] To the surprise of nearly everyone, the album reached number one on 24 January and stayed there for a record-breaking sixteen weeks.

Even more impressively, weekly sales of both albums increased throughout the month of February. During the week of 14 February, the *Titanic* soundtrack sold more than 580,000 units, while Dion's album tallied a sum of 236,000.[31] Buoyed by sales from Valentine's Day shopping, both albums posted huge gains during the next two weeks. By the end of February, the soundtrack was selling a whopping 850,000 copies a week, while Dion's album experienced a slightly smaller sales bulge to 339,000 units. As the two top-selling albums of that week, *Titanic* and *Let's Talk About Love* together tallied more than the combined sales of the eight remaining albums in the Top Ten. As Geoff Mayfield put it, "So large was the growth that, if an album sold only what *Titanic* gained—259,000 units—it would have ranked No. 3 for the week."[32] By the start of March, worldwide sales of the *Titanic* soundtrack reached more than 10 million as the album leaped to number one in some twenty-one countries.

More significant from a promotional perspective, the film's theme song, "My Heart Will Go On," broke broadcasting records by racking up the largest number of radio performances measured in one week. According to data provided by *Billboard*'s Broadcast Data Systems (BDS), Dion's single logged nearly 9,500 spins from some 223 different radio stations during the first week of February. Some stations were playing the song as many as seventy-three times a week or approximately once every two hours. Not surprisingly, with the song reaching some 105 million listeners, "My Heart Will Go On" also broke the record for the largest radio audience ever monitored by BDS.[33]

While Dion's single was largely played within Top Forty formats, the song garnered additional performances in Adult Contemporary and Dance formats through cover versions recorded by Kenny G and Deja Vu respectively. The Kenny G recording was initially intended to serve only as a promotional item, a behind-the-counter premium given away to consumers who purchased Kenny G's *Greatest Hits* package.[34] In addition, radio also began circulating a version of the song that spliced five audio clips from the film. The ploy, which had first succeeded with Bruce Springsteen's recording of "Secret Garden" from *Jerry McGuire* (1996), used sound bites to illustrate the dramatic arc of Rose and Jack's relationship in the film, and it enabled listeners to "relive the three-hour plus film in 4:40 minutes."[35] VH 1 also used this "audio drop-in" technique to create a special video for "Southampton," the second single off the *Titanic* soundtrack.

Like the sales of the *Titanic* soundtrack, the song's airplay was significantly boosted by the popularity of the film. John Ivey, program director at Boston's WXKS, noted that although the song got a great response even before *Titanic* was released to theaters, the mania surrounding the film cemented its popularity among the radio station's largely female listeners. Moreover, Dion's record distributor reported that radio stations were being deluged with listener requests that coincided with the times the film was being let out. According to Hilary Shaev, 550 Music's senior vice president of promotion, moviegoers who had just left the theater were calling to request the song from their car phones.[36] If this is true, it means that spectators were hearing the song as they made their way out of the theater and were calling to hear it again almost as soon as they reached the parking lot.

As of this writing, the *Titanic* soundtrack has chalked up sales of 10 million albums in the United States. A bonanza for all concerned, the album's success has been especially important to Horner and Sony Classical. According to *Variety*, Horner is expected to receive more than $20 million in royalties from sales of the soundtrack, a figure that is comparable to the asking price of major stars like John Travolta and Jim Carrey.[37] The album has also been a major boon to its record company, which on the average sells about five hundred copies a week of works from the canon of Western classical music. Not surprisingly, the *Titanic* soundtrack is expected to bring in more revenues than Sony Classical's entire catalog did in 1997.[38] Moreover, both Horner and Sony Classical expect to receive additional revenues from something we won't see from the film: a sequel. A second album, *Return to Titanic*, was issued in the fall of 1998, its release timed to coincide with the release of the film as a sell-through home video.[39] The album features some cues from Horner's score that were not included on the first album, some of the Irish dance music, and "Nearer My God to Thee," which is played in the film by a string quartet as the *Titanic* sinks.[40] Although sales of *Return to Titanic* will not match that of the first album, it quickly leaped to number two on *Billboard*'s album charts and is expected to become the industry's best-selling soundtrack sequel.

Few people could have predicted the soundtrack's amazing chart run, but then again few people anticipated the film's $1.8–billion gross. Most of the album's fortunes can be traced to the film itself. As Sony Music's president, Tommy Mottola, puts it, "The success of the film was the greatest marketing advantage that any company could have."[41] Yet the album's success should not have been entirely unexpected. After all, the marketing of the album relied on a cross-promotional formula that has been conventional wisdom in the industry for decades. Returning for a moment to the 1979 *Billboard* article that enumerated the ingredients necessary for a hit soundtrack, the *Titanic* campaign had most if not all of them: a big-name composer in Horner, a big-name recording star in Dion, a hit single, a hit movie, and music that is integral to the film. More than that, however, the campaign was also impeccably timed. The tandem release of *Let's Talk About Love* and the *Titanic* soundtrack enabled "My Heart Will Go On" to garner moderate radio play during the crucial period leading up to the film's release. Once *Titanic* was in theaters, both the single and the soundtrack album rode on the film's coattails to the top of the charts. The sales performance of the *Titanic* soundtrack was unprecedented for a film score; the campaign it used to achieve that success most certainly was not.

A Deep Ocean of Secrets: The Form and Dramatic Functions of "My Heart Will Go On"

The commercial fortunes of the *Titanic* soundtrack are only part of the story, however. As I noted earlier, an important aspect of the public's consumption of Dion's recording derived from the film score's ability to elicit recall of one's emotional responses to the film.[42] As any number of industry analysts point out, spectators are more likely to purchase the film's score in its commodity form if the music is "married" to strong dramatic material. For this reason, one must examine a film song's dramatic functions alongside its commodity functions insofar as one cannot be completely understood without the other. In this section, I will take a closer look at the score's four major musical themes in order to highlight the ways in which each serves the film's narrative. In doing so, I intend to show how Horner uses the popular song's form to cleverly intertwine elements from two of the score's main themes. Through this musical gesture, "My Heart Will Go On" brings together several of *Titanic*'s thematic concerns to provide an aural correlative of the film's synthesis of historical spectacle, class politics, and romantic sacrifice.

To begin with, though, a few comments about the score's overall concept and musical style are in order. According to Horner, both he and Cameron wanted to avoid doing a "Hollywood 1940s type big-drama score."[43] On its face, Horner's assertion would appear to be patently absurd insofar as his score shares several compositional and stylistic elements with Hollywood scores of the studio era. First,

Horner's music is structured around several distinct themes and leitmotifs. Second, by using music to reinforce the film's approach to character, setting, and action, Horner's score also adheres to classical conceptions of dramatic appropriateness. Third, although it achieves its effects through slightly different means, Horner's score also strives for and achieves the range of orchestral color and emotional sweep that is generally associated with Hollywood music. *Titanic's* adherence to Hollywood convention is perhaps most evident in the cues that underscore the film's moments of suspense, especially those involving the crew's reaction to the iceberg sighting, the efforts to turn the ship to avoid the iceberg, and in several sequences depicting Rose and Jack's attempts to escape the rising waters below deck. Here, Horner relies on several compositional devices that are the film composer's stock-in-trade: agitato string passages, pedal tones, repeated melodic motifs, and chromatically ascending harmonies.

Having said that, a closer examination of *Titanic's* score reveals a certain substance to Horner's comments. While it does not reject a conception of "Hollywood music" in toto, the score nonetheless deviates from certain aspects of classical tradition. The most important of these deviations is evident in *Titanic's* orchestrations. In order to get away from the string-dominated sound of the classical Hollywood era, Horner relies rather heavily on synthesizer and vocal textures, sometimes combining them with the resources of a more conventional orchestra. In doing so, the composer attempted to create a sound that was at once contemporary and elegiac, symphonic in its emotional sweep, but lilting, melancholy, and ethereal in its more intimate moments.[44] A key component of this sound was provided by the wordless vocalizing of Norwegian singing star Sissel. Horner reports that he became enamored with her voice after hearing her albums, which mix native folk elements with New Age music in a manner that has earned Sissel comparisons with the Gaelic superstar Enya. Not surprisingly, Sissel's involvement in *Titanic* has brought accusations that Horner merely aped the sound of Enya, a charge which has a certain merit when one considers the fact that Cameron used the latter's "Book of Days" in an early trailer.[45] But even if it was true, the similarities between *Titanic's* music and Enya are more or less beside the point. Horner himself admits that such comparisons are pretty much unavoidable for anyone using Gaelic idioms. More important, Horner's mix of synthesizers and vocals neatly positioned *Titanic's* soundtrack to straddle several niche markets, namely, Worldbeat and New Age. In fact, although it is difficult to prove, one might speculate that Sissel's participation played a vital role in the soundtrack's performance in international markets.

In addition to its orchestrations, *Titanic's* music differs from the classical Hollywood score in its handling of leitmotifs and themes. In contrast to something like John Barry's "James Bond Theme," which serves as a kind of aural tag for the series's central character, Horner's leitmotifs tend to develop a looser association between musical ideas and cinematic elements. *Titanic's* major musical themes are rarely tied to specific characters or settings, but rather are linked more generally to a cluster of related motifs and concepts. A good example of this is the twinkly piano motif used to accompany Rose's reminiscence of her experience on

Titanic. This musical motif, the first of four major themes I will discuss, is introduced in the film's prologue during the scene in which Brock Lovett's crew examines the contents recovered from Cal's safe. Although they have failed to find the diamond, Le Coeur de la mer (the Heart of the Ocean), we see the nude sketch of Rose being cleaned, a drawing which at least offers some proof of the diamond's existence. The tinkling piano motif mentioned above first appears under the shot of this sketch and returns shortly thereafter as the older Rose overhears a television report on the exploration of the sunken ship. At least initially, this piano melody appears to be a leitmotif for Rose herself. Subsequent appearances of the motif, however, link it more specifically to Rose as an old woman as well as to the ideas of memory and lost love. This is especially evident in the scene in which Jack shows Rose the sketch he made of Madame Bijou, an elderly Parisian woman who would sit at a bar every night, wearing all of her jewelry and waiting for her long lost love. The tinkly piano motif returns under the insert of Jack's drawing of Madame Bijou, a musical gesture which links her to the elderly Rose. In doing so, Horner's score offers an eerie foreshadowing of what Rose might have become if she had not heeded Jack's urgent plea to survive, marry, and have children.

The second major theme is one that is largely associated with the sea. Although it appears on the soundtrack in several guises, it first appears under the film's opening credits played in unison by a flute and human voice (Sissel). The tune itself is reminiscent of a Celtic sea chantey, a compositional choice which not only highlights the film's British and North Atlantic locales but also serves to musically underline the social divisions depicted in *Titanic*. Much is said in this volume about the film's treatment of class politics, and I have no desire to belabor those points here. Suffice it to say, however, that Horner's score contributes to this characterization by yoking musical signifiers of "Irishness" to the film's representation of laborers and passengers in steerage. This is especially true of the film's source music (i.e., music that occurs within the world of the story), which reinforces this linkage by contrasting the lively drinking and dancing that occurs in steerage with the stultifying conversation and social gamesmanship that occurs during Jack's dinner with the social elite. The former is accompanied by the folk music of an Irish band; the latter, by the ship orchestra's performance of light classics. Moreover, Celtic folk music also accompanies the sequences in which Jack and his friend Fabrizio make their mad dash to board the ship, and during Jack and Rose's journey through the ship's "lower depths" in an effort to elude Spicer Lovejoy, the henchman of Cal Hockley, Rose's fiancé.

While class difference in the film is signaled by the spatial divisions of the ship, especially the differences between those above and below deck, *Titanic*'s music slightly refines those divisions by ascribing cultural values to each side. More specifically, the Celtic touches in Horner's score associate the working class with nature rather than culture, with eroticism and physical pleasure rather than intellectual or commercial pursuits, and with romantic love rather than social propriety. Viewed in this light, the opening cue develops associations with two different but interrelated thematic clusters in the film: one identified with the sea, the mysteries of nature, and the cruelties of fate; the other identified with *Titanic*'s dead, many of whom were poor Irish laborers and passengers. Later appearances of the theme serve to reinforce this elegaic function through a more general association with death. The theme underscores the scenes in which Rose contemplates suicide as she hangs on the railing of the ship's stern; her gradual realization toward the end of the film that Jack has frozen to death beside her; and the montage of the survivors waiting for "an absolution that would never come."

The third major musical theme of *Titanic* is associated with the ship itself, especially those moments that highlight its power and majesty. Elements of this "ship" theme first appear in a couple of brief cues showing Lovett's recovery mission, but the theme gets its most vivid exposition in "Southampton," which plays under the sequences showing Titanic's boarding and departure. It returns shortly after, cued by Captain Smith's order to "Take Her to Sea, Mr. Murdoch." The montage that accompanies this latter version of the theme illustrates the various workings of the ship and culminates in the shots of Jack perched at the ship's prow, arms outstretched, yelling, "I'm the King of the World." Horner's use of synthesized textures is most evident in these two cues, which alternate chordal passages with a soaring, heroic melody. To suggest this sense of triumph, Horner structures the first two bars of his melody around the outline of a D major chord, then follows that with a dramatic octave leap on the tonic. While such wide leaps are a rather conventional device for suggesting heroism, Horner adds a bit of tonal color to the theme by using a low D as a pedal tone. As a result, the metric accents of the melody thus appear to fall on the passing tones rather than on the notes of the tonic triad suggested by the pedal tone. With its synthesized textures and heroic melody, several critics and industry analysts have compared this "ship" theme to Vangelis's popular theme for *Chariots of Fire* (1981).

By far the most important of the four themes, however, is *Titanic*'s love theme, "My Heart Will Go On." As a leitmotif representing the relationship between Rose and Jack, the theme underscores several of the film's most memorable moments, among them the scene in which Rose poses for Jack's drawing; Rose and Jack's first kiss on the prow of the ship; the couple's steamy encounter in the back of a Renault; Rose's tearful good-bye to Jack after climbing aboard a lifeboat; Rose's rescue; and her final dream vision of being reunited with Jack on the ship's grand staircase. As I noted earlier, the emotional intensity of these scenes and their role in furthering the romantic plotline of the film were important factors in coaxing film audiences to seek out the soundtrack. Yet the emotional impact of these scenes was also enhanced by the restraint with which the music is used. Horner's orchestrations for these scenes tend toward smaller ensembles that frequently pit solo instruments against synthesized and orchestral backgrounds. These lighter textures nicely underplay the emotional elements of the love story's most dramatic moments. Instead of the sweeping, melodramatic, and sentimental sounds that we typically associate with Hollywood, Cameron and Horner opt for a quieter, more lyrical, more subdued approach to the orchestration and dynamics of *Titanic*'s love theme.

Yet while Cameron's skillful handling of these scenes brought the necessary emotional connection between music and audience, the theme's commercial prospects were enhanced by certain structural features of the song itself. All of these structural features serve two important functions within the song insofar as they not only furnish it with memorable hooks but also communicate a requisite sense of drama and romantic passion.[46] As was true of the "ship" theme, *Titanic's* love theme also features a dramatic octave leap in the third bar of the song's chorus. The rising and falling shape of the melody here endows the theme with a certain emotive significance, one fraught with feelings of heroism, tragedy, and desire. Moreover, as the tune moves from verse to chorus, the shift from major to minor sonorities serves a somewhat similar function. As Robert Walser points out in his analysis of Bon Jovi's "Livin' on a Prayer," such shifts in modality create a contrast and corresponding tension between two affective states. The octave leap in "My Heart Will Go On"—its "moment of transcendence," to use Walser's phrase—thus coincides with a return to an A major chord, the subdominant in the song's home key of E major. Thus, like the Bon Jovi song, "My Heart Will Go On" uses the modal contrasts between verse and chorus to musically signify the rapturous dimension of romantic union.[47] Finally, a second moment of transcendence occurs with the dramatic key change from E to A flat major that occurs before the last chorus. On Celine Dion's single, this moment is reinforced by a thickening of musical textures and an increase in dynamic intensity. When combined with the rise in pitch, these structural features create one last emotional surge that is ultimately resolved by the song's cadence and the final diminution of its coda.

More important, perhaps, Horner uses a harmonic motif common to all three themes—the "sea" theme, the "ship" theme, and the love theme—to create a thematically and motivically integrated score. The musical figure to which I am referring here is a series of descending chords that move from the submediant to the dominant and back again. This harmonic pattern is used both in the chorus of "My Heart Will Go On" and in the opening phrase of the score's "sea" theme. In addition, a slightly more developed variation of it appears in the chordal passages of the "ship" theme. From a dramatic perspective, such thematic integration offers several advantages to a film composer. For one thing, it endows the score with an overarching sense of musical unity and organicity. For another, it enables the composer to move smoothly from one theme to another and to interweave different themes or leitmotifs throughout the score. By integrating these harmonic and melodic elements, Horner was able to create a score that seems deceptively simple, but in fact contains several kinds of musical and semiotic complexity.

Yet Horner's synthesis of musical themes was also important from a commercial perspective. In Dion's recording of "My Heart Will Go On" and in several cues in the film, Horner rather cleverly incorporates elements of the "sea" theme into the song's introduction and into the transitional passages that move from the song's chorus back to its verse. Through this technique of thematic integration, "My Heart Will Go On" proves to be more than a simple love song. By yoking together musical signifiers of death, nature, fate, and transcendent love, Horner's tune effectively summons up many of the elements that made *Titanic* a commercial success as a film. Through this system of shared musical associations, "My Heart Will Go On" not only reminds us of Jack and Rose's undying love but also brings back *Titanic*'s depiction of class struggle, historical spectacle, epic tragedy, and technological folly.

Conclusion

The commercial success of *Titanic*, both as a film and a soundtrack album, was undoubtedly the major story in the entertainment industry last year. As a score album, *Titanic* generally lacked the commercially savvy sound exhibited by many hit soundtracks, but nonetheless featured a highly regarded composer in James Horner, a bankable recording star in Celine Dion, the promotional backing of Sony Music, and a film that beautifully showcased the score's main musical themes. Moreover, the campaign for *Titanic*'s soundtrack was carefully timed to make the most of its various elements. Through its immediate exposure on radio, "My Heart Will Go On" was able to build positive buzz for *Titanic*, which would later translate to positive buzz for the soundtrack album once the film had topped box offices around the world. In addition, Dion's popularity as a romantic balladeer helped to foreground the film's love story in a way that revised early speculation about *Titanic*'s generic predecessors. Once audiences had heard "My Heart Will Go On," *Titanic* suddenly seemed less like a disaster film (*The Poseidon Adventure*, 1972 or *Earthquake*, 1974) and more like a film that places romance against the backdrop of historically momentous events (*Gone With the Wind*, 1939, or *Doctor Zhivago*, 1965).

Still, "My Heart Will Go On" would have had little impact if it were not so effective within its dramatic context. To paraphrase *Variety* columnist Theda Sandiford-Waller, audiences had a much greater appreciation for the song once they had seen the film.[48] In fact, in communities around the country, radio stations were flooded with requests for the song just after screenings of *Titanic* were let out. Much of this emotional attachment to the song came from Horner's skillful use of it during the film's memorable love scenes, but it also derived from the way in which Dion's recording summoned up many of *Titanic*'s narrative elements. Through Horner's techniques of thematic integration, "My Heart Will Go On" became a complex and multivalent signifier of the film's representations of death, fate, and love.

Yet for all of their dramatic effectiveness, both "My Heart Will Go On" and the *Titanic* soundtrack will best be remembered in their commodity forms. Through the emotional bonds it built with the film's audience, the score came to function as one of *Titanic*'s many souvenirs. As the elderly Rose says in the film's epilogue, "A woman's heart is a deep ocean of secrets." Ultimately, *Titanic* would have no better object to symbolize Rose's heart than Le Coeur de la mer and no better aural object than Horner's "My Heart Will Go On." Like the blue diamond, the song serves as a nostalgic memento of lost love, one that quavers with a sense of mystery and eternity.

Notes

1. Quoted in Chuck Crisafulli, "Chasing Goosebumps," *Hollywood Reporter*, 13 January 1998, 3.
2. Quoted in Fred Karlin and Rayburn Wright, *On the Track: A Guide to Contemporary Film Scoring* (New York: Schirmer Books, 1990), 539.
3. See David Browne, "Star-Ship Enterprise," *Entertainment Weekly*, 13 March 1998, 31.
4. Alan Waldman, "Going for a Song," *Hollywood Reporter*, 26 August 1997, S-12.
5. Ibid., S-66.
6. See Douglas Gomery, *The Hollywood Studio System* (New York: St. Martin's Press, 1986) and Alexander Doty, "Music Sells Movies: (Re) New (ed) Conservatism in Film Marketing," *Wide Angle* 10, no. 2 (1988): 70–79. For a more complete overview of the history of film and music cross-promotions, see my recent book, *The Sounds of Commerce: Marketing Popular Film Music* (New York: Columbia University Press, 1998).
7. Charles Merrell Berg, *An Investigation into the Motives for and the Realization of Music to Accompany the American Silent Film* (New York: Arno Press, 1976), 254.
8. Ibid., 255.
9. Quoted in Andre Millard, *America on Record: A History of Recorded Sound* (New York: Cambridge University Press, 1995), 160. For more on the theme score, see Kathryn Kalinak, *Settling the Score: Music in the Classical Hollywood Film* (Madison: University of Wisconsin Press, 1992), 185–187.
10. See Russell Sanjek, *American Popular Music and Its Business from 1900 to 1984* (New York: Oxford University Press, 1988), 91–114; and Gomery, *The Hollywood Studio System*, 106–110.
11. See Russell Sanjek, *From Print to Plastic: Publishing and Promoting America's Popular Music (1900–1980)* (Brooklyn: Institute for Studies in American Music, 1983), 19.
12. The composers and lyricists for these songs are as follows: "Do Not Forsake Me, Oh My Darlin'" from *High Noon* by Dimitri Tiomkin and Ned Washington; "Love Is a Many Splendored Thing" by Sammy Fain and Paul Francis Webster; "Theme from *A Summer Place*" by Max Steiner.
13. For a more complete discussion of the way in which these multiple versions help to maintain the record industry's profitability, see Tim Anderson, "Which Voice Becomes the Property?: Tie-Ups, Intertexts, and Versioning in the Production of *My Fair Lady*," *Spectator* 17 (spring/summer 1997): 74–91.
14. Mike Gross, "Pix Promotion's Cuffo Ride," *Variety*, 6 September 1961, 45–46. According to Robert Allen and Douglas Gomery, "cuffo promotion" lies somewhere between publicity and promotion. It is not "free" in the same sense as publicity since studios have to pour a certain amount of money into album pressings, rerecording costs, arranging fees, and so forth. However, it is "free" in the sense that studios do not pay radio stations for airplay or record stores for display space. This contrasts "cuffo promotion" with things like premiere parties, promotional tours, or even press junkets—all of which entail costs above and beyond production costs and do not offer any kind of financial return. See *Film History: Theory and Practice* (New York: McGraw-Hill, 1985).
15. Susan Peterson, "Selling a Hit Soundtrack," *Billboard*, 6 October 1979, ST-2.
16. R. Serge Denisoff and George Plasketes, "Synergy in 1980s Film and Music: Formula for Success or Industry Mythology," *Film History* 4, no. 3 (1990): 257–276.
17. The need for a four- to six-week window became most obvious in those situations where this strategy was not used. Problems with the cover art for the *Let's Make Love* soundtrack delayed the album's release until three weeks after the film's premiere. Con-

sequently, the album failed to help the film in key first-run markets. See "This Is 'Love?'" *Variety*, 14 September 1960, 43.

18. For a more detailed explication of this theory, see Denisoff and Plasketes, "Synergy in 1980s Film and Music," 257–276.

19. In the 1980s, there were several films that succeeded without strong cross-promotinal support from a soundtrack. All of the following made over $100 million but had only modest sales for their accompanying albums: *Gremlins* (1984), *Platoon* (1986), *Fatal Attraction* (1987), *Rainman* (1988), and *Lethal Weapon 2* (1989). In 1986, the soundtrack for *Back to the Future* sold barely 500,000 copies despite the fact that the film made more than $200 million and that the album contained a chart-topping single by Huey Lewis and the News ("The Power of Love"). In the 1990s, there were several blockbusters that succeeded without huge albums: *Home Alone* (1990), *Jurassic Park* (1993), *Schindler's List* (1993), and *Independence Day* (1996).

20. Quoted in Ray Bennett, "James Horner," *Hollywood Reporter*, 13 January 1998, 19–20.

21. Browne, "Star-Ship Enterprise," 28.

22. Bennett, "James Horner," 22; and Browne, "Star-Ship Enterprise," 28.

23. Quoted in Browne, "Star-Ship Enterprise," 33.

24. Ibid.

25. According to Peter Gelb, the president of Sony Classical, "New Music in the form of soundtracks and other avenues is what the classical record industry is relying upon for a successful future." Quoted in Catherine Applefeld Olson, "Soundtracks and Film Score News," *Billboard*, 22 November 1997, 19.

26. Catherine Applefeld Olson, "The Reel Thing," *Billboard*, 11 October 1997, 24; and Heidi Waleson, "Classical: Keeping Score," *Billboard*, 18 November 1997, 42.

27. Bennett, "James Horner," 20.

28. Jon Herskovitz and Chris Petrikin, "*Titanic* Preem a Sellout," *Variety*, 3 November 1997, 7.

29. "The Unsinkable Celine Dion," *Billboard*, 7 February 1998, 89.

30. Quoted in Eileen Fitzpatrick, "*Titanic* Makes Big Splash for Sony Classical," *Billboard*, 24 January 1997, 92.

31. Geoff Mayfield, "Between the Bullets," *Billboard*, 14 February 1998, 104.

32. Geoff Mayfield, "Between the Bullets," *Billboard*, 28 February 1998, 90. See also "Shipping the Ship," *Hollywood Reporter*, 2 March 1998, 90.

33. Chuck Taylor, "Dion's 'Heart' Goes On, and On, and On," *Billboard*, 7 February 1998, 5.

34. Melinda Newman, "Sony Classical Enjoying Titanic Success of Hit Film's Soundtrack," *Billboard*, 21 February 1998, 76.

35. Theda Sandiford-Waller, "Hot 100 Singles Spotlight," *Billboard*, 24 January 1998, 94.

36. Taylor, "Dion's 'Heart' Goes On," 89.

37. Michael Fleming, "Fox, Par in Choppy Waters over Cameron's Cash," *Variety*, 5 April 1998, 4.

38. Browne, "Star-Ship Enterprise," 28.

39. Sell-through home videos are priced to be sold directly to consumers. This is in contrast to most home video releases, which are priced for rental and sold directly to video stores. Within this two-tiered pricing system, *Titanic* could be purchased from some online services for under $10 and from stores like Target and Wal-Mart for around $20. Videos priced for rental, on the other hand, typically cost stores between $90 and $110 per tape.

40. Newman, "Sony Classical Enjoying Titanic Success," 76; and Fitzpatrick, "*Titanic* Makes Big Splash," 92.
41. Quoted in Newman, "Sony Classical Enjoying Titanic Success," 76.
42. For more on this aspect of film music reception, see my forthcoming essay, "Movie Music as Moving Music: Emotion, Cognition, and the Film Score," in *Passionate Views*, ed. Carl Plantinga and Greg Smith (Baltimore: Johns Hopkins University Press, 1999).
43. Bennett, "James Horner," 20.
44. Ibid.
45. Browne, "Star-Ship Enterprise," 31.
46. For more on the role of hooks in popular film songs, see my *The Sounds of Commerce*, 15–21.
47. See Robert Walser, *Running with the Devil: Power, Gender, and Madness in Heavy Metal Music* (Hanover, N.H.: Wesleyan University Press, 1993), 121–123.
48. See Theda Sandiford-Waller, "Hot 100 Singles Spotlight," *Variety*, 17 January 1998, 83.

"Almost Ashamed to Say I Am One of Those Girls"

TITANIC, LEONARDO DICAPRIO, AND THE PARADOXES OF GIRLS' FANDOM

MELANIE NASH AND MARTTI LAHTI

Titanic carries all the markers of the prestigious period piece as contemporary blockbuster. It has been heralded as a "vastly ambitious epic" and as standing "at the summit of epic masterwork."[1] Both costing and earning record-breaking sums and sweeping the Oscars, it has evoked comparisons to *Gone With the Wind* (1939) and *Ben-Hur* (1959),[2] and to the work of D. W. Griffith, Cecil B. DeMille, and David Lean.[3] Movies of this kind, commercially successful, critically acclaimed, and often based on famous historical or literary subjects, are generally aimed at and perceived to draw more mature audiences than other contemporary genres (action, comedy, etc.). But in the case of *Titanic*, its apparent filiation with this cinematic grandeur was somewhat at odds with the reality of its audience, which was both young (63 percent under twenty-five) and female (60 percent).[4] While a film that becomes the top-grossing box office hit of all time certainly depends on a vast general appeal cutting across various audience demographics, *Titanic*'s success remains grounded in its young female fans, which as *Newsweek* points out, distinguishes it from most other contemporary blockbusters.[5]

Titanic also attracted exceptional devotion from its viewers, drawing a 20 percent repeat audience against the 2 percent norm. Indeed, by February 1998, only two months after its release, 45 percent of women under twenty-five who had the seen the movie had seen it twice; and 76 percent of all repeat viewers planned to see it again.[6] The *New York Times* notes that "a hefty portion of [*Titanic*'s] repeat business is coming from teen-age girls and younger women, who are seeing the film four or five times."[7] *Seventeen* magazine reports that one fan confessed to seeing the film "an epic 14 times."[8] And *Time* further specifies that girls "generate[d] an estimated 30 percent to 40 percent of the movie *Titanic*'s $580 million U.S. gross."[9] This consuming power of young women was not limited to movie tickets. For instance, demographic research by Sony Classical concluded that girls under fourteen made up the largest market segment buying the *Titanic* soundtrack, too.[10]

The single most important aspect of the enormous appeal of this film to its primary audience, young girls, is the star presence of Leonardo DiCaprio, who plays the part of Jack Dawson. *Titanic* drew heavily on DiCaprio's preexisting fan base of teenage girls in conceiving and addressing its audience, through both generic structures and marketing strategies. But DiCaprio's stardom also brought with it certain elements that sit uncomfortably with this demographic focus. Two contradictory thrusts of his star discourse meet in *Titanic*'s attempts to capitalize on his appeal: his status among girl fans as a pinup heartthrob, and his decided and very public antagonism toward this image. In the face of such contradiction, it is difficult, if not impossible, to understand the popularity of *Titanic* without taking into consideration how girls' fan practices negotiate negative aspects of DiCaprio's star discourse in ways that allow them to enjoy him as a romantic hero and visual spectacle. The fan practices—ranging from pinup collection to rhetorical strategies among Web users—create a sense of community that reinforces and valorizes the desire to see him and, correspondingly, fuels girls' repeat viewings of *Titanic*. In other words, *Titanic*'s success is dependent on its mass teen girl audience's repeat viewings, which were largely focused on DiCaprio's ambiguous star presence and thus relied on a social context of fan practices to negotiate and support such intertextual desires relating to the star.

A $200 Million Teen Movie

Many explanations for *Titanic*'s popularity among girls have been suggested, and not without merit. For instance, director James Cameron is careful to characterize his film as a love story rather than a disaster film.[11] Learning that Mary Pipher endorsed his film's "modern spin" on "the old myth of the damsel in distress being rescued,"[12] Cameron responded: "She should like the movie. I read her book [*Reviving Ophelia: Saving the Selves of Adolescent Girls*] before I wrote the script."[13] Without giving too much weight to authorial intention, it is important to note that *Titanic* does foreground the romance between Jack Dawson and Rose Bukater, despite its historical topic, spectacular special effects, and "disaster" climax. And it certainly resonates with many elements familiar to young girls from larger cultural narratives of teenage life, such as the trope of forbidden love for the "wrong" boy, parental disapproval of the romance, rebelliousness against older authority figures, dating rituals, breaking curfew and other codes of ladylike decorum (spitting, smoking), and so on. Indeed, the film goes so far as to contrive a way of having the shipbound lovers sneak away to "do it" for the "first time" in the backseat of a parked car, complete with steamed windows.

Fan-created *Titanic* fiction, or "fanfic," gives credence to this explanation

The repeat female audience of *Titanic* in the funny papers. Doonesbury copyright 1998 by G. B. Trudeau. Reprinted by permission of Universal Press Syndicate. All rights reserved.

for the film's success, making transparent the extent of this appeal to teen girls' experiences and frustrations. Authors rewrite the *Titanic* story with even greater emphasis on Rose's coming of age. "I'm not a child! I can make my own decisions," Rose declares in Michelle's "My Story." Indeed, in some fan stories Rose gets married, becomes pregnant, and/or gets a job. And many fan-authors choose entry points into their narratives that focus on moments of heightened confrontation between the young lovers and adult authority. For example, in "Jana's Story," Rose even gives "[her fiance's henchman] Lovejoy and [her mother] Ruth the finger before storming out the door." The idea of Rose making adult decisions is entangled in these stories with romantic fantasies of perfect love, as she regularly decides to break her engagement to Cal and succeeds in marrying Jack (either on board the *Titanic* or after the ship safely reaches New York!). The centrality of this coming-of-age love story to girls' pleasures (in contrast to, say, the disaster) is accentuated by the fact that the authors of many of these stories can even ignore what is, for them, irrelevant: the ship's collision with the iceberg. They alter both history and the movie's narrative in favor of a happy ending in their fiction.[14]

Other factors, however, suggest that *Titanic* made its strongest (prerelease) pitch to the teen girl audience by casting young stars, Kate Winslet and, especially, DiCaprio, as its doomed lovers. For example, *Titanic*'s U.S. distributor was fully aware of teenage girls' importance to box office success long before the film's release. The vice chairman of Paramount told the *New York Times*: "In our original concept testing—when we read the concept of the movie over the phone and who was in it—we mentioned Leonardo DiCaprio, and there was a lot of interest in him among girls. . . . When we tested the first trailers, the young girls were the highest quadrant in their interest in seeing the film. And when we screened, the girls were one of the highest-testing groups who enjoyed the movie."[15] Paramount's marketing of the film accordingly emphasized elements (in texts such as the poster, trailers, and TV ads) that were expected to court a young female audience, namely, the romance story and the star presence of DiCaprio.[16] And this strategy's effec-

Leo and his girl fans

tiveness is borne out in the postrelease success of the film specifically among this demographic. The film's high rate of repeat viewings, for example, was mostly credited to DiCaprio by the press.[17] And *Time* noted that largely due to "the patronage of teenage girls, Leonardo DiCaprio recently pulled off the unprecedented feat of starring in two films virtually tied for No. 1 at the box office, *Titanic* and his just released *The Man in the Iron Mask* [1998]."[18] This type of market research and box office analysis strongly indicates the centrality of DiCaprio fans to both the projected and actual success of *Titanic*.

To reconstruct *Titanic*'s special appeal, via DiCaprio, to its girl fans, we have surveyed numerous teen magazines (including *Teen, Teenbeat, 16, Seventeen, Superstars, Gold Collectors Series Entertainment Magazine, Biograph Presents Hollywood's Hottest Hunks, YM: Young and Modern,* and *All About You*) and Web sites where teenage girls read and write about their object of fascination. Indeed, in a readers' poll in *Seventeen* magazine, *Titanic* was named (before its release) the "Film You're Psyched to See in 1997." Speculating on reasons for the voters' particular anticipation of this film, the author of the article asks, "Could it be your strange fascination with the sunken ship? Doubt it. More like your fascination with *Titanic*'s star."[19] It is this preexisting fascination with DiCaprio, mobilized in part through girl-oriented periodicals, that marked *Titanic* as a DiCaprio vehicle, thus ensuring its success.

DiCaprio brought with him to this project an enormous pool of young female fans, some of whom had faithfully followed his career since his teen-idol beginnings on TV's *Growing Pains* (1991–92). Indeed, he was cast on that series to "get it back into . . . teen magazines," according to a DiCaprio biographer who was also the editor of the teen magazine *Dream Guys*.[20] His place in even greater numbers of girls' dreams was clinched, however, by *William Shakespeare's Romeo + Juliet* (1996). While DiCaprio had had critical success in numerous prestigious films—*This Boy's Life* (1993), *What's Eating Gilbert Grape?* (1993), *The Basketball Diaries* (1995), *Total Eclipse* (1995), *Marvin's Room* (1996)—the small, "art" film status of these movies or marginal characters he played (abused child, mentally handicapped boy, drug addict, homosexual poet) did not exactly capture the teen girl imagination to the same extent that his role as Romeo would. As *Seventeen* explains in its readers' poll, in which DiCaprio was named "Celeb You Could Totally Deal with Dating" and *Romeo + Juliet* was voted "Movie of the Year," "He lit up the screen as a pyromaniac in *Marvin's Room*, but it was his emoting as Romeo that got you all fired up."[21]

It is thus not entirely coincidental that teen girls also loved *Titanic*, a film which makes heavy use of the thematic elements—arranged marriage, forbidden love, defiance of parents, secretive consummation, fate, death—of *Romeo + Juliet*, the quintessential teen romance, as well as its quintessential teen idol star. The two films are frequently grouped together as fans' favorites: one girl writes, "I have seen *Titanic* 7 times now and I think it's brilliant and when *Romeo & Juliet* was out at the cinema I saw it 8 times[.] I now have that on video and watch it regularly."[22] Many girls also tend to strongly associate DiCaprio with his characters, blurring any hard-and-fast distinctions in their romantic investments in Romeo/ Leo, Jack/Leo, or Romeo/Jack, for that matter. Wittily pointing up this slippage, an article in *Girlfriend* is titled "Oh Rom-Leo." One girl, Amy, also (jokingly) catches herself in this: "He [presumably Leo] was so . . . perfect. Amazing, wonderful, beautiful, talented. The ultimate lover . . . sweet talking, but he [presumably Romeo] meant it. Completely dedicated to his beloved. . . . Yes, this was Romeo, not Leo, I understand they are separate." And Christina signs off her letter by directly equating DiCaprio with his roles: "Well, on that note[,] 'I'll never let go Leo,' [Rose's words to Jack] and you'll always be our TRUE, 'ROMEO'!!!"[23] This slippage allowed *Titanic* to immediately capitalize on a preexisting fan base of teenage girls whose viewing interest was focused on DiCaprio as a romantic idol. That is, *Titanic* became so popular because it provides an additional context (character, narrative) for girls' ongoing articulation of their DiCaprio fantasies.

Girls also imbue their comments with the tone of his film scenarios, sometimes even replicating the extreme stakes of romantic ardor narrativized in the tragedies of *Romeo + Juliet* and *Titanic*. Evoking *Titanic*'s discourse of salvation through romance, for example, Christina writes, "I could never imagine a life without you in it. . . . I'm glad that every morning I have something to look forward [to. W]hen I wake up to see your [pic] on my wall it's an inspirational sight." Making more direct reference to DiCaprio in *Titanic*, Shannon dreams, "I luv Leonardo! He is the sexiest guy alive! Wouldn't we all like to be Kate Winslet?! Jack Dawson stole my heart in *Titanic*." Synnove calls *Titanic* "the most romantic movie I have ever seen! (That[']s because Leonardo was in it!)" Allowing *Titanic* fantasies to spill over into real-life fan practices, one fifteen-year-old girl, Samantha, tells DiCaprio, "I love you. . . . I can't get you off my mind. I named my teddy Jack that I got for X-mas." And thirteen-year-old Talia writes, "I only want you to know that I love you so much. I have posters of you in . . . my room, I have the [CD] of *Titanic* and I always cry for you whenever I hear the songs." For teen girls, then, both (romantic) anticipation and memories of the film focus on DiCaprio. The popularity of *Titanic* among teen girls must, therefore, be understood in large part as a continuation of a fantasy centering on DiCaprio as a "modern-day Romeo" (to borrow a quickie DiCaprio biography's title).[24]

It has also been argued, however, that *Titanic*'s success with girls rests with Winslet's character, Rose, and the narrative of her liberation: "Her beauty is accessible, not intimidating; women can feel themselves inside her skin. DiCaprio, for all the teen mooning, is there to complement *her*. 'Leo is the candy,' says Cameron. 'But the emotional connection is with Kate's character.'"[25] Exhibitors, however, credit the candy, not Winslet, for the film's enormous box office appeal. Quigley's annual poll (released February 1998) of hundreds of cinema owners reveals that DiCaprio was ranked third among their "top ten moneymaking stars," while Winslet did not appear on the exhibitors' list at all.[26] And *Titanic*'s fans also point to DiCaprio's centrality to its long-running popularity: "Can you believe that Leo didn't get nominated [for an Oscar]," asks one fan, who claims, "Leo has kept TITANIC afloat for the past month and a half! I'm not trying to say that Kate Winslet isn't a great actress but there wouldn't have been a luv-story with[o]ut Jack Dawson, and no one could've played Jack like Leo!"[27] While fans frequently express a strong admiration of and identification with DiCaprio's co-stars, Claire Danes and Winslet, it is clear that, for most, DiCaprio is at the center of their pre- and postviewing interest in *Titanic* and is thus the largest factor in the film's popularity. Indeed, it seems that these women stars function primarily as conduits or stand-ins for girl fans' fantasies about DiCaprio. *Vanity Fair* reports that "countless girls" approach Danes "just to touch a hand that touched his,"[28] and when Danes was named the "Celeb Most Wanted for a Best Bud" in *Seventeen*'s poll, it was with the comment, "When your main topic of conversation is Leo's love life, who knows more than this girl?"[29] Girls find other ways to (playfully or earnestly) write themselves directly into DiCaprio's love life, however. They sign their names as "[L]eo's lover," "Lauren Clinton (DiCaprio)," or "Mrs. DiCaprio (I wish!)."[30] Similarly, they tell other girls that "Leo's MINEEEE!!!!!!"; "I will eventually marry him!!!"; or, "If he ever needed a date I'd be willing to go out with him in a second."[31] And, of course, they express the strong desire to communicate or meet with DiCaprio—a desire which funds their repeat viewings as well as their extratextual fantasies.

While *Titanic*'s textual strategies, as Cameron claims, might privilege Winslet's character as the film's emotional core, extratextual factors including the circulation of fan materials and the star system itself suggest that girl viewers could (and did) choose their emotional focal point independent of the female lead as an object of intended identification.[32] Girls were indeed already "psyched to see"

Titanic long before its release, and for reasons that had nothing to do with Winslet or the (then unknowable) transformation of her character. One DiCaprio fan (and consumer) clearly quantifies this extratextual anticipation: "Dear Leo, I am your BIGGEST fan[.] I have over 300 pictures, 7 movies, 2 books, and both *Romeo and Juliet* soundtracks. . . . I can't wait till *Titanic*, only 23 more days!"[33] And another tells DiCaprio:

> I don't even want to count how many times I've seen *Romeo and Juliet*! I just saw it tonight. . . . I sat there and cried for 30 minutes! I come here on my computer every day and look you up to where I can see all your pictures. I sit there and admire them and pretend I'm Claire Danes . . . or any other girl that you've dated. . . . I can't wait for your new movie, *The Titanic*, to come out, even though I'll probably sit there and cry during that to[o], but just to see your face gives me chill bumps.[34]

This type of "buzz" about *Titanic* worked to focus anticipation as well as later repeat viewings around DiCaprio rather than Winslet or even the romance narrative. And the film's popularity is funded by this discursive climate of excitement, as well as the further opportunities it provided in girl fans' accumulation of props—soundtracks, biographies, pictures—supporting their DiCaprio fantasies. In other words, *Titanic*'s popularity rests in large part on its function within girls' DiCaprio fandom as an additional mise-en-scène for their desires.

Girls regularly play out this erotic investment in DiCaprio through distinctly visual means: the repeated viewings of their two favorite films (*Romeo + Juliet* and *Titanic*) and their collection of literally hundreds of pinup photographs of DiCaprio. "How could I possibly make a Leo page without TONS of pictures?" asks Amy, concluding with an invitation for visitors to "sit back and look at the pretty side of him. Did I say pretty? I mean downright, unbelievably, fantastically, orgasmically, wonderfully, gorgeous. Sigh!" Expressing a sentiment echoed by many others, Jennifer remarks, "This is like the first site I have found with [j]ust pictures and that's all I really need in a web site"; and Corey reports, "I stayed on for about 2 hours [and] I printed about 45 pictures." Many, like Claire and Kimberly, also brag about their fan paraphernalia: "I have 300 and something pics of him," and "I have almost all *Titanic* and Leo books."

Here, collection is an expression of devotion, where quantity of accumulation translates into quality of fandom and the proof of sincerity. It further indexes the extremity of some girls' affective investment in DiCaprio as both erotic spectacle and romantic scenario. Many fans bemoan not yet having access to *Titanic* on video, and Erica even requests "screen savers of [L]eo." Apparently not content with the extensive collection of still pictures and video clips available, one Web site contributor writes, "I think that Leonardo needs to come alive, come out of the computer screen, and kiss us.. . . . . . what a dream."[35] Short of realizing this dream, girls instead sublimate their longings through consumption, not only at newsstands and Web sites but also at the box office. This insatiability of a distinctly visual desire for DiCaprio also plays a role in girl fans' multiple viewings of *Titanic*, thus underwriting the film's fantastic popularity.

Titanic's Reluctant Hero: "The Man in the Teen Idol Mask"?

The visual pleasure DiCaprio offers his girl fans is central to *Titanic*'s success with this majority segment of its audience. And it was largely DiCaprio's star marketing as a collectible pinup that fostered expectations that his films would further fulfill the spectatorial desires thus mobilized. Gracing the covers of various teen and other poster magazines both before and after his appearance in *Titanic*,[36] DiCaprio is clearly sold as an erotic spectacle (and object of romantic fantasy) to a young female audience. For example, *Teen Beat* features a cover picture of "Leo the L♥vable!" with the enticing text: "♥Pin-UP!♥Poster!♥Centerfold! *Plus*—Q&A & Giveaway!" And making explicit *Titanic*'s appeal to teen girls, *Gold Collectors*' special issue on "Leonardo And *Titanic*" promises, "Over 60 Leonardo DiCaprio photos and bonus pullout centerfold inside!"[37]

This kind of emphasis on DiCaprio's pinup status is not limited to teen or picture magazines but sometimes extends to the mainstream press's commentary on him. In fact, DiCaprio is regularly portrayed in a sexualized fashion that underscores his role as an object to be looked at. Janet Maslin goes so far as to call him "a pin-up ready version of angel-faced purity . . . with a physical beauty that reduces the camera to one more worshipful fan."[38] DiCaprio's marketing as a pinup and critical commentary like Maslin's function as aspects of his star discourse that serve and reinforce girls' visual desires and romantic fantasies—the same desires and fantasies that drew them in large numbers to see DiCaprio in *Titanic*.

However important, these desire-reinforcing elements of DiCaprio's star discourse are only one dimension of his public image. Other constituent instabilities, or even directly contradictory discourses, belie DiCaprio's simple appeal as a teen idol. Indeed, *Titanic*'s deployment of the star to guarantee its core audience—a central part of its demographic research and marketing choices—is not as straightforward as it may initially appear, given certain aspects of DiCaprio's persona that implicitly or explicitly demean both the film itself as well as its/his girl fans.

The root of these inconsistent elements may be DiCaprio's pinup status itself, where the proximity to both feminized iconography and to female consumers carries with it certain degrading connotations for male stars. As Richard Dyer has suggested, contradictions that result from the male pinup's violation of the gendered order of looking relations (and attempts to disavow the feminine position of "to-be-looked-at-ness") ultimately lead to further *textual* instabilities.[39] In DiCaprio's case, the "extensive, multimedia, intertextual" dimensions of his star discourse are used to safeguard his masculinity against negative associations with pinup culture, by scorning this heartthrob status (and, implicitly, those who consume his pinups).[40] Before *Titanic*'s release, one biographical piece on DiCaprio noted that, "despite never having played an action hero or a *Beverly Hills: 90210–*style heartthrob, he is still, reluctantly, the idol of many a teenage girl."[41] Even after he appeared in *Titanic*—in the role of both action hero and heartthrob—another article nonetheless reported approvingly that DiCaprio "is not especially comfortable with, and actually dislikes, his image as a movie idol," and further feels "trapped by his romantic image among teen-agers."[42] Presumably, comments such as these would not reinforce girls' consumption of DiCaprio as visual spectacle or romantic scenario, in either photographic or cinematic manifestations. In fact, it might even make them self-conscious about their desires being in conflict with those of their love object.

In addition to DiCaprio's reported reluctance to be seen as a teen idol, there are a variety of other aspects of his star discourse that work against an association with his teen girl fans, some simply expanding beyond the "teen idol" identity but others demeaning this image and its fans. One major aspect of this antiheartthrob discourse is the recurring emphasis on DiCaprio's "great acting," which is praised in direct opposition to his good looks and his girl fans' visual desires.[43] Cameron explains why DiCaprio did not get an Oscar nomination for his role in *Titanic* by saying it was not for any lack of talent but simply "because of his teen-idol image, and because . . . there's a 'resentment of too much stardom too fast,'"[44] implicitly blaming the fans who made the film so popular for its star's devaluation in the Academy's eyes. Rhetorically diminishing the importance of its girl audience, critical commentary on *Titanic* nonetheless suggests that this role marks a departure for DiCaprio from teen roles, crossing into mainstream leading-man status and appealing to a universal audience: one of his "posse" comments, "it's not going to be just 12–year-old girls watching him. It's going to be *everyone*."[45] And *Titanic*'s narrative and visual strategies also work against foregrounding his male pinup image by insistently positioning Winslet as the object of DiCaprio's (artistic and romantic) gaze, and by costuming (and de-costuming) her for the audience's greater attention.[46] DiCaprio's attempts to distance himself from the pinup image made it easier for adult audiences to ignore the film's strong appeals to teen girls and instead view it as more in keeping with a tradition of quality spectacles, such as *Gone With the Wind* or *Ben-Hur*. Arguably *Titanic*'s box office results benefited from this widened appeal to nonteen audiences; but since this type of "broadening" commentary works at the expense of teen girls' interests in DiCaprio, one might expect their continuing patronage of the film to be jeopardized by it.

While some cultural commentators situate DiCaprio's leading-man position in *Titanic* as indicating a newfound maturity, or that he has outgrown his more narrow appeal to young girls, others, in contrast, see this film and DiCaprio's role in it as a regression for the actor, a falling away from his former selection of projects that would garner more serious adult interest. In the long tradition of equating mass culture with (a degraded) femininity and women's consumption,[47] many critics equate *Titanic*'s commercial popularity with a lack of depth in DiCaprio's performance and link this to girls' tastes.

In a similar vein, Peter Travers of *Rolling Stone* actually blames DiCaprio's (vulgarly mainstream) *Titanic* role for his enormous teen girl following, while attempting to dissociate DiCaprio-as-artist from this degrading proximity to the (mass) feminine: "since that box-office juggernaut [*Titanic*] supersized his heartthrob status, DiCaprio has been dreaming up ways to debunk himself as a hunk."[48] Indeed, until the moment he decided to take the lead in *Titanic*, DiCaprio's previous role choices—complex, marginal, or "deep" characters—were regularly invoked to mitigate against any perception of him as purely "surface," the ideally and simply beautiful pinup that girls sought.[49] With telling explicitness, Travers

9 beauty disasters and how to fix them

Seventeen

May 1998

the **Leo**
you don't know:
• his *Titanic* tryout
• his bad boy school days
• and what it's like
to kiss him

quiz: are you
psychic?

the best
swimsuit for
your body

she's your mom
so why is she
competing with you?

on the
set of
Party of Five

**summer
jobs:**
how to be
your own boss

U.S. $2.95 Can. $3.50

Marketing Leo DiCaprio fandom

evokes this opposition in lamenting DiCaprio's *Titanic* fall from anti-teen-idol grace: "DiCaprio is too good an actor for this male-pinup crap. He's always fought it. Look at his pre-*Titanic* roles. . . . Even DiCaprio's failures as the kid gunhand for Sharon Stone in *The Quick and the Dead* [1995] and as the gay French poet Arthur Rimbaud in *Total Eclipse* showed a laudable desire to flaunt [*sic*] convention. *Romeo and Juliet* brought him closer to the romantic mold, but how like

DiCaprio to do an MTV take on the Bard."[50] Travers uses DiCaprio's roles and his "laudable desire to flaunt convention" as a way of further disparaging "this male-pinup crap." He implicitly associates such "crap" with the "romantic mold" of *Romeo + Juliet*, the DiCaprio movie most cherished by teen girls before *Titanic*. Tying his idiosyncratic tastes and professional choices to a hostility toward teens' tastes, DiCaprio himself is quoted as saying that his favorite James Dean film is *East of Eden* (1955), explaining: "'Everyone always says *Rebel Without a Cause* (1955) was his best, but that was just too teenybopper for me.'"[51]

As this last comment indicates, DiCaprio echoes some commentators in both dismissing mainstream popularity and bemoaning his following among girls, while implicitly equating the two. More specifically, where the "great acting" discourse falls short in separating DiCaprio-as-Jack from the teen idol image, belittling the importance of this *Titanic* role to him (and his fans' preference for this leading-man incarnation) takes over. Indeed, *Vanity Fair* reports that, "accustomed to portraying youthful rebels in films such as *Marvin's Room*[,] DiCaprio was ambivalent about taking on the leading-man-cum-action-hero he plays in *Titanic*. He's already hounded by packs of screaming adolescent girls." And this writer continues, "DiCaprio instinctively saw himself as someone other than a big-time, big-budget star who could be hailed on street corners by just . . . *Leo!*"[52] *Rolling Stone* adds to his star discourse's contempt for this ultracommercial, teen favorite, "Was DiCaprio right to fear that *Titanic* would trap him as the man in the teen-idol mask? Was he ever."[53] And DiCaprio's (now abandoned) plans to star in *American Psycho*, as "a yuppie monster who likes to torture and kill women," were reported as precisely motivated by the desire to "tak[e] a role that's far, far removed from *Titanic's* Jack Dawson."[54] Regarding this much-despised role in *Titanic*, DiCaprio is quoted in one teen magazine as remarking that making the film "was like doing construction work,"[55] and elsewhere adds: "After the whole experience . . . I know it's *really* not my cup of tea—all respect to Jim and the actors who do that type of thing."[56] Indeed, it is the very few roles in DiCaprio's oeuvre that girl fans really love that are consistently singled out for disparagement by the actor and the press alike.[57] Girls' apparent awareness of these conflicting elements in DiCaprio's star discourse begs the question of the ongoing and staggering popularity of *Titanic* among them—a question which can only be answered by turning to an analysis of their own fan practices.

Titanic's Mad Leo Teen Fans: The Paradoxes of Being One of Those Girls

Contradictions within DiCaprio's star image might initially seem irreconcilable with his apparent function as the primary draw for teen girls' enthusiastic patronage of *Titanic* and avid consumption of spin-off products as props for DiCaprio-centered fantasies. To understand the continuing popularity of *Titanic* in the face of such disparaging remarks, we need to trace the social reconstruction of girls' desires within their own fan culture. It is this reconstruction process— selective emphasis, appropriation, re-elaboration—that allows girls to take a great deal of pleasure in *Titanic*'s romantic, leading-man incarnation of their favorite pinup, in spite of the negative star and journalistic discourses outlined above. Rather than simply being dissuaded from frequenting DiCaprio's more recent blockbuster films, especially his biggest vehicle, *Titanic*, teen girls were inclined instead to negotiate their viewing position in relation to this marginalization of their desires.

Many have picked up on the discourse of "great acting," for instance, as an alibi for their interest in DiCaprio and, more specifically, in his performance in *Titanic*. References to "great acting" often function as a minor aside, a clearly redundant justification for fandom, or simply as a complement to more prominent expressions of purely visual forms of desire. For example, one typical fan letter (Ari and Amie) reads: "Dear *Teen Machine*, My cousin and I think that Leonardo DiCaprio is so fine! It's hard not to like him, after all, he's a great actor (and a cutie)! Please keep Leo on the cover of all your issues." Indeed, *Teen* magazine's Star Babe Poll playfully points up the use of such legitimizing alibis for girls' fandom in what is presented as a teen insider's decoding of the mainstream language surrounding stardom: "Isn't it great to live in a world filled with charming (*cute*), intense (*sexy*) and talented (*gorgeous*) actors and musicians?" Many fans do not merely "add" such remarks to their appreciations nor simply expand the range of their comments to be more in keeping with a culturally authorized fan position. Instead, they are much more insistent about the primacy or even exclusivity of their interest in DiCaprio's artistry in movies such as *Titanic*. "Nobody could ever play Jack as well as you did," writes Melanie, who then goes on to reassure DiCaprio, "I'm not just saying that because of your good looks or the fact that you['re] the world's sex symbol, but because you have a special talent. Acting."[58] Many girls thus replicate the mainstream media's tendency to contrast his (valorized) talent with his (devalued) teen idol status, as though these appeals are inherently contradictory or at least solicit mutually exclusive generational and/or gendered audiences. While it is very likely that most DiCaprio fans are genuinely impressed by his talents, praise for this aspect of his star image is nonetheless most frequently emphasized rather defensively, as an obvious strategy to differentiate one's fandom from what is perceived to be (other) girl fans' more common (and less appropriate) focus on his looks or his place in romantic fantasies. And this defensive strategy, among others, allows girls to enjoy watching—and rewatching—*Titanic*, without finding themselves interpellated by the critical disdain reserved for those who prefer beefcake to Barrymore.

Titanic's box office success prompted headline discussion of DiCaprio's new standing as a mainstream commercial draw, apparently at the expense of his previously revered status as a serious indie actor. As a result, many girl fans have become self-conscious that their fandom is deemed responsible for this shift and is held in contempt by aspects of DiCaprio's star discourse and the commentary of the mainstream press.[59] In an effort to reconcile their ardent position with this cultural contempt, fans not only adapt the discourse on "great acting" for a legitimizing purpose but also internalize the derisory language applied to them. To cite one brief example of the negative connotations present in journalistic word choice, fans of DiCaprio are often described in turns of phrase evoking animalized or dehumanized masses: "swarms of teenage girls [who] squeal with delight," "flocks of pubescent girls," "hounded by a pack of screaming adolescent girls," [Leonardo is] "catnip to budding teenage girls," "herds of teenage girls," "pubescent riots," "amorous groupies," "throngs of girls," and "hordes of modern Juliets, brand new to puberty."[60] Sometimes fans' use of this same type of language is applied only to other fans en masse. For instance, one Web site contributor invokes the "great acting" discourse to assure Leonardo, "I think you are the best actor in the world. I love the way you get deep inside your characters"; but, she also continues, "I hope you don't think I'm one of those stupid little teenage girls that treat you like a piece of me[a]t by calling you names such as lush Leo even [though] you hate it."[61] This fan is able to reconcile DiCaprio's disapproval of his teen girl admirers with her own choice to see *Titanic* seven times by linguistically separating herself from that demeaned group identity, while legitimizing her own (fanatical) consumption on other bases.

Similarly, terms that negatively connote fandom's near-"insane" excesses (like "gaga" and "obsessed," for example) are used ambiguously, sliding between a means of differentiating one's own fandom from the masses' adoration and an acknowledgment that one's ardor is of a piece with such mass deviance. One girl, Leanne, begs DiCaprio, "Please, please don't class me as a Mad LEO teen fan cozz I'm not, but I am sort of, kinda thing! Whatever! Well anyway I just wanna wish you well in your care[er] and [with] your scre[a]min[g] raving fans!" Another uses age to differentiate herself from some DiCaprio fans: "I think Leo is hot, but after *Titanic* he just got way too much attention, and I'm kinda getting sick of hearing eight year olds go on and on about him, just because everyone else in the world is in love with him."

Variations on the diction "one of those stupid little teenage girls" recur in numerous posts avowedly by teenage girls: "I am one of those girls!" or "I'm ashamed to admit it, but I'm just another stupid teenage girl who has fallen completely in love with this gorgeous and talented creature."[62] Such vacillation between owning and disowning the teen fan identity, and the strong desire to express devotion mixed with the fear of seeming pathologically or excessively invested, are clearly demonstrated in the following post: "Dear Leonardo DiCaprio, Hi, My name is Samantha L. Street. I'm 15. I am just another one of your adoring fans. But I'm sorry, I don't mean to sound like another one of those wom[e]n/girls who chase you around for an autograph or pic., let alone who try to dev[our] you by ripping your shirt off. . . . I love you. Sorry I don't mean to seem like a crazed fan, but I do, I love you with all my heart."[63] Samantha is caught uncomfortably between admittedly being "just another one," but not wanting "to sound like another one." The apologetic identification with, and yet somewhat self-differentiating usage of, disparaging and animalizing descriptions of fandom is employed ambivalently here to normalize the expression of what might otherwise be perceived as excessive, fanatical ardor. This normalizing process is key to *Titanic*'s popularity, since repeat viewing—made legitimate by self-differentiation or apology—is one of fans' preferred means of expressing their ardor.

Talk to Teen Machine!

Teen Machine readers love Leo DiCaprio! Here's a sampling of what you're saying about him!

- Want to get a message to the editors and readers of *Teen Machine*? Just write up your letter and mail it to us! We'll print as many as we can in every issue. (Also, if you want us to include your address to trade photos with other readers, please get your parents' permission first!)

- Write to:
- **Talk To Teen Machine**
- **233 Park Avenue South**
- **New York, NY 10003**

ALWAYS IN MY DREAMS

Dear *Teen Machine*,
I think Leo DiCaprio is so fine! He has it all—good looks, great personality and a wonderful talent for acting. I know every girl my age dreams of Leo showing up at her doorstep with roses. We know this won't happen, but hey, a girl can dream, can't she?
Tawny B.
Cedar Hill, MO

ROOM WITH A VIEW

Dear *Teen Machine*,
These are some pictures of my room because Leo is the best! Do you think you could do a special Leo issue sometime, like a collector's issue, because I have only been seeing a little of Leo in your magazine lately. He needs to be recognized more because *Titanic* and *The Man in the Iron Mask* are great. As you can see by the pictures on my wall, I've been a fan of Leonardo since *Growing Pains*. Thanx!
Ashlee W.
Tempe, AZ

Editor's Note: Thanks for your note, Ashlee! As you can see, we've heard you and the pleas of thousands of other Leo fans. We hope you really enjoy this special Leo issue of Teen Machine. P.S. Cool room!

WANTED: LEO!

Dear *Teen Machine*,
I have a lot of pinups, posters and centerfolds of Hanson, JTT, Devon, Backstreet Boys, Andrew, Matt, Spice Girls and more. But I love Leonardo DiCaprio and I would trade posters (of any of the above and more) for him! He's my fave movie star. I saw *Romeo & Juliet* two times and have already seen *Titanic* three times. It may take a little time for me to get back to you, but don't worry, I will. Thanks.
P.J. Ball
4709 Elsa Road
San Diego, CA 92120

LEO IN A HEARTBEAT

Dear *Teen Machine*,
I would greatly appreciate it if you would include more on Leo DiCaprio in your future issues. I have pinups of JTT, Devon, Hanson and Jonathan Jackson and I would give them all up in a heartbeat for more pix of Leo.
Megan N.
Baldwin, LA

COVER BOY

Dear *Teen Machine*,
My cousin and I think that Leonardo DiCaprio is so fine! It's hard not to like him, after all, he's a great actor (and a cutie)! Please keep Leo on the cover of all your issues!
Ari & Amie
San Ramon, CA

7

Letters to Leo page in a teen magazine

Clearly these rhetorical strategies, like the expressions of love they legiti-mize, ultimately reflect an intense desire to curry favor with DiCaprio. With ei-ther the discourse of "great acting" or negative characterizations of (other) teen fans, contributors are drawing on DiCaprio's reported attitudes toward his work and fans to differentiate themselves from what they know (from devoted reading) he hates. For example, one Web site author refers directly to this type of intimate knowledge of DiCaprio's likes and dislikes and makes her linguistic choices on this basis: "we all know how Leonardo doesn't really enjoy being called 'Leo' un-less you are a close friend. . . . So, out of respect, I will . . . refrain from exces-sively referring to him as 'Leo' in this site."[64] Using a very familiar trope in her opening, another girl writes, "HI! Leo, I'm not one of these girls that goes on about your talent, cause you already know that you have it, so why do people keep tell-ing you!"[65] Fans seek to present themselves as in sympathy with DiCaprio's re-ported annoyance with the type of public attention he has garnered, in hopes of distinguishing themselves from that annoying public. This rhetorical alignment with DiCaprio's feelings is an important tactic in rationalizing or compensating for girl fans'(repeated) enjoyment of *Titanic*, given their knowledge of DiCaprio's public scorn for both this particular film role and its enthusiasts.

These numerous and sometimes convoluted defensive strategies (emphasiz-ing great acting, adopting the derisory language applied to teen fans, and echoing DiCaprio's sentiments in chastising others) clearly suggest a high level of aware-ness among girls of the general disdain that surrounds their DiCaprio fandom. While these defenses allow fans some expression of their desires within a more culturally valued framework and legitimize their pleasure in consuming DiCaprio's disavowed role as Jack, they nonetheless rely on a partial acceptance of the nega-tive evaluation of an important part of their emerging social-sexual identities. That is to say, disparaging aspects of DiCaprio's star discourse and of mainstream press accounts of girls' *Titanic* fandom do not negate nor necessarily diminish their pa-tronage of this beloved film or its tie-ins, as one might expect. These discursive obstacles do demand that girl fans recast, disassociate themselves from, or apolo-gize for their romantic fantasies, visual desires, and their most cherished means of fulfilling them: the collection of pinups and repeat film viewings, which are clearly tied to box office returns. Aware of their precarious position vis-à-vis cul-tural tastemakers and DiCaprio's self-image, then, many girls choose rhetorical equivocation to legitimize their fanatical frequenting of *Titanic*.

However, other teen magazine and fan Web site readers actively seek and apparently find community in their romantic fantasies about DiCaprio and their gratification of more purely visual desires. For example, one girl writes to *Teen Beat*: "Hi! My name is Tracy and I'm 12 years old. I have this incredible urge to write to you and tell you how marvelous I think Leonardo DiCaprio is. . . . Well, the entire reason I'm writing is to tell him, if he's reading, that I'm completely in love with him. And, if it's no inconvenience, to put more pictures of him in your mag. . . . Desperately In Love With Leo."[66] Tracy pulls no punches in emphasiz-ing the nature of her interest in DiCaprio and even points out that she had an "in-credible urge" to share these feelings. While it is possible that many (especially younger) fans are not too familiar with mainstream press accounts of DiCaprio's post-*Titanic* star image, it is equally possible that many are seeking positive rein- forcement of their desires in venues (teen mags, Web sites) that they can trust to be responsive.[67] That is, rather than ambivalently differentiating themselves from the mainstream press's sneering remarks, they seek an alternative forum in which their style and object of fandom can be publicly circulated and valued, and in which their multiple viewings of *Titanic* will be appreciated rather than mocked.

Indeed, some fans even appropriate the semipathologizing language applied to teen fandom, but without any apparent reservations about its implications within a community that shares their rapture. Equating her love for DiCaprio with—and expressing it through—repeat viewings of *Titanic*, Maureen writes, "I am totally obsessed with Leonardo DiCaprio! I have seen *TITANIC* now 7 times!" while Jes- sica boldly announces, "I AM ADDICTED TO LEO!!!!!!"[68] Making frequent use of such opportunities for validation within a like-minded cultural constituency, many girls, it would seem, are as addicted to Leo publications and Leo sites as to DiCaprio himself.[69] Teen Research Unlimited has determined that "among girls ages 12 to 19 . . . 84% read magazines in 1997."[70] More specifically, *Time* reports, "Ever since *Titanic* set sail, 'DiCaprio' has been the most searched-for word on Pathfinder, Time Inc.'s website. . . . Leo searches are especially frenzied from 4 p.m. to 8 p.m. Schoolgirls coming home, I figure." And *Newsweek* adds, "At the peak of *Titanic* mania, AOL says, there was a message posted about Leonardo DiCaprio *every 10 seconds*."[71] This temporal coincidence may further suggest, as our research indicates, that *Titanic*'s popularity and DiCaprio's Web fandom were mutually reinforcing phenomena.

Many girls post to Web sites collectively with friends who already share their DiCaprio fandom on their own terms. Together they seek access to images and a larger group of fans, thus bolstering their desires for DiCaprio and funding the snowballing popularity of *Titanic* among this group. For example, Aimee, Andrea, and Kristen write (without any concern to cloak their true interests): "Leo is sooooo SEXY!!!!!! We would really like to get our hands on some of that SUGARRRR!!!!!! . . . WE TOTALLY LOVE HIM TO PIECES!!!!!!" Girls who write in alone frequently make reference to their friends' DiCaprio fandom or use similar rhetorical strategies to create a needed sense of external support for their desires. When Mary confides that she loves DiCaprio, that "hottie yumillicious babe," she adds that "my buds are crazy about him," and also, "then again who isn't?" In an inversion of pathologizing descriptions of fandom, one fan, Jenn Kelly, enthuses, "Leo is . . . sex-on-legs!! If there's a girl on earth that doesn't love him she must be mad!!!" This creation of a (gendered and age-based) group identity through inclusive language recurs in numerous posts such as "*girls*, he's all mine" and, "Leo was sent down from Heaven for *all us girls* to admire." One fan draws the boundaries of the DiCaprio community more explicitly, policing the support- ive territory she seeks on the Web: "Leo is cute I have to agree. . . . For all you people [who] hate him get a life and fu** yourselves. For the people who like him you rule. LEONARDO IS FINE!"[72] This real or rhetorical support of a peer com- munity—and the vehement exclusion of naysayers—works to legitimize repeat viewing of *Titanic* by normalizing DiCaprio fandom as a majority discourse, despite the mainstream marginalization of girl fans' desires.

Within these created communities contributors can take pride in a certain sense of expertise, closely linked to the dedicated consumption of DiCaprio vehicles: "This site was tha bomb!!" writes Kanoelani, "But I already had most of the pictures of *Titanic*. Probably because I have over a hundred and fifty pics of him." Web site creators address their users in friendly and desire-validating language: "Because he's such a hunk, I've made up a special little page for all you Leo lovers full of links and yummy pictures! Enjoy." And many users leave equally girl-friendly messages in response, sometimes referring visitors to other DiCaprio sites. Daniela signs off with, "keep on being tough, girls need it!"; and Cher writes, "This [p]age rocks!!! . . . Visit *DiCaprio's Domain*, a Page for Leonardo Fanatics." Feeding the dynamics of group fantasy, other girls invite the contemplation of questions such as, "Does Leo really post on this board?" or, if you "saw Leo walking down the street . . . [w]hat would you say or do?" And similarly, two different girls use this forum to offer membership to free newsletters they were separately creating. Dozens of others invite e-pals to share their DiCaprio interest: "I am Leo's wife . . . I wish!!!!! ok . . . I'm 11 and if you want to be my internet buddie then just click on the name. P.S. I'm a girl."[73] Rather than feeling belittled for their interest in DiCaprio, girls articulate a sense of status through accounts of their accumulation of viewing experience and visual objects, which can only be pleasurably shared in this mode of community.

This type of interaction among DiCaprio fans may initially seem (positively) opposed to the self-differentiating or awkwardly apologetic rhetorical strategies that mark many girls' discussions of the star. But, in fact, it speaks to the same problem, despite finding a different solution. The high value placed on participation in the more girl-supportive Web sites symptomatically suggests that teen fans acutely feel the need to (at least try to) insulate themselves from the mainstream contempt for their desires. Indeed, they seek out such (potential) validation and a sense of community in Web sites and teen magazines *because* it is so pointedly lacking elsewhere.

This ongoing creation of a group feeling of belonging is closely linked to the incredible box office popularity of *Titanic* among girls, as well as underwriting their related purchases of *Titanic* merchandise (such as the soundtrack and picture books) and DiCaprio paraphernalia. These community forums fuel not just the individual fan's repeat viewings but the desire to attend within similarly large groups of like-minded girls. As the *New York Times* points out, "Unlike teen-age boys, who attend movies with a friend or two, girls prefer going to theaters in packs."[74] This preference for group consumption finds both an analogous outlet and an important support mechanism in Web site and teen magazine communities. Indeed, this need for validation among one's peers is further symptomatic of girls' culturally deauthorized position vis-à-vis mass cultural objects, compared to their young male counterparts who have been traditionally conceived of as of a piece with, if not identical to, the mainstream market. Hence it is neither surpris-

A whole teen magazine page of Leo merchandise for girl fans

ing (nor incidental to *Titanic*'s success) that girls find ways to seek each other's company in the nearly ritualistic consumption practices that surround this film.

Conclusion: Post-*Titanic* Girl Power?

The incredible commercial impact of *Titanic* has brought girls' movie fandom to the forefront of industry analysts' and cultural commentators' discussions of Hollywood audiences. With both groups quick to pounce on any perceptible trends, sweeping claims have been made for this film as a new precedent in (young) female-targeted productions. One article notes that "*Titanic*'s numbers raised Fox's confidence in the enormity of the women market," while another reports that "virtually every studio is now making, or planning, a handful of films aimed at teenage girls."[75] The president of marketing at Universal Pictures is quoted as saying, "By sheer bulk, the young girls are driving cultural tastes now. They're amazing consumers." And since "the teen-age girl audience is emerging as the most powerful demographic factor driving the success of movies like 'Titanic,'" as one commentator puts it, it is a short step to conclude, as he does, that "Girl Power has seized the entertainment business." Indeed, *CNN/Entertainment Weekly*'s television report, "Girl Power," claims: "Teen girls on average have a disposable income of $103 a week, which can buy a lot of movie tickets, CDs, and designer T-shirts. And these days everybody wants to cash in on the biggest force in viewing and the biggest force in buying: girls. Boy, have they come a long way."[76] By seeing the film both multiple times and within large groups, teen girls were indeed the single largest force driving the box office receipts of *Titanic*. At one level, then, there is no refuting the staggering economic importance of this demographic to the contemporary culture industry in general, nor to *Titanic*'s popularity more specifically.

Even if we accept these claims about Hollywood's rediscovery of a young female audience,[77] being targeted as a lucrative market is not quite the same thing as "driving cultural tastes" or "Girl Power." Despite the alleged proliferation of objects being created for these "amazing consumers," any such marketing trend remains at odds with the continuing critical mockery of girls' genres or desires. Even post-*Titanic*, it would still appear that more DiCaprio fans, for instance, are made to feel like "one of those stupid little teenage girls" than "the most powerful demographic factor." As we have demonstrated, DiCaprio's function as *Titanic*'s chief star lure for girl fans was not unambiguous. In fact, girls were obliged to employ a wide variety of compensatory, defensive, and evasive strategies in order to pleasurably reframe their ardent *Titanic* consumption in the face of negative critical evaluations of their fandom.

Cultural optimists have argued that "since consumerism is the only kind of citizenship they are usually offered, young people use it the best they can, turning the rhymes of hip-hop into shared histories and transforming internet chat rooms into impromptu community forums."[78] But as our analyses of DiCaprio fans' rather conflicted sense of value or belonging suggest, such consumption practices and community forums do not unambiguously empower girls or their taste cultures.

In fact, as we have argued, many girls are unable to simply or gleefully consume even those cultural materials directed at them, and are instead very aware of the stamp of devaluation their fandom carries in this society—or embarrassed by their peers' lack of awareness. They are faced with the paradox of tainting (in the larger public eye) what they love and admire simply through the act of loving and admiring it. These girls are placed in the uncomfortable position of having to negotiate expressions of their fandom under the disapproving lens of the journalistic arbiters of (adult, male) taste and the begrudging (adult, male) recipient of their attentions. And many girls, for the same reason, are also faced with the complementary paradox of trying to remove their love and admiration of a public object into more private, supportive spaces, but with only partial success.

The record-breaking box office of *Titanic* is clearly a product of DiCaprio fandom and the unprecedented repeat viewings such fandom enticed. Tracing the social context of these fans' practices tells us much about the reasons for *Titanic's* popularity, and foregrounds the negotiations required of teen girls as newly found cinematic consumers. While this culture may indeed welcome the (re)emergence of young female audiences in paying admission for the fifth, sixth, or seventh time, it also calls them "swarms," "herds," or "flocks." It can viably praise *Titanic* for having successfully focused on a romance narrative, but "at the *risk* of turning into a women's picture."[79] It is still a culture that can think of no more damning or trivializing criticism of an actor than to point out that he is a "teen idol"; in counterpoint, no greater praise for his skill or seriousness can be demonstrated than to report that he chafes against this identity.

In this cultural context, DiCaprio fandom offers teenage girls ambivalent pleasures: a certain self-conscious trepidation in owning the degraded identity of "fan" (and in risking the defilement of their idol by association), mixed with real opportunities for communal validation and expression of (an otherwise deauthorized) desire. While these girls are well aware that they were primarily responsible for *Titanic's* popularity, they are equally aware that their dominant role in the film's commercial success irrevocably tainted its importance for DiCaprio and many critics. It is because of this paradoxical status of girls' fandom that one young fan can recognize that "Leo is becoming amazingly famous among young teenage girls," while also admitting, "[I'm] ALMOST ashamed to say I am one of those girls."[80]

Notes

1. Kim Masters, "Trying to Stay Afloat," *Time*, 8 December 1997, 87; Wes D. Gehring, "*Titanic*: The Ultimate Epic," *USA Today: The Magazine of the American Scene*, March 1998, 51.
2. David Ansen, "Our *Titanic* Love Affair," *Newsweek*, 23 February 1998, 61; David Denby, "Stacked Deck," *New York*, 23 December 1997, 130.
3. Gehring, "*Titanic*," 51.
4. Ansen, "Our Titanic Love Affair," 60.
5. Ibid. The recent domestic top-grossing films include *Star Wars* (#2), *Jurassic Park* (#4), *Independence Day* (#8), *Jaws* (#11), and *Raiders of the Lost Ark* (#14), which cater to

a predominantly young male audience. One would be hard-pressed to claim that these function primarily as love stories, period pieces, or costume dramas.

6. Ansen, "Our *Titanic* Love Affair," 60.
7. Bernard Weinraub, "Who's Lining Up at the Box Office? Lots and Lots of Girls," *New York Times*, 23 February 1998, E1, E4.
8. Sara Glassman, "The Leo File," *Seventeen*, April 1998, 64.
9. Nadya Labi, "Girl Power," *Time*, 29 June 1998, 62.
10. Eric Boehlert, "*Titanic* Sales On: The Most Successful Movie Score in History Spurs a Concert Tour," *Rolling Stone* 2 April 1998, 30.
11. James Cameron, "Settling Accounts: *Titanic*'s Director Responds to the Charges about His Film," *Time*, 8 December 1997, 92.
12. Quoted in Ansen, "Our *Titanic* Love Affair," 61.
13. Quoted in ibid., 62.
14. See The '*Titanic* Continued' Fan Fiction Library (part of Michelle's Leo DiCaprio Page), http://www.geocities.com/Hollywood/Academy/9204/storypage.html.
15. Weinraub, "Who's Lining Up at the Box Office?" E4.
16. Ibid.
17. Peter Travers, "A New Role for the *Titanic* Star Whom Oscar Forgot," *Rolling Stone,* 2 April 1998, 77.
18. Bruce Handy, "Deconstructing Leo: What the Men Don't Get, the Teen Girls Understand," *Time,* 30 March 1998, 66.
19. Angie Maximo, "Readers' Poll '97: Who Are You Down With? (And Who's Just Down and Out?)," *Seventeen*, July 1997, 80.
20. Grace Catalano, *Leonardo DiCaprio: Modern-Day Romeo* (New York: Bantam Doubleday Dell Books for Young Readers, 1997), 27.
21. Maximo, "Readers' Poll '97," 79.
22. Alana (26 April 1998), Leonardo DiCaprio Online, http://www.leonardo-dicaprio-com/. We have made only minimal corrections to fans' spelling and syntax (in square brackets) in order to maintain readability without sacrificing too much of the flavor of their writing.
23. Zoe Barnes, "Oh Rom-Leo," *Girlfriend*, February 1997, 26–27; Amy Lynn Dott, Amy's Frog and Otherwise Page (www2.trincoll.edu/~adott/); Christina Chudyk (n.d.), Celebrity Corner, http:/virtualvoyage.com/celeb/main.html.
24. Christina Chudyk (n.d.), Celebrity Corner; Shannon Spalding (9 February 1998), Liz's Leonardo DiCaprio Homepage (www.geocities.com/Hollywood/Lot/7020/); Synnove Loftheim (22 February 1998), Liz's Leonardo DiCaprio Homepage; Samantha L. Street (n.d.), Celebrity Corner; Talia Poblete (29 March 1998), Liz's Leonardo DiCaprio Homepage; Catalano, *Leonardo DiCaprio: Modern-Day Romeo*.
25. Karen Schoemer, "A Woman's Liberation," *Newsweek*, 23 February 1998, 64. This identical argument is made about Claire Danes: "But lust aside, it may be Danes's portrayal of Juliet that makes this film so appealing to girls, Luhrmann says. . . . As Angela in the TV series 'My So-Called Life,' Danes gave teenage girls an emotional mirror to stare into. She was clearly of them, not above them. . . . She is lovely, but not an unattainable beauty. . . . Her portrayal is such that teenage girls sitting in the darkened theater may feel suddenly reassured ('If she can snag a Romeo like DiCaprio, maybe there's hope for me, too!'). . . . They rank her with DiCaprio in terms of the film's drawing power." See Inara Verzemnieks, "Like, Way Cool, Romeo; Teen Girls Relate to Screen's Star-Crossed Lovers," *Washington Post,* 8 November 1996, D1.

26. Stephen Holden, "At the Top by Way of a Bottom Line," *New York Times*, 22 February 1998, sec. 2, p. 15.
27. Shannon Spalding (11 February 1998), Liz's Leonardo DiCaprio Homepage.
28. Cathy Horyn, "Leonardo Takes Wing," *Vanity Fair*, January 1998, 75.
29. Maximo, "Reader's Poll '97," 79.
30. See leo's lover (7 April 1998), Lauren Clinton (DiCaprio) (9 April 1998), and Mrs. DiCaprio (20 April 1998), Liz's Leonardo DiCaprio Homepage.
31. See leo's lover (7 April 1998), SARAH (14 April 1998), and Elizabeth Kerper (7 February 1998), Liz's Leonardo DiCaprio Homepage.
32. As mentioned in the main text, *Titanic* fanfic does foreground a deep investment in Rose's liberation into adulthood; but the fact that it easily ignores other less desirable aspects of the film (the iceberg, Jack's death) also points up girls' desire and ability to use the text creatively. And, of course, this fanfic is on a DiCaprio Web site (Michelle's Leo DiCaprio Page). Girls have also targeted other aspects of the film for special attention in defiance of either narrative or star-related determinations: two girls paid a seamstress to make dresses copied in detail from *Titanic* costumes. See Associated Press, "*Titanic* Dresses for Prom," *The Daily Iowan*, 15 April 1998, 2A.
33. Zowi (n.d.), Celebrity Corner.
34. Amy (n.d.), Celebrity Corner.
35. Amy Lynn Dott, Amy's Frog and Otherwise Page; Jennifer (10 February 1998) and Corey (31 January 1998), Liz's Leonardo DiCaprio Homepage; Claire (8 March 1998), Liz's Leonardo DiCaprio Homepage; Kimberly Brown (23 April 1998), Basically Leonardo (www.geocities.com/Hollywood/7178/); Erica (25 April 1998), Liz's Leonardo DiCaprio Homepage; Holly Moore (3 February 1998), Liz's Leonardo DiCaprio Homepage.
36. From May 1997 to May 1998 DiCaprio's photo was on the cover of *Teen Beat* seven times.
37. *Teen Beat*, June 1998; *Gold Collectors Series Entertainment Magazine*, 1998.
38. Janet Maslin, "L'Etat, It's DiCaprio: C'est le Brat-King," *New York Times*, 13 March 1998, E14.
39. Richard Dyer, "Don't Look Now: The Instabilities of the Male Pin-Up," in *Only Entertainment* (London: Routledge, 1992), 103–119. Originally published in *Screen* 23, no. 3–4 (1982).
40. Richard Dyer, *Heavenly Bodies: Film Stars and Society* (Basingstoke: Macmillan, 1987), 3.
41. "DiCaprio, Leonardo," in *1997 Current Biography Yearbook*, ed. Elizabeth A. Schick (New York: H. W. Wilson, 1997), 139.
42. Bernard Weinraub, "DiCaprio, Charismatic Star, Balks at the Idol Image," *New York Times*, 16 March 1998, E1.
43. This "great acting" discourse includes frequent comparisons to male Method actors. A *Detour* (November 1996) cover image of DiCaprio references Marlon Brando in *The Wild One* (1954), an icon of rebellious masculinity, and DiCaprio is even more frequently compared with James Dean. See, for example, Catalano, *Leonardo DiCaprio*, 6, 68, 84; and Weinraub, "DiCaprio, Charismatic Star," E1. Explicitly opposed to his talent, DiCaprio's good looks are portrayed as a burden to be overcome. It is widely reported, for example, that DiCaprio nearly lost the part of a mentally disabled boy in *What's Eating Gilbert Grape?* "because he was considered too good-looking. He saved himself with another strong performance during the audition." See "DiCaprio, Leonardo," 140. See also Aljean Harmetz, "Up and Coming: Leonardo DiCaprio; The

Actor Is Boyishly Handsome, And That's a Liability," *New York Times*, 12 December 1993, sec. 2, p. 16.

44. Ansen, "Our *Titanic* Love Affair," 63.

45. Quoted in Horyn, "Leonardo Takes Wing," 128.

46. But this is not to suggest, of course, that teen girls or other fans were unable to take pleasure in the spectacle of their choice (DiCaprio!). As the first and third sections of our article demonstrate, voyeuristic objectification and identification alike are processes that have as much or more to do with intertextually elaborated spectatorial desires (for example, in star-related fan materials) than textually constructed looking relations.

47. See Andreas Huyssen, "Mass Culture as Woman: Modernism's Other," in *Studies in Entertainment: Critical Approaches to Mass Culture*, ed. Tania Modleski (Bloomington: Indiana University Press, 1986), 188–207.

48. Travers, "A New Role for the *Titanic* Star," 77.

49. Indeed, one might argue that many Method actors (to whom DiCaprio is compared)— Marlon Brando, James Dean, Montgomery Clift—similarly profited from "alienated" roles and "deep" characters, as well as from the patina of studied "great acting" to disavow their uncomfortable status as sex symbols.

50. Travers, "A New Role for the *Titanic* Star," 77.

51. Quoted in Catalano, *Leonardo DiCaprio*, 89.

52. Horyn, "Leonardo Takes Wing," 71 and 72, respectively. DiCaprio's reported treatment of these fans also demonstrates his contempt for his status as a teen idol. For instance, one article recounts the posse's dumping water on girls waiting under DiCaprio's hotel balcony: "Sometimes Jonah Johnson would open a window, look down at their honest, trembling, Polly Magoo faces, and throw water on them. 'They *loved* it,' swears Johnson." See Horyn, "Leonardo Takes Wing," 75. DiCaprio himself suggests a misogynist motivation for this kind of action: "'I tease girls and try to get some power trip going and show them I'm the dominant one,' says DiCaprio, explaining his method of dealing with amorous groupies." See Christine Spines, "I Would Die 4 U," *Premiere*, October 1996, 138.

53. Travers, "A New Role for the *Titanic* Star," 77.

54. Frank DiGiacomo, "The Selling of Leonardo DiCaprio," *New York Observer*, 15 June 1998, 3.

55. Cathy Garrard, "Everything Leo: His Top Secrets Revealed," *YM: Young and Modern*, May 1998, 79.

56. Horyn, "Leonardo Takes Wing," 72, 75.

57. Beyond disowning *Titanic*, numerous articles and interviews go back in time to disparage his TV beginnings as a teen idol (and, by association, fans of these texts) as clearly beneath DiCaprio: "Only 10 and already becoming a favorite of teeny-bopper magazines," one magazine reports, "Leo was nonetheless bored with his vapid assignments." See "Deconstructing Leonardo: Leonardo DiCaprio's Rise to Superstardom!" *Biograph Presents: Hollywood's Hottest Hunks #2* 1, no. 8 (1998): 8. Another claims that his role as Luke on *Growing Pains* "proved illuminating to DiCaprio. 'I got to know what I don't want to do. . . . I had these lame lines—I couldn't bear it, actually.'" See "DiCaprio, Leonardo," 140, quoted from Rob Tannenbaum's interview with DiCaprio, "What's Eating Leonardo Dicaprio?" *Details*, March 1995, 174–178, 226. DiCaprio's remarks even about his critically acclaimed films favored by teenage girls are equally explicit in this attempt to deemphasize or mock his appeal as a pinup.. Witness DiCaprio's much-reproduced remark about *William Shakespeare's Romeo + Juliet*: "If this hadn't been a contemporary spin on *Romeo and Juliet*, I wouldn't have done it I

didn't want to be leaping around in tights." See Kim Cunningham, "Such Sweet Sorrow," *People*, 25 November 1996, 184. See also Catalano, *Leonardo DiCaprio*, 4, 85. Or DiCaprio on being dubbed "Hollywood's hot new heartthrob": "Well, it isn't a label I placed on myself." See Catalano, *Leonardio DiCaprio*, 110–111.

58. Ari & Amie, San Ramon, California, "Cover Boy," Letter to *Teen Machine*, August 1998, 7; "Star Babe Poll," *Teen*, May 1998, 57. Original emphasis; Melanie (n.d.), Celebrity Corner.

59. Some teen magazines surprisingly do include some similarly contemptuous elements of this discourse—and *Hollywood's Hottest Hunks #2* even foregrounds such disdain for teens in trying to dissociate itself from this category of publication: "teeny-bopper magazines (hey, we are *not*!)" (8). But in contrast to the mainstream press, when teen magazines provide information on DiCaprio's dislike of girl fans or their favorite texts, it is generally recast as something positive about DiCaprio, such as fame not going to his head, his modesty about his good looks, or his desire for privacy. See, for example, Jim Shevis, "Leonardo DiCaprio: Serious Actor, Serious Heartthrob," *Gold Collector Series Entertainment Magazine*, 8, or Garrard, "Everything Leo," 80. Furthermore, Catalano's DiCaprio biography (again courting teen girls) regularly takes DiCaprio quotes out of context or uses carefully selected material to suggest the opposite of what mainstream sources claim. See, for example, Catalano's spin on DiCaprio's feelings about *Titanic,* 104, 110–111, or his TV roles, 20–21, 29, 32. And many magazines find ways to recontextualize any anti-teen-idol information within features (gushing headings, pinup photos, sections of love letters to Leo, etc.) that belie its larger implications. *Teen Machine*, August 1998, for example, recently reprinted a photo of a fifteen-year-old DiCaprio holding an issue of *Teen Machine* in his hand. The caption reads, "As you can see, he was pretty tight with *Teen Machine* even back then!" (22), suggesting that DiCaprio (still) approves of this circulation of his image.

60. Respectively: Shevis, "Leonardo DiCaprio," 26; Jesse Green, "Fresh Blood: Leonardo DiCaprio," *New York Times Magazine* 12 February 1995, 28; Horyn, "DiCaprio Takes Wing," 71; ibid., 72; Catalano, *Leonardo DiCaprio*, 65; "Our Fabulous 50," *People* 11 May 1998, 77; Spines, "I Would Die 4 U," 138; Weinraub, "DiCaprio, Charismatic Star, Balks at the Idol Image," E1; Russell Baker, "Those Fetching Guys," *New York Times* 27 March 1998, A19.

61. Alana (26 April 1998), Leonardo DiCaprio Online.

62. LEANNExxx (n.d.), Celebrity Corner; Anon. (13 April 1998), Liz's Leonardo DiCaprio Homepage; Raingirl (Sarah) (25 March 1998), Liz's Leonardo DiCaprio Homepage; Jessica (obsessed) (4 February 1998), Liz's Leonardo DiCaprio Homepage.

63. Samantha L. Street (n.d.), Celebrity Corner.

64. Absolut DiCaprio (a.k.a. Absolut Leo), www.geocities.com/Hollywood/Studio/5524/.

65. Sugarbery (26 April 1998), Leonardo DiCaprio Online.

66. Tracy T., Mesa, Arizona, letter to *Teen Beat*, June 1998, 93.

67. Web sites are hit and miss, in this regard, for many are also dismissive of teen girl fandom in their construction (e.g., Absolut DiCaprio; Completely Unofficial Leonardo DiCaprio Home Page, http://www.dicaprio.com); most sites have virulent anti-Leo or anti-teen-fan contributions; more or less all have contributors using the self-differentiating strategies that implicitly deride teen fans or their areas of interest; and a number of Leo sites go in directions teen girls don't want to go (e.g., gay porn). Still, girls come to know the sites where their interests are fed and encouraged and revisit them faithfully for support.

68. Maureen (25 April 1998), Basically Leonardo; Jessica (4 February 1998), Liz's Leonardo DiCaprio Homepage.

69. At one point, there were four different DiCaprio-related books on the *New York Times* best-seller lists, in addition to five *Titanic*-related books. See the *New York Times Book Review*, 29 March 1998, 28. And this is, of course, on top of the endless teen magazines that regularly feature DiCaprio material. Since *William Shakespeare's Romeo + Juliet*, DiCaprio has played second fiddle only to the teen rock group Hanson in magazines of this type.

70. Labi, "Girl Power," 62.

71. Joshua Quittner, "Looking for Leonardo," *Time*, 4 May 1998, 25; Brad Stone, "The Keyboard Kids," *Newsweek*, 8 June 1998, 72 (original emphasis).

72. Aimee, Andrea, and Kristen (2 February 1998), Liz's Leonardo DiCaprio Homepage; Mary (25 April 1998), Liz's Leonardo DiCaprio Homepage; Jenn Kelly (27 April 1998), Basically Leonardo; Joe (girl) (4 February 1998) and Cameerom (9 March 1998), Liz's Leonardo DiCaprio Homepage, our emphases; Taz (22 April 1998), Basically Leonardo.

73. Kanoelani (31 January 1998), Liz's Leonardo DiCaprio Homepage; Mouse's Sexy Homepage (www.hitech.net.au/mouse/); Daniela Hutwagner (16 April 1998), Liz's Leonardo DiCaprio Homepage; Cher (28 April 1998), Mouse's Sexy Homepage; Jolt Girl (28 April 1998), Leonardo DiCaprio Online; Emmy (27 April 1998), Leonardo DiCaprio Online; Charisse (26 April 1998) and Susan Locke (16 February 1998), Liz's Leonardo DiCaprio Homepage; Froggy (25 April 1998), Mouse's Sexy Homepage.

74. Weinraub, "Who's Lining Up at the Box Office?" E4.

75. David Ansen, "The Court of King Jim," *Newsweek*, 13 April 1998, 70; Weinraub, "Who's Lining Up at the Box Office?" E4.

76. Weinraub, "Who's Lining Up at the Box Office?" E4, E1; "Girl Power," produced by Grace Kahng, *CNN/Entertainment Weekly*, originally aired 9 July 1998 on CNN.

77. This premise is by no means universally accepted. Weinraub notes that "the movie industry's rediscovery of the young female audience is greeted with cynicism in some quarters. The consensus is that this audience was always there, but never fully acknowledged until lately" ("Who's Lining Up at the Box Office?" E4). And Ansen reports skepticism as well as cynicism: "Indeed, not everyone sees a reawakening. 'It's complete bulls— that they've rediscovered the female audience,' insists one executive [who believes there is still much resistance to producing such films]. . . . Amy Pascal, head of Sony Pictures, thinks 'it's disgusting' to think that anyone has to rediscover the female audience. . . . 'How can we be rediscovered? . . . It's patronizing. But it's true. Every time a women's movie does well, they rediscover us'" ("The Court of King Jim," 71).

78. Ann Powers, "Who Are These People, Anyway?" *New York Times*, 29 April 1998, D8.

79. Janet Maslin, "*Titanic*: A Spectacle as Sweeping as the Sea," *New York Times*, 19 December 1997. Our emphasis.

80. Raingirl (25 March 1998), Liz's Leonardo DiCaprio Homepage.

"Something and Someone Else"

The Mind, the Body, and Sexuality in *Titanic*

PETER LEHMAN AND SUSAN HUNT

$\mathcal{P}$erhaps the biggest cliché about *Titanic* is that the film's success derives from James Cameron's decision to structure it around a love story. Rather than simply present an action, special effects extravaganza, Cameron opted to tell a tale of romantic love of epic proportions against a well-known historical backdrop of equally epic disaster. It would seem, then, that *history plus romance equals success*. While it is obviously true that foregrounding the love story is part of *Titanic*'s extraordinary box office success, such a formulation has little or no explanatory value since it bypasses any analysis of either the nature of that love story or the historical event.

To move beyond this critical impasse, we will analyze *Titanic*'s love story in relationship to two quite different traditions: (1) love stories that may powerfully appeal to a fantasy wherein a working-class man awakens sexuality within an attractive, upper-class woman, and (2) 1980s and 1990s male action-adventure films. However, *Titanic* departs significantly from several of the major conventions of both traditions. These departures from convention include a realignment of the mind/body split inherent in such love stories and a divergence from the expected body types of the male romantic leads within both traditions. The manner in which the love story of *Titanic* draws upon but differs from these two primary traditions helps explain the film's particular appeal for teenage girls. It has been widely acknowledged that an unusual part of the film's box office success was based upon the repeat audience of teenage girls who characteristically went to the theater in groups.

Titanic refashioned the body and characterization of the working-class lover and the male action hero in such a manner that a type of character that teenage girls normally cared little or nothing about suddenly became intensely attractive to them. Keeping this in mind, we think it is important to acknowledge the importance of *Titanic*'s lovemaking scene and how it is structured to appeal in an unthreatening manner to this key segment of the audience. Our analysis also shows that some of the conventional elements of a powerful masculinity that have been banished *from* the film are successfully displaced onto a marketing strategy that includes discourses surrounding the making *of* the film.

Cameron was, of course, almost exclusively identified with the action cinema genre prior to *Titanic*. Yvonne Tasker notes that 1980s muscular male action cinema with its emphasis on the display of the male body has its precedents in such films as the "B" movie Tarzan series. She notes: "What does distinguish the action cinema of recent years is its transition into big-budget operations. . . . It is the sheer scale of the budgets, the box-office success, and of the male bodies on display, that seems to have shifted in the Hollywood cinema of the 1980s."[1] Given the trend Tasker identifies and Cameron's filmmaking background, the predictable thing for the screenwriter-director to do would have been to make *Titanic* yet another 1980s and 1990s–type male action film. Despite the fact that the audience knows the ship is doomed and many lives will be lost, Cameron could have displayed the powerful body of an action hero as he rushes around, helping others, defeating unsympathetic characters. We can only speculate as to how successful such an approach would have been, but it is clear that Cameron's somewhat surprising decision to resist such predictability enabled him to fashion *Titanic* in such a way that it could become the unprecedented hit it did.

Tasker also observes "a tendency in recent Hollywood production towards the development of hybrid genres."[2] It is precisely such a hybrid of genres that Cameron created in *Titanic*, by combining a love story of a woman's sexual awakening with the action-adventure film (itself a kind of hybrid). It is not only the manner in which Cameron combined these two traditions that accounts in part for *Titanic*'s success but, rather, the manner in which he departed from central elements of 1980s and 1990s films operating within both of those traditions. In so doing, he styled a love story with appeal not only to men and women but specifically to the repeat teenage girl audience.

"You Are Very Pretty"

The success of the film's love story appears to stem from Cameron's awareness that the body of *Titanic*'s male star, Leonardo DiCaprio, could not replicate the masculine body type that had so dominated 1980s and 1990s action-adventure cinema, a genre to which he had made a major contribution as a director. After being implicated in establishing that powerfully built male body as the norm in a specific cinematic generic context, Cameron here shifts away from it, and does so within a film that not only critiques the notion of the awesome spectacle of phallic male power, but does so through the eyes and mouth of a desiring woman who mocks that very ideal. Thus, *this* love story simply could not have been told with Arnold Schwarzenegger or even Bruce Willis in the DiCaprio role of Jack Dawson.

Titanic, then, seems to be an action-adventure love story with a different kind of male hero, one who lacks the excessive body-focused spectacle of impressive phallic masculinity. In sharp contrast to the "male bodies on display" that Tasker discusses, DiCaprio's body is never displayed, not even in the film's lovemaking scene. Indeed, the way in which the film dwells on his attractive face threatens to make him, not Kate Winslet, the actress who plays the part of young Rose Bukater, the focus of visual pleasure. Several Web site parodies make light of *Titanic*'s reliance on DiCaprio's attractive face as a source of viewer pleasure. In *"Titanic—The expurgated version"* Web site parody, when Leonardo meets Kate, he says, "You are very pretty," and she replies, "Thank you. So are you." "I know," he says. "Prettier than you, in fact."[3] One of the *"Titanic* Parody Pictures" Web site pages, with a reference to the film's sketching scene, shows DiCaprio's face with an emphasis on his eyes as the cartoon bubble reads, "She looks almost as good as me! . . . almost." In another panel of them dancing on the lower deck, the cartoon bubble for DiCaprio reads, "*GRUNT* Kate . . . I think it's time you laid off the *WHEEZE* Twinkies. . . . "[4] Both these parodies recognize that he is "prettier" than she. Indeed, in yet another parody, published in the magazine *Grand Royal* and reported in *Entertainment Weekly*, Vincent Gallo went further, calling DiCaprio "a good looking girl."[5]

The first two Web-site cartoon pictures are also related in calling attention not only to how the casting of DiCaprio has the unusual effect of centering his "beauty" but also to how that effect is inseparable from the casting of Winslet as Rose. Winslet's body is overweight in relation to contemporary Hollywood and cultural norms of female beauty. In other words, one of the consequences of not having a conventionally beautiful female lead is the intensification of DiCaprio's boyish good looks as a replacement for the female star as a traditional source of cinematic pleasure.

Our argument about Cameron's casting of the leads and his use of DiCaprio in *Titanic* is not meant to imply that this phenomenon is either original within Hollywood film history or that male body types in general can always be simply categorized as either attractively powerful or pathetically and/or comically weak. Steven Cohan notes that the "irresistible good looks" of Cary Grant were an important part of his post–World War II films: "Often giving Grant the glamorous build-up usually reserved for female stars, his films of this period play up his desirability as a male through the close-ups that introduce him and make his face comparable to the female lead's."[6] There are and always have been a variety of masculinities and star body types represented within the Hollywood cinema. Our analysis, however, situates *Titanic* in relationship to two genre traditions achieving popularity in 1980s and 1990s cinema that centrally define this "hybrid" film and help explain the film's success.

If DiCaprio's face is important to creating the film's appeal to audiences, there is also another important aspect to Rose's depiction as a woman—her age. Rose is represented by two bodies, two faces. One is young (Winslet) and one, old (Gloria Stuart). In the frame story, both Rose and *Titanic* are old, "relics" of their former selves. One shot makes this chillingly clear. The camera pulls back from underwater images of the ship's wreckage to Rose narrating her story; her wrinkled face clearly echoes the ship's wreckage. The film thus implies that the

Jack's nude portrait of Rose, drawn by James Cameron himself

elderly Rose's face and body constitute a withered wreckage of femininity. Furthermore, the manner in which she moves slowly or not at all in the frame story contrasts with the vibrancy represented in the beginning of the flashback, where Rose's youthful perfection of visage at age seventeen is surrounded by the warmth and bustle of the maiden voyage of the ship. Indeed, it is the Lovett crew's fascination with their discovery of an erotic sketch of a female nude within the *Titanic* wreckage that motivates the entire plot, and everyone's interest in the "old lady" seems rooted in that youthful image of her past.

In a culture that attributes much of women's power to their beauty, age, of course, is the enemy. Contrasting an elderly woman with her once youthful beauty is itself a form of punishment not unprecedented in recent Hollywood film. At the end of *Edward Scissorhands* (1990), for example, a wrinkled, elderly Winona Ryder reflects back upon her memories of the youthful central character played by Johnny Depp. This is very similar to the elderly Rose reflecting back on her lost, youthful lover. Both these women have had their "moment" of intense love and spent the rest of their lives with a sense of its loss. Our observation of the loss of their beauty only compounds their loss of the loved one. Cameron successfully uses this heightened sense of double loss to appeal to his female audience. Such frame stories, evident also in *The Bridges of Madison County* (1995), another film highly successful with female audiences, add emotional intensity to what is already an intense love story.

The precise nature of that love story in *Titanic* demands analysis, especially in the way in which Cameron's film reworks the story of the lower-class, working man who awakens the restless upper-class woman's sexuality. The body types of leading characters figure significantly both in the love story and in the intersecting action-adventure plot in which the male hero saves the woman. Also of interest in attempting to understand the film's appeal is *Titanic*'s lovemaking scene and the manner in which the sexual empowerment of the central male character relates to the working-class, "body man" tradition. Finally, it is important to address the means through which Cameron and the studio somewhat contradictorily turned the making of the film itself into a type of action-adventure story successfully celebrating the modes of masculinity and male heroism that have been eliminated from much of *Titanic*'s narrative.

"How Did He Know That Your Legs Would Bend Back That Way?"

The popular appeal of the love story in *Titanic* hinges on the film's representation of Rose as trapped in and eventually liberated from her deadening social world. Indeed, tropes of entrapment and escape are woven throughout the narrative: characters repeatedly escape from handcuffs, break through locked gates, and open and relock a safe. Entrapment is the central dilemma of the film's upper-class heroine, who strives to free herself from a restrictive fiancé and repressive lifestyle. *Titanic* naturalizes the notion that women would want to escape upper-class boredom through the narrative technique of undermotivating Rose's sense of entrapment: Old Rose briefly narrates her discontent in voice-over; then we see young Rose acting restless and snooty only once before attempting suicide. Cameron simply presumes the audience knows the dreads of such a life.

The theme of freedom is visually expressed in perhaps the most well-publicized image from the film: Rose, supported by Jack, and apparently enjoying the sensations of movement, wind, mist, and height, stands on the railing of the *Titanic*'s prow with her arms outstretched from her body. While this image is an engagingly romantic representation of Rose's journey to personal liberation, a dramatic low angle of Rose as she stands beneath the Statue of Liberty after surviving *Titanic*'s sinking represents her ultimate liberation. The extreme low angle shot rhymes with an earlier image in the film, that of the *Titanic*'s captain standing proudly against a railing with one of the ship's phallic smokestacks behind him. Because Captain Edward J. Smith is depicted as being complicit with self-serving, aristocratic men who are blamed for *Titanic*'s disaster, the formal rhyme between the two shots visually encapsulates Rose's oppression. It helps communicate that Rose is initially caught in a world of conventionally patriarchal men (and women) who ignore, patronize, control, and abuse her.

Such strategies visually position *Titanic* as sympathetic to females like Rose in their desire for freedom from the conventional and the patriarchal. To support this, dialogue such as, "Of course it's not fair. We're women. Our choices are never easy," suggests something of a protofeminist consciousness. On another level, however, the film's author, Cameron, is set up as a benevolent "father" who will offer a solution to young Rose's problems—and to those of the teenage girls in the audience who may be experiencing their own sense of entrapment as they search for a self-identity that will move them from the troublesome adolescent position between childhood and adulthood, dependence and independence.

The narrative solution to Rose's oppression is located in the character of Jack, who, she says, saved her in a number of ways. While he is the one who guides her arms into the outstretched position at the ship's prow, this shot also rhymes with yet another earlier shot. Jack took the same position and shouted what becomes the film's signature line, "I'm the King of the World!" By anointing Jack—the penniless, third-class passenger—"king," Cameron links Rose's liberation to the working class and a body-oriented world, while her oppressors are associated with the upper class, with its refined language and body-repressing world of the mind. Rose's fiancé, Cal Hockley, and *Titanic*'s most distinguished first-class passengers, enjoy a dinner of gourmet food and champagne at the captain's table as they engage in verbal sparring and "mind games." The men then retreat to a first-class lounge—without the women—to talk business and politics over cigars and brandy. The following scene provides the visual exemplar of the film's split between the world and men of the mind and the world and men of the body. Jack takes Rose to steerage for a "real party." The loud Irish folk music renders conversation virtually impossible. Along with male beer guzzling and arm wrestling, this world does include women in the exuberant, frenzied fun of folk dancing.

This representation of a mind/body duality in *Titanic* is consistent with a narrative pattern deeply embedded in twentieth-century Western culture. It is important to understand both the nature of this pattern and why it holds such appeal for so many people. To understand the success of *Titanic*, one must also understand the manner in which Cameron was able to modify it in a way that held particular appeal for teenage girls. In this story pattern, a conventionally attractive woman is discontented to the point of psychological instability, primarily because of her marriage or engagement to an intellectual man (often coded as upper class). The woman's restlessness is revealed to be sexual in nature when she is quickly attracted to a "man of the earth" who later awakens her dormant sexuality. The "earth man," coded as working-class, is more of the body than of the mind.

A seminal text illustrating this pattern is D. H. Lawrence's 1928 novel *Lady Chatterley's Lover*. Wealthy Clifford Chatterley—paralyzed and impotent from a war injury—ultimately cannot satisfy his wife, Connie, sexually or spiritually, even though she thought herself adjusted to his situation. Lawrence describes Clifford and Connie as having "lived in their ideas and his books," and Connie "quite liked the life of the mind, and got a great thrill out of it."[7] Through an affair with one of Clifford's intellectual cronies, Connie attains sexual pleasure, but she realizes her life is empty after meeting the working-class Mellors—a gamekeeper in Clifford's employ. Connie describes her first sighting of him as a "visionary experience . . . [he was] not the stuff of beauty, not even the body of beauty, but a lambency, the warm, white flame of a single life, revealing itself in contours that one might touch: *a body*."[8] Connie has a sexual affair with Mellors and is so fulfilled by him that she leaves Clifford. The characterizations in *Lady Chatterley's Lover* of the "mind man," the body man, and the woman they both love are recapitulated in many recent films, as they are in *Titanic*.[9] But *Titanic* does more than simply recapitulate; it reformulates a key aspect of the body man: Mellors is not "the stuff of beauty," but the same cannot be said of DiCaprio in *Titanic*.

Although not new as a film phenomenon, movies centering on a similar mind/body split have proliferated in the 1980s and 1990s. These films were made by women (such as Jane Campion) as well as men; they range from big-budget Hollywood tales (*Legends of the Fall*, 1995) to international art cinema (*The Piano*, 1993; *Sirens*, 1994; and *Antonia's Line*, 1995). In all of these relevant film examples, and *Titanic* as well, intellectual upper-class men cannot satisfy the principal female characters' longings.

In *Sirens*, Estella's (Tara Fitzgerald) husband, Tony (Hugh Grant), is marked as childish. Tony—an intellectual minister who reads *Decline of the West* in the privy—gets car sick, stumbles around, and breaks things. The excessive childishness and impulsiveness of the educated, upper-class men in these films connotes a lack of full masculinity and sexuality, something that heightens the contrast between them and the "body men." The mind/body narratives also intersect with films that focus primarily on a duality between the upper class and the middle or lower class. In these films, the wealthy are often depicted as mentally unstable and unhappy as in *Reversal of Fortune* (1990), for instance. In films such as *Overboard* (1987), *Pretty Woman* (1990)*, Regarding Henry* (1991), *Sabrina* (1995), and *Mrs. Winterborne* (1996), the lives of the bored, superficial, unscrupulous, arrogant, and/or neurotic wealthy are improved through contact with lower- or middle-class people and lifestyles.

Working-class, body-oriented men succeed where the intellectual, upper-class men fail. They respond to the women's desires and fulfill them, primarily through their sexual expertise. Mellors is depicted as having an instinctive knowledge and sensitivity of the female body and his lovemaking regenerates Connie's enthusiasm for life—a life that was deadened with Clifford. Lawrence vividly describes how Mellors's body and lovemaking technique bring Connie to exquisite orgasm. In this tradition, Jack, too, sexually satisfies Rose because, like Clifford in *Lady Chatterley's Lover*, Rose's husband-to-be, Cal, is "royalty," but he is marked as deficient. Cal is depicted as arrogant, a class snob, and a misogynist. When he senses Rose is unhappy, he tries to buy her affection with the priceless Heart of the Ocean diamond (Le Coeur de la mer). Cal's most egregious quality is his abusiveness: he overturns a table to intimidate Rose, slaps her, and ultimately tries to kill her when he learns of her affair with Jack. Cal's impulsive brutality is similar to that of the industrious New Zealand colonist Stewart (Sam Neill) in *The Piano*. His wife, Ada (Holly Hunter), is an accomplished pianist, but he chops off one of her fingers with an ax after he learns of her affair with Baines (Harvey Keitel), a neighbor who has "gone native."

In keeping with this pattern is *Legends of the Fall*. However, in this film, the deficiency of Samuel (Henry Thomas)—the Harvard-educated fiancé of the beautiful and refined Susannah (Julia Ormond)—is defined as childishness rather than brutality. When Samuel enlists in World War I, his two brothers join as well to protect him, but Samuel volunteers for a dangerous mission and is killed. After Samuel's death, the "body brother" Tristan (Brad Pitt) returns home from the war and begins a sexual relationship with Susannah, who was drawn to him at their first meeting. The montage sequence depicting their first night of lovemaking shows

Tristan actively and skillfully performing in a manner that repeatedly brings Susannah sexual pleasure. We can assume that Samuel would not have performed so well as to evoke this response from Susannah because, earlier in the film, we see him shyly consult Tristan about "being with" her before marriage. Tristan says: "I recommend fucking" (rather than "being with"), a response that embarrasses Samuel, but "fucking" is something that later Susannah clearly enjoys with Tristan. We can also assume Susannah's sex life was unsatisfactory with Tristan's brother Alfred (Aidan Quinn). After Tristan left her to tour the world, Susannah married Alfred, a businessman and politician, but she is morbidly unhappy with him and their upper-class lifestyle. Tristan succeeds where two brothers fail, thus doubling his potency.

The superior sexual performance of such body men is also articulated in several other recent films. In *The Piano* Ada is initially repulsed by the body man Baines. He is illiterate, but his sensitive sexual advances excite her, and she eventually has passionate sex with him. On the other hand, Ada's husband, Stewart, is so sexually repressed that he cannot respond to her sexually even though he wants her to "come to him." Tony, the man of letters in *Sirens*, is also depicted as a poor lover: he is shown bobbing on top of Estella while she lies still with her eyes open. Her sexuality is awakened by the tanned, muscle-shirted handyman, Devlin, whom she saw nude and masturbating. She later goes to him and is sexually satisfied. In *Moonlight and Valentino* (1995), Rebecca's (Elizabeth Perkins) college professor husband dies suddenly. In the difficult transition period following his death, she has an affair with a man (Jon Bon Jovi) who is painting her house. She describes the sex to her friend as "amazing" and "too delicious." Rebecca's friend asks, "How did he know that your legs would bend back that way?" and she replies, "Men like that just know these things." When Rebecca speculates that the painter is "really an artist—an oil painter who just paints houses as a sideline," he replies, "No, I'm a house painter. I paint signs as a sideline." Thus, he is firmly dissociated from the mind.

What is the appeal of this pattern? Why are contemporary film audiences willing to accept the notion that working-class, body-oriented men are "naturally" better lovers than upper-class intellectuals? One reason may be that this pattern relates to a general suspicion that intelligent and educated people are socially (and physically) awkward nerds (or "brainiacs"). The mind/body narrative patterns support widely circulated cultural clichés that are expressed in "everyday" means such as the popular bumper sticker: "My kid beat up your honor student." The films with these patterns support and reinforce belief systems to which young people are exposed on a regular basis.

But this explanation does not account for the particular popularity of Jack Dawson/Leonardo DiCaprio with teen audiences. Though not so extreme as Tristan in *Legends of the Fall*, Jack, like other body men, lives outside community and family and prefers the company of "the other" (in Jack's case, Europeans and workingclass people). Jack is an orphaned only child who likes his rootless existence traveling around the world performing manual labor—a fact he enthusiastically conveys to *Titanic*'s upper-class passengers. The rebellious, antisocial quality of Jack and other body men may have a certain cachet with teenagers, who often distance themselves from their parents' lives in order to locate their own identity.

Jack is associated with the body when we see him dancing at the steerage party; nevertheless, as a body man, he deviates from this traditional masculine representation in a number of significant ways. Earth men are frequently seen disrobed, revealing their toned bodies. Jack/Leonardo is unclothed in one lovemaking scene, but only one arm and shoulder are partially visible. *The Piano* and *Sirens* show full frontal male nudity as Baines and Devlin stand immobile in front of the camera. Though DiCaprio's body is not revealed, it is obvious that he is thinner, less developed, and much more lithe than the earth men of other recent films.

Perhaps the most striking difference between Jack and other body men in the pattern is that they are primarily manual laborers while Jack is primarily an artist (he *is* the artist that Rebecca hoped the house painter would be in *Moonlight and Valentino*). Jack's status as an artist somewhat disrupts the traditional mind/body split in such love stories, but even in that capacity, he is far from being intellectually engaged. Jack was in Paris at the height of the modernist movement, a time when artistic style and political action coalesced. While Rose purchased work by Picasso, Monet, and Degas, Jack seems not at all influenced by the Parisian artistic community. He draws bodies in a highly conventional, realist style—a style against which the philosophical artists rebelled. Perhaps, most telling in linking him to other earth men, Jack's sketches are all female nudes and body parts.

Since Jack does not have the muscled earth man body that attracts women in other mind/body narratives, what is it about him that impresses Rose? From her intensified gaze, Rose clearly sees "something" in Jack from their first interaction. This kind of immediate response to the common man who seems uncommon can be traced back to *Lady Chatterley's Lover*: "[Connie] wondered very much about him [Mellors] . . . he seemed so unlike a working-man . . . although he had something in common with the local people. But also *something* very uncommon."[10] In *Titanic* what is this *something*? Rose is taken with the frenetic bodily energy she experiences at the steerage party she and Jack attend. She dances wildly in a smoke-filled room with crowds of working class men and women. Jack's playfulness delights her: he teaches her how to spit and describes how they will someday drink cheap beer, ride a roller coaster till they throw up, and ride horses like real cowboys. The feeling of an amusement park ride is simulated by the camera when Rose and Jack spin in circles while holding hands on the impromptu dance floor. The two of them run gleefully like children through *Titanic*'s corridors. Rose is impressed by Jack's energy, his playfulness, and his sense of fun—all qualities embodied by an uncommon common man. For adolescent audiences, Jack's playful quality may speak to the element in their psyches that clings to childhood. Perhaps, more significantly, Jack's association with "partying" supports a widely accepted cultural model of fun and pleasure that hinges on sport, speed, and somatic sensation.

The only physical vitality Cal displays is violent: slaps and physical threats. In fact, Cal is dramatically associated with isolation and stillness through the film's cutting patterns. He is shown alone surveying his stateroom's private promenade immediately after a scene in which Jack negotiates a bustling corridor to enter a third-class state room he shares with three other men. Rose and Jack's frivolity at the steerage party is intercut with rigid and restrained images of Cal and the other upper-class men conversing in a drawing room. Such a subtle visual denigration of the mind's potential as a locus of erotic energy appears more fully in other films that set up the mind/body opposition.

In *Antonia's Line*, when Antonia's daughter wants to get pregnant without commitment, she chooses a black-leather-jacketed motorcyclist who repeatedly makes love to her in the course of a few hours and immediately impregnates her. In turn, Antonia's brilliant granddaughter picks up a man in a college pub who is shown frenetically expounding philosophical, intellectual hypotheses. The next shot after they leave the pub together is of the man standing naked on the sidewalk with a newspaper over his genitals after she has thrown him out of her apartment. Further underscoring the cultural cliché that intellectuals make poor lovers, the narrator says over these scenes: "She experimented with a few intellectuals but found them wanting . . . nor was she compensated physically." She ends up having a child with her childhood friend who is a good lover but not an intellectual.

In privileging Jack's masculinity so dramatically over Cal's, Cameron ultimately supports an anti-intellectual ideology—an ideology that resonates strongly in American culture. Jack's position is one that lauds emotion over intellect. In establishing the mind/body dichotomy in this manner, Cameron plugs firmly into the popular fantasy that drains the mind domain of energy and precludes the imagining of intellectual activity as stimulating, erotic, or even fun. Those qualities are attached instead to the party in steerage. When he urges Rose to dance, she says, "I don't know the steps," to which Jack replies, "Neither do I. Go with it. Don't think." At the dinner on the upper deck, Jack makes a banal statement denigrating critical thought: "You learn to take life as it comes at you. To make each day count." At one point Rose tells Jack that when the ship docks, she's getting off with him. Jack replies, "This is crazy," to which Rose responds in a manner echoing Jack: "I know. It doesn't make any sense. That's why I trust it."

Dismissed as the "snake pit" is the world of the mind represented by Cal, and also Thomas Andrews, J. Bruce Ismay, and other "real life" men on the *Titanic* such as Benjamin Guggenheim and John Jacob Astor. This "snake pit" dismissal is uttered by the socially questionable nouveau-riche matron, Molly Brown. Obviously, the first-class world of cigars, cognac, and conversation could be presented as one of pleasurable vitality rather than deadly boredom, and just as obviously, Rose could find erotic fulfillment with a man from that world. And, indeed, the film potentially contains such a man in the character of Andrews, the designer of the *Titanic*.

Cameron seems to present a contradiction in his project of privileging working-class Jack by creating Andrews as a kindred spirit to Rose. Andrews is the only upper-class diner (along with Molly Brown) who is amused by the impertinent comments Rose makes to the White Star managing director, J. Bruce Ismay, about *Titanic's* size. Though she publicly impugns the *Titanic*, Rose's private remarks to Andrews are positive: "The ship is a wonder, Mr. Andrews, truly." In many ways, Andrews is the upper-class, educated equivalent of Jack in that they are, in a sense, both artists. They are even linked visually: they both have significant interactions with Rose on the elegant stairway to the upper-deck dining saloon and while standing in front of clocks.

Perhaps the most compelling similarity between Andrews and Jack is that they both have astute perceptive abilities, as does Rose, who comments on Jack's artistic ability, "You have a gift, Jack. You do. You see people," to which he replies, "I see you." Andrews compliments Rose on her keen observation about the inadequate number of lifeboats, saying, "Rose, you miss nothing do you?"[11] Although Andrews may appear to be a father figure, his place within the narrative structure makes it clear that Cameron could just as easily have made him a younger, potential lover for Rose—one who attractively represents the world of the mind. Although Jack and Andrews are linked, the relationship between Rose and Andrews functions ultimately to emphasize the educated, upper-class man's impotency in comparison to working-class potency. Jack was able to motivate Rose and effect her survival in a way that Andrews could not. As the ship is sinking, Andrews's parting words to Rose are "I'm sorry that I didn't build you a stronger ship."

Thus, by blocking the potential of the upper-class male to offer any intellectual, romantic, (or technological) comfort to Rose, the film suggests that the only solution to Rose's oppression—to her very survival—lies in the anti-intellectual domain of frenetic bodily activity, and it is this aspect of the traditional mind/body split that holds such deep-seated appeal. Yet the film's central image of Jack and Rose on the prow sensuously feeling the rush of the wind complicates this formulation. In contrast to the wild dancing and heated sex below deck, their pose is assumed on the upper, first-class deck and actually implies a creative *synthesis* of mind and body. The pose is not purely physical nor highly active but involves the intellectual dimension of a metaphor in its birdlike sense of flight. Thus the "arms-outstretched" image mediates between the hyperphysicality of the lower deck and the antiphysicality of the upper deck. Indeed, this scene of Rose responding to a liberating body experience immediately follows one where she witnesses a mother teaching her small daughter etiquette by manipulating her posture to rigidly conform to an upper-class standard. Even though Rose's and Jack's bodies in the prow scene are not as physically active as in the lower-deck dancing scene, the prow scene reinforces the film's emphasis on liberating bodily experiences.

If this image of two bodies "in flight" is perhaps the single most popular image from *Titanic*, the question remains, what types of bodies are foregrounded here? Is this a pose, for example, that would resonate in the same way with Schwarzenegger or Willis in the place of DiCaprio? Or Demi Moore or Linda Hamilton instead of Winslet? Indeed, would the love story work its box office magic if the star pairing was Schwarzenegger and Hamilton or Willis and Moore? The casting, particularly in regards to star body types, tells us much about how the film's love story constructs its appeal and, in turn, secured *Titanic*'s immense popularity.

"It Doesn't Look Any Bigger than the *Mauretania*"

That DiCaprio is no Schwarzenegger or Willis was not lost on critics or parodists of the film. The popular press discussions surrounding *Titanic* return repeatedly to the issue of DiCaprio's youthful slender body, a body which shows no signs of muscle building or countless hours sweating at the gym. Throughout the 1980s and 1990s, many actors prepared for action-adventure roles by literally transforming their bodies. Indeed, Willis's body in *Die Hard* (1988) is virtually unrecognizable from the body he displayed in the popular television series *Moonlighting* or in his first two theatrical features, *Blind Date* (1987) and *Sunset* (1988). Similarly, when Keanu Reeves appeared in *Speed* (1994), he evidenced a new, pumped-up body not previously seen in such films as *My Own Private Idaho* (1991).

Cameron played a major role in installing the powerful male bodybuilder norm that came to characterize the heroic centerpiece of 1980s and 1990s action cinema. The founding fathers of the phallically powerful, hyperbuilt body were Schwarzenegger and Sylvester Stallone, and Cameron's work with Schwarzenegger in *The Terminator* (1984), *Terminator 2: Judgment Day* (1991), and *True Lies* (1994) is a central component of the Schwarzenegger oeuvre. (He also co-authored the screenplay for *Rambo: First Blood Part II*, 1985). Indeed, *The Terminator* was a crucial film in transforming Schwarzenegger into a superstar. But Cameron was equally if not more influential in shaping the 1980s and 1990s female action hero as well. In *Aliens* (1986), Cameron revived the heroine, Ripley, of the original *Alien* (1979), which was groundbreaking in its depiction of women in male action films. In both films, Sigourney Weaver plays Ripley, a member of a space mission. In *Alien*, she is represented as an active, intelligent equal of the male crew. Until the final sequence, her body is never erotically displayed. Cameron's revival of this character seems like a warm-up for the role played by Hamilton in *Terminator 2*. In that film, Cameron fully transfers the familiar male bodybuilder physique onto the female heroine, Sarah Connor, played by Hamilton, who, like Schwarzenegger, looks like someone who spends most of the time weight lifting.

Cameron's previous films, then, have been caught within the larger cultural mind/body polarity and dialectic. It is helpful to consider such masculinity and the issue of size that figures so prominently in Cameron's *True Lies* for three reasons. First, this film sheds light on what will become Cameron's obsession with these issues in *Titanic*. Second, it helps us understand why at this precise moment, *Titanic*'s dramatic shift away from the powerful bodybuilder physique was so successful with audiences, for it is strikingly obvious at first glance that neither DiCaprio nor Winslet in *Titanic* could be accused of bodybuilding. Their defiantly nonbuilt body look (his is scrawny, and hers is soft and fleshy) is an important clue to understanding Cameron's successful development of the love story in *Titanic*. Cameron seems to have accurately sensed that, after well over a decade of Hollywood's representation of a body culture and powerful, "built" bodies, the public would respond to a refreshing change. Third, given the pivotal nature of *Titanic* in Cameron's work, it is not surprising that this shift involves some contradictions. Cameron, as we shall see, does not simply abandon one form of masculinity for another.

In *True Lies*, Schwarzenegger plays a government secret agent who catches up with a used car salesman (Bill Paxton) pretending to be an agent. When Schwarzenegger scares the man into accounting for why he is an impostor, the man blurts out that he has a "little dick" and wets his pants. The image of this terrified pretender-to-true-masculinity with a little penis juxtaposed with Schwarzenegger's powerfully muscled body represents the twin poles of masculinity constructed within our culture: a powerfully impressive phallic masculinity (Schwarzenegger) and its pitiable, comic collapse (Paxton pretending to be the real thing). Audiences generally break into howls of laughter when the salesman blurts out that he has a little dick, thus sharing the underlying cultural assumption that a small penis is the most embarrassing sign of masculine failure.[12]

Despite the seeming simplicity of the opposition between true masculinity and pretend masculinity in this scene, *True Lies*, in fact, works to erode that very distinction. Schwarzenegger lives in fear (for good reason, it turns out) that his wife is having an affair, which implies that he is somehow inadequate and unable to fulfill her needs. Furthermore, for all his muscular power, he enlists not only a friend but millions of dollars' worth of government high-tech gadgetry to catch his wife in the act. Stated simply, he lives in fear and so is not unlike the used car salesman who wets his pants. Thus *True Lies*, like *Titanic*, is caught within an unresolved contradiction about masculinity: on the one hand, it wants to affirm a powerfully phallic masculinity; on the other hand, it implies that such masculinity is not what it is cracked up to be. Schwarzenegger, as much as Paxton, is a pretender, though in the end the polarity between them seems fully reinstated when Schwarzenegger once again makes Paxton wet his pants out of fear. It is unimaginable that Schwarzenegger (or his character) could have a small penis or wet his pants out of fear or that the size of his penis could explain his masculinity as it does the car salesman's.

If *True Lies* maps its concerns with size and masculinity literally on the male body, *Titanic* displaces that concern (with one major exception) symbolically onto the ship and even onto the discourse surrounding the production of the film itself. When young Rose is first introduced in the flashback, she says somewhat contemptuously of the *Titanic* upon first seeing it, "I don't see what all the fuss is about. It doesn't look any bigger than the *Mauretania*." Her fiancé quickly informs her, "It's over a hundred feet longer than the *Mauretania*." The importance of size, then, is established at the very outset in the "body" of the film, and there are two quite different and incompatible discourses of size that we hear. The first, based upon a woman's perception, belittles the supposed glory of the ship's spectacle. As a counter, the man responds with a precise measurement: "over a hundred feet." This first exchange, in other words, introduces a gap between female perception and male proof.[13]

As the *Titanic* leaves the harbor, Cameron visually reinforces its size with a shot of two small sailboats dwarfed by the massive ship that fills the frame. The juxtaposition of the sailboats with the *Titanic* recalls the juxtaposition of Paxton with Schwarzenegger's body in *True Lies*; in both instances, the latter appears to embody the awesome spectacle of power that eclipses the former. But, as with *True*

Lies, the truth is somewhat different. Both the verbal exchange about size and the visual emphasis upon it make the *Titanic* itself like a body. This equation becomes explicit in the frame story when a man says in his re-creation of the ship's sinking: "Finally she's got her whole ass sticking up in the air." The ship is referred to throughout as a "she," though a "she" constructed by males who invested a great deal of pride and ego in their creation. Indeed, the frame story even constructs the investigation of the sunken ruins as a voyeuristic masculine enterprise. "Are you seeing this, boss?" an assistant asks as a robot's arms caress the body of the ship. The navigator of that robot wears "snoop vision" as he probes the wreck, an act comparable to Schwarzenegger's secretly watching his wife while hidden behind a two-way mirror in *True Lies*.

The moment in *Titanic* that specifically links the ship's body to the symbolic significance of male preoccupation with size occurs during the first dining scene. "She's the largest moving object ever made by the hand of man in all of history," one of the ship's makers remarks. Molly Brown asks, "Hey, who first thought of the name, *Titanic*? Was it you, Bruce?" "I wanted to convey sheer size and size means stability, luxury, and above all strength," comes the reply. "Do you know Dr. Freud, Mr. Ismay?" Rose replies. "His ideas about the male preoccupation with size might be of interest to you." Rose refers to the popularized notion of Freudian psychology wherein men who, for example, drive big cars are overcompensating for a small penis. As with *True Lies*, then, the subject of masculinity and sexual size emerges overtly in the dialogue, although the explicit reference mocks the male preoccupation rather than glorifies it. Rather than be "impressed" with the *Titanic*, Rose cynically attributes its element of masculine phallic spectacle to insecurity and lack.

A representation of powerful masculinity associated with a "phallic" spectacle does, however, emerge somewhat contradictorily within the film's lovemaking scene. Furthermore, media hype and publicity surrounding the film celebrate the very type of masculine spectacle that amuses Rose. A consideration of those contradictory aspects of the film and its publicity offers a clue to the film's success, which, in part, hinges on simultaneously presenting a refreshingly different kind of masculinity while recuperating conventional masculinity.

"I'm the King of the World"

In recent years, masculinity scholars such as Gaylyn Studlar, Dennis Bingham, Steven Cohan, and Peter Lehman have cautioned against simple generalizations about the representation of the male body (e.g., it is always active and never objectified for visual pleasure).[14] They have also cautioned against viewing masculinity as simple, fixed, and powerful. Far from such a simplistic, hegemonic view, they have described and analyzed differing forms of masculinity, many of which coexist at the same time and some of which come to the fore at a given historical moment.

The question of *Titanic*'s break with a traditional mode of Hollywood masculinity is raised by Ellen Goodman, who notes: "In the old days, heroines were generally swept off their feet and gone with the wind by heroes like Clark Gable. A true woman was supposed to swoon with gratitude whenever John Wayne uttered another monosyllable. But today they are looking for something and someone else. Say, for example, Leonardo DiCaprio."[15] Goodman refers to classical Hollywood in a somewhat oversimplified manner that overlooks such romantic leads as Cary Grant, discussed above, Paul Henreid in *Now, Voyager* (1942), and James Stewart in *The Philadelphia Story* (1940). But it is precisely Cameron's sense of this "something else" that helps explain the success of the film's love story and reveals its reworking of elements associated with both the lower-class/upper-class love story and the male action hero of the 1980s and 1990s. Not only is DiCaprio no John Wayne, he is not Keitel nor Schwarzenegger.

Lovemaking scenes are particularly important within the tradition of stories wherein the working-class body man awakens and satisfies the upper-class woman's sexuality. As we have demonstrated, a central element of the appeal of such stories is the fantasy that these men intuitively possess a sexual power and physical skill that educated, upper-class men lack. As the sexually satisfied woman in *Moonlight and Valentino* says, "Men like that just know these things." *Titanic* includes a lovemaking scene that places Jack within that tradition. While a key ingredient in the appeal of the love story, this scene suggests a number of contradictions about masculinity and the male body. Understanding how Cameron negotiates these contradictions provides more clues as to how the love story is constructed to contribute to *Titanic*'s phenomenal success with audiences.

Writing about the love story, Goodman attempts to link *Titanic*'s most sexually explicit scenes to the film's particular appeal to adolescent female audiences. She writes: "After all in this movie, Kate makes a choice between the fiancee [sic] who wants to dominate her and the steroid-free artist who enables her liberation. Even the love scenes have a gentle and misty mutuality. When Kate takes off her clothes, Leo draws her instead of assaulting her. She does the initiating in her own time. Is Leo adored by the young female audience because he is a harbor for their sexual awakening?"[16] Goodman is perceptive, but she does not go far enough in analyzing either the nude-sketching scene or the lovemaking-in-the-car scene. It is, of course, true that Jack draws instead of "assaults" Rose when she first takes off her clothes, but it is crucial to note that this scene is followed immediately by the sex scene. Rather than any significant delay in the consummation of their sexual relationship, the sketching scene serves as foreplay to Rose and Jack's having "the real thing." The discreet scene of sketching as foreplay takes place in a well-appointed, first-class stateroom, and the "real thing" on the lower deck in the backseat of a car, the latter commonly regarded as a place where teen sex and loss of virginity occur. Rose initiates the sex, but Goodman does not pay careful attention to what type of sex follows. "Gentle" and "misty" describe only one aspect of the scene, and not the most interesting aspect. When Rose initiates the sex, Jack is pretending to be her chauffeur, a working-class role reminiscent of Mellors and other "hired" body men. Although the actual lovemaking is nearly elided, two images stand out in the scene: first and foremost is the image of the Renault's window, steamed from the hot sex going on in the cold car, and Rose's hand coming up into the frame and slowly sinking and clawing the glass on the way down. Second, when Cameron dissolves to the interior of the car after the lovemaking has ended, sweat covers the lovers' bodies, and we hear panting on the soundtrack: they have had physically demanding sex.

The *Titanic* Parody Pictures Web site amusingly but astutely gets to the heart of one of the contradictions at the center of this lovemaking scene. As "Kate" cradles "Leo" in her arms, the cartoon dialogue bubbles read, "Don't feel bad . . . that was the best thirty seconds in my entire life," and "Sorry about that. But they say it happens to all men sometimes. . . ."[17] Cameron's film represents the lovemaking scene as highly physical, with steamy windows, sweat-drenched bodies, and panting sounds as proof that this event lasted longer than thirty seconds. The cliché of highly physical and satisfying sex at their first encounter conforms entirely to the fantasy of the working-class body man awakening and fulfilling the upper-class woman's sexual desires. True to the formula, the body man performs perfectly and manages to do so even as he is fleeing for his life. (Cal's henchman is pursuing Jack and Rose as they retreat to the backseat of a car to make love for the first time!) Just as certainly as Cal can't arouse his fiancée's passions, let alone fulfill them, Jack does both in the most incredible of narrative circumstances.

This scene allows Jack to be read as a highly conventional figure of masculinity who possesses phallic sexual power at the moment that it is most needed. Stated simply, the kind of hyperphysical sex that Jack performs would be in keeping with that of the lower-class, earthy body man or of the phallically powerful male action hero. But within the logic of the film's development of Jack, what we might expect is what Goodman would call a "gentle" lovemaking scene or even one with an emphasis on an alternative form of erotic activity and satisfaction. Despite Goodman's emphasis on the narrative delay and on Rose's initiation of sex, the lovemaking scene itself emphasizes conventional sexual intercourse, with the man delivering a highly active, satisfying performance. The steamy windows, sweaty bodies, and panting breathers are closer to porn (indeed, there even is a porn film entitled *Steamy Windows*) than they are to any alternative form of eroticism.

This sexual contradiction in the film's representation of masculinity risks becoming explicit in the frame story when Rose introduces the flashback of posing nude (without Jack touching her) by remarking, "It was the most erotic moment of my life; up until then, at least." As the scene in the car indicates and her lines suggest, however, highly physical sex is clearly much more erotically fulfilling for her than being sketched. So while Jack is presented as an attractive "soft" alternative to dominant masculinity throughout much of the film, in the sex scene, he is suddenly empowered with the very qualities he seems to lack. As Rose herself remarks in the frame story, "Jack Dawson saved me in every way that a person can be saved." Similarly, in *True Lies*, Schwarzenegger is presented as vulnerable and in need of great powers to control his wife, but his phallic potency is restored with a spectacular rescue of his family, followed by another humiliation of the car salesman.

What holds true for the sexual contradictions within *Titanic* also holds true for Cameron's way of talking about his film. It is, to say the least, ironic that a film that mocks male preoccupation with size was promoted and received within a marketing context that glorified these qualities. Indeed, the promotion of the film sounds like a brag at the *Titanic* first-class dinner table. Both the studio and Cameron have, in effect, been saying, "I can assure you it's the largest moving picture ever made by the hand of man in all of history." Another applicable line to be adapted *from* the film to describe the film might be, "I wanted to convey sheer size, and size means stability, luxury, and above all strength." Even while it was still in production, *Titanic* was touted as the most expensive movie ever made, and much of the film's publicity attempted to "convey sheer size." This discourse of male pride in the size and difficulty of the production, as well as the preoccupation with the film's huge budget and record-breaking box office receipts, culminated at the Academy Awards ceremony, where Cameron accepted the Oscar for best picture, one of the film's eleven wins that night. Cameron waved the statue above his head and declared, in a repetition of Jack's line from the film, "I'm the King of the World."

At that moment, the gendered sexual contradictions that underscored the film were dangerously close to being laid bare. These contradictions frequently indicate how a film successfully negotiates treacherous ideological terrain—the contradictions mask ideological difficulties, denying social and cultural reality. This is true, for example, within many of the romances featuring working-class body men, which is why these stories deserve the moniker of "fantasies." There is no logical reason to believe that less-educated, poorer men make better lovers than educated, economically successful men. Indeed, sensitivity and erotic creativity may very well be qualities one would more likely find among educated, successful men. The very appeal of fantasy, however, depends on denying the complexities of social realities.

The same holds true of the contradiction between the film itself and its promotion. Cameron has his cake and eats it too. In a successful negotiation of contradictions not perceived negatively by the public or the media, he simultaneously critiques a dominant notion of powerful, phallic masculinity by offering an alternative to it, while also recuperating and celebrating that very form of masculinity. As a consequence, he could not have chosen a better word than "king" to describe himself. Along with Cameron's royal self-proclamation, everything about the sheer size of the budget, the production, and the box office records make Cameron and his film just like the *Titanic* and the masterminds who built the ill-fated ship. Indeed, one can easily imagine Rose telling Cameron: "[Freud's] ideas about the male preoccupation with size might be of interest to you." Despite his efforts to align himself with Jack, Cameron actually seems more like the smug J. Bruce Ismay, bragging about his masculine accomplishments, and he invites comparison to any of the powerful men of business and finance whom Rose sarcastically calls "masters of the universe."

Titanic, then, is a complex and frequently contradictory mixture of traditions of representing the mind, the body, and sexuality. The film does indeed offer "something and someone else." The "something" else is a reformulation of the lower-class "earth/body man" from that of a physically overbearing manual laborer to that of an artist, embodied in the "someone else" of DiCaprio. Cameron's innovative reworking of the lower-class body man as a sensitive, attractive, boyish artist enabled this narrative fantasy to strike a particularly responsive chord in teenage girls. The decision to present the hero as a boyishly unthreatening figure necessarily also meant abandoning the conventional body type of the male action hero and the discourse of size and power that went with that body. Indeed, as we have shown, Cameron actually seems to mock and critique that discourse within the film.

Titanic's success, however, must also be understood as being inseparably linked to a concern with (and desire for) masculine size and power that was displaced from the film's love story onto promotional discourses about the film. Cameron, the studios, and the press all combined to impress the public with the very kind of masculine spectacle of size that Rose refuses to be impressed with. Unlike Rose, the public was not skeptical about the value of a spectacle—in this instance, one focused on the size and meaning of the budget, the breaking of box office records, and even the "heroics" of a filmmaker who forfeited much of his salary to complete the film. The conventional male action hero may be nowhere in sight in *Titanic*, yet many stories circulated in the press about Cameron's throwing himself into the *Titanic* project with near maniacal commitment and against all odds, even saving the production itself. Taking this into account, it would be more accurate to say, perhaps, that although Arnold Schwarzenegger is nowhere around and the burly earth man has been banished from the film's story, in some sense James Cameron guaranteed the success of *Titanic* by playing those familiar masculine roles himself.

Notes

Special thanks to Gaylyn Studlar and Kevin S. Sandler for their many editorial suggestions and to Kathy Vlesmas, Peter Lehman's graduate research assistant, for her excellent work and intense enthusiasm for *Titanic*.

1. Yvonne Tasker, *Spectacular Bodies: Gender, Genre, and the Action Cinema* (New York: Routledge, 1993), 2.
2. Ibid., 57.
3. Sue Zahn, "*Titanic*—The expurgated version." (www.angelfire.com/ak/TitanicLeo/titexpur.txt).
4. Phineas Bog, "*Titanic* Parody Pictures." (www.angelfire.com/ak/TitanicLeo/titpic2.html & titpic1.html).
5. "Raging against the Machine," *Entertainment Weekly*, 24 July 1998, 52.
6. Steven Cohan, *Masked Men: Masculinity and the Movies in the Fifties* (Bloomington: Indiana University Press, 1997), 30.
7. D. H. Lawrence, *Lady Chatterley's Lover* (1928; reprint, New York: Bantam, 1968), 17 and 35.
8. Ibid., 68. Emphasis added.
9. Among the many other related films are: *Moonstruck* (1987), *At Play in the Field of the Lords* (1991), *A River Runs Through It* (1992), *I.Q.* (1994), *Stargate* (1994), *Angels and Insects* (1995), *Executive Decision* (1996), *The Nutty Professor* (1996), *Phenom-*

enon (1996), and *Tin Cup* (1996). This discussion of the mind/body split is drawn from Susan Hunt's essay "Matter over Mind: Assaulting the Masculine Intellect," in *Masculinity in Bodies, Movies, and Culture*, ed. Peter Lehman (New York: Routledge, forthcoming).

10. Lawrence, *Lady Chatterley's Lover*, 70. Emphasis added.

11. Cal, however, fails in the arena of vision. Jack (wearing a borrowed tuxedo) attends an upper-deck dinner as payback for saving Rose and instantly adapts his manner to conform to upper-class posturing after observing the affect of others. Cal, on the other hand, does not even recognize Jack as he looks directly at him while walking by. He also cannot see why Rose is melancholy, and does not see that Rose is lying about why she slipped from the rear of the ship (but his working-class manservant does).

12. Peter Lehman discusses this aspect of *True Lies* in "In an Imperfect World Men with Small Penises Are Unforgiven: The Representation of the Penis/Phallus in American Films of the Nineties," *Men and Masculinities* 1, no. 2 (1998): 123–137.

13. This discourse of measurement echoes the medical discourse of penis size measurement that Peter Lehman documents and analyzes in *Running Scared: Masculinity and the Representation of the Male Body* (Philadelphia: Temple University Press, 1993). The scientific discourse of measurement replaces individual perception and evaluation with a seeming standard of objective truth about size. Measurements, not a woman's perceptions, will determine what is big and what is small.

14. See Gaylyn Studlar, *In the Realm of Pleasure: Von Sternberg, Dietrich, and the Masochist Aesthetic* (Urbana, University of Illinois Press, 1988) and *This Mad Masquerade: Stardom and Masculinity in the Jazz Age* (New York: Columbia University Press, 1996); Dennis Bingham, *Acting Male: Masculinities in the Films of James Stewart, Jack Nicholson, and Clint Eastwood* (New Brunswick: Rutgers University Press, 1994); Steven Cohan, *Masked Men*; and Peter Lehman, *Running Scared.*

15. Ellen Goodman, "Movies Showcase New Male Role Models, but It's Mostly Women Watching." *Arizona Daily Star*, 10 May 1998, F2.

16. Ibid.

17. Bog, "*Titanic* Parody Pictures," titpic3.html.

Women First

TITANIC, ACTION-ADVENTURE FILMS, AND HOLLYWOOD'S FEMALE AUDIENCE

PETER KRÄMER

$\mathcal{A}$n important aspect of Hollywood's hold on the public imagination is its ability to generate, from within the films themselves, the very terms in which its major releases are going to be discussed. For James Cameron's long-delayed disaster movie *Titanic*, which was announced to be the biggest and most expensive film ever, critics' tendency to use the title and story of a film to describe and judge its qualities and meanings as well as its performance at the box office did not bode well. One could already see the headlines in the industry's "bible," *Variety*: "Cameron's Latest Sinks without a Trace" (in case of a complete box office disaster, without even the obligatory big opening weekend generated by the hype surrounding the film), or "*Titanic* Makes a Big Splash—and Then Goes Under" (in case of a big opening weekend, followed by a drastic drop in attendance caused by negative word of mouth).[1] The explanations for poor box office performance would be given by the film itself. In the same way that the *Titanic*'s builders were obsessed with size and technology when constructing the largest man-made vehicle, contemporary Hollywood could be accused, especially but not only when making *Titanic*, of valuing quantity (more money, more spectacle) over quality, technology (special effects and the mechanics of large-scale filmmaking) over humanity. And in the same way that the ship's very size led to its doom (because it was too slow in turning away from the iceberg) and the disregard of its owners for the dangers of seafaring and for human lives (failing to provide enough lifeboats) led to numerous deaths, the film's bloated spectacle and the filmmaker's disregard for characters and their experiences could be seen as the reasons for its death at the box office after having hit the iceberg of public rejection. The film thus provides its critics with a ready-made discourse ideally suited for a devastating critique both of the film itself and of contemporary Hollywood in general.

Instead, however, on 23 February 1998, eight weeks after the film's release, the cover of *Newsweek* activated a different set of meanings from the film to tell a success story that is without precedent: "The *Titanic* Love Affair: Steaming toward $1 Billion at the Box Office." By using the film's title as an adjective, this line suggested (and the cover story inside the magazine confirmed this)[2] that what is so spectacular and majestic about *Titanic* is not the ship itself or the sophisticated technology used to bring it and its demise to the screen, but the love that the film portrays in its story and generates in its audience. The *Newsweek* cover shows Kate Winslet holding on to Leonardo DiCaprio, with the *Titanic* barely visible in the background, which implies that it is precisely because of the film's foregrounding of the romantic couple that audiences have started their love affair with it (rather than being simply awed or exhilarated by the disaster); this love affair, moreover, is going to last a long time, making sure that, unlike the ship, the movie is never going to sink but will steam on to become the highest-grossing film of all time. Indeed, five weeks later, *Variety* reported that on 14 March *Titanic* had overtaken *Star Wars* (1977) as the all-time top-grossing movie at the U.S. box office.[3] While the *Star Wars* total of $461 million included revenues generated by several rereleases between 1978 and 1997, in the fourteenth week of its first release *Titanic*, boosted by a record win of eleven Oscars at the Academy Awards ceremony on 23 March 1998, sailed past the $500–million mark, with no end to its steady box office performance in sight.[4] Even more impressive was the film's performance in foreign markets, where already by the beginning of March, it had topped the $556–million foreign earnings of the previous international top grosser, *Jurassic Park* (1993), to become, just as *Newsweek* had predicted, the first movie to have a combined gross in domestic and foreign markets of $1 billion.[5]

However, industry observers also noted that these figures fail to take rising ticket prices into account, and, if domestic gross were adjusted for inflation, the undisputed champion at the American box office remains *Gone With the Wind* (1939), which happens to be another epic love story centering on one woman's emotional experience in catastrophic historical circumstances.[6] *Newsweek* linked the two films by declaring that "*Titanic* is the *Gone With the Wind* of its generation," and it further noted that, not unlike the story of Scarlett O'Hara, the narrative of *Titanic* focused on "a woman's liberation," appealing primarily (but not exclusively) to a female audience.[7] In doing so, the magazine confirmed that, like *Gone With the Wind* in 1939, not only is *Titanic* the movie event of the year and the decade, it may in fact be an event of such magnitude that it could change the course of American film history,[8] by returning female characters and romantic love to the center of the industry's big releases and also by returning female audiences to the central place in Hollywood's thinking that they had once occupied in its golden age but which they lost to the young male audience in the late 1960s.[9]

In this essay, I will explore some of the textual and contextual determinations of this potential historical turning point. First, I discuss production trends in contemporary Hollywood leading up to *Titanic*, with particular reference to the previous work of James Cameron and to the cycle of female-centered action-adventure films that the success of his earlier films initiated. Second, I analyze the ways in which the marketing of *Titanic* and the film itself have tried to engage audiences, with an emphasis on the role played in this process by love, the act of storytelling, and female subjectivity. Finally, I take a closer look at the film's performance at the box office and at its audience, concentrating on female cinemagoers and linking the success of *Titanic* to the female appeal of Hollywood's blockbusters of the past. I argue that *Titanic* is the culmination of the recent cycle of female-centered action-adventure films as well as a long overdue return to the big-budget romantic epics of Hollywood's past, and that the film's marketing and its story self-consciously set out to woo female cinemagoers without alienating Hollywood's main target audience of young males in the process. Furthermore, like many of the most successful products of popular culture, the film (supported by the surrounding publicity) explains itself to its audiences, offering them guidance on how to understand and enjoy *Titanic*.

Action-Adventure Films

The poster for *Titanic* declares it to be "A James Cameron Film," adding, so as to be sure that everybody knows what this means, that Cameron is "the director of *Aliens* [1986], *T2* [1991] and *True Lies* [1994]." Cameron is one of the few filmmakers working in contemporary Hollywood whose name may be recognized by more than a few critics and film buffs.[10] For those who do recognize the name (and even for those who do not, the films listed on the poster will evoke a similar response), it stands for some of the most spectacular and most expensive action-adventure films of all time, usually made with a more or less pronounced science fiction slant, including a heavy emphasis on futuristic technology and special effects. Not only does Cameron's work include some enormous box office hits, but, unusually for action films, it has also received considerable critical acclaim.[11] For example, Cameron's sequel to Ridley Scott's *Alien* (1979) was the seventh-highest-grossing film of 1986 (with U.S. revenues of $81.8 million); it was written and directed by Cameron and produced by his then wife, Gale Anne Hurd; and it earned the female lead, Sigourney Weaver, an Academy Award nomination for best actress and won in the visual effects category.[12] Following the disappointing performance of *The Abyss* in 1989 (earning $54 million, against a budget of $45 million, which was one of the highest in that year),[13] Cameron, in 1991, broke records with the sequel to his 1984 film *The Terminator*. *Terminator 2: Judgment Day* was the biggest hit of the year, and its gross of $204 million made it the twelfth most successful film of all time, while its $95–million budget was the highest ever.[14] In 1994, Cameron easily topped this record with the $120–million budget for *True Lies*, which was the third-highest-grossing film of the year in the United States with $146 million.[15]

Thus Cameron is perhaps *the* outstanding representative of the most important production trend in contemporary Hollywood—the action-adventure film.[16] Since the success of *Jaws* (1975) and *Rocky* (1976), action-adventure films have consistently received the biggest budgets and the widest releases of all Hollywood films; they have generated the highest star salaries (for performers such as Sylvester Stallone and Arnold Schwarzenegger) and accounted for about half of the Top Ten films listed in the annual box office charts during the last twenty years.[17]

Like most classificatory terms in contemporary Hollywood, "action movie" or "action-adventure" is a label that can be applied to a wide variety of films, ranging from films featuring a superhero or a mismatched pair of cops, to movies about a man and a woman falling in love during an exciting adventure, and even comedies featuring an apparent loser who eventually asserts himself; these films can be set in a mythical or historical past, in the present, or in the future.

Within the action category, there are also a number of basic requirements that audiences would expect to be fulfilled. The story typically revolves around a series of physically threatening tests and trials for the protagonists, in which they quite frequently get hurt, even seriously injured, often losing control over their situation for extended periods, before they finally manage to triumph over their adversaries by beating or killing them. Most important, these tests and trials and the final triumph are staged as largely self-contained spectacles. The actors engage in an outstandingly athletic, acrobatic, or simply violent performance, presenting a series of amazing stunts, in which they (apparently) inflict damage on each other and/or the set, or in which they narrowly escape such damage. At the same time, in these sequences the filmmakers self-consciously display the tricks of their trade with rapid editing, fancy camerawork, collapsing sets, and all manner of special effects (from back projection to computer-generated images). The intended effect of this spectacle on audiences is amazement and excitement about the magical possibilities of the cinema and about the potential of the human body. At the same time, the audience is meant to be drawn both into the fear and suffering of the protagonists in the early stages of the narrative and later into their triumphant violence and its attendant satisfaction (which may verge on outright sadistic pleasure at seeing the bad guys suffer and die). The films' iconography centers on weapons and the human body, indeed the human body as a weapon and the weapon as an extension of the human body. The key image usually is that of a seminaked muscular human body, tense and about to explode into action.[18]

Audience research has confirmed the commonsense view that action-adventure films primarily appeal to young males, looking for physical action on the screen and excitement in the theater, and they are largely disliked by women, who tend to prefer films dealing with characters and emotions such as romantic comedies, dramas (e.g., melodrama and costume drama), and musicals.[19] Contemporary Hollywood has generally marginalized these traditional female-oriented genres by limiting their production and marketing budgets (often only a fraction of the budget for major action-adventure films) and by giving these films a comparatively narrow release outside the main cinemagoing seasons (whereas action-adventure films typically hit vast numbers of screens during, or in the period leading up to, the Christmas and summer holidays).

At the same time, however, Hollywood has made a concerted effort to attract female viewers to action-adventure films. Beginning with *Star Wars*,[20] the industry has produced a steady stream of films that combine some of the qualities and concerns of the action-adventure movie with those of the traditional children's or family film, so as to reach a more broadly based audience, including both regular moviegoers (teenagers and young adults, especially males) and infrequent moviegoers (parents and children, especially females). Since the late 1970s, almost every year one or two family-adventure movies have actually achieved this feat, and these films have consistently topped the end-of-year box office charts as well as the list of all-time top grossers, easily outperforming youth-oriented action-adventure films. Family-adventure movies indirectly appeal to women through their children, who will often be accompanied to the cinema by their mothers or other female caretakers, and the films also directly aim to address women through a highly emotional concern with familial relationships on the screen (which mirror those in the movie theater).[21]

In sharp contrast to the family-adventure films, which are still almost exclusively focused on young males, the second main strategy for attracting women to action-adventure films is to promote a female character to the status of main protagonist. Arguably, it was the success of Cameron's *Aliens* in 1986, featuring Sigourney Weaver as a reluctant warrior who eventually turns into a supreme fighting machine, which first signaled to the industry that female-centered big-budget action-adventure films were a viable option, and this signal was confirmed by another Cameron film in 1991.

While *Terminator 2* features the biggest of all action heroes (Schwarzenegger) and replicates some of the main thematic concerns of the most successful family-adventure movies,[22] it is also a woman's story.[23] Not only does Sarah Connor fully participate in the action, skillfully handling weapons and other machinery, displaying her muscular and sweaty body, suffering extreme pain, and triumphing in the end; she also mediates all of this action for the viewer with her voice-over commenting on the action from a superior vantage point throughout the film, communicating her thoughts and feelings and also drawing conclusions about the significance of events. Furthermore, it is her subjective vision of judgment day (the imminent nuclear devastation of the planet) that is presented to the audience during the credit sequence and later on in the film, quite literally making the viewer enter Sarah Connor's mind to share her most traumatic experiences.

This also happens at the beginning of *Aliens*, when without being aware of it, the viewer inhabits Ripley's mind; it is only after she has replayed the trauma of the first film, with an alien bursting out of her own stomach, that the events on the screen are revealed as her nightmare. With its references to childbirth, moreover, this nightmare has clearly gendered overtones. The rest of the film is effectively the story of a woman who suffers from a trauma that she can only overcome by restaging it in real life; she must confront the alien creature at the root of the terror that haunts her, who turns out to be a mother protecting her offspring. But the film is also the story of a woman who wakes up from a long sleep to find that everyone she has ever known is dead, and who in the course of her subsequent adventure forges an emotional bond with a child, for whom she is willing to die (much like the alien mother she confronts).

Aliens and *Terminator 2*, then, do not simply move a woman to the center of their narrative; they also deal with what are traditionally perceived as female issues (childbirth and mother love), and they explicitly set up the world and action of the film as an extension of the female protagonist's subjectivity.[24]

This is true of several subsequent action-adventure films, which in the wake of the success of Cameron's films have strengthened the role of the female lead, even if they do not go as far as displacing the male protagonist. For example, the rise of Sandra Bullock to superstardom is, arguably, closely tied to the way in which her character in *Demolition Man* (1993) or *Speed* (1994), while apparently merely serving as a sidekick to the action hero, is in fact also positioned as the one whose wish the film fulfills, and thus as the very source of the action presented on the screen. At the beginning of the main story of *Demolition Man*, Bullock's character, in a tight close-up, wishes for some action, just before violence erupts into her otherwise totally pacified world, and toward the beginning of *Speed* she declares that she loves and misses her car, asks the bus driver to drive all over the vehicles blocking the way, and later, when she finally sits in the driver's seat again, admits that she has had her driver's license revoked for speeding, which is exactly what she is forced to do from then on.[25]

Furthermore, the runaway hit of 1996, *Twister*, earning $241 million in the United States (with a $91–million budget), which only *Independence Day* managed to top in that year, not only is a kind of remake of the classic comedy of remarriage *His Girl Friday* (1940), but also sets up and thus motivates the whole action story by first depicting the traumatic experience of a young girl who sees her father being carried away by a tornado, a trauma which she has to replay endlessly in her later life so as to master it.[26]

The significance of this childhood scene becomes more obvious when compared with a similar scene at the beginning of *Contact* (1997), in which the girl, who is first shown trying to contact other radio amateurs with her CB radio, asks her father whether the radio will ever allow her to reach her dead mother; the film answers this question (somewhat ambiguously) by allowing her later on in life to meet a vision of her by-then-dead father as a result of her total professional dedication to radio astronomy and her belief in alien life forms. Furthermore, the film's opening shot (the camera pulls back from earth into the farthest reaches of the universe and then emerges, without a discernible cut, out of the girl's eye) specifically locates the whole universe in her mind.[27]

Thus both *Twister* and *Contact* declare their stories to arise from, and to be an exploration of, the minds of young girls. With numerous explicit and implicit references to their literary predecessors, these films connect up with the great and immensely popular tradition of turn-of-the-century girl adventurer stories such as *The Wonderful Wizard of Oz* (L. Frank Baum, 1900) and *Peter Pan* (J. M. Barrie, 1904 play, 1911 novel), which is, after all, the story of Wendy's adventure told from her perspective, as well as the slightly earlier *Alice's Adventures in Wonderland* (Lewis Carroll, 1865) and *Through the Looking-Glass* (1872). What all of these classic stories have in common is that, by fantastic means, they realize the girl's (implicit or explicit) wish to escape the limitations of her everyday domestic life and to participate in adventures usually reserved for boys, while also, among many other things, exploring her relationship with her parents and other authority figures as well as her own future role as a parent. By drawing on these girl adventurer stories as well as on closely related female-centered fairy tales and classic romantic comedies, then, in recent years several successful action-adventure and science fiction movies have provided an antidote to the boys' stories that otherwise dominate the output of contemporary Hollywood, capturing the imagination and the admissions fees of female audiences.[28] In doing so, these films, especially the previous work of Hollywood's foremost action director, James Cameron, have prepared both male and female moviegoers for the biggest adventure of them all.

Titanic

During its long gestation period, which was characterized by reports about an escalating budget (worse even than the $160 million spent on that other notoriously overbudget ocean-based spectacle *Waterworld* in 1995) and by several delays of the planned release date from summer 1997 toward the end of the year, *Titanic* appeared to be an extension of Cameron's previous concern with superexpensive action spectacles. Only this time, it seemed, Cameron had gone too far, giving in to megalomania, going crazy, losing control of the project, which some sources insisted would eventually cost a totally unprecedented $250 million.[29] Cameron's project came to be seen as the movie equivalent of the all-too-big, overexpensive, and disaster-bound vehicle that was its subject. Indeed, when the film finally came out in the United States on 19 December 1997, the accompanying publicity highlighted the fact that Cameron had gone to the bottom of the ocean to film the real wreck (footage of which is included in the opening section of the film); that he had meticulously re-created the original ship and had then effectively sunk it all over again; that he was a crazy, dictatorial, and supermacho guy obsessed with realism, pushing his technical crew and his actors to the limit, making them suffer almost as if they were going under with the real *Titanic*.[30]

The film delivers on the publicity's promise of spectacular physical action after about 100 of its 194 minutes, when the *Titanic* hits the iceberg and slowly begins to sink, with people on the ship only gradually becoming aware of this fact.[31] The remainder of the film operates almost as a self-contained one-and-a-half-hour action movie, in which two protagonists (the young lovers Rose Bukater and Jack Dawson) have to deal with a human antagonist (Rose's fiancé, Cal Hockley, supported by his sinister henchman, Spicer Lovejoy), while also having to fight with the elemental forces unleashed by the collision with the iceberg (rising water levels, increasing social chaos, a collapsing man-made structure, the icy cold). The antagonist's actions start out as being merely deceptive (framing Jack for the theft of a diamond) but soon become physically threatening. Spicer leaves Jack handcuffed to a pipe on a lower deck of the sinking ship facing certain death, and after he has been freed, Cal tries to shoot him and Rose. Yet unlike other action-adventure films, in *Titanic* the actions of the antagonist do not serve as a primary focus of the film, and they do not culminate in a climactic showdown with the protagonists; instead they form a subplot to the much grander confrontation between the lovers and the elements.[32]

This confrontation, however, has many of the characteristics of the action film. For long periods, first Jack alone and then Jack and Rose together are placed in extremely dangerous situations, having little or no control over what is going on, while the spectacular sets of the film are systematically destroyed all around them. However, through intelligent, skillful, and courageous physical action (Rose getting an ax and cutting Jack loose; Jack diving for a key and opening a gate while the water rises to their necks; Jack always knowing exactly where to run and Rose being able to keep up with him), the couple not only escape imminent death but also regain a measure of control. When the ship finally turns upright, they lie safely and relatively calmly on the railing at its stern, while others below them are falling to their deaths. In fact, in this most self-conscious display of the power of special effects to (re)create what appear to be impossible images (the aft section of an ocean liner standing upright and then smoothly sinking into the water), the protagonists are placed not so much as participants in the action, but as spectators of it, much like the film's viewers in the movie theater. From fear and suffering and the excitement of physical action, the film here shifts registers to sheer amazement about, and perverse delight in, the magic of cinema.

The next scene, after the ship has finally disappeared into the ocean, again focuses on the plight of the protoganists and in particular on their physical vulnerability as they float in the water (Jack fully submerged, Rose on a piece of debris), slowly freezing to death without, apparently, any options for decisive action being left. However, after Jack's death, Rose, in a final move combining intelligence, determination, and courage, dives back into the water to get to a nearby corpse whose whistle she uses to attract the attention of the only lifeboat that has returned to the scene of the disaster looking for survivors—and thus she saves herself.

This conclusion is in line with the emphasis on strong female characters in the previous work of Cameron and in the cycle of female-centered action-adventure films initiated by it.[33] In fact, throughout the last ninety minutes of *Titanic*, Rose fully participates in the physical action, shedding clothes to be able to use (and also to display) her body to greater effect, skillfully employing an ax, even hitting people, and running, wading, and swimming in a most unladylike fashion. Moreover, much like Ripley in *Aliens*, Rose is not satisfied with saving herself. She twice gets the chance to leave the sinking ship, and on both occasions, she goes back into the bowels of the *Titanic* to save her loved one (or to die with him), just as Ripley goes back, immediately after having narrowly escaped the clutches of the alien brood, to save Newt, the little girl she has adopted.[34]

What drives Rose, Ripley, and the other heroic women in Cameron's films is not professionalism, nor the desire for public recognition, nor a general selflessness (although all of these might play a part at one point or another), but primarily, it would seem, the intense emotional bond they have established with one particular person. *The Terminator* culminates in Sarah Connor's loss and commemoration of her beloved protector from the future who is the father of the child she is pregnant with, while in *Terminator 2* his death in the past is a concrete reminder of the imminent destruction of most of mankind in the near future, the knowledge of which Sarah Connor has to live with, while she tries to reconcile her responsibility for the future with her love for her son. In *Aliens*, as we have seen, Ripley forges an intense emotional bond with a child, whom she is not prepared to lose under any circumstances. On a different note, both *The Abyss* and *True Lies* are stories about marital discord, in which the couple's involvement in spectacular action finally brings them back together again. In all of these films, then, romantic or mother love are at the center of the narrative, providing an emotional counterpoint to the thrill of spectacle. What makes *Titanic* different is that the first one hundred minutes of the film are given over to the love story without any violent action in sight, and that the publicity and advertising for the film highlight romance as a major attraction.

The trailer that played in movie theaters for months in advance of the release clearly indicated that there would be more to *Titanic* than the spectacle of disaster and heroic action.[35] The audience is presented with one of the survivors of the disaster in a contemporary setting, and together with her, they are asked: "Are you ready to go back to *Titanic*?" The motivation for this question is the quest for a priceless diamond, which is depicted in a nude drawing of that same woman made during her journey on the *Titanic*. However, the past story that the trailer begins to unfold is not so much about material goods (although the splendor and luxury of the ocean liner are displayed in rich, sensuous detail), but about a woman torn between two men, a rich fiancé and a poor artist, and about her desire for freedom and a different way of life. When the trailer finally gets to the spectacular images of the sinking of the *Titanic*, it has already established that this spectacle is intimately connected with, and needs to be understood in relation to, the fate of the young lovers.

In interviews at the time of the film's release, Cameron explained the connection between the love story and the spectacular disaster further. For example, he told the readers of *Cinefex*, presumably made up of people whose interest lies first and foremost with the technical aspects of filmmaking: "I thought it was not artistically interesting to just follow a bunch of historical characters, never really getting involved in the event at an emotional level. I figured the best way to get in touch with the emotion of the event would be to take one set of characters and tell the story as a love story—because only by telling it as a love story can you appreciate the loss of separation and the loss caused by death."[36] Elsewhere, he stated, "I like using hard-core technological means to explore an emotion."[37] Thus Cameron emphasized that for him technological spectacle is not an end in itself, to be appreciated in its own right, but a means to the end of character-based storytelling and of engaging the audience's emotions; and the staging of a disaster in which 1,500 people died does not merely provide a good context for heroic individual action, but it is an occasion for the vicarious experience of tremendous loss and for the mourning of that loss.

Such expositions of Cameron's view of filmmaking were a central feature of the marketing of the film as a different kind of action movie. Cameron's most comprehensive statement is his foreword for the book about the making of *Titanic*. On the one hand, he writes about his extensive research on the topic, which culminated in several dives to see and film the actual wreck; on the other hand, he emphasizes his personal response to this encounter: "I was overwhelmed by emotion. I had known the event so intimately from my research, and now I had been on the deck of the ship itself, and it just flooded over me. I wept for the innocents who died there. That night I realized that my project, my film, was doomed to failure if it could not convey the emotion of that night rather than the fact of it."[38]

Since "the deaths of 1,500 innocents is too abstract for our hearts to grasp," Cameron argues, it was necessary "to create an emotional lightning rod for the audience by giving them two main characters they care about and then taking those characters into hell." By making them lovers and having one of them die, he could make more tangible the sense of loss experienced by everyone who lost a loved one on the *Titanic*. In turn, the "terrible majesty" of the sinking of the *Titanic* would move the couple's love to a higher level: "The greatest of loves can only be measured against the greatest of adversities, and the greatest of sacrifices thus defined," writes Cameron.[39] While the love story translates the disaster into human terms, the disaster gives the couple's love a mythical dimension.

This mutually reinforcing relationship between the *Titanic* legend and the love story is nicely captured by the poster for the film. It shows a young couple, the woman looking down thoughtfully with half-closed eyes, the man standing behind her, nestling his head on her shoulder and neck, eyes closed and lost in his embrace of her body. The image indicates both the intimacy and the distance between them, the ecstacy of romantic union and the melancholy of loss. Their disembodied heads float above the bow of a giant ship, which seems both to support their union, holding them together, and to push through between them, cutting them apart. "Nothing on Earth Could Come Between Them" reads the tag line, a phrase with multiple meanings and complex ironies. At first sight, it would seem the statement is simply wrong, because the whole point of the film is that an iceberg and the ship's sinking will come between them. However, a closer examination of the statement reveals that, strictly speaking, these young people meet and fall in love not on earth but on water. And while their class differences are likely to have kept them apart if they had stayed on solid earth or, indeed, if they had returned to it (after their meeting on the ship), these differences are magically overcome on the floating microcosm of the *Titanic* and are erased forever precisely by the young man's death. While disaster and death appear to come between them, they actually are that which makes their love eternal, keeps them together forever, at least in the woman's heart.

Following a twenty-minute modern-day prologue, the film dedicates the next eighty minutes (until the ship hits the iceberg) to the telling of Rose and Jack's love story, with a few more or less casual references to the imminent disaster inserted to keep up an overall sense of anticipation. This part of the film operates, much like the later action part, almost as a self-contained movie, a melodramatic costume drama about young lovers kept apart by a hierarchically organized social order, with elements of romantic comedy (in the often playful interaction between

Rose and Jack, and in their lighthearted transgression of social norms) and even of the musical (in one memorable dance sequence). The focus of this melodrama is clearly on Rose, whose present-day voice-over occasionally comments on the action, explaining the state of mind of the young woman on the ship who is so desperate about the social role she is trapped in (a respectable lady, a future wife and mother, a man's prized possession) that she contemplates jumping overboard to escape it.

It is her dramatic gesture of climbing over the ship's railing, ready to jump, that allows, and indeed forces, Jack to enter into a conversation with her, bridging the social gap that had previously been pointed out to him as being unbridgeable. Jack convinces Rose to come back on the deck by linking his own fate to hers; if she jumps, he will have to jump after her, and they will probably both die. This pact establishes a powerful bond between them, which transcends the difference in their social status that the members of her class then immediately want to reestablish.

After a brief misunderstanding (his rescue is interpreted as a rape attempt), Jack is rewarded for his good deed with an invitation to the upper-class, upper-deck world Rose inhabits, and while he makes a good impression with his new clothes and his spirited declaration about the joys of life, it is the invitation he extends to Rose to join him in turn for a party on the lower deck that provides a glimpse of the life Rose seems to be longing for—unrestrained, full of energy, fun, and excitement. These excursions into each other's world continue, with barriers being erected by her fiancé to be overcome first by Jack's decisive action (he adopts a disguise to get close to her) and then by Rose's. She joins him in the evening at the bow of the ship, puts her fate into his hands (he holds her so that she can have the experience of flying) and takes it back into her own hands, by first posing nude for him in her fiancé's cabin, and then escaping with him to the very bottom of the ship, past the engines, to the holding deck where she drags him onto the backseat of a car (which may be her fiancé's) to make love. This is certainly a fitting conclusion to their socially transgressive affair, but it leaves open how they will present themselves to the world around them and how they will be able to live together in a sharply divided society with powerful enemies and without any obvious source of income.

This issue does not, however, have to be addressed, because soon afterward, the ship hits the iceberg and the film's focus on the love triangle is gradually displaced, as already discussed, by a basic concern for survival and commitment in the face of overwhelming elemental forces. In the process, Rose is willing and able to keep her end of the bargain Jack struck with her during their first meeting: if one jumps, the other jumps as well. First, it is Rose's turn to go to Jack and save him, and then, when she is in the safety of a lifeboat and he lies to her about his own chances of getting away, she returns to die with him, strictly adhering to the terms of their original agreement.

In the end, however, when Jack has saved her a second time by getting her off the ship and onto a piece of debris, he manages to dissolve their pact and convince her that she has to live while he is going to die. When she saves herself in the end, it is a somewhat ambiguous conclusion to their love story, because it is her love for Jack that made her want to die with him (if they can't both live)—and it is her love of life (a life of adventure that she had mapped out in her previous conversations with Jack) that eventually allows her to pull away from Jack's corpse and certain death. Thus romantic love is shown to be a force potentially as deadly as the icy water, but it is also portrayed as a life-giving force, which gives back to Rose the will to live (which she had abandoned when the two lovers first met) and, more precisely, the will and confidence to live her own life, unrestrained by the social conventions of the day. When Rose decides to save herself, the potentially deadly selflessness of a woman's romantic love is transformed into the selfishness of her love of life. Perhaps there is a price to pay for this salvation. When the present-day Rose talks about the guilt of the survivors looking for redemption without ever finding it, she may also be referring to herself (although she never admits to it). After all, Jack has had to die and their romantic pact had to be broken for Rose to be able to live.

The ambiguities of Rose and Jack's love story on the *Titanic* can be seen as the driving force behind the present-day framing story, which takes up the first twenty minutes and the last seven minutes of the film and is also present in the main body of the film (its love and action parts) through the voice-over and several inserts. Picking up on, and going beyond, the various narrative devices (such as dream sequences, voice-overs, and childhood prologues) used by the female-centered action-adventure films discussed above to present the action as a part or extension of the female protagonist's subjectivity, *Titanic* squarely presents most of its action as a story told by a woman who invites her audience on the screen and in the theater to share her memory and thus to enter her mind.[40]

While the setting of the story on the *Titanic* gives it historical solidity, its bare outlines sound more like the stuff of adolescent female fantasy: a hopeless young woman is saved by an attractive young man, who miraculously appears out of the darkness just when she is about to kill herself;[41] after many adventures, he heroically dies so that she can live and be free. Behind this romantic tale, however, lies a more sinister wish-fulfillment fantasy. Right from the start, the *Titanic* is presented as the very emblem of the society that so restricts Rose's life that she does not want to go on living. Her voice-over declares that while for others it was "the ship of dreams," for her it was "a slave ship taking me back to America in chains"—unless, of course, something would happen to this ship along the way. Furthermore, in one scene she explicitly identifies the ship with oppressive phallic power, telling its owner, J. Bruce Ismay, that Freud's "ideas about the male preoccupation with size may be of interest to you." Whether she admits to it or not, Rose does want this power, this society, and thus this ship to be destroyed so that she can be free—and in a roundabout way this is exactly what happens.[42] Behind the romantic dream of an adolescent girl lurks the nightmare of suppressed female rage. Rose's story is also a cautionary tale about the destructive power women may unleash on an oppressive patriarchal order.[43]

However, this is not at all what Rose's on-screen audience want to hear. Indeed, Rose is only asked to tell her story because treasure hunter Brock Lovett is looking for clues as to the whereabouts of the priceless diamond (called the Heart of the Ocean) she was wearing in the drawing he found while scavenging the wreck of the *Titanic*, expecting to find the diamond itself. While the motivations of the 101–year-old Rose for telling her story are not initially made clear, the film contrasts her very self-consciously with Brock and his male crew, against whom she has to assert her right to tell the story the way she wants it to be heard. When she is shown a computer simulation of the sinking of the *Titanic* by Brock's assistant, she appreciates his technological and scientific effort yet states that for a participant "it was a somewhat different experience." And when Brock interrupts her after the first half-sentence of her tale ("It's been eighty-four years . . . "), she asks sharply whether he wants to hear the story or not. She then concludes the sentence, "but I can still smell the fresh paint." She claims the authority of the traditional storyteller who talks of things in the past with precision and insight and commands absolute attention.

Interestingly, Brock, who here is reduced to being part of her audience, not only had previously been in control of the action (the investigation of the wreck and the subsequent television appearance which Rose responds to) but also had started out as a kind of storyteller himself, a filmic storyteller at that. When his submersible approaches the wreck at the very beginning of the film, he films the approach and himself with a video camera, commenting pretentiously on what is happening, his pretentiousness being highlighted by his assistant with a hearty "you're so full of shit, boss." Brock can be seen as a stand-in for director James Cameron, another man obsessed with the *Titanic* who did go down to see and film the wreck, and a filmic storyteller who takes command of complex technology to achieve his goal. What happens in the prologue is the undercutting of Cameron's position, first by the comments of Brock's assistant and then, more importantly, by his reluctant handing over of the role of storyteller to Rose. It is as if Cameron declared that this story and this film belonged to the woman on the screen, and also, by implication, to the women in the audience.

Throughout the prologue, Brock is presented as a problematic figure, willing to spout platitudes for the video or television camera, so as to disguise his true intentions, which are purely materialistic. He is a treasure hunter, and the diamond is the treasure he is hunting. However, while he listens to Rose's story for clues about the diamond, during the few cutbacks to the present in the main body of the film, he seems to lose interest in his initial objective, getting involved in the human drama instead. In the end he fails to ask Rose the crucial question (which would have been: what happened to the diamond?), because he has realized that the wreck of the *Titanic* he has been scavenging and the story Rose tells him are not to be seen in terms of the wealth that can be gained from them, but have to be engaged with on a different level altogether. After having heard out Rose's story, he turns to her granddaughter and states that he has been dealing with the *Titanic* for three years, but, he says: "I didn't get it. I never let it in."

What exactly he is referring to is not explained, but there are a number of candidates the audience might fill into the blank spots provided by the word "it," especially if they have read Cameron's widely circulated statements about the film (as discussed above) and know that he gave up his profit participation so as to be able to finish his labor of love the way he wanted. Obsessed with money and technology, Brock Lovett/James Cameron had initially refused to acknowledge that the disaster of the *Titanic* was about people, about their death or suffering or sense of loss; he never let in the emotions attached to catastrophic and extreme experiences (and, one might add, after hearing Rose's story, he never let in the love that can blossom even, and especially, in the midst of disaster). Brock's statement is mapping out the very process Cameron underwent from first getting fascinated with the disaster of the *Titanic* to ultimately realizing that it had to be told as an intimate story about love and loss. It is also a self-reflexive declaration to the audience that *Titanic*, the movie, should be seen not as technological spectacle put on for material gain, but as an exploration of human experience and the power of love, and a sharing of this experience and of this power between filmmaker and audience. Thus the film itself replicates the publicity discourse surrounding it, identifying *Titanic* as a different kind of blockbuster.

This is all very well, but what is in it for Rose? Despite a long life, which could be expected to have muted the memory of her brief affair, Rose, at the age of 101, still is at one with her dead lover. This is because, as she says, he "saved me in every conceivable way," and she owes her rich and varied life, which she so carefully documents with the photographs she takes everywhere (recording the things she discussed with Jack, like riding a horse and flying), to him. Jack himself, however, is dead; moreover, his role in her life has never been acknowledged. It is not only that Rose might feel guilty for having survived when Jack had to die, but it is also that to the outside world she pretended that he never existed in the first place, and hence she has reason to feel doubly guilty. Therefore, nearing the time of her own death, Rose returns to the ocean and for the first time tells Jack's story, thus bringing him back to life for herself, while also giving him life for the first time in the eyes of the outside world. Perhaps it is her way of looking for redemption.

After telling Jack's story, she returns the diamond (named the Heart of the Ocean), the search for which gave rise to the film, to the heart of the ocean, where she last saw her lover. What had started out as an object of material value in the opening sequence and acquired a series of shifting meanings in the course of the film (her fiancé gives it to her to remind her of the right he has over her body; she reclaims her body wearing only the diamond when she asks Jack to do a drawing of her; she denies her status as a man's possession by returning the diamond to her fiancé's safe) finally has been transformed into a token of this woman's eternal love. By letting the diamond drop into the ocean, she confirms that she has given her own heart to the very ocean in which her lover rests. With the diamond sinking to the ground as her lover once did and as she had originally promised to do, she can now die herself, as if belatedly fulfilling her part of the death pact, yet she does so at peace in a warm bed, as Jack had promised her at the time of his own death.

Before she dies, in her mind Rose projects a union that never could take place in reality: the two lovers uniting, across the class divide, on the grand staircase of the *Titanic*, in front of an audience that is socially integrated, including passengers from all decks, and that applauds their union. While this celebration of love and social integration could never have taken place in reality, in her dream, which is yet another version of the film she has made possible for the audience, they can.

The movie audience is addressed in a complex way here. Throughout the film they have been presented with mirror images of themselves on the screen, which guided their responses: the research ship's crew so deeply moved by the tale, the treasure hunter who learns an important lesson about material and emotional values, and the applauding crowd at the end of Rose's dream. But they have also been closely identified with Rose herself, the teller of the tale. When Rose dies, having made her peace with the past, the image fades to white, which is the white of the paper on which Jack drew her picture and also the white of the screen onto which the film is projected. By sharing in Rose's transition from dream to death, the movie audience dissolves its connection with her and begins to awaken from the dream of the film to the reality of the movie theater and of the blank screen in front of it. Like Rose, who dreams of love and social harmony to the very end, the audience is encouraged to take the memory of love away from the film, not the recollection of a spectacular disaster. And like Rose, the audience will perhaps be redeemed by this memory of love for their guilty desire to see and enjoy the disaster and the death of 1,500 people.

The Female Audience

The world premiere of *Titanic* took place on the opening night of the Tokyo International Film Festival on 1 November 1997, which signaled right from the outset that, even more so than regular Hollywood productions, *Titanic* was aimed at the world market and that it was a prestige production as well as a superexpensive blockbuster.[44] *Variety* reviewed the film two days later, with the American release still, quite unusually, more than one and a half months away.[45] The review, which rose to the occasion by being itself of epic length, was generally optimistic about the commercial prospects of the film, predicting that it would reach "the largest possible public" and was "certain to do exceptionally well at the box office." Yet it was also concerned about some inconsistencies (the marginalization of British characters in favor of American ones, "vulgarities and colloquialisms that seem inappropriate to the period and place"), which "seem aimed directly to the sensibilities of young American viewers," thus potentially alienating older and non-American audiences. This again signaled that *Titanic* was not like other Hollywood blockbusters, whose primary address of young Americans does not normally raise concern in the trade press; *Titanic*'s audience, however, was to be truely international and mature.

The film's long delayed American release on 19 December 1997 confirmed its exceptional status. The first weekend, which is considered all important for Hollywood's major releases as a reliable predictor of overall box office performance, generated a good, but by no means record-breaking, gross of $28.6 million.[46] In fact, this figure would appear to be all too small when compared with the $50 million for the opening weekend of *Independence Day* (1996), the $56 million for *Mission: Impossible* (1996), or the $53 million for *Batman Forever* (1995).[47] Furthermore, while *Titanic* received a wide release playing in 2,674 theaters, this was less than the circa 3,000 theaters for *Independence Day*, *Mission: Impossible*, and *Batman Forever*, and much less than the record of 3,500 set by *The Lost World* only a few months earlier.[48] However, unlike the typical steep decline in revenues for these and other blockbusters, the box office receipts for *Titanic* did not drop off significantly after the weekend, and the film ended its first week with a gross of $53 million. Then, quite astonishingly, the box office figure for the second weekend improved on that for the first one by 24 percent, whereas the figures for *Independence Day*, *Mission: Impossible*, and *Batman Forever* had shown a drop of 30 to 60 percent.[49] While the third and fourth weekend saw a slight drop in *Titanic*'s revenues, the results were still higher than on the opening weekend, and the film also continued to perform strongly during the week (not just on weekends).[50] Amazingly, the four-day fifth weekend then saw a significant increase to over $30 million, which is unprecedented in Hollywood history.[51]

By this time, it was perfectly clear that *Titanic* had managed to combine the performance characteristics of two production trends in contemporary Hollywood: the big splash of the action-adventure movie aimed primarily at young males rushing to see the film on the opening weekend, and the ability to make waves of the "sleeper" hit, usually a romantic comedy, serious drama, or weepie aimed primarily at women, who tend to wait for recommendations from their girlfriends and whose attendance several weeks into the release give the film what the industry calls "legs."[52] By starting out at a high level and staying there for many weeks, *Titanic*'s box office receipts were bound to break all existing records in the United States. Furthermore, the film's foreign release early on confirmed predictions about its international reach, and its status as a prestige film also was soon cemented with a record eight Golden Globe nominations only a few weeks after its American release (the film went on to win four awards, including best drama and best director) and with a record fourteen Academy Award nominations in February.[53]

The scale of *Titanic*'s success, and the exceptional way in which it was achieved, provoked a strong response both in the trade press and the general press, culminating in the *Newsweek* cover story. Early attempts to explain the *Titanic* phenomenon pointed out the importance of older audiences, especially those "who rarely leave home to see a film," and of repeat attendance: "unusually, older viewers are going back to see *Titanic* for a second time, in the same way teen viewers return to see action blockbusters."[54] In part, this attendance pattern could be explained with reference to *Titanic*'s status as a prestige film, because older cinemagoers are known to value critical reputation much more than younger ones. *Newsweek*, however, argued more specifically that women were the audience that was turning *Titanic* into the biggest movie hit ever. Calling the film "a shipboard weepie," "a chick-flick period piece," "a tragic romance," a "passionate love story framed by the epic sweep of a true historical event," the article pointed out that the film was unique in the industry's chart of all-time domestic top grossers for being first and foremost about romantic love.

Before *Titanic* broke into the Top Ten, the group included: *Star Wars* at number one with $461 million, followed by *E.T* (1982), *Jurassic Park*, *Forrest Gump* (1994), *The Lion King* (1994), *Return of the Jedi* (1983), *Independence Day*, *The Empire Strikes Back* (1980), *Home Alone* (1990), and *Jaws* (1975) at number ten with $260 million.[55] While most of these films (especially *Forrest Gump*) contain an element of romantic love, not one of them was marketed or perceived primarily as a love story.[56] The reason for this may be male prejudice against, and dislike of, love stories, which is another commonsense view held by Hollywood executives and confirmed by audience research. With Hollywood's overall output geared toward a primary target audience of young males, it is not surprising that love has been marginalized in the narratives and the marketing of most of the industry's major releases and biggest hits. It is against this backdrop that the success of *Titanic* is so remarkable, yet this backdrop also helps to explain the film's success.

For thirty years now, Hollywood's major releases have addressed themselves primarily to a young male audience, and with comparatively few and mostly only modestly successful exceptions, women have not been given films in their preferred genres, but have largely been expected to accompany their male partners or their children to the movies, going along with the film choices of others rather than making their own. Since the early 1970s, industry observers have persistently criticized Hollywood for its neglect of the female audience; at the same time, changing demographics have created an important mature female audience for the movies (especially important because among older couples, unlike young couples, women are perceived to be the ones who select the film when going to the movies). Yet even when this large and growing female audience, in the exceptional year of 1990, created two of the biggest hits of all time, *Pretty Woman* and *Ghost*, Hollywood refused to reconsider its basic conception of the female audience as either a niche market or an adjunct to the young male audience. Consequently, the industry's output of romantic comedies, dramas, and musicals, and especially of high-profile releases in these genres, has failed to meet the considerable demand of women for such films.[57] This failure meant that a ready-made audience of women for a major new women's film came into existence, waiting for the one movie that could meet their demands and send a signal to the industry as a whole. Marketed as an epic love story and concerned with the complex narrative exploration of female subjectivity, of romantic and other feelings, *Titanic* was that film.

Newsweek's research on the film's audiences confirms that *Titanic* has attracted a predominantly female audience, with 60 percent of all tickets sold to women, many of whom (especially younger ones) have seen the film more than once and keep coming back for more.[58] The film would indeed seem, and is certainly perceived, to belong first and foremost to women: Rose on the screen and the female majority in the theater. And since *Titanic* is not one of the modestly budgeted romantic comedies or dramas that contemporary Hollywood usually produces for its female audiences, but the industry's major release of the year written and directed by one of its most distinguished filmmakers, the success of the film also has wider implications. The film not only returns women to the cinema but, in a way, also returns the cinema to women, declaring them to be the most important audience, and expecting males to go along with their female partners, rather than the other way round.

This is indeed a "return," not a historical innovation. Until the mid-1960s, Hollywood had viewed women, especially mature women in charge of regular movie outings with their husbands and children, as the key audience for the cinema, and it had serviced this female audience with a range of films, including the industry's most important releases.[59] For example, the biggest hits of the 1930s, which also were among the most expensive and most highly acclaimed films, were *Gone With the Wind* and the animated fairy tale *Snow White and the Seven Dwarfs* (1937); in the 1940s, the top hits were the male-centered topical melodrama *The Best Years of Our Lives* (1946) and the female-centered Western melodrama *Duel in the Sun* (1946); in the 1950s, the sentimental religious epics *The Ten Commandments* (1956) and *Ben-Hur* (1959); and the top films of the first half of the 1960s were the musical *The Sound of Music* (1965) and the epic melodrama *Doctor Zhivago* (1965).[60] Indeed, in 1965, the list of all-time top-grossing movies (not adjusted for inflation) looked like this: *The Sound of Music* at number one, followed by *Doctor Zhivago*, *Ben-Hur*, *The Ten Commandments*, *Gone With the Wind*, *Mary Poppins* (1964), *Thunderball* (1965), *Cleopatra* (1963), *Goldfinger* (1964), and *Around the World in 80 Days* (1956) at number ten.[61]

While the two James Bond films heralded the future emphasis on action-adventure movies addressed primarily to young males, the top positions were held by great love stories, dealing with romantic and/or religious love (the love of God), often centered on a strong female protagonist and set in times of great political and social upheaval. It is this tradition that Cameron explicitly tried to link *Titanic* with, by listing it in interviews as one of his most important inspirations and by evoking it in the film itself: "I'd been looking for an opportunity to do an epic romance in the traditional vein of *Gone With the Wind* and *Doctor Zhivago*, where you're telling an intimate story on a very big canvas."[62] Thus *Titanic* is not just an evocation of the true story of the *Titanic* and of its times, but also an evocation of Hollywood's past, of a neglected tradition of filmmaking that clearly subordinated spectacle to emotion and put women (and, one might add, children) first—much like the crew of the sinking ship.

The question remains, however, whether the film's success will indeed change the course of American film history, leading to a full-scale reorientation of Hollywood away from its focus on the young male audience and toward women. Early indications are that, as with the *Titanic*, Hollywood's inertia may well be too big for the industry to be able to change course. Already executives say that the film's success will only lead to ever more expensive action-adventure movies, not to more female-oriented films.[63] Even Cameron himself has stated that he sees *Titanic* as a one-off, "a singular picture," after which everyone is likely to return to business as usual.[64] To paraphrase Brock Lovett, it is possible that they simply won't get it, that they will never let it in.

Notes

Work on this essay was made possible by a fellowship from the Amsterdam School for Cultural Analysis, Theory and Interpretation (ASCA). A version of this essay was presented at the ASCA conference "Come to Your Senses!" Amsterdam, May 1998.

1. For a systematic and historically wide-ranging introduction to the blockbuster phenomenon and the patterns of release and box office performance in contemporary Hollywood, see Thomas Schatz, "The New Hollywood," in *Film Theory Goes to the Movies*, ed. Jim Collins, Hilary Radner, and Ava Preacher Collins (New York: Routledge, 1993), 8–36.

2. David Ansen, "Our *Titanic* Love Affair," *Newsweek*, 23 February 1998, 44–50.

3. Leonard Klady, "*Titanic* Wins Domestic B.O. Crown," *Variety*, 23 March 1998, 8. For the American trade press, the domestic market includes Canada. All subsequent references in this essay to the American or domestic market therefore also refer to Canada.

4. Timothy M. Gray, "Ship's Oscars Come In," *Variety*, 30 March 1998, 24; Leonard Klady, "Oscar Adds to *Titanic* Treasure," *Variety*, 30 March 1998, 9. *Titanic*'s Oscar tally ties with the eleven awards won by *Ben-Hur*. At the time of the last revisions for this essay, *Titanic*'s domestic gross was over $600 million. *Variety*, 21 September 1998, 10.

5. Leonard Klady, "Cameron's Billion-$ Baby," *Variety*, 9 March 1998, 26. What is perhaps even more astonishing is that by the end of the film's theatrical run, the film's foreign gross of over $1.2 billion topped the total of $913 million that *Jurassic Park* had grossed in foreign *and* domestic markets. As reported in *Variety* on 21 September 1998, *Titanic*'s worldwide box office cumulative was $1,807,259,583.

6. Leonard Klady, "Tara Torpedoes *Titanic* as the Real B.O. Champ," *Variety*, 2 March 1998, 1, 105. The adjusted domestic gross of *Gone With the Wind* is listed as $1.3 billion (in 1998 dollars). Even if the earnings of various rereleases of the film were deducted, the film's gross would still dwarf that of *Titanic*.

7. Ansen, "Our *Titanic* Love Affair," 47; Karen Schoemer, "A Woman's Liberation," *Newsweek*, 23 February 1998, 50.

8. For a discussion of the crucial role of the cinematic "event" throughout film history, see Peter Krämer, "The Lure of the Big Picture: Film, Television, and Hollywood," in *Big Picture, Small Screen: The Relations between Film and Television*, ed. John Hill and Martin McLoone (Luton, England: John Libbey Media, 1996), 9–46.

9. For a historical survey and critical discussion of the marginal status of the female audience in contemporary American cinema, which takes into account research on audience preferences and habits, production trends, and debates within the industry, see Peter Krämer, "A Powerful Cinema-going Force? Hollywood and Female Audiences since the 1960s," in *Hollywood Audiences and Cultural Identity* (working title), ed. Richard Maltby and Melvyn Stokes (London: British Film Institute, 1999).

10. Cameron's status is confirmed, and problematized, by the fact that the poster for the Kathryn Bigelow–directed *Strange Days* (1995) implied that it was in fact a James Cameron movie so as to generate more interest in the film. This strategy did not work, however, and the film was a disastrous flop (earning $8 million in the United States against a budget of $39 million). Information on box office revenues and budgets is taken from the German magazine *steadycam*, which derives its figures from the American trade press; see "In Zahlen," *steadycam* 31 (spring 1996): 12.

11. For selected critical responses to, and basic credits for, the films discussed below, see Christopher Tookey, *The Critics' Film Guide* (London: Boxtree, 1994). There is also considerable academic literature on Cameron's films.

12. Box office information is taken from "The 1980s: A Reference Guide to Motion Pictures, Television, VCR, and Cable," *The Velvet Light Trap* 27 (spring 1991): 81; information on the Academy Awards is from John Harkness, *The Academy Awards Handbook* (New York: Pinnacle, 1994), 266–267. A brief sketch of Cameron's career is provided in Robyn Karney, ed., *Who's Who in Hollywood* (London: Bloomsbury, 1993), 70.

13. "In Zahlen," *steadycam* 15 (spring 1990): 10. *The Abyss* was again written and directed by Cameron and produced by Gale Anne Hurd, whom he did, however, split up with during the production of the film.

14. Budgets and box office revenues for 1991 are from "In Zahlen," *steadycam* 21 (spring 1992): 15–16. Information about all-time domestic top grossers (not adjusted for inflation) is from Leonard Klady, "Tara Torpedoes *Titanic* as the Real B.O. Champ," 105; *Terminator 2* is number twenty-three on this list, but eleven of the films above it were released after 1991. Cameron cowrote and directed the film.

15. "In Zahlen," *steadycam* 29 (spring 1995): 8–9. Cameron again directed and adapted the screenplay from the 1992 French film *La Totale!*

16. By using the term "production trend" rather than "genre" for the classification of films, I follow Tino Balio's example. Production trends can be identified both by textual features (such as story, iconography, and forms of spectacle) and extratextual features (such as target audience, release pattern, budget, cultural status, and key personnel). See Tino Balio, *Grand Design: Hollywood as a Modern Business Enterprise, 1930–1939* (New York: Scribners, 1993), 179–312.

17. For a more detailed analysis of the budgets, release patterns, and box office success of action-adventure films, which compares this production trend with various kinds of films addressed to women, see Krämer, "A Powerful Cinema-going Force?"

18. For extensive discussions of the action film, see, for example, Yvonne Tasker, *Spectacular Bodies: Gender, Genre, and the Action Cinema* (London: Routledge, 1993) and Susan Jeffords, *Hard Bodies: Hollywood Masculinity in the Reagan Era* (New Brunswick: Rutgers University Press, 1994).

19. See, for example, various surveys from the 1970s and early 1980s discussed in Krämer, "A Powerful Cinema-going Force?"

20. On the marketing of *Star Wars* to a diversified audience (including older people and women) rather than to a limited audience of young males, see Olen J. Earnest, "*Star Wars*: A Case Study of Motion Picture Marketing," *Current Research in Film: Audiences, Economics, and Law*, vol. 1, ed. Bruce A. Austin (Norwood, N.J.: Ablex Publishing, 1985), 1–18.

21. For an extensive discussion of this production trend, see Peter Krämer, "Would You Take Your Child to See This Film? The Cultural and Social Work of the Family-Adventure Movie," in *Contemporary Hollywood Cinema*, ed. Steve Neale and Murray Smith (London: Routledge, 1998), 294–311.

22. The film is a kind of wish-fulfillment fantasy of a boy from an incomplete and dysfunctional family, who almost gets to save the universe and almost finds a new father, yet has to say good-bye to him in the end, which leaves him with the single mother with whom he is now reconciled. The parallels to, for example, *E.T.* and *Star Wars* are striking.

23. In fact, *Terminator 2* can be seen as a reworking of one of *the* key female stories in Western culture: what is Sarah Connor, who has given birth to the future savior of humankind (after having become pregnant under rather mysterious circumstances), if not a modern version of the Holy Mary; except that in this version of the story, the mother

interferes with destiny, saves humankind herself (with a little help from her friends), and thus takes the role of savior away from her son.

24. Interestingly, both *Aliens* and *Terminator 2* are sequels to films that can be seen as sci-fi variants of the slasher movie, as discussed in Carol Clover, *Men, Women and Chainsaws: Gender in the Modern Horror Film* (Princeton: Princeton University Press, 1992). Slasher films, such as *Halloween* (1978), revolve around a monstrous figure who goes around systematically killing people, usually teenagers, until a somewhat androgynous, strong young woman, the "final girl" in Clover's terminology, finally manages to stand up to the monster and kill it (albeit only temporarily; the monster is invariably revived). Ripley and Sarah Connor (the heroines of *Aliens* and *Terminator 2*, respectively) are the big-budget action-movie versions of the slasher's "final grl." While slasher films were originally addressed very specifically to a young male audience, there is considerable anecdotal evidence that they found a secondary audience in young females, watching these films in groups during slumber parties and similar social occasions. These viewing habits may well have prepared the way for a later female demand for action heroines.

25. While the Sylvester Stallone vehicle *Demolition Man* barely made it into the Top Twenty for 1993, with United States revenues of $56 million (against a budget of $58 million), *Speed* was the seventh-highest-grossing film of 1994 with a $121 million gross (and a moderate budget of $31 million); "In Zahlen," *steadycam* 26 (spring 1994): 9–10; *steadycam* 29 (spring 1995): 8–9.

26. "In Zahlen," *steadycam* 33 (spring 1997): 19–20. At the end of its domestic release, *Twister* was the twelfth-highest-grossing film of all time in the United States, according to *Screen International*, 7 February 1997, 42.

27. With a $100–million domestic gross, *Contact* was number eleven in the end-of-year box office chart for 1997; *Variety*, 5 January 1998, 96.

28. It also has to be noted, however, that most of the female-centered action-adventure movies in recent years have flopped. The Geena Davis vehicle *Cutthroat Island* (1995) about a female pirate, for example, cost about $100 million and grossed only $10 million in the United States. The results for the equally expensive action-adventure films *The Long Kiss Goodnight* (1996), another Geena Davis vehicle, and for the Sandra Bullock vehicle *Speed 2* (1997) were not much better. Recent family-adventure films centered on girl protagonists such as *Matilda, Harriet the Spy,* and *Fly Away Home* (all 1996) performed moderately at best; "In Zahlen," *steadycam* 31 (spring 1996): 12; *steadycam* 33 (spring 1997): 21. There is a particularly strong resistance in the industry to make films centered on the exploits of young females. As one shocked film producer recently reported: "Somebody at one of the studios once said to me 'Don't bring me any girl protagonists.' . . . I asked if I brought *Wizard of Oz* would they reject it. And they said yes." Quoted in Dan Cox, "Family Fare, Adult Price," *Variety*, 7 April 1997, 9.

29. These comments are based on a wide range of press materials encountered throughout 1997. The figure for the budget has been inflated; it is probably close to $200 million.

30. See, for example, the following reports in the British press, which are based on interviews with Cameron and/or publicity material: Sarah Gristwood, "Sink or Swim," *Guardian* (London), 2 January 1998, sec. 2, pp. 2–3; "Jim'll Fix It: The World's Biggest Liner's Hit an Iceberg. Cut to Demented Director," *Observer* (London), 11 January 1998; Simon Hattenstone, "A Screaming Director, Freezing Water, a Cast Driven Crazy, and Danger on All Sides. Who'd be the Chief Stuntman on *Titanic*?" *Guardian* (London), 23 January 1998, sec. 2, p. 4. See also the issue of the special effects magazine *Cinefex* dedicated to *Titanic*, the first article of which is summarized as follows

on the contents page: "*Titanic* is an apt title for the latest film from director James Cameron, denoting not only the subject matter of the picture, but the scope of the endeavor, as well. On his odyssey to bring the story of the 1912 maritime disaster to the screen, Cameron went to the bottom of the North Atlantic to photograph the actual *Titanic* wreck, then reconstructed the celebrated ship, almost full-size—and sank it!—at a studio built expressly to house the massive production." Don Shay, "Back to *Titanic*," *Cinefex* 72 (December 1997).

31. The following analysis is based on several viewings and the detailed synopsis of the film in Todd McCarthy, "Spectacular *Titanic* a Night to Remember," *Variety*, 3 November 1997, 7, 106; compare with Richard Williams, "Waving Not Drowning," *Guardian* (London), 23 January 1998, sec. 2, p. 7, and José Arroyo, "Massive Attack," *Sight and Sound*, February 1998, 16–19.

32. By focussing on elemental forces, the film harks back to the disaster movie cycle of the 1970s, although there are also important differences (mainly having to do with the centrality of the couple rather than of a larger group of people), which would be worth exploring further. Compare with Nick Roddick, "Only the Stars Survive: Disaster Movies in the Seventies," in *Performance and Politics in Popular Drama*, ed. David Bradby, Louis James, and Bernard Sharratt (Cambridge: Cambridge University Press, 1980), 243–269.

33. While the critical response to *Titanic* does not seem to pick up on this defining theme of Cameron's work, some of the publicity did highlight his liking of strong women, referring, however, not so much to his films as to the women he married: Gale Anne Hurd, Kathryn Bigelow, and Linda Hamilton. See Gristwood, "Sink or Swim," and "Jim'll Fix It."

34. No doubt, this theme can be found in most of Cameron's work, including his script for *Rambo: First Blood Part II* (1985), in which Rambo, just after he has narrowly escaped the bad buys, returns to the POW camp to save its inmates. Structurally, the similarities between *Rambo II* and the rest of Cameron's oeuvre are striking, although ideologically they would appear to be at opposite ends of the spectrum.

35. The following comments are based on the trailer shown in movie theaters in Britain and The Netherlands, which I presume to be the same as the one shown in the United States.

36. Quoted in Shay, "Back to *Titanic*," 16.

37. Gristwood, "Sink or Swim," 3. Compare with similar statements in "Jim'll Fix It" and "Captain of the Ship," *Preview*, November–December 1997, 16–21.

38. Ed W. Marsh, *James Cameron's Titanic* (New York: HarperPerennial, 1997), ix.

39. Ibid., vi.

40. However, in typical Hollywood flashback fashion, the film actually shows several events that Rose neither attended nor knew anything about.

41. In fact, Jack is first seen immediately after the voice-over has declared that Rose was screaming inside, but no one could hear her, at which point the ship's horn "screams" and the film cuts to Jack, as if the ship was calling him on her behalf, as if her relayed internal scream brought him into existence even.

42. There is yet another way of looking at this. Throughout the film, Rose is closely identified with the ship, which "screams" on her behalf and is, just like Rose, a prized possession of powerful males; in one scene Rose is also presented as the ship's figurehead. The sinking of the *Titanic*, then, would appear to be an extension of Rose's earlier death wish. Furthermore, the two are linked through the motif of virginity: The *Titanic* is on her maiden voyage, and Rose is still a virgin; the *Titanic*'s voyage comes to an end

shortly after Rose has lost her virginity. Thus the story of the film moves from Rose's sexual objectification and her suicidal frame of mind (in which she turns her anger against herself) to her sexual liberation and the externalization of her aggressive impulses in the spectacle of the ship's destruction. The connection between her sexual liberation and death is also hinted at by the peculiar postcoital exchange in which she points out to Jack that he is shaking, and he replies, as if he had been severely wounded: "I'll be okay." Of course, in the end he won't.

43. While traditional girl adventurer stories prefer the construction of an alternative world to the destruction of the real one, contemporary female-centered action-adventure films revel in the destructive power of female forces (which may or may not be directed against an identifiable patriarchal order): the alien mother and her brood in *Aliens*, the nuclear devastation of the earth which is endlessly replaying in Sarah Connor's mind in *Terminator 2*, the devastating female-identified tornadoes in *Twister*.

44. Jon Herskovitz and Chris Petrikin, "*Titanic* Preem a Sellout," *Variety*, 3 November 1997, 7, 11.

45. McCarthy, "Spectacular *Titanic* a Night to Remember," 7, 106.

46. *Variety*, 5 January 1998, 16.

47. "In Zahlen," *steadycam* 30 (winter 1995): 15; *steadycam* 31 (spring 1996): 12; *steadycam* 32 (winter 1996): 25.

48. That *Titanic* "has bucked the trend of ballooning playdates" was noted in *Variety*, 26 January 1998, 21.

49. Ibid., 5 January 1998, 13, 16.

50. Ibid., 12 January 1998, 13; and 19 January 1998, 13.

51. Ibid., 26 January 1998, 12. Statistics about the "highest weekend grosses after fourth week of wide release," which show *Titanic* way ahead of the competition, appear on 21.

52. Compare with Schatz, "The New Hollywood," 25–36.

53. See Paul Karon, "*Titanic* Steams on with 4 Globes," *Variety*, 26 January 1998, 20; and Ansen, "Our *Titanic* Love Affair," 47. While the release of *Titanic* was not supported by, and did not feed into, a merchandising craze typical of youth and child oriented blockbusters, Ansen points out that by February, 10 million units of the orchestral soundtrack album had been shipped worldwide and that the glossy paperback version of *James Cameron's Titanic* had been at the top of the *New York Times* best-seller list. Even the film's ancillary products had an air of prestige.

54. *Screen International*, 16 January 1998, 37.

55. Klady, "Tara Torpedoes *Titanic* as the real B.O. Champ," 105. There is considerable overlap with the list of *international* top grossers. The most up-to-date version that I could find is from June 1996, which is before the rerelease of the *Star Wars* trilogy in 1997 and before the release of the superhits *Independence Day*, *Twister*, *Men in Black* (1997), and *The Lost World* (1997). The list has *Jurassic Park* at number one with $913 million, followed by *The Lion King*, *E.T.*, *Forrest Gump*, *Ghost* (1990), *Star Wars*, *Aladdin* (1992), *Indiana Jones and the Last Crusade* (1989), *Terminator 2*, and *Home Alone* at number ten with $454 million; *Variety*, 3 June 1996, 70.

56. In fact, elsewhere I have argued that most of these films are family-adventure movies whose primary concern is with familial relationships, with a particular emphasis on parents' love for their children and children's love for their parents. See Krämer, "Would You Take Your Child to See This Film?"

57. Compare with Krämer, "A Powerful Cinema-going Force?"

58. Ansen, "Our *Titanic* Love Affair," 46–47. A striking statistic is that "45% of all the women under 25 who have seen the movie have seen it twice," and it is assumed that most of them were adolescents. Quoting experts on the development of adolescent girls, the article highlights the importance both of the design of Jack's character (as a vehicle for Rose's liberation) and of DiCaprio's performance for the movie's appeal to this audience segment. According to a poll cited in *Variety*, prior to the release of *Titanic* both Winslet and DiCaprio were actually relatively unknown to the general public, yet they were considered rising stars by those who recognized their names; *Variety*, 15 December 1997, 73. DiCaprio can be seen as a teen idol much like many pop stars. Yet his appeal goes beyond this, for even *Vanity Fair* could not help declaring him to be "simply the world's biggest heartthrob," quoting Winslet's statement that he is "probably the world's most beautiful-looking man." Cathy Horyn, "Leonardo Takes Wing," *Vanity Fair*, January 1998, 54–59, 112–114; quotes from title page and 112.

59. Compare with Balio, *Grand Design*, 1–12, 179–312; Richard Maltby with Ian Craven, *Hollywood Cinema: An Introduction* (Oxford, England: Blackwell, 1995), 10–11.

60. Joel W. Finler, *The Hollywood Story* (New York: Crown, 1988), 276–277.

61. Ibid. In inflation-adjusted charts, most of these films still hold top positions. See Klady, "Tara Torpedoes *Titanic* as Real B.O. Champ," 105.

62. Cameron quoted in "Captain of the Ship," 18. Also see Gristwood, "Sink or Swim."

63. Leonard Klady, "H'wood's B.O. Blast," *Variety*, 5 January 1998, 1, 96.

64. Quoted in Shay, "Back to *Titanic*," 76.

"Size Does Matter"

Notes on *Titanic* and James Cameron as Blockbuster Auteur

Alexandra Keller

*Every time I make a movie, everybody says it's the most expensive film
in the film industry.*
—James Cameron

Motivational Preamble: Why People the World Over Have Spent Two Hours and Seventy-four Minutes Watching a Boat Sink . . .

People went to see *Titanic* to experience a stunningly executed, special-effects-laden, working-class-loving, owning-class-hating, strong-willed-heroine-driven, romantic tragedy that, what with Kate Winslet running up and down flooded hallways wielding an ax, almost doubled as a swashbuckling sea picture. They went because Leo DiCaprio is apparently the sexiest thing anyone has ever seen since whoever was hot last month. They went because Cameron is a computer effects master who seldom makes you feel as if you're watching the effects of a computer (read: YOU ARE THERE!). They went because, as the tag line said about Jack Dawson and Rose Bukater, but which also came to be true about the audience and the movie, "Nothing on Earth Could Come Between Them." People seem also to have gone to see *Titanic* for other reasons as well, reasons that were more reflexive and, well, postmodern. They went to see the visual signifier of all that meticulousness, detail, obsession, and realism they had read about.

I went to see what the most expensive movie in the world looked like.

Now, I've read Don DeLilo's *White Noise*, and to that extent, I knew what I was in for. When the central character of that novel, a professor of Hitler Studies, goes to visit the most photographed barn in the United States, the question is raised as to why this quite ordinary barn is the most photographed of its kind. The answer is, natch, that it is the most photographed because it is the most photographed.

Given how long it took for *Titanic* finally to slide off the list of weekly top-grossing films (it still reappeared occasionally on slow weeks), it makes plenty of sense that after the first wave of people went to see what the most expensive film looked like, a whole new wave of spectators went to see what the most profitable film might be like to see.

It must also be said that this sort of tautology and reflexivity is something of an autoportrait of Hollywood at the end of its first century. Bloated, over budget, preening, egomaniacal, and yet sometimes yielding stunning results, not only in spite of but also *because* of all these things. The paragon of mass-produced, mass-disseminated, mass-received art and entertainment, Hollywood (and most of the rest of us) nevertheless cleaves to traditional, prefilmic concepts of individual genius. And Cameron is exactly the man to paint Hollywood's fin-de-siècle self-portrait. And that was something I (and many others) just had to see.

I also went to *Titanic* to see whether it was as good, or bad, as the press was saying. When I read *New York Times* film critic Janet Maslin's assessment that it was the greatest epic film Hollywood had produced since *Gone With the Wind* (1939), I assumed that either she was right, and that it would therefore be an equally twisted document of the social realities of our age, or else that she was wrong, and was about to crash and burn just as Bosley Crowther had when he said *Bonnie and Clyde* (1967) marked the end of decent filmmaking in the United States.

I also went to see *Titanic* because it is more than an event movie (though it is assuredly that). I went to see two hours and seventy-four minutes[1] of the traces of a story that was not only about a ship that sank but about a movie that might.[2] I went to see a story about an obsessed director. I went to see the traces of his obsession in detail, an obsession that in the case of the failed blockbuster *Heaven's Gate* (1980), was the sign of an ego gone disastrously out of control, but that in the case of *Titanic* seemed to register with the audience as a measure of Cameron's devotion to bringing his public the most immediate and intimate experience possible. Paradoxically, this intimacy with the ship *Titanic*, its journey, its passengers, and its foundering, seems only to have been increased by the scale of the production, the film's very largeness, and this, too, contributes to explaining *Titanic*'s popularity.

I went to get an eyeful of the romanticism outside of the film that evidently matched the inside: Cameron's devotion to and love for the ship at the bottom of the ocean was at least as intense as Rose's love for her boy at the bottom of the sea. This love and devotion segued nicely into Cameron's apparent love and devotion for his audience (see above).

Mostly, I went to see capital. For there is even more to the reflexivity of the portrait of capital, perhaps, than there is to *Titanic* as a portrait of Hollywood. Cruise ships like the *Titanic* are, as Roy Grundmann calls them, "floating signifiers of capital." Especially since they present microcosms of class structure, transporting whole societies in miniature from port to port (the mouths and anuses of nineteenth-century industrial capitalism), cruise ships are collapsed forms of signification, capitalist mechanisms not unlike classical Hollywood entertainment itself, which in its late stages (think TV's *The Love Boat*) obscures its own means, engines, and

Floating signifier of capital: *Titanic* T-shirt for sale on the Internet

logics of production. Though the contours of capitalism have changed since the *Titanic* era, indeed, perhaps because they have changed so much, *Titanic* seems to offer a compellingly comforting mirage for millions upon millions of late capitalist spectators.

But most assuredly, by the time I went to see *Titanic* at the end of December 1997, there was no doubt that I was going to see a James Cameron blockbuster.

Points of Embarkation

This essay moves us toward a partial explanation of the unprecedented popularity of *Titanic* by examining what this popularity has to do with two important and interrelated factors: Cameron's auteuresque imprint on the film, and *Titanic*'s status, both before and after release, as a blockbuster film. To talk about Cameron as an "auteur" is to acknowledge how very far film culture has come from the original usage of that term, which connoted a director whose singular, guiding vision was strong enough to merit the status of artistry, even in the popular entertainment format of cinema. To talk about *Titanic* as a blockbuster is to speak about how the film has irrevocably changed what that category means. To talk about both auteurism and the blockbuster in the same thought is to implicate the one in the other, which is to suggest that as the notion of the auteur has become broader, the conception of the blockbuster has become more discernible (sometimes) as something like a genre, and certainly as a format with quite familiar protocols. To talk about auteurism and the blockbuster together is to be speaking of a hybridization of categories only conceivable under postmodern conditions. For under postmodernism, both the concept of the auteur and that of genre have indeed mutated far from their original intentions (originality itself being highly suspect these days).

The useful thing about auteur and genre criticism for getting a fix on Cameron and *Titanic* is that, as organizing principles, they very efficiently address how *Titanic*, a film that seems on its face generically anomalous in the largely science-fiction and action-oriented works of the Cameron oeuvre, is actually very much in the Cameron groove. And what I want to suggest here is that, increasingly, Cameron's groove has been money itself, Guy Debord's image of accumulated capital. Just as John Ford made his mark in the western, and Alfred Hitchcock spoke through the thriller, so Cameron seems to have gravitated toward the blockbuster as his format.[3] Cameron has pushed the edge of the blockbuster envelope many times before. But this time he may well have exploded it. *Titanic* may, to paraphrase the language of the fighter pilots in Tom Wolfe's *The Right Stuff* (a blockbuster book that in 1984 did *not* translate into a blockbuster movie), be the first blockbuster film to break the sound barrier. But that barrier itself is not a fixed demarcation. It is, rather, one endemic to, and reflective of, postmodern conditions, the very conditions which produce both *Titanic* and the viewing subjects who account for its extraordinary popularity.

Any mention of postmodernism inevitably invites and incites anxiety about what precisely the "p" word means. There are two fundamental traditions vis-à-vis the term "postmodernism," one critical of it and one celebratory, albeit in a cautionary fashion. Postmodernism can be looked at conservatively (negatively) and progressively (positively). Where its critics (e.g., Fredric Jameson, Terry Eagleton, Jürgen Habermas, Hal Foster) see an epistemology marked by a breakdown of tastes and standards, its proponents (e.g., Craig Owens, Linda Hutcheon, Charles Russell, Robert Venturi) see an expansion or deemphasis of, and a challenge to, those very same things.[4] Looked at conservatively, postmodernism has led to the breakdown and fragmentation of the subject beyond repair. It (and its adjunct poststructuralism) marks a devalorization of genius and of the author—of the very fact or possibility of authorship. And perhaps most seriously, postmodern conditions are often cited as the cause of society's failure to invest in progress and history. Looked at progressively, postmodernism's ostensibly fragmented subject (whose unification was always an illusion anyway) is capable of far greater social and political radicality than ever before. Postmodernism subverts the control of any dominant ideology that might lead to the formation of oppressive cultural canons, and has made possible a more diverse and democratic approach to historical discourse, in which power is not a precondition of the right to historicize.

Titanic, like Cameron's career as a whole, manifests the more negative view of postmodern practice, in which spectacle replaces history, consumption takes the place of political action, and the signature merely appears to represent a signer. The visceral experience of watching *Titanic* spurs its viewers not toward historical investigations of the early twentieth century, or even of their own present, but instead to another viewing of the film. Any progressive message about class that the film claims to hold does not incite its spectators to pay more attention to the plight of contemporary Jack Dawsons, but rather to consume as commodity (and therefore ultimately dispose of) the social message of *Titanic*, such as it is. And Cameron's pretensions to the status of auteur, his altogether successful (for now) bid to be "King of the World," have less to do with art and entertainment than with power itself.

All of this—history, capital, and subjectivity—come under the sway of *Titanic*, but that film is only the most accomplished of a longer chain of narratives that have similar effects. *Titanic*, as the world's most successful blockbuster, so expertly reframes its proposed concerns of romance, class, gender equality, technical prowess, and historical accuracy as sheer commodity that it has become as ubiquitous and as all-encompassing as global capitalism itself. It presents its viewers with extremely pressing and vital issues in an ostensibly rigorous historical context. But by tacitly framing its concerns in terms of consumption, it offers its audience the easy way out, while still leaving them with the impression that they have participated in something of vital importance. This spectacular aspect of *Titanic* is, I think, essential to understanding the film's popularity. "It is the sun which never sets over the empire of modern passivity. It covers the entire surface of the world and bathes endlessly in its own glory."[5] Debord was defining the spectacle in those lines, but he might just as well have been speaking of *Titanic*, its maker, and its format.

What We Talk about When We Talk about Blockbusters

The American Heritage Dictionary defines a blockbuster as "something, such as a film or book, that sustains widespread popularity and achieves enormous sales." This, surely, is a rather modest definition for the *Titanic* phenomenon, though it certainly fits. It also fits—far more snugly—a growing number of movies and cultural events. Thomas Schatz proposes that blockbuster films are "those multipurpose entertainment machines that breed music videos and soundtrack albums, TV series and videocassettes, video games and theme park rides, novelizations and comic books."[6] In a general context, this is, of course, an excellent description of the way blockbusters of any medium ultimately bleed far beyond their original form into many corners of everyday life. But it does not describe the *Titanic* phenomenon very well. *Titanic* is considerably less of an "entertainment machine" than most blockbuster movies—what theme park ride could possibly come out of this film that would be tasteful enough to get off the drawing board?[7] And in some sense this makes it an exception that proves the rule. There does exist a stereotypical blockbuster because we expect our blockbusters to be experientially onomatopoetic, which is to say, we expect them to bust our blocks, and certainly films like *Star Wars* (1977), *Jurassic Park* (1993), *Independence Day* (1996), *Men in Black* (1997), and Cameron's *Terminator 2: Judgment Day* (1991) do that. We tend to expect them to be loud and noisy, and to have impact that is visceral first, emotional second, and intellectual a very, very distant third. Largely we think of action films, science fiction, and adventure films—exactly what Cameron does—when we think of blockbusters. Or rather, when the studios lay out that much money, they are not going to do it on quiet films, even if the profit potential is almost as great. So at some level, blockbusters also have both a broad generic definition as well as an aesthetic and generic attitude.

There is, then, a big difference between films that make a truckload of money and films that are blockbusters, and some of that has to do with reaching the audience at a certain volume. If it were just a question of cost-to-profit ratios, it would be fair to say that *Four Weddings and a Funeral* (1994) and *The Full Monty* (1997) were also blockbusters, since not only do they both hover around the $200–million mark (which seems to be the new magic number) in ticket sales, but their profits also far exceeded what they cost to make. By this logic, Cameron's original *Terminator* might modestly fit the bill, having made $37 million on a budget of only $6.4 million. But this cannot be the full picture: as massive as the profit margins are for these inexpensive films, there is no *Four Weddings and a Funeral* culture, no *Full Monty* ethos. *Titanic*, more than any film since *Star Wars* or *Raiders of the Lost Ark* (1981), has both. Moreover, unlike Indiana Jones or the projected nine *Star Wars* films, *Titanic* stands alone, with no real possibility of a sequel. This may, in fact, have something to do with its popularity. Knowing there is no real possibility of a sequel, spectators had better get it now if they are going to get it at all. Insofar as a sequel almost always requires at least a memorial, or mental re-viewing, of the film that preceded it, it might be suggested that *Titanic*'s repeated viewings by many spectators is in some small part a replacement for the sequel that can never be.

Of course, there is obviously more to the blockbuster dynamic, and increasingly the issue is not just the magnitude of profit but the magnitude of outlay as well. (Imagine your average studio exec hollering at the top of his lungs, "Ya gotta spend money to make money!!") Some blockbusters, to be sure, are quieter than others, and the *buster* part of that neologism seems hardly to apply. These films are more like blockburrowers. For example, *The Full Monty* and *Good Will Hunting* (1997) made their money quietly and/or slowly, *Good Will Hunting* in particular initially relying as much on word of mouth as advertising (as did *Four Weddings*). Not so with *Titanic*.

With *Titanic* there could be no such thing as word of mouth, no quiet building of support for a cinematic gem discovered by a lucky few who became disciples spreading the news. The film had no secret and was unknown to no one. Everything about *Titanic* was prespoken. The success of *The Full Monty* had much to do with "I just saw the most charming British film last night." *Good Will Hunting* thrived on "and you know those two hotties, Ben and Matt, wrote it too. They actually *wrote* it!" *Titanic*'s word of mouth was bold headlines in the mainstream press, which picked up steam right about when the film missed its original release date of 2 July 1997. And even when the copy spoke favorably of the film's quality, the slug lines and ribbons predominantly whispered—no, they shouted—doom. In its August 1997 issue, *Premiere* ran a story called "Cameron's Way," which was announced on the magazine's cover with a ribbon screaming "*Titanic* Panic! What's Really Going Down."[8] The article was one of many that spoke of Cameron's meticulous devotion to detail and his relentless pursuit of the perfect reconstruction of the ship, using the original blueprints. In *Premiere*'s December issue, the month *Titanic* was released, the extensive feature was titled "Magnificent Obsession," and the slug line read, "The closer he gets to the brink of disaster, the nearer director James Cameron gets to filmmaking genius. Dispatches from the set of 'Titanic.'"[9] Dispatches. As if the journalist were reporting Michael Herr–style from Vietnam. Nevertheless, in that article, more prespoken word was put forth: about the $3 million that Twentieth Century Fox had given the director so he could dive down to the actual *Titanic twelve times*; about the technology, such as a crush-proof camera, that Cameron invented just for the shoot; about the replica of the *Titanic* constructed (at 90 percent of scale) in the world's largest water tank (also constructed for the shoot); about the PCP in the chowder. Lest anyone think that Cameron was a no-sacrifices free-spender, he also repeated the information that he had given back his salary, or, as he put it, "I'm doing it for free."[10]

Months later *Premiere*'s rhetoric reversed itself utterly. When it became clear the film would likely crack the billion-dollar mark, *Premiere* ran a story called "Cameron Is God," in which it was less than tacitly suggested that Cameron, having given up his back-end deal, should now be rewarded with a sizable bonus for turning the world's most expensive film into the world's most profitable.[11] Likewise, *Entertainment Weekly* Monday morning quarterbacked *Titanic*'s success, seeking to learn lessons for next time from a sui generis event.[12] Indeed, so radically has *Titanic* altered the expectations for and contours of the blockbuster that, though profits were actually up industrywide from the previous summer, 1998 was nevertheless considered an unspectacular year, since no film had cracked the $200–million mark. As *Entertainment Weekly* began its article on the subject:

> It will go down in history as the summer the blockbuster turned lackluster. Halfway to Labor Day, something strange is happening in entertainment: This year's putative event movies are taking their sweet time cracking the $150 million mark, and it looks increasingly unlikely that *any* of the films will see $200 million. . . . Even the most sun-struck event-movie devotees are detecting the scent of blockbuster breakdown in the air.[13]

To toll the death knell of the blockbuster is not only unwise but also unoriginal, and is unlikely to be any truer now than it has ever been. The pertinent point is that next to *Titanic*, these high-grossing films now appear less successful, and this seems to be affecting audience perceptions of them. Two full seasons later, audiences were still "imprinted" with *Titanic*, and the largeness of the typical blockbuster could not distract them. Another way to look at it is that in the wake of *Titanic*, as *Entertainment Weekly* put it, audiences were suffering from "chronic post-blockbuster fatigue syndrome."[14]

Titanic makes clear that at the end of the twentieth century, the blockbuster film has a two-part definition. Obviously, any film that makes enough money, especially one that does it quickly and dramatically enough, is regarded as a blockbuster, and this quality is only amplified by a film's potential market tie-ins—for example, *Star Wars* and *Batman* (1989)—which extend public consciousness of and desire for the film into other aspects of life from fast food to Halloween costumes to bedsheets. But it is only with the release, press, and success of *Titanic* that the other side of the definition becomes absolutely clear—as does the fact that this aspect of blockbusters is relatively new (suggesting that blockbusters are indeed mutating into something as distinct as a genre). A film can be a block-buster before it is even released, and even if it does not make any money, pro-vided enough time, money, and industrial and popular attention are invested in it and focused on it. Even before it was released, *Titanic* was, in that sense, already the biggest blockbuster of all time.

As a result of this two-part description, blockbusters need to be looked at not only in terms of success but also in terms of failure. For every Hollywood boom there is a bust. The boom: *The Ten Commandments* (1956). The bust: *Star!* (1968). The boom: *Star Wars*. The bust: *Heaven's Gate*. It is this last boom-and-bust couplet that seems most relevant to *Titanic*. The generation of blockbusters out of which *Titanic* might be said to mutate is obviously that of *Star Wars*, but the parent nobody talks about is *Heaven's Gate*. We tend to deal with film history and its phases in terms of what worked, looking at failures as cautionary tales of what *not* to do again, and regarding successes as the keys to formulas that, muta-tis mutandis, can repeat themselves. But this positive focus (and I am overstating the case somewhat) gives us an incomplete picture. Blockbusters that fail can be just as influential in their voice-from-beyond-the-grave way. *Heaven's Gate*, after all, is, at least mythically, the film that sunk the western for all time—or at least for the duration of the Reagan-Bush years. And while *Titanic* is in many ways discernible as a descendant of *The Ten Commandments/The Godfather* (1972)/*Star Wars* line, it is just as much the successful offspring of Michael Cimino's epic fail-ure. Cameron's now-legendary attention to detail, his insistence that everything from the carpets to the lifeboat davits come from the same manufacturer as the real *Titanic*, his certainty that, even though no one on or off the screen would ever see them, the luggage tags had to be authentic down to the handwriting—all smacks of Cimino's similar maneuvers for *Heaven's Gate*. Never mind that whereas *Heaven's Gate* was being funded by the minor, if prestigious, studio of United Artists, *Ti-tanic* had the backing of two studio titans, Twentieth Century Fox and Paramount. Moreover, Cameron's insistence on a period piece, on a romantic epic, a genre so contrary to his area of proven expertise, as well as his insistence that the audience would not only sit still but be emotionally absorbed for as long as it took him to tell that story, even if was well into next Sunday, smacked of Cimino's insistence on spending his *Deer Hunter* (1978) Oscar clout to make a western—the one genre that in the 1970s was undeniably on its way out.[15]

But here is where the films part ways. *Heaven's Gate* was too political, too left-wing populist, to appeal to a film culture that was at that point strafed as much by the opposition to the Vietnam War as by the war itself. *Titanic* is, at the end of the day, utterly apolitical, or, at any rate, differently political from its own very overt claims, which resemble those of *Heaven's Gate* itself. *Heaven's Gate* anchored its politics firmly in the conventions of the western genre (even if those conven-tions were, by that point, as much those of the counterwestern), using those very conventions to effect a critique of the dominant ideology. *Titanic*, emerging as it has under the conditions of full-blown, even late-stage postmodernism,[16] also frames its epic story in the generic framework of the historical romance. The difference is the enthusiastic nostalgia of *Titanic*'s generic attachment—a nostalgia symptomatic of a big chunk of postmodern cultural production, though by no means all of it. The ease with which *Titanic* presented history, via nostalgia, as an eminently consumable commodity goes a long way toward explaining its popularity.

In any case, as if it weren't enough to attribute to *Titanic*'s success the "failure" of films like *Godzilla*, *Armageddon*, and *Lethal Weapon 4* (all 1998), there was a second wave of film journalism that seemed to stem from a thwarted desire to see *Titanic* dead in the water. Inspired by the film's nonfailure, *Premiere* ran a story about ten films that bombed, but shouldn't have.[17] Earlier in the year, *Entertainment Weekly* did a story about the ten-biggest box office losers of all time.[18] So *Titanic* inspires critical and journalistic ink not only in response to its success but also in response to its lack of failure, in a sort of what-iffing usually reserved for historical figures like Christopher Columbus. In many ways *Titanic* is both anomalous and inevitable. It is the apotheosis (so far) of life under blockbuster culture.

To be sure, blockbuster films precede blockbuster culture. *The Birth of a Nation* (1915), *Gone With the Wind*, *The Ten Commandments*, and *Lawrence of Arabia* (1962) are blockbuster films that were not linked to a larger cultural firmament with a blockbuster mentality. Schatz notes the intensification of the blockbuster mentality in the period following World War II. But it seems to me that this was largely limited to the cinema and certainly was not the key of life. Nevertheless, it is through blockbuster film that a larger blockbuster culture emerges. As Schatz suggests, the genealogy of the postwar blockbuster film can be broken down into distinct generations, which arguably starts with *The Ten Commandments* and *The Sound of Music* (1965). These were followed transitionally by *The Godfather*, whose historically removed setting and equally dramatic on-set stories and rumors, combined with the great success of Mario Puzo's novel, prepared the film to be one of the first "event movies." It is one that clearly finds its echo in *Titanic*, having garnered both critical and financial success, as well as having brought undebatable star status to its previously lesser-known young leads. But the line between these blockbusters and what follows also points to another element of *Titanic*'s lineage. As Schatz notes, *Jaws* (1975) established new protocols for the blockbuster film, including saturation marketing, the idea of the summer hit, the focus on younger filmgoers. *Star Wars* and *E.T* (1982) were produced and marketed with this in mind. *Titanic* smacks of all three. Indeed, that *Titanic*'s much ballyhooed Fourth of July opening weekend slipped away in a fog of Cameronian tinkering, fine-tuning, obsession, and expenditure, leaving its expectant young fans in the lurch, may actually account for increasing its popularity. Forced into a spectatorial coitus interruptus, the fans' appetites may only have been further whetted.

Schatz also suggests that the success of this second generation of blockbuster films "signaled a crucial shift in moviegoing and exhibition that accompanied the rise of the modern 'shopping center.'"[19] The unification of the cinema and the shopping mall brought into full relief what had been latent ever since the beginning of cinema: film was—and is—a commodity and is subject to the same exigencies and impulses. A movie can, therefore, be designed, and focus-grouped, as well as made. Indeed, *Titanic*—though putatively the result of one mad genius's efforts to see his vision through to the beautiful end, no matter what it took, no matter what the studios said, no matter who got hurt, no matter what it cost him, including his salary and his marriage—is also a marketer's dream.[20] The influential National Research Group divides audiences into five demographic quadrants (under age twenty-five, over age twenty-five, male, female, and "ethnic"). A film like *Godzilla* would typically draw from two quadrants (male, under age twenty-five), as would *Hope Floats* (1998)—(female and over age twenty-five). According to Edward Jay Epstein, "The Holy Grail was a film like *Titanic*, which appealed to all five quadrants."[21] Not only is *Titanic* evidently a film for all, it is a *product* for everyone, the ice cream flavor nobody dislikes, and of which everyone wants seconds.

Even if blockbuster culture's sine qua non is multinational corporate capitalism, which seems to homogenize almost everything in its path, the culture did not appear simultaneously with its cause (or, perhaps more accurately, its guiding, motivating structure). Blockbuster culture also heralds the rise of Ronald Reagan, as well as the events that ultimately brought about a national desire for him: Vietnam and its protests, Watergate, inflation, the oil crisis, President Jimmy Carter's frontally ineffectual heroics both at home and abroad, the spiritual malaise of which he spoke. It arises in its coherent, recognizable form, complete with ideological propositions and social protocols in two happenings, both occurring in 1977: *Star Wars* and the traveling King Tut exhibit—"coming soon to a museum near you!"—sponsored by the Los Angeles County Museum of Art. These two seminal events had the curious effect of accidentally looping into each other, the first overtly plugging ancient mythological and mytho-historical themes and ideas into up-to-the-minute special effects, the second transporting wholesale an ancient culture and its attendant mythologies and histories into the contemporary framework of consumer capitalism. Both events came with wholly aggressive, carefully thought out marketing plans.[22] So that in leaving either *Star Wars*, the movie, or "King Tut," the exhibition, you did not really need to leave for good; you could own action figures, trading cards, scarves, and personalized cartouches. Hell, you could even sing along with the Steve Martin song about the king. The Force was always with you.

Simultaneous to increased niche marketing is the desire, shared by corporations and cocooners alike, also to have moments of simulated common ground, and here is where blockbusters from *Terminator 2* to the traveling Monet retrospective in 1985 come into play. One wants to call them cultural moments, but they simply are not, or rather are not simply cultural moments. Increasingly these moments do not occur in the sociopolitical sphere, but rather in the realm of consumption, in the purchase of experience. You go to see water lilies, but you do not leave until you are wearing the water lilies on a tie. Before postmodernism broke down the distinctions between high and low art, it whittled away at the barriers between culture and consumption. And twenty years after the release of *Star Wars*, an audience that had never before seen it on a big screen finally did so, and six months later returned to the theaters to see its echo in *Titanic*. As David Walsh of the World Socialist Web Site wrote, picking up on the general tendency of such films to express a form of unanimity endemic to the Blockbuster Age:

> The very fact of its initial popularity (aided by media manipulation) helps a film like *Titanic* to become *immensely* popular. "It is attractive to me because it is attractive to others; I have seen something extraordinary and tragic in the film because others have seen it." This is not so much conformism, although that enters into it, as the desire for affiliation, for some unifying element, when the new social affiliation and the new basis for unifying humanity have not appeared to the vast majority.[23]

Titanic's financials show how this blockbuster culture has been taken to a new plateau, one that reflects the increasing power and prevalence of virtual experience. Despite the success of the soundtrack, and despite the fact that *Titanic* items can be purchased through the J. Peterman catalog (that bastion of virtual [neo]colonialism), compared to the *Star Wars* and *Batman* franchises, the consumer tie-in market for *Titanic* diffused profit making away from the studios. Yet it is precisely the intersection of consumer ethos with lack of studio-generated consumption that contributes to *Titanic*'s popularity—the film actually benefits from the having little to sell. What remains the big moneymaker for the *Titanic* franchise, sans Happy Meal, is the movie itself. Without Kate and Leo action figures, one is compelled to work out the desire, endemic to blockbuster culture, to consume *Titanic* by seeing it again. The evanescent nature of film-going is such that it is always an insufficient replacement for the presence of a material object, so the compulsion is, of course, to see *Titanic* again and *again*. If you cannot hold it, you can at least behold it.[24]

La Politique des auteurs and the Politics of James Cameron's Authorship

Cameron has until now worked exclusively in the genres of science fiction and action-adventure. *Titanic* is neither of these, though, like many generically hybrid films, it borrows heavily from both. And yet it seems to be recognizable to both critics and the public as a "James Cameron Film." This, I think, is for a number of reasons. First, Cameron has been extremely consistent in his ideological concerns and his narratological way of expressing them. Second, Cameron's ideological and narrative propositions are expressed in a quite consistent visual and aesthetic style. Third, Cameron's "vision" has increasingly had less to do with traditionally marked genres (e.g., sci-fi) and more to do with sheer scale of production and profit, making Cameron's films blockbusters no matter what else they also are.

In the seemingly idiosyncratic *Titanic*, we have, in fact, the clearest articulation yet of the bottom line of Cameron's auteurist mark: his milieu is the blockbuster. By strict definition, a blockbuster is not a genre on the order of, say, the woman's melodrama. But the blockbuster *as spectacle* begins to approach genre status. By spectacle I do not only mean *Titanic*'s large-scale set pieces, especially the sinking of the ship, nor its emotions writ large, such as Jack's sacrificial gesture of love. Nor do I simply mean, in a more traditional sense, those moments in a film that, by inducing sheer visceral response, momentarily arrest (and are arguably mutually exclusive with) narrative altogether, though I certainly do intend both of these things as well. But additionally, and crucially, I mean spectacle in Guy Debord's sense: "The spectacle is *capital* to such a degree of accumulation that it becomes an image."[25]

What *Titanic* appears to put on offer for the spectator's consumption as image is a commodified version of history—history as spectacle. Indeed, the "history" functioning in *Titanic* seems very virtual, very nostalgic, in Jameson's sense. And this, it would seem, has some fairly important political implications, which contribute to the magnitude of the film's popularity. It is in the film's politics that we begin to start circling the airport of Cameron's auteurism—what it is that he is saying in the consistency of his "vision," and why his films are consistently popular. I do not want to claim that Cameron is an auteur on the order of Hitchcock. But then again, I am not altogether comfortable claiming that Hitchcock is an auteur on the order of Hitchcock. Which is to say, following Peter Wollen, that the director's authorial presence is not a presence at all, but a metonymic contraction under which the film's effects are organized.[26] Given the huge numbers of people who work under the sign of Cameron, this seems an especially crucial retooling of the method originated in the 1950s by the editors of *Cahiers du cinéma*. The way auteurism folds the genres in which a director works neatly into his style (think John Ford and westerns), also operates here. It would seem that, for all that auteur criticism has obviously been about personal authorship, genre has always been all but the sine qua non of discussing an author and remains so in the postmodern era of generic hybridity.

The hybridity that marks the postmodernist vision also marks Cameron's, most obviously in the Terminator, who is a hybrid of human and machine. But postmodernism's most profoundly evident hybrid state is the current condition of what Rick Altman calls "genericity."[27] Because Cameron's previous films have tended to be not generic hybrids but quite straightforward action or science fiction films—or clear syntheses of the two—other consistencies in his style have been overshadowed or camouflaged. One of the most interesting is his highly debatable feminism—I would go so far as to call it virtual feminism. Cameron's version of femininity, proposed in the figure of the take-no-prisoners woman, may be atypical for Hollywood but ultimately does not disturb its patriarchal imperative. In this it is eminently nonthreatening, therefore consumable, and therefore popular.

Nation critic Katha Pollitt has suggested that *Titanic* actually offered its female adolescent spectators a peculiar but undeniable form of feminism. "Within the context of Hollywood films," she suggests, "*Titanic* is a feminist movie."[28] Pollitt perhaps knows that radical feminism for Hollywood stops with *Thelma and Louise* (1991), and therefore suggests that Rose is a marked improvement, since her road trip, unlike the gals in the turquoise convertible, does not end with a fatal swan dive. Nor is she otherwise compromised, having to choose between the job she loves and the man she . . . loves. Rather, Pollitt concludes, *Titanic* is:

> a women's fantasy—of costless liberation brought to you by a devoted, selfless, charming, funny, incredibly handsome lover. He teaches you to spit, awakens your body and soul, points you toward a long, richly eventful future and dies, beautifully, poetically and tragically—but not before he tells you that freezing to death in a sea full of corpses was worth it because it brought him to you. "He had to die," said one friend of mine, "because otherwise he would have disappointed her down the road." I had the same thought: How many happy artists' wives can you think of?[29]

Pollitt is obviously somewhat befuddled by the feminist message in *Titanic*, as am I right along with her.

Walsh takes a quite different view, one which has implications for the film's feminism: not only, states Walsh, is *Titanic* a film without any artistic merit,[30] its popularity is in some sense predicated on this fact—in spite of the cries of myriad Titaniacs that this is the greatest film ever made. And, in fact, this does offer a convincing explanation for why blockbusters work the way they do at this particular sociohistorical moment, as well as why *Titanic* works even better than the rest of them. "One of the difficulties in the situation" of *Titanic*'s popularity, continues Walsh,

> is that the same low cultural level that has produced the film has, to a large extent, produced the public reaction to it. . . . There is nothing "mystifying" about such a relatively vacuous film winning tremendous popularity. On the contrary, no other film would fill this particular bill. It is *Titanic*'s emptiness that allows the audience to invent a film, and a world for itself in the course of those three-and-a-quarter hours or as many viewings as it takes.[31]

Walsh's estimation of the film suggests that *Titanic*'s "girl power" exists as one of many potentially infinite spectatorial projections. The audience "invents the film," implying that the spectator is the author of this film, not Cameron. And a film without a single author would appear to be artistically worthless, though that is hardly the only reason Walsh supplies. Indeed, it is this repeated viewing that, for Walsh, keeps the film from being great, despite the fanatical affection of its return viewers.

> If the film were truly great, as its admirers claim, it would be impossible for *anyone*, of any age, to see it five, ten, or even more times. A great film, by definition, is a demanding film. One cannot rush back and see a work; one needs to recover from the experience and assimilate its contents.[32]

I will assume Walsh has never heard of cinema studies, or at any rate lumps it in with Santa Claus and the Easter Bunny.

I cannot go as far as Pollitt and give over, even cautiously, to the feminism in *Titanic*, not even during Ruth Bukater's exquisite corset string–yanking monologue in which she spells out to her daughter the complexity of a woman's lot in modernity. But the alternative, that *Titanic* is a tabula rasa on which people project whatever they please, seems to me nearly as untenable. For *Titanic* does have a politics, but I do not think it is altogether what either Pollitt or Walsh claim. *Titanic's* politics fit its blockbuster profile, and in this Walsh is correct when he suggests it does aim to leave itself open to the widest spectrum of spectatorial interpretations possible—within a certain acceptable range. But Pollitt is nevertheless absolutely right that the ideological linchpins of Cameron's films are usually his heroines, which may account for why a significant body of women would already have been familiar with Cameron's work before *Titanic*. *Titanic* may be exceptional in Cameron's work for a fan base mainly consisting of teenage, Leonardo DiCaprio–addled girls, but this does not mean that his earlier science fiction and action films, masculinist though they are at a generic level, have not actively invited female spectators.

If Cameron indeed has other auteuresque consistencies in his films, one of the most important remains his heroic, and very often buff, female protagonists. If *The Terminator's* Sarah Connor (Linda Hamilton, a.k.a. the future-ex-Mrs. Cameron) was the first of these heroines, she was latent until *Terminator 2*. In between, Cameron made *Aliens* (1986), which turned Sigourney Weaver's Ripley from director Ridley Scott's more measured, stately, and almost intellectual force in *Alien* (1979) into a contemplatively pumped up rebel, who, it happens, has spent some time training at the Yale Drama School. In *The Abyss* (1989), Mary Elizabeth Mastrantonio takes guff from no one and seems to take an almost existential pleasure in relentlessly being called a bitch. Then again, in Cameron's world, you would have to be one to design, build, manage, and save a colossal oil-rig-cum-deep-sea-exploration-unit, and keep control of it when both the oil company and the navy want it. In *True Lies* (1994), even Jamie Lee Curtis's Little Susie Homemaker, Helen Tasker, is man enough to throw punches not only at the enemy (male and female) but also at her husband, for lying to her so patronizingly all these years.

But Mastrantonio is still a bitch, Curtis hits like a man rather than like the fury of a woman she becomes, Weaver's major motivation to heroic action is almost exclusively maternal, and Linda Hamilton, for all her action-hero antics, is nowhere near as good a mother to her son as Schwarzenegger's Terminator is. All of which is to say that Cameron's fierce women are always pressed back into the service of patriarchy, pleasantly reaffirming the way things are in a manner equally palatable to both women and men. Cameron's big fake-out, his ability to make these women do something on a par with a gender striptease, is that, time after time, his heroines use their spunk and force to maintain the status quo.

In *Titanic*, Winslet's high-spirited, loogey-hocking wannabe heiress (or, more to the point, *don't*-wannabe heiress) is as independent, smart, idiosyncratically beautiful,[33] sexy, powerful, (fill in another complimentary adjective here, like an especially flattering Mad Lib), as Cameron's previous leading women. And yet again, Rose, a powerful but pleasing figure of the feminine, ultimately serves both patriarchy and the owning classes she appears to spurn in favor of Jack and all he represents. All Cameron films have a kind of bait-and-switch when it comes to their heroines, and in *Titanic* the change-up comes in the form of the necklace, the famous Heart of the Ocean, and the jewel's ultimate fate.

In the end, Rose the adventuress has led a life both like Jack's and like the one he wanted her to lead. But it is the rich version of that life. By leaving us with the image of an anonymous postrescue Rose, which we connect to the Bohemian image of a much older Rose at the potter's wheel, Cameron urges us to believe that Rose has really renounced her class. But she has not rejected her class at all, only its most obviously repugnant values. These values (boorishness, materialism, a tendency to treat people, especially women, like objects) are no less prevalent in the nonfilthy rich, though you would never guess it from Cameron's depiction of the folks in steerage. As the pictures she has brought to her stateroom on the present-day ship narrate—Rose the Hollywood starlet, Rose the Jane Bowles–esque desert explorer, Rose the aviatrix avoiding the Bermuda Triangle à la Amelia Earhart—Rose has led an adventurous but *expensive* life. Paralleling the Picassos, Degases, and Monets she brought into her stateroom earlier in the film, these are pictures of a life only slightly less privileged than the one she gave up.

And it is at the end of this idiosyncratic but nevertheless lush life that Rose throws away the Heart of the Ocean. Tossing away the necklace is, it seems to me, a slap in the face to Jack's memory and yet, oddly enough, also an aspect of the film's popularity.[34] Sure, sure, the necklace is contraband, the insurance company would be on her in a minute, and legal hijinks would ensue. But in her final impish gesture, she is not acting like Rose or even like Jack. She is acting like Cameron. Rose's ultimately wasteful gesture of throwing away the diamond (and luxury is nothing if not about waste) may be very expensive ideologically, but to the audience it only costs the price of a movie ticket. Pretty economical. Given how much Cameron has spent on the film (a fact which virtually every audience member would have known), and given that the final act of narrative closure is one in which Rose performs an act of waste that is only the prerogative of the very, very rich, the audience is, for a very small fee, made momentary shareholders in this upper-class ethos, while still being allowed the moral high ground of those in steerage.

The Blockbuster as Virtual History

Capping any understanding of *Titanic*'s popularity vis-à-vis Cameron's status as a blockbuster auteur must be the way in which Cameron uses the magnitude of the blockbuster to reinforce the magnitude of History and therefore the rock-solid reality of his version of events in *Titanic*. That is, in *Titanic* he has solidified the conventions of what might best be termed the Blockbuster Historical Paradigm. I want to bring us back to the rather obvious point that, dovetailing with the spectacle of the *Titanic* going down, is the fact that the *Titanic* really went down one night a long time ago. Which is to say that one reason *Titanic* may have been more of a surefire winner than the press originally made it out to be before all the money started rolling in is that it has come to its audience as *virtual history*. Virtual history, a uniquely postmodern entity, in which a presentation of past events comes to the viewer so loaded with detail that there can be no refuting it, seems to take the place of historical discourse. This is partly because of the realist aesthetic that has long been endemic to mainstream narrative cinema, and partly because of certain attendant ideological values and effects of historical narrative—the accretion of facts as a way to "prove" that something (history) happened.

Indeed, cinema's capability to represent mimetically and kinetically leads to what historian Robert Rosenstone calls film's slide into "false historicity."

> [This] myth of facticity, a mode on which Hollywood has long depended . . . is the mistaken notion that mimesis is all, that history is in fact no more than a "period look," that things themselves *are* history, rather than *become* history because of what they mean to a people of a particular time and place. The baleful Hollywood corollary: as long as you get the look right, you may do whatever you want to the past to make it more interesting.[35]

In this, *Titanic* is a particularly intense instantiation of this false historicity. The obsessive rendering of *accurate* detail that is the aesthetic hallmark of *Titanic* is not so far removed from that of classical history painting and shares with that tradition of cultural production many of the same ideological traps. This amounts to a piling on of seemingly "authentic" details that distract from the potential unreality of the larger ideological or historical framework of the narrative. This tautology is supported by what Roland Barthes termed the "reality effect."[36] Art historian Linda Nochlin had applied Barthes's notion to certain trends in eighteenth- and nineteenth-century French Academic painting, concluding that

> such details, supposedly there to denote the real directly, are actually there simply to signify its presence in the work as a whole. As Barthes points out, the major function of gratuitous, accurate details like these is to announce "we are the real." They are the signifiers of the category of the real, there to give credibility to the "realness" of the work as a whole, to authenticate the total visual field as a simple, artless reflection.[37]

Though she refers to Orientalist painting, in which the West constructs an imaginary and disempowered version of the East, Nochlin's claims apply just as well to *Titanic*, and with little alteration.

This virtual history opposes itself to a more contentious and radically postmodern version of cinematic historicization, in which the facts are not simply strung together like beads but are also reflexively contested, or, at any rate, lead to such contestation, debate, and discussion around the film. There is such historical discourse at work in contemporary cinema: *JFK* (1991), *Malcolm X* (1992), and *Schindler's List* (1993) have all provoked extensive public discourse both in the media and in people's "real lives." *Titanic*, even more than the equally detail-oriented and accuracy-focused but far less expensive *Dances with Wolves* (1990)—a film that was also proportionately far more profitable—seeks to wash the viewer in the well-tested formula of Academic painting:

obsessive detail + grand emotion = ideological stupefaction

The formula still works. *Titanic*'s narrative and visual coding are weighted down with an apparently never-ending succession of accurate details, and this has the paradoxical effect of buoying up spectators, allowing them to float with ease through an experience without any attendant historical anxiety. When this lack of anxiety is enhanced by emotional catharsis on an epic scale, it is particularly easy to sway an audience to a particular ideological position, since they have no idea that any ideological argument is being made at all.

The ease with which *Titanic*'s ideological arguments can be made also has to do with the particular way the event has already been configured as history. Unlike, say, Vietnam, the sinking of the *Titanic* was not the kind of national trauma that has dogged the nation and preoccupied the culture ever since it happened. On the contrary, it has, I think, become rather fuzzy in the national memory, not unlike the Johnstown Flood or the crash of the Hindenburg. This very fuzziness, this lack of either direct identity-based connection (e.g., Jews and the Holocaust) or iconicity (e.g., the image of the naked little girl running from a napalm attack and Vietnam), allows for a profound conflation between historical recognition and emotional response. This conflation goes quite a distance in explaining the intense connection audiences have had to *Titanic*, the fictional narration of an event that was tragic, to be sure, but not globally, culturally, socially traumatic.[38] Yes, as Cameron opined in his screenplay, the sinking of the *Titanic* "signaled the end of the age of innocence, the gilded Edwardian age, where science would allow us to master the world." Cameron, it would seem, is trying to master it still, and this extends to his implicit notions about history, notions which run directly, explicitly counter to those articulated by Oliver Stone in *JFK*.

Stone's own approach to history is certainly provocative, even when he is not agitating, as he is here.

> What is history? Some people say it's a bunch of gossip made up by soldiers who passed it around a campfire. They say such and such happened. They create, they make it bigger, they make it better. I knew guys in combat who made up shit. I'm sure the cowboys did the same. The nature of human beings is that they exaggerate. So, what is history? Who the fuck knows?[39]

Cameron, on the other hand, is not only antirevisionist but, apparently, anti-interpretation.

> Stone has an interesting philosophy. His view is that history is so fucked up, it's a consensus hallucination. So he will create an equal but opposite untruth to try to counteract the untruth that we live with. It's a bullshit theory. I think if you just do what's fuckin' right and accurate to the best of your knowledge, it will ring true.[40]

At least they can agree that any discussion of the idea of History must include the word "fuck."

What Stone would call interpretation, Cameron deems untruth. Moreover, doing what's "right and accurate" appears to be perilously free from morality, ethics, and ideology. For Cameron to get the facts of the ship correct, down to the last detail, means—to him—that whatever ideological structure falls out will also be right, accurate, and, one assumes, natural, organic to both the ship and the narrative. Cameron's is, then, the quintessential blockbuster approach to history. Do I mean to suggest that less accuracy is better? Certainly not, but in the case of *Titanic*, the facts that present themselves as facts are paradoxically always already interpreted, and at the same time not in need of interpretation.

Cameron's particular approach to history in *Titanic* is the culmination of the way he sees things. Cameron prefers to look at things in a particular way. His outlook is distinct. And this manifests itself quite literally. Among the many other important tropes of a Cameron film, including the skewed feminism and the stunning, never-before-been-done technological innovation, perhaps the most crucial, both in terms of *Titanic*'s consistency in the work of the director and in terms of its success, is the notion of prosthetic vision and its implications. Cameron has never made a film without prosthetic vision. *Titanic* is no exception, and here, where it is least obvious, it might be most important. For in *Titanic*, Cameron's use of prosthetic vision manifests what Robert Burgoyne and Alison Landsburg call "prosthetic memory." Prosthetic memory, writes Burgoyne, "describe[s] the way mass cultural technologies of memory enable individuals to experience, as if they were memories, events through which they themselves did not live."[41] Burgoyne singles out *Forrest Gump* (1994, another atypical blockbuster on the order of *Titanic*) as a film that uses prosthetic memory to create a false history of the 1960s in which the personal drama of Forrest Gump replaces the turmoil, pain, and social effect of everything from the Vietnam War and its protests to the string of assassinations from John F. Kennedy to Malcolm X. The implications of *Titanic*'s prosthetic memory may be less dire, simply because the event itself does not have the import of "the Sixties." But the note it strikes is no less false and may be even more so since it is part of a larger aesthetic tradition presented under the sign of Cameron.[42]

In *The Terminator*, we are presented early on with the now famous red field of Schwarzenegger's cyborg vision. All visual information is mediated, and text breaks the world down into data—animal, vegetable, mineral, terminal. This method of negotiating the world visually is distinctly nonhuman, distinctly technological. In *Aliens*, Ripley sees a great deal of the initial marine incursion on a number of video screens, which transmit what each soldier sees (as well as the vital signs of each—*Terminator* redux) as she sits safely inside a protective vehicle. Cameron specifically aligns her view with that of Corporal Hicks's camera, with whom she will later form something of a couple. In *The Abyss*, in a direct precursor to *Titanic*, there are little video-camera-rovers that swim through the depths of the ocean, moving ahead of divers, a pair of scouting eyes through which Ed Harris and Mastrantonio see both the oceanscape and, at times, each other. In *Terminator 2*, the cybervision is back, but there is also a lengthy scene in which we observe Sarah Connor undergo some slightly sadistic psychiatric testing. Yet our vision is often mediated by a video screen, which highlights the clinical power and detachment of her doctor, but also shows us a pathos the doctor cannot see. In addition to all the high-tech, high-falutin' night sights befitting a secret agent's mission in *True Lies*, the *Terminator 2* video probe repeats itself as Schwarzenegger anonymously verbally tortures his own wife as he sits behind a two-way mirror. The audience often sees her through a video feed and the glass simultaneously, as well as on a television screen that abstracts her image to highlight heat-emitting areas—predictably, tears.

We can go further and include *Strange Days*, the script he wrote and produced for then-wife Kathryn Bigelow.[43] The film's premise revolves around the ability to "jack in," or plug other people's visual and sensory experiences, which have been stored on disc, directly into one's own brain, a kind of hyped-up virtual reality complete with snuff films.

In all of these films, this prosthetic vision simultaneously, and often paradoxically, both further distances the spectators by adding another layer of vision to the experience of watching a film, and brings them closer, by reminding them through this now-conventional coding that they are, in fact, engaged in the act of watching a movie.

This thematic of mediated vision reappears in *Titanic* as Brock Lovett, captain of the present-day dive crew, cynically delivers a dramatic, made-for-the-Discovery Channel narrative to accompany the roving camera's investigations into the ship. But prosthetic vision in *Titanic* is not just the technological; it is the historiographic as well. The visual aid technologies embodied by the underwater *Mir* exploration crafts—which lead the crew (remaining safe and dry inside their submersible) to the safe in which lies the drawing of young Rose—move the crew (and the spectators) not only between viewing paradigms but also between two eras. And this, too, is utterly typical of Cameron.

Why? Well, for one thing, with the exception of *Aliens*, all these films take place in the present, and *Titanic* is no exception. Cameron, whatever else he is, is not a modernist, nor even simply a postmodernist. He is *presentist*, and this is especially evident in *Titanic*, his single period piece, his one and only foray into history and the past. As *New Yorker* critic Anthony Lane pointed out in his review of *Titanic*, the film about a sinking ship was actually more like the two *Terminator* films than it was a "fresh departure" from them, because in all three, Cameron is "obsessed by the bending and shaping of time."[44] And this obsession with time becomes, in the case of *Titanic*, an obsession with history.

Cameron's obsession with history in *Titanic* brings us back to the status of both film and director as participating in the more conservative strain of postmodern cultural production. As historian Patricia Nelson Limerick has suggested, "Each age writes the history of the past anew with reference to the conditions uppermost in its own time."[45] What marks postmodern historicism, including that performed under the sign of cinema, is a consciousness of these conditions as factors in the shape of discourse. Although every age before this one wrote in reference to its own circumstances, it did not do so with such a clear knowledge of the intimate relation between *what* the history was, *for whom* the history was produced, and *whom* it served to produce it in that particular way. I certainly do not wish to suggest that historical discourse and historiography have never before had any element of self-consciousness at all—Herodotus and Thucydides are nothing if not aware of their own status as historians, as different as the implications of that term might have been at the time. Simply by debating the conditions of postmodernism, and by agreeing, despite disagreements over the utility of postmodernity, on the modes attributable to and provoked by it, and the implications for social and cultural futures (both local and global), we acknowledge that this *episteme* differs from what preceded it. It need not be hyperbolically claimed that postmodernism and postmodern forms of historical discourse are marked by a break from modernist modes, or premodernist modes, or any modes at all. Rather, certain traits, tendencies, models, paradigms, and methods, which may long have existed, are simply becoming dominant or prevalent *in proportion* and *in relation* to other traits, tendencies, and so on. It is dangerous to claim uniqueness, even (especially) in the context of the "nothing-new-under-the-sun" mood that is one of the markers of the late twentieth century. Postmodern historiography, then, is distinct from, but continuous with, previous historical modes. It is distinct not so much in its difference but in how it achieves its ends through its means in a context that has shifted markedly since the end of World War II and, in a more accelerated way, since 1968.

But in Cameron's case, I want to suggest, it is not so much a question of a heightened consciousness in telling history or a revisionist desire to critique it. Rather, it is a nearly rabid desire to *own* history, which Cameron wants to reinvest with that capital "H." In so doing, Cameron is far more like the invidious Cal Hockley, whose desire to own Rose not only made him a capitalist pig, but also reduced her to an allegorical figure (not altogether progressive or feminist in the context of the film), and far less like his hero Jack Dawson, whom he has been so reviled for quoting during one of his many Oscar acceptance speeches.[46] When Cameron makes ownership claims on history, his desire to be "King of the World" is not about identifying with his young, beautiful, and doomed working-class artiste, nor even the object of Jack's affections. It is about having his masses and putting one over on them too. This should not suggest, however, that audiences mindlessly cottoned to *Titanic* like lambs to the slaughter. Rather, it seems perfectly plausible that the film's popularity stems in part from an audience identification with Cameron himself and a desire by some of the viewing public to own history as well.

This is a partial indication of how blockbusters and the people who make them are some of the staunchest significations of the complexity of postmodernism. Where high- and low-art barriers are broken down, the relation between capital and culture can become simultaneously transparent and altogether invisible. Both happen in *Titanic*. Blockbuster films, or "event movies," such as *Titanic* are no different from the rest of blockbuster culture in this respect: these cultural "events" take the place of historical events. They aspire to become history not by doing anything but by appearing, or passing, as history. And in this they are exemplary postmodern simulacra. The claim to be the event comes before the event itself and, thus designated, becomes the event (in attendance, ticket sales, expense, profit, merchandise, consumer ethos). It does not become history, as it pretends; it replaces history. One of the great ironies of *Titanic* and its extraordinary global popularity is that the actual sinking of this ship today would probably be a smaller blip on the historical radar screen than the film about it has been.

Notes

1. That is indeed the running time that was printed in most of the papers I saw from New York to San Francisco, reflecting the studios' consensus that most Americans would be scared off if they saw a three-hour viewing experience in front of them. Short Attention Span Theater indeed.
2. So the loss of life that would have incurred if *Titanic* sank at the box office would probably have been limited to James Cameron swan-diving off the Twentieth Century Fox building in Studio City, but the loss of *livelihood* associated with the bankrupting of two major studios was another drama entirely. Somewhat mimetic of the *Titanic* disaster itself, the studio executives would get their golden parachutes, and the grips and gaffers would be left looking at the holes in their socks.
3. Cameron's obvious self-consciousness as an auteur (real or pretend) is evident in *Titanic* from the get-go. In an early, sepia-toned, silent cinema–style scene, Cameron appears, Hitchcock-like, as a filmmaker turning the crank of his camera, quietly documenting the embarkation proceedings.
4. See, for example, Linda Hutcheon, *The Politics of Postmodernism* (New York: Routledge, 1989); Hal Foster, ed., *The Anti-Aesthetic: Essays on Postmodern Culture* (Port Townsend, Wash.: Bay Press, 1983); Fredric Jameson, *Postmodernism, or, the Cultural Logic of Late Capitalism* (Durham, N.C.: Duke University Press, 1991).
5. Guy Debord, *Society of the Spectacle* (Paris: Rebel Press, Aim Publications, 1987), paragraph 13. Originally published as *La Société du spectacle* (Paris: Editions Buchet-Chastel, 1967).
6. Thomas Schatz, "The New Hollywood," in *Film Theory Goes to the Movies*, ed. Jim Collins, Hilary Radner, and Ava Preacher Collins (New York: Routledge, 1993), 9–10. While sometimes numbers driven to the exclusion of larger social phenomena, Schatz's account of the blockbuster film is nevertheless exemplary.
7. Doubtless the folks on Madison Avenue tried just the same. Maybe they abandoned their efforts when they realized that nobody would want to supersize their Coke at McDonald's when that would mean getting an even bigger picture of the frozen Jack Dawson on the cup.
8. Anne Thompson, "Cameron's Way," *Premiere*, August 1997, 63–64, 110.
9. John H. Richardson, "Magnificent Obsession," *Premiere*, December 1997, 125.
10. Ibid., 128.
11. Anne Thompson, "Cameron Is God," *Premiere*, April 1998, 44.
12. Benjamin Svetkey, "In the Wake of *Titanic*," *Entertainment Weekly* at http://www.ew.com/features/ 980206/titanic/index.html.
13. Andrew Essex, "Summer . . . What a Bummer," *Entertainment Weekly*, 24 July 1998, 22.
14. Ibid., 23.

15. One may, in fact, pair the success of *Titanic* with any number of failures for slightly different reasons: *The Postman* (1997) not only because it was one of the biggest bombs of all time, but also because it was the bomb of the year the same year that *Titanic* set sail; *Cutthroat Island* (1995) because it really is the biggest bomb of all time, losing about $100 million.

16. We appear, at least in film culture, to be experiencing a second generation of post-modernism. If *Blade Runner* (1982) was both praised and lamented for its postmodern aesthetic—one that drew from a myriad of cultural and historical references apparently (and this I question) without any regard for actual history—films like Luc Besson's *The Fifth Element* (1997) take it one step farther, constructing themselves intertextually through intertextual references to films (like *Blade Runner*) that are themselves almost wholly intertextual.

17. Simon Brennan, et al. "Noble Failures," *Premiere*, August 1998, 80–87.

18. Tim Purtell, "They Were the Bomb," *Entertainment Weekly*, 15 May 1998, 115–116.

19. Schatz, "The New Hollywood," 19.

20. In the kind of do-si-do now perfectly familiar to anyone who knows anything about Cameron's private life, Cameron's marriage to *Terminator* star Linda Hamilton ended as the result of his affair with *Titanic* co-star Suzy Amis.

21. Edward Jay Epstein, "Annals of Commerce: Multiplexities," *New Yorker*, 13 July 1998, 37.

22. For a concise and myth-busting account of George Lucas's very canny approach to cre-ating a Star Wars consumer ethos, see M. Pye and L. Miles, "Cashing in on *Star Wars*," *Atlantic Monthly*, March 1979, 47–54.

23. David Walsh, "*Titanic* as a Social Phenomenon," World Socialist Web Site, presented by the International Committee of the Fourth International (www.wsws.org/arts/1998/feb1998/titanic.shtml), 25 February 1998.

24. "The movie itself" carries with it notions of purity and autonomy that don't actually extend to *Titanic*. For the idea of the blockbuster also carries in it, for the cultural in-telligentsia, insinuations of corruption and bastardization. A blockbuster show of Monet may bring Monet to the people, but those ties certainly are not in the spirit of cultural enlightenment.

25. Guy Debord, *Society of the Spectacle*, paragraph 34.

26. Peter Wollen, *Signs and Meaning in the Cinema* (Bloomington: Indiana University Press, 1969).

27. Rick Altman, "A Semantic/Syntactic Approach to Film Genre," in *Film Genre Reader*, ed. Barry Keith Grant (Austin: University of Texas Press, 1986), 33.

28. Katha Pollitt, "Women and Children First," *Nation*, 30 March 1998, 9.

29. Ibid. There is something to be said for the death of Jack as the site of pleasure for many teenage girls. Not only do they get to experience the joys of young love and romance writ large, they also have the far more illicit and subversive catharsis of watching the boyfriend, whom they know will ultimately cease to be that perfect, die. As Lucia Bozzola has put it to me, "One day Jack Dawson was going to sketch the wrong one-legged hooker, and it was all going to be over anyway." These younger female specta-tors therefore get the enjoyment of vengeance without the pain of betrayal. So the repeat viewings also have to do with the desire to repeat the pleasure of witnessing Jack's death.

30. Here it is hard to see how Walsh can discount the incontrovertible advances in special effects, or the beautiful fades between the wreck of the ship and its former glory, or even the very Eisensteinian shots of plates crashing out of their cupboards in slow

motion, or the surreal presentation of perfectly set dinner places floating on the watery surface where the table used to be. But just as the unprecedented breadth of *Titanic's* success has led to an acknowledgment of fans who were previously unconsidered, it has led, for better or worse, to a widened critical discourse, an expanded critical base which it would be equally unwise to ignore.

31. Walsh, World Socialist Web Site.

32. Ibid.

33. Snaps for Cameron at least on this: he has never cast a typically beautiful female star in any of his films. Linda Hamilton, Sigourney Weaver, Mary Elizabeth Mastrantonio, Jamie Lee Curtis, and Kate Winslet are, in a variety of ways, gratifyingly wide of the mark of what audiences seem to want in their Hollywood femininity—young, or recut and liposuctioned to look it, buxom, and yet rail thin everywhere else, delicately bobbed nose, and blond, blond, blond.

34. I will not take this kind of what-iffing any farther. Too many Titaniacs have done it more vividly than I ever could. Still, a good friend of mine insists that somewhere in Cameron's unused footage is a shot of the necklace sinking to the ocean floor and landing—plop!—next to the pair of handcuffs Jack wore.

35. Robert Rosenstone, *Visions of the Past: The Challenge of Film to Our Idea of History* (Cambridge: Harvard University Press, 1996), 60.

36. Roland Barthes, "L'effet de réel," in *Littérature et réalité*, ed. Gerard Genette and Tsvetan Todorov (Paris: Editions du Seuil, 1982), 81–90.

37. Linda Nochlin, "The Imaginary Orient," *Art in America*, May 1983, 123.

38. Assuming, just for the sake of argument, that the sinking of the *Titanic* really is seen as a global trauma, it is only a testament to the power of Euro-American capitalism and culture to claim such universality. Something like the 1998 tsunami in Papua New Guinea, in which whole villages were wiped out, dwarfing the death toll of the *Titanic*, will no doubt be (has been) swiftly forgotten in the West, while those in the South Pacific will be reminded of the *Titanic* for years to come.

39. *Esquire*, November 1991, 93, quoted in Hayden White, "The Modernist Event," in *The Persistence of History*, ed. Vivian Sobchack (New York: Routledge, 1996), 37.

40. Quoted in Richardson, "Magnificent Obsession," 130.

41. Robert Burgoyne, *Film Nation: Hollywood Looks at U.S. History* (Minneapolis: University of Minnesota Press, 1997), 105. See also Alison Landsburg, "Prosthetic Memory: *Total Recall* and *Blade Runner*," *Body and Society* 3–4 (1995).

42. Indeed, in *Titanic*, Cameron seems to equate memory, even a fictitious one, with experience. As Cameron stand-in Brock Lovett's contemporary ocean explorer asks the older Rose in an early scene, "Are you ready to go back to *Titanic*?" The idea that to remember is equal to going back certainly has implications for the video release of the film.

43. Musing on his four wives, three of whom have achieved fame in the movie industry, we must retool that old adage to say that, in Cameron's case, behind every great man there are several great women.

44. Anthony Lane, "The Shipping News: *Titanic* Raises the Stakes of the Spectacular," *New Yorker*, 15 December 1997, 156–157.

45. Patricia Nelson Limerick, "Turnerians All," *American Historical Review* 100 (June 1995): 708.

46. It is a testament to the power of image over text in *Titanic*, as well as to the weakness of Cameron's script, that most people did not seem to know he was quoting his own film on that night to remember.

Heart of the Ocean

DIAMONDS AND DEMOCRATIC DESIRE
IN *TITANIC*

ADRIENNE MUNICH AND MAURA SPIEGEL

*I*n the penultimate scene of *Titanic*, the centenarian Rose slips out onto the deck of the *Keldysh* research vessel late at night, clothed only in a white nightgown, brushed nostalgically by those same ocean breezes that, eighty-four years earlier, wafted her dress when Jack Dawson, her drowned lover, encircled her in his arms. Climbing delicately onto the stern railing, she opens her hand to reveal a secret, her possession of the precious diamond, Heart of the Ocean, the object of this high-tech salvage expedition. Audiences invariably gasp as she confidently lets the gem go and watches it sink silently into the watery depths.

Since everything in the highly self-conscious *Titanic* is intended to excite, dazzle, or in some way gratify the audience, we look for the strategy behind this gesture that appears commonly (if superficially) to disgruntle viewers for its profligacy. It is no overstatement to claim the diamond's centrality in the film's symbolic system. This unifying object changes in meaning as the object itself passes through different levels of the film's plotting. It is first the primary object of Brock Lovett's treasure hunt, then the prized possession of industrialist Cal Hockley, and then a sentimental reminder of Rose Bukater's liberating love for Jack Dawson. Not only does the Heart of the Ocean carry the movie's ostensible message about proper and improper relations to wealth and property, and even to life itself, but it also embodies its thematic of secrets, memory, access to the past, and the female heart. Like the fetish it is, the diamond's commodity and symbolic value signifies even beyond the movie's plot, extending to lived reality, as the movie interacts with history, with movie history, with the media, and with the audience and its desires.

Titanic's phenomenal popularity rests in large part on its epic embodiment of a quintessential American dream, a dream saturated with desire as well as aspiration.

As Hollywood films have traditionally done, *Titanic* gratifies a magnetic attraction to wealth while appealing to higher American values, exposing the poverty of riches and honoring the *important* fulfillments, those particularly created by and accessible to the middle classes. The movie uses an excessive gem as a shifting symbol that ultimately represents what in this essay we call "democratic desire."

Democratic desire in various ways is pitted against cruel capitalism and masculine hubris. Individual fulfillment and survival become a woman's story, filled with nostalgia and, in place of a survivor's guilt, the obligation to live life to the fullest. Substituting a nostalgia about notions of masculine chivalry (good, knightly men sacrifice their lives for women and children and love) for other kinds of feminine liberation, the movie gives us the diamond, which initially represents cold, unfeeling possession, and transforms it in the course of three hours to a relic of love, a priceless object of sentimental value alone.

From the first moments of the film, we inhabit the world of the diamond, which at the outset is the world of the sea. Following sepia images of the ship's sailing, we see a screen of solid color, deep sparkling blue, as of a screen-wide diamond, and only gradually do we realize that we are underwater, looking up at the searching headlights of submersibles that descend to the *Titanic* on the ocean's floor. The entire visual field thus signals the diamond, a brilliant reversal, for, rather than the diamond symbolizing the ocean, the ocean symbolizes the diamond. Actual technology and a real ship provide the entry into the movie's symbolic system.

The flashback to the crowded dock takes us right to the heart of the early twentieth-century class system and into the world of white America's subject formation. The class struggle as well as the American success story are depicted spatially within the ship, whose passengers include immigrants departing for the United States, along with those who have achieved material success. In sailing on the "ship of dreams," the European poor are seeking to throw off their class chains. While the audience watches, the film constructs us as desiring, democratic subjects: we, the viewers, joined in a more perfect union.

Those relatively few whose ancestors could have inhabited the upper deck can take pride in their lineage, while the majority, whose ancestors filled steerage, can glory in what their forebears endured and what they in turn have become. All can feel confident of having gone beyond the class strictures in which classes know their place, to create a democratic society where wealth and position exist as possibilities "for all." A new kind of desire in the movie's terms, democratic desire, emerges with the creation of a "classless society" that believes in the attainability of its desire.

In democratic desire, the film's ideal honors a classnessness that nevertheless depends on a melodramatic structuring of class, where the rich by and large stand for callous materialism, exploitation, yet utter dependence on the lower orders and on women as signs of their own superiority.[1] Having more warmth, generosity, and sexuality, lower classes and women can transmit enduring values to the upper classes, whose "good" women, in serving the patriarchal system, dampen their elemental fire. Their training enslaves them to their wealth and privilege. All

"Heart of the Ocean"™ Necklace.

75 carats.
The Hope Diamond
is only 45.

Exact replica of astonishing heart-shaped pendant necklace worn by Rose De Witt Bukater (as portrayed by Kate Winslet), and lost at sea, in the movie "Titanic."

Length: 18 inches. Comprised of 84 brilliant faux diamonds linked together in precious platinum-like rhodium-plate settings.

Fairly enormous heart-shaped blue faux 75-carat diamond solitaire, encircled by a single row of faux diamonds, is detachable, enabling necklace to be worn alone *sans* large solitaire, when mood so dictates.

"Heart of the Ocean" Necklace (Nº. HRT10322). Note: Authorized replica with a certificate from Twentieth Century Fox. Hinged presentation box. Price: $198. (The original necklace: $3+ million.)

Deferred Billing. No payment 'til June 1, 1998 if you order now.

The Heart of the Ocean: On Kate and on sale. J. Peterman Company *Owner's Manual* no. 68, fall 1998.

these components in *Titanic* are embodied in the enormous deep-blue diamond, in its transformation from cold and "malevolent" symbol of capitalist patriarchy to glittering souvenir of Rose's erotic awakening, and ultimately to an (eroticized) symbol of American fulfillment.[2] The longest and most flattering shot of the diamond is given to us in the seconds before Rose drops it into the water, and once it is submerged, it is shot from below, radiating a light from its center. At the beginning of the movie, we look into the heart of the diamond. At its end, we gaze into democratic desire.

The diamond's final descent into the depths spatializes the diamond's social line of descent from European royalty to a middle-class woman with a rebellious spirit, and even the jewel's movement out of the filmic frame into lived reality. In its design, the rare gem resembles the Hope Diamond, the most famous diamond in the United States. Like the Hope, the *Titanic* diamond is surrounded by white diamonds and is suspended from a necklace containing about sixty more diamonds, all set in platinum. The rich industrialist Cal gives its history (as had Brock earlier), specifically linking it to the Hope. According to him, the Heart of the Ocean was once part of the great French Blue (a part of the French crown jewels). The real French Blue weighed 67 1/2 carats when it was stolen in 1792. This lineage is also associated with the Hope Diamond, which is believed to have been cut from the French Blue. What might have been part of the French diamond surfaced in London, the earliest documentable date being 1813. It weighed 45 1/2 carats and fits the description of the gem known as the Hope Diamond, which now rests in glory in the Hall of Gems at the Smithsonian Institution in Washington, D.C.[3]

When he presents the diamond to his fiancée, Rose, Cal endows his diamond's lineage more certainty than in fact is possible, for no diamond carries a "gemogram" giving its parentage. It bears no sign of its origins. For the democratic purposes of *Titanic*, however, the Heart of the Ocean must descend from royalty, from kings in fact. In ending his legend of the diamond, Cal grasps the scepter of modern royalty: "It's for royalty. We are royalty, Rose." Royalty, that is, power and money, have moved to the United States, where, according to Cal, "men make their own luck."

Cal assumes his title when he buys the diamond and rightly names the passing of royalty to the American rich. Historically, the transfer of royalty to American democracy was dramatized in the auction of the French crown jewels in 1871, when Tiffany bought up most of the treasure, signaling that America and Americans were going to be the diamond buyers of the future. In 1901, Hope, a titled Englishman in debt, sold the diamond to an American firm, Joseph Frankel's Sons.[4] In 1909, three years before Cal buys the Heart of the Ocean, Cartier opened a branch in New York City.

The Hope diamond is the keystone of what passes as America's crown jewels and royal treasury, the gem collection in the Smithsonian Institution, the repository of national history. Since the Hope diamond first arrived there in 1958 as a gift of Harry Winston, Inc., it has been the Smithsonian's major public attraction. According to the curator of the gem collection, "They come in such numbers that, in the peak of the tourist season, the crowds far exceed the capacity of the room in which the diamond is kept."[5] A new hall of gems was opened in 1998 to accommodate the crowds. Hordes of Americans who view the Hope bear a somewhat different relation to it than do Europeans who view the crown jewels of their nations' treasuries. Although they share a fascination with extraordinarily large or unique gems, coming simply to stare at relatively small objects of disproportionate worth, they differ in their symbolic access to them. For if a subject of England, say, views the Koh-I-Nor diamond in its setting of a royal crown, he or she recognizes either proud and national, or imperial subjection. But an American gazing upon the Hope sees an object of personal empowerment, of potential possession; he or she can (theoretically) attain a gem of such magnitude.

Winston wanted the United States to have a gem collection comparable to but surpassing the royal treasuries of Europe. As a canny salesman-promoter, Winston, who for security reasons never allowed his face to be photographed, fortified the image of diamonds in his lavish New York store, which he called a salon, and through extensive publicity about his clientele which included both European royalty and Hollywood stars. In contributing to an American gem collection with his extravagant gift of the Hope diamond, Winston sought to retain the gem's aura and prestige while making it commercially accessible to an expanded market. With the Hope diamond, the Smithsonian collection became not only a sign that the seat of power had switched from Europe to the United States, from a monarchy to a democracy, but also a sign that the great jewel commerce had switched from royal houses to rich Americans.

Within the logic of the film, however, Cal's purchase of the diamond does not represent a democratizing spirit, but rather a capitalist adoption of European-styled classism and exclusion, predicated on a wealth built upon exploitation (in pre-union steel manufacture), as well as a sense of ownership that derives its pleasures from the sustained consciousness of what others cannot have. Cal treasures Rose, like the diamond, as a commodity, traded to him by her mother. In the melodramatic triangle of Cal, Rose, and her mother, the diamond functions as a sign of the young woman's subordination within the upper-class system, where women function as signs of men's wealth and potency. Cal presents the diamond to Rose as a surprise, including her in his possession of the new world. But Rose does not assent to Cal's valuations; her response, "It's overwhelming," recalls to the viewer her cutting comment in an earlier scene regarding Freud's interpretation of the "male's preoccupation with size." Rose accepts the diamond, but it is the task of the plot to transform the diamond's meaning, to recast class and gender relations so that the diamond includes women and the nonrich in its democratic creed.

Despite Rose's efforts to resist the constricting plot into which she has been written (emphasized when her mother tightly laces her into a corset), signs suggest that Cal has had his way with her, that this maiden has lost her virginity on this maiden voyage before her love scene with Jack in the backseat of a car. Cal's sexual possession of Rose is suggested in the breakfast scene where he says, "I had hoped that you would come to me last night." In his violent eruption, he remarks, "You are my wife . . . in practice if not yet by law. So you will honor me, as a wife is required to honor her husband." Cal gives Rose the diamond following, presumably, their first night together, and following her subsequent melodramatic halfhearted suicide attempt. The diamond, which in an early version of the script Rose describes as "a dog collar," degrades her, drives home her position as purchased object.

Rose's rebellion finds its object in Jack, from whom she draws courage and a model of agency. As an embodiment of American liberty, Jack is multiply coded. As an artist he exists outside the class system, observing all classes and putting them in their place. He is a natural aristocrat who "cleans up like a new penny," according to Molly Brown, a knight whose chivalric code requires that he rescue the damsel in distress. He also knows how to play with the masses—cards, games, dances. But Jack, an orphan, is actually neither classless nor working-class; he emerges, the film suggests, from the solid middle class of the Middle West. Bohemia here is itself linked to the middle class and to upward mobility (consider in this light the reference to that unknown artist, "somebody Picasso"). Rose herself, in her old age, has traded the jewels of the elite for "arty" Native American handcrafted silver and semiprecious stones. We first encounter her as the camera focuses on her hands working a piece of clay; as the camera tracks back, she is situated in a very comfortable house, a middle-class house where the television is aimlessly blaring, while her granddaughter, Lizzy, is busy at housework. A middle-class life, the movie tells us, *is* the creative life. The middle class in this film is the unmarked site of fulfillment; so thoroughly do its values saturate the film that they are naturalized, almost invisible. The large second class of the real *Titanic*'s passenger list disappears in the movie portrayal.

Following her mother's stern admonitions and Rose's pained relinquishment of Jack in the gymnasium, there is a scene in the dining room, where Rose focuses on a mother teaching an exquisitely dressed little girl of about seven or eight years how to sit without touching her chair back, how to place her napkin in her lap. This image of the construction of upper-class femininity drives Rose back to Jack, who stands alone at his symbolic perch at the prow of the ship, where he embodies the spirit of unencumbered youth and freedom, where the poor but talented man with a future is (as he anoints himself) "King of the World."

But Jack's form of liberty is not limited to vagabondage and a philosophy of making each day count. According to the film's (male) perspective, he is a feminist, a position he has arrived at through his art.[6] As an artist, he knows women; his drawing has taught him to see into their souls. He does not want to buy women diamonds; he wants them to own themselves. His drawing, "Madame Bijoux," a pensive woman of a certain age sitting at a table, alludes to such sympathetic views of the demimonde as Manet's *The Plum* and Degas's *L'Absinthe*. Jack gave her that name, he explains, because she sat "wearing every piece of jewelry she owned, waiting for her long-lost love. Her clothes were all moth-eaten." Madame Bijoux is Rose's antitype, while Jack's attitude toward her indicates that he finds her a curiosity, a static model, whose lost love stops her life. Her story poses an antinostalgic object lesson against Rose's future.

In the nude scene, where Jack draws Rose wearing only her diamond, the film sends out a number of messages regarding Rose's rebellion. It redraws Madame Bijoux, for Rose in odalisque pose as "Miss Jewel" wears nothing and eventually will wait for no one. The gesture plainly links her body and the diamond as Cal's possessions, in a contract that the eyes of another man will revoke. Additionally, she is taking the diamond out of Cal's system by turning it, for the moment, into an erotic adornment, which will forever be linked to Rose's sexual agency. The scene neatly reverses the logic of the male gaze, as Rose shifts her position from model to purchaser of the drawing. In addition, Rose is no passive receiver of the male gaze; she is the erotic subject of the scene, not only in control of events but explicitly aroused. Again, reversing gender roles, Rose remarks, "I believe you are blushing, Mister Big Artiste."

In the camera's remarkable treatment of Rose's eye at the close of this scene, where the camera moves into an extreme close-up of young Rose's deep blue iris, rests there for a significant moment, and emerges from old Rose's eye, we find a metonymic linkage of the diamond, the heroine, and the ocean itself, each containing impenetrable depths. Diamonds worn by women can suggest the perishability of feminine beauty as the vastness of the ocean refers to the perishability of human life. In this equation, Rose's old age signifies the ephemerality of memory (paradoxical because Rose's memory is "photographic") and the inevitable experience of loss. It is from this resonance that the movie's most poignant moments emerge, and hence the diamond falls into the sea. (Note that the blue eyes of both of the lovers are marked against the deadened brown of Cal's.)

These blue eyes of Rose's, the movie is intent upon reminding us, are our gateway to the past, to the glory of the *Titanic*, to its vivid and pulsing reality. The eyes, human and aging, are presented as the visual trope for the film itself, the re-creation through the human imagination, of the spectacle of the film. Cameron demands that we recognize a contrast between the high-tech research vessel and its benighted quest, and the grand and miraculous journey of the film, its vitality and passion in contrast to the "forensic" analysis of computer simulation. This titanic production began as a twinkle in Cameron's eye. The vanity of human endeavors might not have escaped Cameron himself. At that necessarily evanescent moment when he accepted the Academy Award for best director, Cameron quoted Jack's youthful illusory sense of power: "I am the King of the World." The pathos of his remark (particularly given artist Jack's fate) was universally lost when Cameron was castigated for his arrogance, while the press reporting on his comment did not bother to pick up the allusion.

The diamond trope, now firmly linked to a host of themes, is again expanded by old Rose's remark that "a woman's heart is an ocean of secrets." By the logic of the narrative, those to whom old Rose is speaking do not of course see what we see. The tiny tape recorder Brock switches on when Rose begins to tell the story makes a visual pun for the incredible feat of scale that the movie will achieve—as does the bowl of goldfish that Rose brings aboard the *Keldysh*. The audience, thus, possesses a grander vision, the epic vision of the movie. As the audience peeps through the tiny porthole of Rose's eye to the grand spectacle, we are admitted to a secret—history's secret, the secret of the past. The ostensibly erased stories of Rose, Jack, and of the Heart of the Ocean are locked in that secret past. And, of course, by the logic of the film, the audience alone (all hundreds of millions of us) is brought into the secret of the diamond's final dispensation. In these multiple gestures the film both flatters the position of the viewer and valorizes itself as creative medium, separate and distinct from the technology and money upon which it depends. Jack's drawing of Rose was actually drawn by Cameron, and the hand we see making the sketch is his.

The contrast between cold technology and male economic pursuit, on the one hand, and the creative medium of film, the female spirit, and the realm of authentic experience, on the other, is further pursued in the film's framing narrative. The frame shows us the construction of better manhood (and better movies) through the transforming tale of the *Titanic* as recounted by a liberated woman. Brock's quest for the diamond is shown to be a sterile one. "It's payday boys," he says as he watches the robot take the safe. The camera finds his slow smile as he mutters, "Oh, baby, baby, baby," but there is no issue in this male-robot love affair. It is Rose who must teach these men the lesson of the *Titanic*, who must teach them how to cry. At the point of his enlightenment, Brock, the seeker for the sign of crass male materialism (a kind of late-twentieth-century, and hence more tractable, blue-eyed version of Cal), ruefully fondles and then discards a cigar he had planned to smoke once he had the diamond in hand. With its earlier allusion to Freud, and its scenes of the captains of capital smoking their cigars, the movie pursues its logic, that the male preoccupations with size, money, and life in general as competition (as the slimy director of the White Star Line says, size means "stability, luxury, and strength") are phantoms in the pursuit of personal fulfillment. After Rose finishes her story and the listeners cry, Brock says, "Three years I kept looking for *Titanic*, but I never got it. I never let it in." Without the irony of the formidable gross excesses of its cost overruns, this movie's message lands on the side of feeling over possession, of authentic—if fleeting—experience over technological simulation.

In contrast to the cynical, pseudodocumentary style of Brock's video-narration at the beginning of the film (called "bullshit" by him and his assistant), we have Rose's storytelling, which, in Cameron's hands, takes us into the depths of a woman's heart. The analogy is drawn between the healing, educative function of Rose's story on her listeners and that of the film's effects on us, the viewers, with Rose's as the voice-over reinforcing the female perspective on its truth. Spending unimaginable sums for vast profits, this movie claims to give us something that money cannot buy.

This message, that *Titanic* is far more than another Hollywood blockbuster, that it is an *experience*, is not really a new strategy in the history of film marketing. In this case, the film's promotion has included a very active development of what might be called "the director's myth." (A comparable example is that of the prominent circulation of Francis Ford Coppola's ravaging travails of his own personal war in the making of *Apocalypse Now* [1979].[7]) We learn the story of Cameron's having given up profit-percentages and his director's fee at the point where the film was in danger of being "cut off" by the studios. Cameron's sacrifice was made, we are to understand, in order to ensure the *authenticity* of the film (he would bridge no compromises to its verisimilitude), and in this gesture, he establishes a resonant continuity with the film's messages about seeking the authentic over and above mere profit.

Titanic's theme song delivers this message of transforming a hard diamond heart into pulsing human ones, its sentimentality asserting, "My Heart Will Go On." On one level, the song's Irish wailing tones perhaps honor the "fifteen thousand Irishmen who built this ship." (Reaching into present time and experience, at the end of the credits, in a telling parallel, the Mexican workers who constructed the *Titanic* model are named.) On another level, the song echoes the film's revision of a traditional plot of doomed but great love by asserting triumph over tragedy. Celine Dion, singing the song at the Academy Awards ceremony, wore Asprey London's real reproduction of the movie's paste Heart of the Ocean, actual gemstones moving the fetish into the marketplace.[8] In this epic, the commercial is not always separated from the love song of democratic liberation.

Titanic advances the long history of entertainment-as-simulated experience. Inching closer to the *real* in the *actual* footage of the *Titanic*, submerged and claimed by the ocean (while mocking, in Brock's monologue, the documentarist's false-earnestness, hinting that the *real* is not to be found in that film genre), in its much publicized verisimilitude, and in the you-were-there effects achieved with the help of computer graphics, this movie offers us a fresh impression of real make-believe. The narrative, as observed, problematizes the relation between what is true and what is merely accurate, between verisimilitude and authenticity, by thematizing modes of engagement with the past. But the film also problematizes the relation between reality and realism.

By the logic of the film, the diamond is part of *Titanic*'s fiction, and like the hero and heroine, it leaves no traces. It is plotted as part of the voyage's secret history, which is returned from the movie's *real*, at the movie's end, to the realm of imagination. Further complicating our experience of *Titanic*'s real make-believe is the constant slippage in the film between fact and fantasy, between reality and romance, history and legend. The movie gains untold force from *not* being a fantasy, not being a conventional disaster film; its romance plot rests firmly within the facts of history.

In presenting the authentic as real objects and real facts, but simultaneously suspending the very idea of authenticity, *Titanic* achieves an ontological status that is indeed postmodern. Advertisements in the *New York Times* sell reproductions of the newspaper from the day after the ship's sinking (separated by pages from ads for the film and for the Broadway show of the same name). The movie's frame and the selling of the 1912 newspaper create a time warp where one can inhabit both times at once.[9] Time is collapsed, where an actual object, the newspaper, can be held or seen, as in the scenes in the movie of the actual wreck.

Along with the movie's verisimilitude, serving an American fantasy of one's ability to have it all, the Heart of the Ocean, which began its existence as a piece of paste designed by Asprey London, travels not from the past to the present but from the fiction into the world, having been transformed into a real gem en route. Following the movie's spectacular success, Asprey London produced a *real* Heart

Inhabiting both times at once: The grave of *Titanic* victim J. Dawson filled with
bouquets from "Jack Dawson" mourners

of the Ocean. Because no blue diamond of that size (which in the film, at 56 carats, exceeds the size of even the Hope diamond) could be found, the real Heart of
the Ocean is now a sapphire, which the jewelers painstakingly located in Sri Lanka.
After resting on Celine Dion's bosom, the jewel was auctioned off for over $2 mil-
lion, the proceeds going for AIDS research, an example of the commercial and
philanthropic uses of Hollywood ideology. Ten other jewelers, according to Internet Web sites, offer replicas for sale.

Available for purchase through the J. Peterman catalog for considerably less
($198) is a "trade-marked" and "authorized" paste version of the original, which
comes "with a certificate from Twentieth Century Fox, in a hinged presentation
box."[10] The copy blurs the boundary between reality and film, *as if* the original,
real piece of jewelry, supposedly a real gem, were actually lost. The catalog thus
articulates democratic desire by replicating and selling what once was lost but now
is found. The people can reenact the scene of possession. J. Peterman, *lui meme*,
articulates the nostalgia inherent in democratic desire in his catalog philosophy:
"People want things that are hard to find. Things that have romance, but a factual
romance about them." Peterman knows about nostalgia, for he ends his catalog
"philosophy" thus: "Clearly, people want things that make their lives the way they
wish they were."[11]

Many in the film's audience, more materialistic and nostalgic than the heroine, cannot comprehend why she should throw the diamond into the sea and not
capitalize on its value, if only to dispense her fortune to philanthropic causes. As

we have shown, the diamond becomes the sign of her independence from her inherited value system, including the philanthropic role. But Rose's gesture, like most of her acts, alludes to other plots. An American epic, with an embedded love plot (like all classical epics), *Titanic*'s love plot alludes liberally to love stories, such as that of Dido and Aeneas, where one lover, conventionally the woman, dies so that the survivor can learn the lessons of life. In such legendary doomed medieval romances as that of Lancelot and Guinevere, Tristan and Isolde, even Abelard and Héloise, the woman belongs to a patriarchal figure (King Arthur, King Mark, Héloise's father). The tale contrasts that kind of power relation with the woman's desire to transgress the system itself, as represented by the subversive affair. In these stories, the deaths or punishments of the lovers traditionally restore patriarchal order.

In the American version, however, one eventually can have what is lost, and the new order is less patriarchal. Rose, the heroine, never loses Jack, for her entire life after the *Titanic* upholds his vision of her. The photographs old Rose brings aboard the *Keldysh* make this point explicit: Rose beside a plane (Jack's singing "Josephine and Her Flying Machine" into her ear before they first kiss); Rose on a horse, not sidesaddle, in front of a roller coaster (their conversation about the Los Angeles pier Jack used to frequent and his promise to teach her to ride horses and roller coasters); Rose with her family (his dying demand that she survive, have children, live long). The Heart of the Ocean speaks of the love that lasts beyond the grave.

Rose's flinging away her fabled diamond recalls the diamond plot in Alfred Tennyson's epic of Victorian England, *Idylls of the King*, a retelling of the Arthurian romance, with its pervasive allusions to the *Aeneid*'s theme of the founding of a new empire. The movie stands in a similar relationship to contemporary American culture as the poet laureate's work stands to the mid–nineteenth century, a similarly materialistic age. Large fortunes were being made by new groups of people, as in the 1990s. Tennyson's poem was written as a national allegory, using what had become a national myth in King Arthur. *Titanic*, too, takes what has become an American myth for its foundation. And although there is nothing in Tennyson's poem comparable to the plot or structure in *Titanic*, both scripts add to their given material—the Arthurian legend in the *Idylls*, and the historical event in *Titanic*—diamonds calculatedly tossed into the water to symbolize conflicts within cultural values.[12] Tennyson added the tournaments of diamonds to his Arthurian material, diamonds being a symbol of the key sexual relationship of his epic. The plot centers on Lancelot's adulterous love for King Arthur's wife, Guinevere, as the sign of national corruption.

Thinking that her knight has been untrue, Guinevere throws nine diamonds into the river. Throwing away the diamonds he has won for her constitutes her rejection of his adulterous love and ultimately her repentance and retreat into a nunnery. Tennyson uses the diamonds as a sign of desire at a time when diamonds were becoming more accessible to purchase by the increasingly wealthy middle class and when that class was consolidating its power. Hence the diamond functions as a signifying agent, not only of the content of the epic plot but of its cultural context. Large, perfect, and with an ancient pedigree, it has a brilliance that tantalizes Victorian readers, both to wonder at the womanly sensibility that could throw away such riches and to agree with the premise of renunciation of its symbol as degraded womanhood. At the same time, many a reader could aspire to owning and wearing the stones previously reserved for aristocracy.

The diamond in *Titanic* is a similar addition to the historical material, and it, too, points to a similar class formation where new people make unimaginable fortunes and look to display their riches in symbols of gross excess. Within the fashion system, jewels are the ultimate sign of that excess (democratized) wealth.[13] And like the Victorians with Guinevere, the *Titanic* audience sighs when Rose casts her diamond into the waters. Back it goes, back to her lover and back to its atavistic namesake. For in this rewriting of Guinevere's act, Rose has already renounced the debased, materialistic lover. She has already reclaimed the diamond for her own sign, her agency in life, which cannot, however, finally free its meaning from a conventional love plot. Her great love, who has authorized her agency, turned into a ghost, enabling her to choose life in the name of his bodiless spirit. Sailing beneath the Statue of Liberty, she renames herself "Rose Dawson." By taking on her spiritual husband's name, she enters into respectable idealized marriage, freeing herself from enslavement to the protocols of the rich, the well-born, and European-inflected mores. Thus, in Rose's hand, the diamond signifies her kind of freedom, her individuality, her independence—not only by having the diamond but by throwing it away.

In the closing images of the film, in Rose's dream, a dream of heaven, signified by the white light of eternity, we gaze up into the *Titanic's* gloriously restored white leaded-glass dome. The white light that fills the screen for the film's final frames recapitulates the opening by magnifying the searching headlights. Rose, dressed in white, swathed in colorless, pure diamonds, kisses her lover on the great sweeping staircase, where he waits for her in front of the clock. All the people of all classes who were lost on the *Titanic* gather in first class to witness the kiss and to beam their approval. The kiss lasts forever in that solid portrayal of eternity. Heaven, as in one version of millennial fundamentalism, is material. We are drawn up in our ideal bodies, perfect and bejeweled, to kiss our lovers, fondle our children, and adore each other. There is no class division, but all classes aspire to luxury. The ship's dome has become the celestial sphere, while the grand staircase to the first-class dining room has become the stairway to paradise. Heaven is the upper deck.

In a movie that plays upon an irony of the unsinkable ship and thus destroys the notion of permanence, the diamond stands for the irony of endless time, for whatever permanence can mean. As something more enduring than the steel ocean liner, than human life and memory, the blue diamond signifies the transformation of object into legend. It falls to its source, the heart of the ocean, only (like King Arthur) to return again. *Titanic's* diamond constructs democratic desire as obtainable both when we have it and when we give it up. And yet again when we can buy some form of it. The Heart of the Ocean replaces the bald eagle as a more enduring, less endangered American symbol of the people getting and keeping things that make their lives the way they wish they were. In a stunning rewriting of the advertising ploy that convinces Americans not to put their diamonds into free play as commodities,[14] for their meaning transcends commodity value, *Titanic*'s plot *and* its marketing of the diamond show that the democratic desire it signifies is forever.

Notes

1. For an explanation of the cultural meanings of cinematic melodrama as "the modern mode for constructing moral identity," see Jackie Byars, *All That Hollywood Allows* (Chapel Hill: University of North Carolina Press, 1991). On page 11, Byars writes: "Usurping the place of religious education, melodrama has operated since [the 1950s] as a site for struggles over deeply disturbing materials and fundamental values. Melodrama became for the Western world the ritual through which the social order is purged and sets of ethical imperatives are clarified."

2. The word "malevolent" appears in an early draft of Cameron's script, in the director's characterization of the first appearance of the gem.

3. In 1642, Jean Baptiste Tavernier bought a deep blue diamond weighing 112 3/16 carats, believed to have come from the Kollur Mine in Golconda in India. He sold it to Louis XIV, who had it cut in 1673. The newly cut stone was triangular (sometimes described as heart or drop shaped) and weighed 67 1/2 carats. It was then officially named the Blue Diamond of the Crown. See Susanne Steinem Patch, *Blue Mystery: The Story of the Hope Diamond* (Washington: The Smithsonian Institution, 1976), 33–34.

4. Patch, *Blue Mystery*, 36.

5. Ibid., introduction by Paul E. Desautels, curator, National Collection of Gems, 9.

6. First-wave feminism passed through the Left Bank before World War I, although Jack's brand of feminism is clearly second-wave American feminism, directed primarily at giving middle-class, mainly white women a voice.

7. "I sent a telex to Francis telling him that because I loved him, I would tell him what no one else was willing to say, that he was setting up his own Viet Nam with his supply lines of wine and steaks and air-conditioners, creating the very situation he went there to expose. That with his staff of hundreds of people carrying out his every request, he was turning into Kurtz—going too far." Eleanor Coppola, *Notes: On the Making of Apocalypse Now* (New York: Simon and Schuster, 1979), 177. For a thorough treatment of the film's reception and the status of the director's image, see Jon Lewis's *Whom God Wishes to Destroy: Francis Coppola and the New Hollywood* (Durham, N.C.: Duke University Press, 1995).

8. The tradition of stars borrowing jewels from Harry Winston, Paul Flato, Cartier, and other such firms dates back to the early years of the star system. Diamonds were lent not only for gala events, like the Academy Awards, but also for the movies themselves. Movie credits carried the jewelers' names prominently, making them familiar to moviegoers across the nation. Joan Crawford, Paulette Goddard, Claudette Colbert, and others posed for magazine ads for these firms, often wearing their own purchases. The use of real diamonds in the world of Hollywood make-believe was a consistent practice until the 1950s. See Maura Spiegel, "Hollywood Loves Diamonds," in *The Nature of Diamonds* (Cambridge: Cambridge University Press, 1997), 199–207.

9. In the Halifax cemetery where approximately one hundred *Titanic* dead are buried, the grave of one "J. Dawson" has become a shrine filled with bouquets from "Jack Dawson's" mourners.

10. The J. Peterman Company, *Owner's Manual*, no. 63 (summer 1998): 25+.
11. Ibid., 1.
12. Byars presents an argument that might explain the diamond addition in the two epics in terms of their melodramatic elements: "Using shared public symbols, this ritual that is melodrama resolves not crises of order but crises within order." See *All that Hollywood Allows*, 11.
13. Gilles Lipovetsky in *The Empire of Fashion* (Princeton: Princeton University Press, 1994) discusses the democratic process inherent in the fashion system. His idiosyncratic, highly suggestive argument has influenced the strategies in this essay.
14. Under the control of DeBeers, ordinary diamonds do not usually constitute an investment, for their original inflated cost usually exceeds their resale value. But if ordinary people regularly sold their diamonds for cash, they could flood the market and undermine the global price-fixing of the DeBeers cartel. See Edward Jay Epstein, *The Rise and Fall of Diamonds: The Shattering of a Brilliant Illusion* (New York: Simon and Schuster, 1982). In early modern Europe, famous jewels retained their commodity value. The Medicis, investors in great gems, had no compunction in selling them when they needed money. Gems, even those most treasured, were sold. Isabella D'Este's famed green diamond, made into a fabulous jewel by Cellini in the early sixteenth century, was sold when money was needed. Similarly, Eleanora of Toledo, who married Cosimo I de Medici, collected jewels of great value as an investment, not forever. Francis I of France established the tradition of securing jewels to the family and established the royal treasury. Most of the historical information above is from a lecture by Martha McCrory, "Dynasties and Diamonds: Court Jewelry of the Italian Renaissance," American Museum of Natural History, 24 November 1997.

Ship of Dreams

CROSS-CLASS ROMANCE AND THE CULTURAL FANTASY OF *TITANIC*

LAURIE OUELLETTE

Titanic is an epic, a love story, a special effects extravaganza; according to some critics, it is also a "subversive" commentary on American class politics. Calling *Titanic* "an exercise in class hatred that few European socialists would dare to display," the *Economist* speculated that with "Ronald Reagan no longer in the White House, wealth looks more vulnerable to criticism than a decade ago." The conservative *National Review* panned *Titanic* as "leftist propaganda," protesting its view of the rich as an unflattering caricature. Similar objections catapulted *Titanic* into the editorial pages of distinguished national newspapers. Commentators writing in the *Washington Post* charged director James Cameron with "kindergarten Marxism," and in another article, with celebrating a dangerous "vast leveling" of democracy where the "lowest common denominator is exalted, and anything that smacks of manners or intelligence is suspect." Not all high-level observers were so disturbed. Columnist Frank Rich of the *New York Times* equated *Titanic*'s popularity with a backlash against greed, warning modern-day robber barons to take note "how a tycoon's arrogance plays in the court of American opinion."[1]

The issue of class plays an important role in the *Titanic* phenomenon, but rather than triggering class consciousness or resistance, the film actually works in the *opposite* direction by mystifying the causes and continuities of inequalities. Cameron's claim that *Titanic* stops just "short of Marxist dogma" implies that the film critiques dominant class relations—and invites controversy in the process—but critique is safely focused on the snobbery of a few loathsome first-class characters.[2] Likewise, *Titanic* dramatizes vast socioeconomic disparities within the microcosm of an ill-fated ocean liner, but it presents the class structure of a bygone era as un-American and easily overcome by personal gumption and fairy-tale romance. *Titanic* encourages viewers to simultaneously enjoy and reject the special privileges of wealth and stature, as epitomized by the concluding dream sequence, where the ship's third-class passengers have joined their betters on the steps of the grand staircase to unanimously applaud the once forbidden love affair between Jack Dawson and Rose Bukater. At a time when the American middle class is growing smaller and the gap between haves and have-nots is growing wider, *Titanic's* romantic resolution of class may be pleasurable—but it is hardly subversive.

If commentary directed at an influential slice of the public equates the phenomenal success of *Titanic* with percolating class rebellion, promotion and publicity directed at moviegoers tells a different story. The best-selling *James Cameron's Titanic* coffee table book, the Twentieth Century Fox *Titanic* Web site, and the countless celebrity profiles, articles, and reviews generated by the film magnify the message that class is at once glamorous, temporary, superficial, and passé. Although the publicity and media commentary surrounding *Titanic* cannot tell us how actual viewers made sense of the film, it does offer a telling ideological framework for analyzing class as an important factor in the film's popularity.[3] As a complement to textual analysis, critical commentary, publicity, and promotional tie-ins (such as star interviews) implicated in selling the film can show us how a number of intersecting class mythologies were articulated by publicists, filmmakers, performers, and critics in their effort to define the "meaning" of *Titanic* for audiences.

My main argument is the following: while *Titanic* ostensibly addresses the class prejudice of the distant past, it also promotes the illusion that the United States is now a classless society—or what cultural critic Benjamin DeMott calls the "myth of the imperial middle."[4] As Elizabeth Traube argues, for Hollywood films to become commercially popular, they must penetrate "everyday thought" and negotiate the "socially-conditioned imaginative needs" of audiences.[5] Cross-class romance is not a new Hollywood theme, but *Titanic's* blockbuster success warrants special attention to how and why this narrative trope meets the current imaginative needs of a broad spectrum of audiences. I attribute *Titanic's* popularity to its ability to finesse the growing dissonance between myth and reality. Today, more than any point in recent history, socioeconomic trends and policies directly undermine the illusion of American classlessness. Corporate downsizing of white-collar workers, the dismantling of social welfare programs, "niche" marketing and a fragmentation of consumer culture, exclusive "gated" communities, and the exportation of living-wage manufacturing jobs overseas are among the factors that threaten not only the American dream of class mobility but also the once-taken-for-granted guarantee of middle-class security. By reconstructing and symbolically dismantling the steep class hierarchy of the Gilded Age, *Titanic* taps into a contemporary "structure of feeling," or a series of anxieties and resentments, that are lived and felt by many people but are not yet politically coherent.[6]

Titanic aligns a cross section of viewers with a promise of classless love, without questioning the capitalist forces working against equality, mobility, and middle-class security. It does so by constructing an "us versus them" opposition against boat-hogging villains who flaunt their vast fortunes and status markers and by displacing class relations onto romantic hurdles and victories. *Titanic* soothes the prospect of class polarization by inviting viewers to identify with love-struck characters who rise above, "upend," transcend, or renounce proscripted class lines, and by disassociating undue class privileges and prejudices from "Americanism." By unpacking the ideological intersection of class and romance, we can see how the *Titanic* phenomenon speaks to a range of class-related tensions, from economic want to cultural biases; from the displacement of postindustrial blue-collar labor to a white-collar middle-class "fear of falling."[7] These parallels need not be explicitly named (or even consciously recognized by viewers) to play an important role in *Titanic*'s cultural currency.

American Class Mythologies

Before we elaborate on *Titanic*, it is useful to consider the relationship between class and myth. In his illuminating critique of the denial of class in the United States, DeMott defines class as the "inherited accumulation of property, competencies, beliefs, tastes and manners that determines, for most of us, our socioeconomic lot in life and our share of civic power."[8] This definition mirrors sociologist Pierre Bourdieu's argument that in capitalist democracies, class power is reproduced by the uneven allocation of economic capital as well "cultural capital," or socially approved knowledges, competencies, tastes, manners, and intellectual dispositions acquired through family socialization and extended years of education.[9] Class is a "central organizing feature" of life under capitalism, but Americans—especially those on the wrong end of power relations—are encouraged to think otherwise.[10] As DeMott argues, Americans "can't think straight about class" because class differences are perpetually displaced, rationalized, or obscured by the illusion of *classlessness*.[11]

While European nations tend to acknowledge class differences, the United States downplays them. Inherited privilege (whether economic or cultural) is especially contested, says DeMott, because our national ideals of equality, freedom, and mobility are difficult to reconcile with the inequalities produced by capitalist socioeconomic arrangements. For this reason, class mythologies—or cultural meaning systems that draw selectively from the past to naturalize a particular understanding of the present—are especially powerful in the United States.[12] Mythologies are not conspiratorial or "invented" by Hollywood directors; they are socially produced fictions that circulate widely through the educational system, political discourse, and media culture, helping to legitimate unequal power relations.[13]

Class mythologies provide the symbolic material for "discounting the evident social differences" in our midst, says DeMott. The central mythology is that class is un-American. Since its founding, explains DeMott, the United States has symbolized freedom from European class structures. The national credo of equality of opportunity defined people as "their abilities, not their stations," promising all Americans (provided they were white males) the chance to compose "their own nature and destiny" regardless of birthright.[14] The rise of industrial capitalism was said to affirm this ideal with the rags-to-riches biographies of "self-made" robber barons. We can still see this validating logic at work in the distinctly American admiration for "new money."

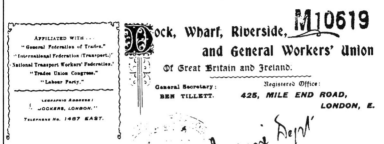

RESOLVED.

The Executive of the Dock, Wharf, Riverside & General Workers' Union hereby offers it's sincere condolences to the bereaved relatives of the Third Class passengers of the S/S "Titanic", whose tragic sinking we deplore. We also send our sincere regret to the relatives of the Crew, who were drowned. We also offer our strongest protest against the wanton and callous disregard of human life and the vicious class antagonism shown in the practical forbidding of the saving of the lives of the third class passengers. The refusal to permit other than the first class passengers to be saved by the boats, is in our opinion a disgrace to our common civilisation.

We therefore call upon the Government and the Board of Trade to insist on the provision of adequate life-saving appliances in boats. rafts and belts, which shall not only provide means of safety to the passengers, but to the whole members of the ship's staff.

We express our regret that in order to save time and cost, at the risk of life, shorter and quicker routes were insisted on, in spite of the knowledge of the presence of ice.

We trust the saving of so many first class passengers lives will not deaden the solicitude of the Government for the lives of those who belong to the wage earning classes, and call upon the members of the Labour Party to force upon the Government the necessity of proper protection to the lives of all mariners and all passengers, irrespective of class or grade.

Signed for the Executive.

BEN TILLETT.

Bereavement letter to relatives of third-class passengers from the Dock, Wharf, Riverside, and General Workers' Union, circa 1912

Americans admire success, especially in unexpected places, but they have always been rather fickle about the overt display of class privilege. For one thing, the American Dream proposed that "no one enjoyed privileges that others could not share, and everyone achieved a success equivalent to merit."[15] The "Judeo-Christian warning," says Jackie Byars, "that it is easier to pass a camel through the eye of a needle than to get a rich man into heaven," and the American dogma "work is honorable, wealth is decadent," also temper popular respect for anything smacking of aristocracy or the leisure class.[16] By the late nineteenth century, says DeMott, Mark Twain was encouraging Americans to "jeer at rich culture values," and there is still a popular convention that despises people who "give themselves airs" and takes "wry satisfaction" when status seekers get what they deserve.[17] The media's disdainful view of the decadent consumption habits and snobbish attitude of Leona Helmsley, the hotel mogul jailed for tax evasion, is a typical example. In short, the quest for upward mobility is valued in the United States—but efforts to elevate one's self too far above the masses are not.

Industrial capitalism fundamentally subverted the possibility of class equality by concentrating vast wealth in the hands of the few, and by creating a deskilled working class with little chance for mobility. As cultural historian Alan Trachtenberg argues, the "incorporation" of the United States during the late 1800s and early 1900s created economic conditions that no longer supported the spectacular rise of "captains of industry" or even small-scale entrepreneurship for the many who were interested.[18] While the expanding professional-managerial middle class entered white-collar corporate employment, working-class immigrants entered the factories, and a relatively stable class structure was institutionalized in the United States.[19] Class differences that served the interests of corporate capitalism were masked by the mythology that class could be transcended—it was only temporary.

According to Trachtenberg, the iconography of the American West (e.g., rugged individualism, self-reliance, the pioneer spirit) and the popular success stories propagated by writers like Horatio Alger infused the American Dream with new possibilities. Alger's advice to the would-be "self-made" man emphasized hard work and character as the paths to entrepreneurial success (or at least middle-class security secured via corporate employment). However, Alger's tales also stressed luck as an important factor in one's destiny. For men who lacked opportunities, there was always the hope of "magical outside assistance."[20] For women without means, marrying up was the equivalent of a lucky break. Cross-class romance (or "gold digging" as it was less charitably called) was a staple fantasy promoted by the nascent mass culture industry, one that lives on in films such as the remake of *Sabrina* (1995), in which a chauffeur's daughter romances the sons of her father's wealthy employer. According to Stanley Aronowitz, the shift to a postindustrial economy—and the resulting decline of blue-collar labor—has coincided with a new twist on this mobility fantasy. Citing films like *Dirty Dancing* (1987), about a working-class dancer who becomes romantically involved with an upper-middle-class, female resort guest, he argues that mediated representations of working-class men are also increasingly apt to displace class transcendence onto sexual relations.[21]

The promise that virtually anyone can transcend the class into which he or she is born pervades American media culture, and the "humble origins" claimed by many politicians, celebrities and CEOs contributes to its "capacity to energize the mind," says DeMott.[22] But as he persuasively argues, the fantasy of ascent now coexists with newer class mythologies that affirm American classlessness in different ways. These mythologies center on the erroneous assumption that the United States is now a vast middle class that encompasses all but the outer fringes of society, where any remaining "pockets of inequality" are located. What distinguishes the newer class mythologies from conventional rags-to-riches stories, according to DeMott, is that both the worthy poor and the superrich desire a place in the "imperial middle." With the exceptions of criminals, "deviants," and "arrogant fools," all are readily assimilated.[23]

Class differences that defy the logic of the imperial middle are smoothed over by what DeMott calls the "omni syndrome," or the idea that class is so fluid and superficial as to be practically meaningless. The illusion of "mastering the flux," he explains, is a variation on the American Dream that makes the pecking order seem "less confining and inhibiting." Whether slumming or hobnobbing, people of different classes intermingle and even temporarily become the "other" in recent films. For example, *Romy and Michelle's High School Reunion* (1997), a comedy about pink-collar women who borrow a fancy car, don business clothes, and "become" upscale professionals for the weekend, is an example of how characters effortlessly "step from above to below and vice versa," instilling "confidence that each has access to all" and that "social distance is unreal."[24]

Stories that present class labels as irrelevant and misleading complement the omni sensibility, says DeMott. In such scenarios, lower-class characters who feel insecure or who are treated as inferior "upend" higher-ranking classmates, colleagues, or romantic competitors by displaying superior gifts or character traits. *Good Will Hunting* (1997)—a film about an uneducated young janitor at Massachusetts Institute of Technology who is discovered to be a mathematical genius intrinsically smarter than the upper-class coeds who sneer him at the local pub—typifies the way "upending stories" can feel subversive in their confirmation that "strata are evanescent and meaningless."[25] But as DeMott observes, such stories affirm the illusion of classlessness by downplaying the importance of class inequalities.

Class "renunciation" stories go a step farther by presenting class privilege as attainable but unenviable, says DeMott. In these story lines, characters who are momentarily tempted by "lofty visions" of wealth or sophistication come to realize that class really does not matter. The modern film version of the classic Charles Dickens novel *Great Expectations* (1998), about a poor fisherman who becomes a famous New York artist only to find his dream world pretentious, painful, and disappointing, is a typical Hollywood renunciation story. A variation on this theme features conventionally successful characters who pursue downward mobility as the route to personal happiness. In the romantic comedy *Bed of Roses* (1995), for example, a businessman quits his high-powered job to deliver flowers because he enjoys life in the slow lane and making people smile (only later do we learn that the modest-appearing hero also owns the flower shop). From above or below, the prevailing message is that class is transcendable, superficial, unenviable, or simply unreal.[26]

Keeping these intersecting class mythologies in mind, we can now see how *Titanic*, a film charged with promoting "leftist propaganda," actually promotes the illusion of classlessness, and how it does so in multiple but complementary ways that contributed to its enormous audience appeal.

Class Is Un-American

Congruent with DeMott's analysis, the central mythology promoted by *Titanic* is that class is un-American. Class differences are the narrative tension that drives the film, both in the romance that develops between Jack and Rose and in the struggle over lifeboats. Viewers' pleasure hinges on the establishment and resolution of these differences. Nationalism sets the stage: by coding the rigid class hierarchy governing the ship as rooted in European aristocratic traditions, *Titanic* alternately codes the United States as classless in spirit—if not yet in practice. Similarly, by periodizing the Gilded Age, the film invites viewers to observe overt class differences and prejudices—and then dismiss them as anomalies of a bygone era.

With her California ranch home, blue jeans–wearing granddaughter, and unpretentious attitude, old Rose is an archetype of the "imperial middle." Through her memories, however, we are introduced to a very different young Rose, a society belle about to board a transatlantic luxury ship with her mother, Ruth Bukater, and her fiancé, Cal Hockley, heir to a steel fortune. The wedding party, which is returning from a shopping trip to Europe, drives up to the Southampton loading dock in a swanky Renault. They are dressed to the hilt, the men in subdued but obviously expensive suits, the women in elaborate traveling clothes. Welcomed by old Rose, viewers enter their world of luxurious furnishings and crystal chandeliers, nobility and millionaires, humble servants and extravagant meals. *Titanic's* first-class setting is far removed from the icon of classlessness, and (as some critics protested) its sharp contrast to the ship's minimalist steerage accommodations is made all the more dramatic by the absence of "second-class" people and quarters from Cameron's script. However, lingering camera shots, coupled with old Rose's friendly narration, invite one and all to enjoy the luxurious splendor of the "ship of dreams" without intimidation. We might be technically outclassed, but there's no reason to feel we're unwelcome—except for the un-American attitude of snobbish elites who want to monopolize wealth and status for themselves.

Rose dreads the life that awaits her as Cal's bride (to-be), but neither vast wealth nor the capitalist system that produces it are the crux of the problem. The "narrow-mindedness" of the rich is what brings Rose to the brink of suicide, and Cal is the most pretentious and ostentatious of the bunch. Cal, importantly, is no self-made millionaire; he is a man of the leisure class who lives off his inheritance, and he is deeply wedded to European-style, aristocratic class distinctions. He books the ship's most expensive suite to impress the elite, coifs his hair and his eyebrows, employs servants, and would not dream of mingling with people below his station. Cal is immediately unlikable, not because he is rich, but rather because he thinks himself intrinsically above the masses. When he presents Rose with the 56–carat Heart of the Ocean, a huge diamond necklace that belonged to Louis XVI, he explains: "It's for royalty, Rose—we are royalty." Cal's class attitude goes against the American Dream and its newer version in the omni sensibility of the imperial middle.

Rose and her mother, Ruth, are members of the "old money" Northeastern elite—the closest thing the United States has to an aristocracy—and they are also coded as European by their formal gestures and facial expressions, courtly costumes, refined way speaking, and social attitudes. Jack first spots Rose strolling on the first-class promenade, dressed in a wispy, elegant gown that emphasizes her corseted hourglass figure. She looks like a princess, and she is filmed from below, a vantage point that visually communicates her self-assured social superiority. Rose is a confident young woman: She talks back to Cal and earns his wrath for lighting a cigarette at the dinner table. But her demeanor is scripted and spoiled, especially with Jack. Even at the moment he saves her from plummeting into the ocean, she talks down to him in a clipped and condescending tone as if he were a servant. Later, she determines him "rude" and "uncouth" for his violation of the rules of proper gentlemanly behavior. Rose's sense of class superiority would make her highly unlikable in these early scenes if we did not know she eventually becomes a sweet old woman who behaves in the classless American way.

The casting of Kate Winslet, a British actress with a "snooty cinematic pedigree" and "cachet with the Merchant-Ivory crowd," in the words of one journalist,[27] contributed to Rose's upper-brow European coding. Commentators often cited Winslet's British nationality as evidence of her good breeding, constructing symbolic associations that overlapped with her screen character.[28] When Winslet appeared on *Good Morning America*, she was asked to confirm that "every piece of cutlery" used in *Titanic* was an accurate reproduction, a question that presumed she, like Rose, was equipped with the cultural capital to make such assessments.[29] Similarly displacing class onto national differences, Winslet was also quoted in several print venues as half-worrying that Leonardo DiCaprio would perceive her as a "starchy Brit who recites Shakespeare left and right and absolutely insists on drinking tea in the afternoon."[30]

Ruth is a secretly destitute but socially arrogant Philadelphia society matron who is pressuring Rose to trade on her "good family name" by marrying Cal (as *People* magazine was sure to note, the actress who played Ruth, Frances Fisher, was also born in England).[31] Ruth looks down on Jack because he is traveling in steerage, and she also draws a firm line between the upper class and the merely rich. She hobnobs with the likes of the countess of Rothes and snubs the "vulgar" Molly Brown, the newly monied first-class passenger whose husband struck gold out West.

The distinction between old and new money insisted upon by Ruth is an important theme in *Titanic* and is one of the ways the film aligns working-, middle-, and "humbled" upper-class viewers against class hierarchy without prompting a reassessment of capitalism. As Bourdieu argues, the signifiers of old money (titles of nobility, good taste, social confidence) cannot be bought—they are inherited through family socialization. And as Demott notes, this inevitably exclusive process, epitomized by Ruth, is far more contested within American media culture than the narrow distribution of wealth, which is made to seem reasonable and fair by the credo of "equality of opportunity." *Titanic* reproduces this narrow and ultimately nonthreatening opposition to class power by emphasizing the selfish arrogance of the ship's social elite, but not the monopolized accumulation and control of economic capital or the government that makes it possible. Significantly, the brassy-talking nouveau riche Molly Brown is one of the few sympathetic first-class passengers.

White Star Line's managing director, J. Bruce Ismay, is shown to be a charter member of the socially respected upper class, when he more accurately belongs to the new middle class of managers and professionals that arose during the period Trachtenberg refers to as "incorporation." Likewise, Ismay's foolish insistence that *Titanic*'s maiden voyage break speed records to "make headlines" despite ice warnings is attributed to his personal arrogance, as opposed to the profit-oriented values of his corporate employer.

The erasure of corporate capitalism from the "cause" of the *Titanic*'s sinking is paralleled in the attribution of class prejudice to individual—and very European—character flaws in the ensuing struggle over lifeboats. Scenes of third-class steerage passengers locked behind gates as water gradually fills the lower cabins are juxtaposed with moments of supreme snobbery above deck. Ruth hopes the boats are not "too crowded" and hopes they will seat according to class. When Cal learns there are not enough boats for everyone, he presumes the "better half" will be served first. To doubly ensure his safety, he bribes a steward with a huge wad of bills and then pretends to be a doting father to a crying toddler. J. Bruce Ismay is also shown sneaking into a vessel reserved for women and children. Molly Brown is, significantly, alone among the first-class survivors in her empathy for the drowning masses, reiterating *Titanic*'s distinction between American new money (good) and European-style inherited privilege (bad).

Cameron has been accused of "distorting" the facts surrounding the loss of life in an attempt to "politicize" the *Titanic* story. On the *Titanic* Web site he describes the disaster as the "first time class was translated into body count, and published for all the world to see." The *Titanic* book further asserts that "everyone knew where they belonged, up and down the social classes or up and down the decks. . . . when the ship sank, people realized that a certain amount of exploitation had been going on." This interpretation appears to critique the status quo, but it is rendered politically benign by the presumption that class was a phenomenon of the past caused by coldhearted, status-obsessed individuals. On the *Titanic* Web site, Twentieth Century Fox claims that the sinking of the ship marked the end of "acceptance of class as a definition of birthright," implying that American class issues have since been resolved. Film critics also wrote about class as if it were a relic from the past. In a typical example, Janet Maslin of the *New York*

Times praised Cameron for "furthering the illusion that the privileged past had re-turned to life."[32]

This view of class hierarchy encourages working- and middle-class viewers to project everyday class resentments and the coldhearted decisions of faceless capitalist bureaucracies onto un-American characters who lived long ago, and who ultimately got what they deserved. Old Rose assures us that Cal shot himself in the stock market crash of 1929, and the *Titanic* book informs fans that J. Bruce Ismay's arrogance and cowardice were exposed by the popular press, furthering the idea that justice was served. Meanwhile, the construction of Jack as a penni-less free agent offers an American-coded counterpoint to the flawed European sen-sibilities Cal and his despicable ilk represent. Through Jack's forbidden romance with Rose, *Titanic* shows class differences transcended, upended, seen through, and eventually leveled. Thus, the film displaces the popular fears and resentments of an American audience polarized by class inequality.

Class Is Temporary

Closely related to the illusion that class is un-American is the mythology that class is temporary. Molly Brown's upward mobility affirms that there is a better life in the United States for the poor immigrants traveling in steerage, and Jack shares this promise by association. While Jack is technically traveling third class, he is only a "subordinate" in the mistaken eyes of *Titanic*'s snobbish elite. Part of the popularity of the film is no doubt related to the fact that viewers are encour-aged to see Jack as an autonomous individual who occupies a social space not defined by rigid class labels—a living symbol of the American Dream.

As we have seen, luck is a vital component of achieving the American Dream, according to popular mythologies, and it is also central to Jack's self-assured opti-mism. The scene where Rose boards the *Titanic* in the arrogant manner of a wealthy European aristocrat is immediately followed by the scene where Jack wins his pas-sage on the voyage in a "lucky" game of barroom poker. While the overprivileged Rose feels trapped by her pending marriage to Cal, Jack is willing to bet every-thing he owns on a game of chance because, as he tells his best friend Fabrizio, "when you have nothing, you have nothing to lose." With his crumpled clothes and unshaven chin, Jack keeps company with barflies and rowdy immigrants like Fabrizio, but as he proudly informs a health inspector, he does not warrant the degrading check for head lice required of other third-class passengers because he's an American. Unfazed by his lowly accommodations, he symbolizes the promis-ing spirit of the "very small" Statue of Liberty Fabrizio spots during their romp on deck.

Unlike the sweaty, British-accented workers who shovel coal in *Titanic*'s in-dustrial steam engine room, Jack possesses a talent that distinguishes him from the certainty of working-class wage labor: he is an artist. His mix of artsy sensi-tivity and rugged self-reliance can (depending on the class backgrounds of *Titanic* viewers) signify a bohemian disregard for status or the early American frontier spirit. Either way, Jack possesses talent, luck, and character traits that transcend

Titanic's steep class hierarchy. His economic insecurity is shown to be voluntary, temporary, and exciting, not structural, stigmatized, or painful. For Jack, poverty is an adventure. From his perspective, he is the "King of the World."

Chance is central to Jack's distinctly American worldview. He does not mind being poor, working from place to place on "tramp steamers and such," because he enjoys the thrill of not knowing what hand he is going to be dealt. Jack's blind trust in fate conceals the social and economic factors that structure life's possibilities—and encourages viewers to do the same. Similar to Horatio Alger's tales, his hopeful classless attitude hinges on "outside magical assistance." While a dubious prospect for most Americans, this faith in the openness of fate also underscores the highly favorable assessment of Jack in the media. For example, the *Titanic* scene excerpted by National Public Radio's *Morning Edition* to illustrate its favorable review of the film emphasizes the thrill of chance represented by Jack over the dead weight of certainty represented by Rose—a message that glamorizes poverty, affirms the possibility of class mobility, and soothes audience worries of involuntarily falling from a secure middle-class livelihood.[33] Jack sees life as filled with lucky possibilities that simply appear out of the blue. As he tells his fellow dining companions: "I've got everything I need right here with me. I've got the air in my lungs and a few blank sheets of paper. I mean I love waking up in the morning, not knowing what's gonna happen or who I'm gonna meet, where I'm gonna wind up. Just the other night I was sleeping under a bridge and now here I am on the grandest ship in the world having champagne with you fine people."

Luck is also a determining factor in Jack's romance with Rose. "You'd as like have angels flying out of your arse to get next to the likes of her," scoffs the Irish immigrant who notices Jack staring at Rose from a deck below. Fate proves him wrong—a point that is emphasized on the *Titanic* Web site, which describes the scene where Jack comes upon Rose contemplating a jump into the freezing ocean with the logic: "Through their chance meeting, class lines blur for one telling moment to allow these two strangers to establish a powerful bond." This romantic blurring requires one of the central characters to move up or down the ship's class structure, as determined by Hollywood conventions. What distinguishes *Titanic* from most cross-class romances is that both upward and downward mobility are represented: Jack's accesses the ship's socioeconomic elite and even temporarily becomes upper class himself through his sexual relationship with Rose. Rose, on the other hand, eventually "renunciates" her upper-class status to be with Jack.

Titanic's love scenes unfold within the luxury of first class, a setting that enables all viewers to enjoy the splendor of the "ship of dreams," and working-class male viewers, in particular, to vicariously transcend their class via Jack's intimate relations with a glamorous and classy woman who "belongs" to a more powerful man. Cameron explicitly encourages this reading when he calls *Titanic* a "gender-bending twist on the Cinderella myth."[34] And so it is: Jack flirts with Rose during their leisurely stroll on the first-class promenade, catches her eye in the posh first-class dining saloon, and then defies the ship's social hierarchy by slipping her an invitation to meet with him later. He sketches her not in his cramped steerage bunk but in the lavishly decorated luxury suite Cal paid for, as she wears only the blue diamond necklace Cal associates with royalty. Jack and Rose's flight through the ship's engine room, where they brush up against British workers toiling hard to propel the enormous ship, is immediately followed by the scene where they make love in Cal's Renault. Jack initially takes the role of the chauffeur in the front seat; Rose pulls him into the passenger seat, and Jack "takes her to the stars." In so doing, he transcends working-class industrial labor and the less "manly" service jobs that have increasingly replaced it in today's postindustrial economy. This symbolically loaded moment makes it possible to read *Titanic* as a sexualized male mobility fantasy. In a telling example of this reading from popular culture, one entertainment magazine summed up *Titanic* with the "upending" narrative: a "skinny steerage passenger . . . wrests a fleshy poor little rich girl from her dastardly beau."[35]

Titanic is also a renunciation story, in that Jack temporarily enjoys the luxury and glamour of wealth through his association with Rose, but he does not aspire to become superrich or socially elevated like Cal. He is quite cheerfully penniless and homeless. *Titanic* goes a step farther than most renunciation tales by presenting his situation as the epitome of the independence and adventure Rose longs for. The credibility of this representation hinges on the inequities of gender. Rose's perception of being "taken back to America in chains" is fostered by the restrictions she experiences as a "well-bred" young woman—a caveat that makes it easier to see class privilege as a hardship. Cal orders meals for Rose without consultation, ridicules her budding interest in modern art, and threatens to censure her reading material when she cites Freud to mock male obsession with the size of *Titanic*. If Rose was once enamored with her fiancé, she has grown weary of him and the other men of her class, who spend their evenings dressed in tuxedos, drinking expensive brandy, and congratulating themselves for being the "masters of the universe." She is also utterly bored with the feminine pursuits of her social set—including the elaborate society wedding her mother is planning.

Jack's adventuresome spirit is what initially attracts Rose. When she learns he is an aspiring artist who has spent time in Paris (or what Jack irreverently refers to as "old Paree"), she begins to see him less as a subordinate and more as someone she wishes to emulate. Rose listens intently as Jack tells her of peddling his portraits on the Santa Monica pier, riding the roller coaster, and drinking cheap beer, and wonders why she cannot be more like him. Ironically, what Rose comes to desire for herself is not the gritty working-class womanhood of her maidservant Trudy or the immigrant women in steerage. What she wants is what Jack represents: the historically male-coded freedom to pursue the American Dream. Thus, the appeal of *Titanic's* romance to audiences is dependent on the mystification of socially imposed gender limitations as well as the mystification of class.

This point becomes clearer when we consider the masculinized, downwardly mobile nature of her transformation. Jack learns that Rose rides horses sidesaddle, as is customary for women of her class; in an exaggerated western drawl that momentarily subverts her feminine, Northeastern upper-class identity, she makes him promise to teach her to "ride like a man." Jack also teaches Rose to "hock it back" and spit like a man, a lesson both agree has not been taught to her in "finishing school." Rose's decision to be with Jack is cemented during the scene where she observes a first-class little girl being instructed on the dainty ritual of afternoon tea; she learns to sit up straight and fold her napkin in the proper, ladylike way. When Rose defies Cal and Ruth to pursue her steerage love interest, she also gains some of the freedom and optimism that defines Jack as classless in spirit and will-fully (and only temporarily) poor. Rose lets her hair down, becomes more casual in her speech, body language, and facial expressions. She drops her pretentious attitude and—in an especially symbolic gesture of her new freedom—gives Cal's brute manservant the finger.

The gender inequalities that inspire Rose's rebellion invite women and girls to reject patriarchal ideologies by supporting her flight from Cal and his authori-tative world. But this oppositional stance, as constructed by *Titanic*, also requires that viewers accept the notion that class is a temporary, inherited privilege both unimportant and unenviable. While the female counterpoint to *Titanic*'s male mobility fantasy works quite differently, Rose's transformation complements the illusion of American classlessness, and this complementary role was further em-phasized by extratextual discourse. The *Titanic* book, for example, describes Rose's attraction to Jack with a reversal of the rags-to-riches scenario, telling fans: "They share so many of the same passions for life, which he's already attained, and to which she's aspiring." Many film critics similarly framed poor Jack's "boyish adventurousness" as "just the cure for what's ailing Rose."[36]

Jack inspires Rose to see herself in the masculine spirit of the American Dream, but his character is what captures her heart. Character was also important to Alger's success formulas, and *Titanic* draws from this popular culture legacy by emphasizing Jack's caring sensibility as a factor in the clichéd adage "love con-quers all." Whereas Cal feels he owns Rose and equates love with expensive jew-els, Jack treats her as an equal and is responsive to her interests, problems, and desires. The contrast between her two lovers foregrounds the politics of romance, but it also presents classless love (but not class critique) as a mechanism for over-coming inequalities.

This underlying message helps account for *Titanic*'s broad audience, includ-ing male viewers not typically drawn to the melodramatic woman's film. Even view-ers (such as middle-class teenage girls) who are primarily drawn to *Titanic*'s love story are encouraged to accept comforting class mythologies. Rose's choice to be with Jack allows such viewers to vicariously experience a more sensitive, thoughtful, and respectful lover—provided they dismiss class differences as unimportant. *Titanic* promotes the idea that "true love" exists independent of class relations, obscuring the way money, social status, and education influence dating and mar-riage patterns. The ideological framework constructed by Twentieth Century Fox and popular commentary magnifies this message, suggesting that undue class privilege is a personal burden that can be romantically overcome. According to Cameron, for example, it is Rose's emotional connection with Jack that "transforms this sort of Edwardian first-class geisha who is dying on the inside into this spirited young woman on the cusp of a new life."[37]

Jack's death has the potential to rupture the myth of the American Dream, to the extent that Rose's grief upon discovering his frozen corpse enables viewers to feel the visceral effects of class prejudice. Jack freezes to death in the water after the sinking even though many half-filled lifeboats float nearby, their passengers refusing to rescue those struggling in the water for fear of being submerged. Rose's grief upon discovering that Jack has succumbed is overwhelming. However, the potential to share her grief and understand the link between Jack's death and class prejudice is blunted by the ideology of romantic individualism.

The competition between Jack (sensitive poor boy) and Cal (rich snob) over Rose intersects with the struggle over lifeboats, displacing biases and inequalities onto character differences and romantic choices. Cal's heartless disregard for third-class passengers who will be left for dead cements Rose's moral respect for Jack, but her frantic leap out of a lifeboat is inspired by passion and love—and a nagging suspicion that Cal is lying about Jack's personal safety—not the politics of survival. The skewed odds of survival on the *Titanic* meant that a third-class male stood a one-in-ten chance of surviving, whereas a first-class female stood a nine-in-ten chance. Reiterating this distinction, Cameron has said, "I've emphasized those odds so the audience will understand exactly what kind of sacrifice Rose makes when she chooses to be with Jack."[38] The uncertainty of reaching safety is not the only consequence; Rose's defiant declaration that she would rather be Jack's "whore" than Cal's wife catapults her fiancé into a violent rage, and his frenzied attempt to harm the young lovers is almost as threatening to their well-being as the freezing waters of the Atlantic. But Cal cannot keep Rose from her steerage lover; even after Jack's death, Rose becomes Rose "Dawson." Tragedy does not subvert *Titanic*'s romantic resolution of class polarization but infuses it with additional emotional intensity. In the words of one reviewer, "If we didn't care about its young lovers, nothing else in *Titanic* would matter."[39]

Class Is Superficial

It is possible to read *Titanic* as a comeuppance of aristocratic elites, a glamorization of economic insecurity, a sexualized male mobility fantasy, a class renunciation story made more credible by gender politics, or a combination thereof. These different but complementary ways of upending or dissolving class (at least temporarily) may help account for *Titanic*'s broad popularity. In all cases, however, the film pits inherited privilege against new money and European-style class hierarchies against the spirit of the American Dream. In so doing, it pits "us" against the loathsome first-class characters upon whom capitalist forces are displaced. Here, I want to show how this process intersects with a newer class mythology that positions all viewers as part of the imperial middle. While *Titanic* constructs a line between steerage and first class, it also promotes the notion that identity is independent of class, and anyone can access and temporarily become the "other" upon command.

Cross-class romance is key to constructing an omni sensibility, to use DeMott's term. In addition to possessing talents (such as a familiarity with modern artists that upends Cal's arrogant ignorance) and personality traits that transcend *Titanic*'s class structure, Jack mingles easily with people above and below him on the socioeconomic pecking order. Just as Jack "really sees" the down-and-out French women (one-legged prostitutes, drunken barflies) he draws in the nude, he sees through the mask of status and money and recognizes the real Rose. But *Titanic*'s faith in unconditioned individuals does not show class to be the product of culture rather than nature, in the critical sense demonstrated by Bourdieu. It presents the very appealing idea that class differences do not matter because they are at once misleading, fluid, and unreal, and in so doing makes class hierarchies seem less powerful.

The long process of class socialization emphasized by Bourdieu is obscured by *Titanic*'s utopian view of artifice. Jack's ability to "pass" as a member of the upper-brow social elite is a telling example. When Cal invites his steerage acquaintance to dinner in the first-class dining saloon, assuming he will serve as a foil to point up the superiority of his betters, Molly Brown warns Jack he is "about to go into the snake pit." But her proclamation that the young man "shines up like a new penny" with some hairstyling and her son's tuxedo sets the stage for Jack's stunning transformation. The audience enters the "snake pit" from his perspective, and we see him take his social cues from fellow diners. When Rose arrives, he graciously bows, takes her gloved hand, and lightly kisses it, explaining, "I saw that in a nickelodeon once." Jack hobnobs comfortably with his betters, and he is not intimidated by the millionaires and aristocrats Rose flags: Benjamin Guggenheim, John Jacob Astor, Sir Cosmo and Lady Duff Gordon, and the countess. With some coaching from Molly Brown ("just start from the outside and work you way in"), he masters first-class dining etiquette, including an array of eating utensils to rival "the implements of a surgeon."[40] *Titanic*'s elite presumed "he was one of the club," explains old Rose of Jack's successful makeover. Even Cal, with a look of surprise on his face, must admit his steerage guest can "almost pass as a gentleman." Jack's adaptability allows viewers to pleasurably imagine that they too could adapt successfully to a more lavish and glamorous social universe. This scene promotes the fantasy that anyone can cross class lines by merely appropriating the cultural signifiers of privilege. More subtly, it divorces class from economics, suggesting that class is ultimately nothing more than its symbolic dimensions.

The same ideas underscore the pronounced extratextual attention to *Titanic*'s re-creation of first-class culture during the Gilded Age. This discourse focuses exclusively on style, leaving political and economic issues (such as the monopolization of wealth and the power of corporations) untouched. For example, the *Titanic* book describes in considerable detail how cast members learned to successfully pass as bonafide upper class—a focus that suggests class is passé and based on pretense. Actors were tutored by a specialist in the elite manners and mores of the Edwardian years and a short video, *Titanic Etiquette: A Time Traveler's Guide*, played in the wardrobe building, informing the cast how to walk, eat, and behave properly.[41] Similar attention was given to *Titanic*'s first-class costumes and grooming customs—the ultimate symbols of a "person's stature" during the Gilded Age—in the *Titanic* book and on the Web site. Because these stylistic markers of class signify the exclusivity of the past, not the present, voyeuristic attention to them does not undermine, but instead contributes to, the myth of contemporary American classlessness. This myth, in turn, helps account for the popular appeal of the film.

Jack's ability to master the look and style of first class is tempered by his disinterest in pretending to be "one of the club." When Ruth sneeringly asks about the accommodations in steerage to expose the "true" class of the handsome guest, he jokes about the rats without embarrassment. Jack does not hesitate to give the *Titanic* as his "current address," for the wealth and status markers that obsess his dining companions do not especially matter to him. On one hand, Jack's courage to "be himself" shows up the pompousness of people like Cal, for even Jack's first-class companions find him quite charming, much to Cal's chagrin. But as DeMott argues, characters like Jack complement the omni sensibility, with its emphasis on fluidity and access to all, by proving class differences to be unimportant and unreal, not unjust or politically charged. In other words, the myth of classlessness underscores Jack's pleasant visit with the gilded elite and his amiable rejection of its norms on personal grounds. DiCaprio's star persona as an all-American teenage heartthrob contributed to Jack's classless spirit. Whereas Winslet was familiar with formal etiquette, DiCaprio was reported to have turned to the sea of forks and asked, "Which one of these do I use to lobotomize myself?" a joke that presumes his similar ability to pass, but his preference for the culture and temperament of the imperial middle.[42]

The "real party" Jack and Rose attend together in the steerage public room safely celebrates working-class folk culture. Far removed from the iconography of the imperial middle and without noting contemporary class differences, working-class traditions are coded as ethnic and "vestigial," and the audience knows they are destined to "pass away."[43] The scene also provides further testament of Jack's class fluidity. Jack is not an ethnic immigrant, but he adds "spice" to his life by socializing with *Titanic*'s low cultural "others." The steerage party also allows Rose to sample, and temporarily become one of the vivacious people below deck—an "omni" invitation that is vicariously extended to viewers. Rose takes repose from her class and gender socialization by drinking beer, smoking, and dancing wildly to the swinging pace of Irish folk music—a sharp contrast to the subdued classical melodies performed in the dining saloon. She rejects the rules that dictate her behavior above deck, but when need be she can also use her training in ballet to "top" the masculine prowess of burly third-class arm wrestlers (standing *pointe* on her toes proves she's as tough as they are). In short, slumming offers Rose freedom and excitement without requiring her to adopt a permanent working-class identity or experience any of the hardships of working-class life. She sheds her glamorous but restrictive clothes and the "porcelain doll" identity they impose on her to become a kindred soul with Jack's down-and-out Frenchwomen, but then her upperclassness is reasserted when she makes love to him in a rich man's automobile.

The presumption that fluidity and flux offer freedom from class labels was also articulated around Winslet's star persona. While the American media stressed her Britishness as a sign of her good breeding, Winslet rejected this fixed identity by acknowledging the glamour of the film's formal dinner party but then citing the steerage party as her favorite scene.[44] In a *Rolling Stone* profile, she was reported to curse, smoke, and pick her feet and confessed to peeing in the water during the filming of *Titanic*, subverting her image as a snooty upper-class Brit. Pointing to her beat-up pair of Harley-Davidson biker boots, she told the magazine's reporter, "This is me."[45] As with her *Titanic* character, it is Winslet's privilege that enables her to appropriate the cultural markers of working-class male bravado without also enduring hardship or prejudice—and still wear a lavish *Titanic*-style evening gown to the Academy Awards ceremony. But in extratextual discourse, as in *Titanic*, class is not only un-American and temporary, but also so superficial as to be virtually meaningless.

Conclusion

Far from inciting class rebellion in its millions of viewers, the *Titanic* phenomenon affirms, at a moment of growing class polarization, that the United States is still a classless society, an imperial middle. The class mythologies that support the notion of an imperial middle promote an "us versus them" opposition that encompasses, in different ways, all but the most intrinsically flawed individual characters. Likewise, all but the most self-consciously arrogant viewers are invited to witness, and vicariously participate in, the dismantling of European-style hierarchies by identifying with cross-class lovers, accessing their different worlds, and witnessing the artificial line between them collapse. *Titanic* is unusual in that its creators explicitly capitalized on the rhetoric of class struggle—a telling decision at today's historical juncture. But as we have seen, the displacement of systemic inequalities and their historical continuities onto the trials and tributes of fairy-tale romance hardly constitutes a Marxist critique.

In the end, Rose finds hope in the Statue of Liberty that awaits her in New York. She arrives back in the United States penniless and homeless, with only the tattered clothes on her back, but she has been liberated from class chains by Jack. Her downward mobility is but temporary—a necessary step in her pursuit of the American Dream. As we learn from the photographs on her bureau, she does indeed learn to "ride like a man" and even fly an airplane. Rose becomes an actress in New York; later, she becomes a comfortable middle-class artist, just as Jack might have been.

In her dying dream, Rose meets Jack again on the *Titanic*'s grand staircase. Rose is young once more, back in her 1912 attire, and Jack is in his working-class clothes. But this time, the *Titanic*'s third-class steerage passengers have joined the ranks of the wealthy in the ship's most famous first-class setting. Class differences no longer matter to anyone on the *Titanic*, nor to the long-parted lovers now joined in death: one and all applaud the once forbidden romance. The "leveling" fantasy that underscores this scene and the entire film is dangerous—not in the antielitist and purportedly "threatening" or socially subversive way argued by alarmed commentators, but in the sense that it distorts and obscures the realities of class. The final scene could be read as undermining any desire to take action in the real world that could correct socioeconomic disparities. As DeMott asserts, "Where changing one's class is seen as feasible, where class is understood as really a disguise, class cannot be a major player in great undertakings. It's of the margins, peripheral; of the shadows, murky; a figment; a mirage."[46] *Titanic* trivializes and flattens class differences, rather than politicizing them. It works on a fantasy level to reassure us that class is, indeed, "of the shadows," a "mirage" unimportant, ultimately, to two attractive lovers and to their admirers, whether the latter are a ghostly assemblage of *Titanic* passengers or contemporary film viewers numbering in the millions.

Notes

1. See "Room at the Bottom," *Economist*, 3 January 1998, 30; James Bowman, "Sinking Ships," *National Review*, 26 January 1998, 36; Ken Ringle, "Integrity Goes Down with the Ship," *Washington Post*, 22 March 1998; Tim Page, "A *Titanic* Division: Gross Excess Drags Down this Bilgy Blockbuster," *Washington Post*, 1 March 1998; Frank Rich, "Soak the Rich," *New York Times*, 27 December 1997.
2. Quoted in Ed W. Marsh, *James Cameron's Titanic* (New York: HarperPerennial, 1997), 73.
3. My analysis of the extratextual framework surrounding *Titanic* draws from Marsh's best-selling book (which features a foreword by Cameron), the Twentieth Century Fox Web site (www.titanicmovie.com), and approximately two dozen articles, celebrity profiles, and reviews. It is cited hereafter in the text as the *Titanic* book.
4. Benjamin DeMott, *The Imperial Middle: Why American's Can't Think Straight about Class* (New Haven: Yale University Press, 1990).
5. Elizabeth Traube, *Dreaming Identities: Class, Gender and Generation in 1980s Hollywood Movies* (Boulder, Colo.: Westview, 1992), 70. Traube argues, and I agree, that analyzing Hollywood films from the contextual perspective of a historical moment, and the specific ideological conflicts that it produced for men and women, avoids the limits of textual analysis and the presumption that audiences can make their own interpretations of films outside the parameters of what Antonio Gramsci called "hegemonic" or commonsense meaning-systems. For more on cultural hegemony, see Gramsci, *Selections from the Prison Notebooks* (New York: International Publishers, 1971).
6. Raymond Williams defines a structure of feeling as "a change of presence" distinguished from formally held worldviews or ideologies in that it is lived and felt. It is a "social experience which is still in process, often indeed not recognized as social but taken to be private, idiosyncratic, and even isolated." See *Marxism and Literature* (Oxford: Oxford University Press, 1977), 132–133.
7. Barbara Ehrenreich, *Fear of Falling: The Inner Life of the Middle Class* (New York: HarperPerennial, 1990).
8. DeMott, *The Imperial Middle*, 10.
9. Pierre Bourdieu, *Distinction: Toward a Critique of the Social Judgment of Taste* (Cambridge: Harvard University Press, 1984).
10. Sut Jhally and Justin Lewis, *Enlightened Racism: The Cosby Show, Audiences, and the Myth of the American Dream* (Boulder, Colo.: Westview, 1992), 70.
11. DeMott, *The Imperial Middle*, 9–10.
12. Ibid.

13. My understanding of myth draws from Roland Barthes, *Mythologies*, trans. Annette Lavers (New York: Noonday Press, 1972) as well as from John Fiske, *Television Culture* (New York: Routledge, 1987), 14–15, 133–134.

14. DeMott, *The Imperial Middle*, 29, 150–154. For more on early national ideals with respect to class, see chapter 9, "History: The Fate of Autonomy," 149–170.

15. Robert Weibe quoted in DeMott, *The Imperial Middle*, 42.

16. Jackie Byars, *All that Hollywood Allows: Re-Reading Gender in 1950s Melodramas* (Chapel Hill: University of North Carolina Press, 1991), 216.

17. DeMott, *The Imperial Middle*, 33, 71.

18. Alan Trachtenberg, *The Incorporation of America: Culture and Society during the Gilded Age* (New York: Hill and Wang, 1982).

19. For more on the rise of the professional-managerial class, see John and Barbara Ehrenreich, "The Professional-Managerial Class," in *Between Labor and Capital*, ed. Pat Walker (Boston: South End Press, 1979), 5–48.

20. Trachtenberg, *The Incorporation of America*, 11, 81. For more on popular success literature and Alger's advice in particular, see Judy Hickey, *Character Is Capital: Success Manuals and Manhood in the Gilded Age of America* (Chapel Hill: University of North Carolina Press, 1997).

21. Stanley Aronowitz, "Working Class Culture in the Electronic Age," in *Cultural Politics in Contemporary America*, ed. Ian Angus and Sut Jhally (New York: Routledge, 1989), 135–150.

22. DeMott, *The Imperial Middle*, 34.

23. Ibid., 41–54.

24. Ibid., 73–94, esp. 75, 79.

25. DeMott, *The Imperial Middle*, 64.

26. Ibid., 57–72, esp. 64.

27. Paula Paresi, *Titanic and the Making of James Cameron* (New York: Newmarket Press, 1988), 103.

28. See, for example, "The Women of *Titanic*," *People*, 23 February 1998, 52–53; and Anita Bush, "Was Leonardo Robbed?" *Entertainment Weekly*, 6 February 1996, 38.

29. *Good Morning America*, ABC Television, 9 January 1998, transcript 950191178.

30. Quoted in Marsh, *James Cameron's Titanic*, 80. Winslet makes a similar remark in *Rolling Stone*. See David Lipsky, "The Unsinkable Kate," *Rolling Stone*, 5 March 1996, 45–49.

31. "The Women of Titanic," 52–53.

32. Janet Maslin, "A Spectacle as Sweeping as the Sea," *New York Times*, 19 December 1997, sec. E 1, p. 1.

33. *Morning Edition*, National Public Radio, 18 December 1997, transcript 950187551.

34. Quoted in Marsh, *James Cameron's Titanic*, 98.

35. "*Titanic*," *Interview*, January 1998, 49.

36. Maslin, "A Spectacle as Sweeping as the Sea," 1.

37. Quoted in Marsh, *James Cameron's Titanic*, 85.

38. Quoted in ibid., 77.

39. Jeff Shannon, "*Titanic*" (review), *Sidewalk Seattle*, n.d. (http://seattle.sidewalk.com).

40. Marsh, *James Cameron's Titanic*, 36.

41. Ibid., 88–90. The Twentieth Century Fox *Titanic* Web site featured a similar discussion.

42. Quoted in Marsh, *James Cameron's Titanic*, 96.

43. Traube, *Dreaming Identities*, 106–107. Traube is discussing the occasional vogue of ethnic blue-collar culture in Hollywood films, but her analysis is also applicable here.

44. See Marsh, *James Cameron's Titanic*, 94. Winslet also said on *Good Morning America* that the steerage party was her favorite scene.

45. Lipsky, "The Unsinkable Kate," 48.

46. DeMott, *The Imperial Middle*, 39.

Bathos and the Bathysphere

On Submersion, Longing, and History
in *Titanic*

Vivian Sobchack

bathos [Gk = depth] 1. Depth, lowest phase, bottom. rare.
2. Rhet. Ludicrous descent from the elevated to the commonplace; anticlimax.
3. A comedown; an anticlimax; a performance absurdly unequal to the occasion.

bathysphere [comb. form of Gk bathus deep] n. a large strong submersible
sphere for deep-sea observation.
—Oxford English Dictionary

Le monde est grand, mais en nous
il est profond comme la mer.
(The world is large, but in us
it is deep as the sea.)
—R. M. Rilke

*H*ow can we possibly account in a truly compelling way for the monumental popularity and emotional impact of James Cameron's *Titanic*? Various "explanations" of the unprecedented mass (indeed, global) appeal of the movie seem somehow partial and thin and, in their sum, do not really touch upon what precisely it is about the film that has deeply moved so many people (not all of them teenage girls) to tears, to gestures of reenactment, and even to reading history. While many elements have clearly contributed to the film's popularity across a broad demographic range (its epic scope, its dramatization of a particularly mythicized but real historical event, its generic hybridity as romance/action/costume/special effects melodrama), taken together they still do not seem to "explain" the extraordinary emotional impact *Titanic* has had on the vast majority of its audience.

Yet if we listen to this audience describe their cinematic experience and its aftermath (recorded in various reviews, news reports, Web sites, and e-mail postings),

The Fairview Lawn Cemetery in Halifax, Nova Scotia

we are left even more at sea. *Entertainment Weekly* reports, for example, that one fifty-two-year-old male visitor to the Fairview Lawn cemetery in Halifax, Nova Scotia, where *Titanic* passengers are buried, "went from headstone to headstone writing down names." His explanation: "After I saw [the movie] I decided I wanted to do this." A young woman visitor says, "The graves remind fans that *Titanic* 'is not fiction. It really touches you.'"[1] Web sites on the film, divided in their emphasis (but not their obsession) along gender lines (females privileging the fictional romance and costumes and males the factual history and technology), are nonetheless united in their attempts to memorialize a deeply felt *cinematic* experience—usually underscored (and overscored), no matter the gender, by sound bites of Celine Dion singing "My Heart Will Go On."

Across a range of responses, common description of the *Titanic* experience reduces again and again to three interrelated articulations: "It's really old-fashioned and romantic," "It made me cry," and "It really happened." In this context, one is bemused at the bathos and banality of this reduction in relation to the magnitude and extremity of audience response: an unprecedented array of repetitive and mimetic activities that include not only repeated viewings of the film and construction of innumerable commemorative altars to it on the World Wide Web, but also the aforementioned pilgrimages to victims' gravesites, mass purchase of replicas of Heart of the Ocean necklaces, and reenactments of scenes from the movie such as throwing the replicant necklace into the sea or leaning precariously off the bow of cruise ships, arms outstretched. Indeed, one hears radio news items about cruise ship captains warning passengers about the dangers of just such imitation after "one woman fell off and drowned,"[2] and then reads in *Avenues*, the Automobile

Association of America's travel magazine, of the "unexpected irony . . . that a movie about history's most infamous sea disaster is partly responsible for an unprecedented boom in cruise ship bookings."[3] Given such extreme behavior and the bathetic vagaries of "It's really old-fashioned and romantic," "It made me cry," and "It really happened," one wonders, most of all, exactly what is the referent of "it" in these phrases.

This phenomenological and powerful "it" is what I wish to address and describe more precisely in what follows. I want to argue that this "it" refers to a poetic profundity in *Titanic* as complex and moving as it is also retrograde. While the film's critics have accurately pointed to *Titanic*'s superficial historicism, ludicrous dialogue, and over-the-top melodrama, I suggest these elements are not where the film's poetic power and emotional force are located. Rather, its poetic depth and complexity emerge from two significantly correlated features. The first is the absolutely crucial *frame story*, which, set in the present day, narratively encircles the irreversibility of the historical past—reconstituting it in the "roundness" of the film as a whole as a felicitous and comforting "eternal return" that undoes catastrophe and death. The second is the film's particularly *resonant imagery*, which functions as a quite literal "medium of exchange" between the film's two temporal registers of present and past and its two spatial registers of vast and small— and thus allows for their *reversibility*. These two correlated features constitute *Titanic* as perhaps the most deeply felt and yet bathetic disaster movie ever made.

Indeed, both the elevated emotion generated by the *Titanic* catastrophe and the bathetic resolution generated by the film's romantic mode find ready expression across a range of anecdotal reports. For example, a cruise line official descends from the elevated to the bathetic when he tells an interviewer, "As far as we're concerned, *Titanic* is not a downer . . . but a love story that is inspiring people to book a cruise."[4] And leading actress Kate Winslet ascends from the bathetic to the elevated when she tells *Rolling Stone* that, watching *Titanic* with a real audience, she "wept flood buckets. Absolute buckets. . . . It's fantastic thinking that I've been such a big part of it, and it's probably going to go down in history."[5]

Winslet is right in ways she cannot imagine. *Titanic* ultimately functions in its whole less as a linear and teleological historical narrative than as a literal *bathysphere*, a round and protective submersible device that can "go down in history" at the cost of a few tears (well, buckets of them) and little danger. Given the film's particularly canny narrative structure and poetic imagery, it allows audiences a hermetically safe way not only to immerse themselves in the literal depths of the ocean to re-collect the historical past and emplot it in the romantic mode,[6] but also to immerse themselves in the emotional clarity of an "age of innocence" undampened by the murky ambivalence of contemporary irony (even as it is drowned in a sea of tears). Beneath its surface bathos, then, if only for a moment, *Titanic* "raises" both itself and all that seems irrecoverable and "old-fashioned" to a large majority of its present audience: that is, an elevated sense that historical existence (and narrative) is infinitely immense in meaning and transcendent power, and an elevated sense that emotional existence (and poesis) is infinitely deep and lasting in intimacy, immediacy, and immanence. And all this without anyone getting the "bends."

Because of its particular structure and imagery, *Titanic* has touched contemporary audiences longing for something not readily available or particularly credible in the age of irony at the end of history: namely, "authentic emotion" felt as "historic experience." This longing ultimately confuses the "histrionic" and "historic" with the "historical." In other words, *Titanic* is a highly effective cultural expression of what Susan Stewart, in *On Longing: Narratives of the Miniature, the Gigantic, the Souvenir, the Collection*, calls—with specific reference to bourgeois sentiment and the longing to feel (rather than understand) the singular "aura" of history in a capitalist economy of mass production—"the social disease of *nostalgia*."[7] Stewart defines nostalgia as

> sadness without an object, a sadness which creates a longing that of necessity is inauthentic because it does not take part in lived experience. Rather it remains behind and before that experience. Hostile to history and its invisible origins, and yet longing for an impossibly pure context of lived experience as a place of origin, nostalgia wears a distinctly utopian face, a face that turns toward a future-past, a past which has only ideological reality. . . . [The] nostalgic's utopia [is] a utopia where authenticity suffuses both word and world.[8]

However briefly, *Titanic* as a whole offers such a nostalgic utopia, its narrative structure not only enabling a *descent* into and *submersion* in the "past" as an "impossibly pure context of lived experience," but also enabling a very present and contemporary *search* for this "place of origin." Indeed, as an effect of its bathyspheric and rounded frame story, *Titanic* contains the utopian dream of a "future-past," while also—despite or because of this future-past's catastrophic curtailment—generating a "past-perfect" and a longing for its perfect repetition in the future, a future-perfect. It is hardly surprising, then, that many in the audience, seeking the lost "authenticity" of *Titanic*'s "word and world" once they leave the theater, turn to gestures of reenactment. In sum, the depths to which *Titanic* sinks is quite different from the depths it achieves.

Going Down in History

Given its resonant complexity of structure and function, it is somewhat strange that, compared to emphasis given other constituent elements of the film, *Titanic*'s frame story has received relatively little attention as other than an expository device—and it certainly has been given no great credit as structurally essential to the film's extraordinary emotional appeal. For example, José Arroyo, who has written perhaps one of the few extended considerations of the frame story, is begrudging at best. First, he questions "the decision to let Rose live to be a hundred years old, in order to tell us the story."[9] And then he writes:

> The exploration of the wreck of the *Titanic* and the interaction between [Brock] Lovett [the leader of the salvage expedition] and old Rose takes up a fair amount of running time at beginning and end of the film, and as

a narrative device is not without its uses: the audience can be given contextual information on the history of the ship and its passengers, moving
between past and present, while several questions can be set in motion.
What happened to the necklace? What happened to Rose?

But such benefits do not make up for the device's shortcomings. The
good things one remembers in the framing-device sections are few: an abstract shot of submarines resembling spaceships descending toward the final frontier; a cute robot maneuvering its way through the silt-covered
remains of the wreck; computer graphics vividly illustrating what happened
to the ship when it hit the iceberg. This section is still not worth the screen-
time that it occupies.[10]

Arroyo goes on to further criticize the frame story because he views Lovett
and the salvage crew as they listen to Rose as providing a "surrogate" audience
whose rapt faces are meant to instruct the movie's audience on how they should
feel. This device is considered shamelessly "pre-emptive," "hackneyed," and "manipulative." As Arroyo puts it: "The director should have trusted the audience to
make the link between the past and the present."[11]

Yet, I would claim, it is precisely this highly manipulative and on-screen linking of past and present that makes the framing device so critical to *Titanic*'s emotional appeal and extraordinary success. Going far beyond mere preliminary
exposition, the film's frame story serves a number of extremely significant narrative
functions. On the one hand, it serves both literally and metaphorically as a *submersible* device that allows both viewers and characters in the present to slowly
descend and relocate themselves in a "lost" past history both public and private;
on the other, it serves literally and metaphorically as a *spherical* device that encircles and contains both the past and present and the public and private, adequating
each to the others and constituting them all as reversible. In both functions, it also
constitutes the entire film as a *protective* device—one that allows for a mediated
but seemingly "authentic" experience, one that keeps real trauma, but not real emotion, at bay.

In her discussion of the "social disease of nostalgia," Stewart notes that nostalgia is always inauthentic in its goals. That is, while a real feeling, it is also a
form of false consciousness insofar as it seeks fulfillment in an impossible origin
and ostensibly desires to fill a perceived absence and lack it really wishes to maintain. As the desire to return to a "pure" past that never was, as "the desire to desire,"
nostalgia compulsively generates its own repetition and yet is always disappointed
by the results: "Nostalgia is the repetition that mourns the inauthenticity of all repetition." That is, insofar as repetition can never return itself to its origin to again
become a "first time," Stewart suggests that "we find that . . . *disjunctions of
temporality* . . . create the space for nostalgia's eruption."[12]

Titanic's emplotment is based precisely on just such "disjunctions of temporality" that "create the space for nostalgia's eruption" and for its repetitions—
disjunctions that the film as a whole rather cannily attempts to adjudicate and
synthesize with monumental, if momentary, success. In this regard, the frame story

is absolutely critical. Indeed, the frame story's present descent into the ocean and the past is *doubly* disjunctive: first in temporality and, again, in motivation. We begin in the present with a salvage expedition that uses scientific knowledge and high-tech "bathyspheres" to descend into the depths of the ocean, their goal to explore the wreck of the "real" *Titanic* and find a priceless necklace with a blue diamond pendant called the Heart of the Ocean. In the context of this very public and objectively motivated mission, however, we also are soon introduced to old Rose ("101 years old"), who identifies herself not only as a *Titanic* survivor but also as someone who has an intimate and subjective connection to the Heart of the Ocean. Thus she joins the expedition; but her descent into the past, however mediated by high technology and publicly narrated to Brock Lovett and the salvage crew, is intensely personal and her motivations private.

From the beginning (and finally at the end) of the frame story, our "going down in history" to locate the *Titanic* is doubly moving and doubly emplotted: on the one side, a public, objective, scientific, and technological voyage of capitalist salvage and historic *re-collection* and, on the other, a private, subjective, humanist, and emotional journey of bourgeois memory histrionically reconnecting with the personal past through *souvenirs*. What makes this frame story even more complex, however, is that this dual and dialectical descent into the *immense depths of the ocean* and the *intimate depths of the past* is itself *doubly synthesized* at the more inclusive level of the film as a whole. This synthesis is accomplished by— and, indeed, concretely resolves itself as—both the historical wreck of the real *Titanic* (in all its docudrama ambiguity) and the Heart of the Ocean necklace. These objects (as well as certain others) are synthetic; that is, they serve as the *material* and *common* ground of both present and past, both public collection and private souvenir (a distinction to which I will later return).

Two and a half miles down on the ocean floor, the real, "authentic" *Titanic* (access to which is always mediated, thus marking its irrecoverable loss to immediate experience) is at once the nostalgic object of the film's histrionic narrative desire and the nostalgic object of James Cameron and his crew's historic cinematic desire. Indeed, the highly mediated footage of the real *Titanic* continually undermines both the narrative "transparency" of the salvage crew's descent to the ocean floor and the myth of "direct" contact with the ship. In other words, we become aware of Cameron and his crews' own bathyspheric descent into the depths of the ocean to film not only the framing narrative and the remains of the historical *Titanic*, but also their own contemporary acts of cinematic exploration. Thus, at one and the same time, looking at the footage of the remains of the ship, we are brought both physically closer to the past and temporally more distant from it. It is precisely this irresolvable experiential paradox presented by the real *Titanic* that becomes poetically foregrounded in the frame story and generates nostalgic longing for a temporal proximity with the past that is impossible to achieve. And it is precisely this paradox that finds resolution in the film's breathtaking computer graphic dissolves—not only between the present and past, but also between the different ontological and epistemological relations we have to what we distinguish as history and fiction. For brief instants (indeed, in one, the blink of an eye), the temporal disjunctions that constitute nostalgia are resolved through their dissolution: desire itself is fulfilled, and narrative is at "one with its object."[13]

Intimate Immensity, or the Heart of the Ocean

This momentary resolution of such disjuncture in *Titanic* is as much spatial as it is temporal, as much categorical as it is particular, and again is highly dependent upon the frame story to provide the gaps in space and time as well as between categories of desire. In part, the film's very powerful poesis emerges from its ability to construct its *motifs* (whether historically or fictively generated) into a *system of objective exchange* that serves to mediate between past and present, between the "here" and "elsewhere" of both characters and audience, and between objective and public existence and subjective and individual experience. Perhaps the most striking examples are the sea, the ship itself, and the Heart of the Ocean— the first a medium that *surrounds* and the latter two material objects that *circulate between* both past and present narratives. All three are highly resonant for characters and audience alike. There are other intermediary objects as well—not only the obvious drawing of young Rose but also the more subtle motifs of the *Titanic*'s fireplaces, its fragile china, and its doors. Indeed, the latter allow us, through computer graphic poesis, literal and metaphoric passage from the isolation and quietude of the present depths of the sea to the public bustle and expansiveness of a recollected past and then back to its loss once again. Considering "the dialectics of inside and outside" in *The Poetics of Space*, Gaston Bachelard notes that the poetic image of a door has two modes of being, "awakens in us a two-way dream, that is doubly symbolical." He asks, "And then, onto what, toward what, do doors open? Do they open for the world of men, or for the world of solitude?"[14]

Correlative with this system of objective exchange, *Titanic*'s poesis also emerges from its construction of a *system of subjective reversibility* and, therefore, equivalence between extreme oppositions. These oppositions include the past and present resolved by the rounded framing of the narrative and the computer graphic dissolves, as well as the large and the small, the immense and the intimate, the horizontally broad and the vertically deep. Pointing to how "macrocosm and microcosm are correlated" by certain poetic images, Bachelard notes, in particular, that "transpositions of size . . . give a double life to poetic space."[15]

Certainly, the *Titanic* itself (wreck and ship) generates this double life and poesis: it is at once and alternately both miniature and gigantic. Stewart tells us that the miniature is "a metaphor for the interior space and time of the bourgeois subject"; it is removed from "lived historical time" and "tends toward tableau rather than narrative, toward silence"; it presents a "still and perfect universe," "whose anteriority is always absolute, and whose profound interiority is therefore always unrecoverable."[16] Found in the present, the wreck of the *Titanic* is just such a miniature—the Heart of the Ocean—resting in ultimately unfathomable solitude like a single boot or doll's head or china cup on the vast expanse of ocean floor. Nonetheless, lost in the past, the *Titanic* is also gigantic. Even as, in the blackness of night, we watch it break apart and go down into the sea and history, it still dwarfs its passengers, still expands and overwhelms space in spectacular display mode. Indeed, Stewart sees the gigantic as a metaphor not only for "the abstract authority of the state" but also for "the collective, public life," and she locates it "at the origin of public and natural history."[17] "Represented through movement, through being in time," unlike the miniature, the gigantic "represents the order and disorder of historical forces"; it points to "the body's 'toylike' and 'insignificant' aspects"; it "envelops us, but is inaccessible to lived experience" since its "modes of exaggeration tend toward abstraction."[18]

This transposition of size and of the poetic values of intimacy and immensity, of the miniature and the gigantic, is perhaps most concretized in the Heart of the Ocean necklace, which stands as the film's crudest and yet also most subtle example; for the diamond is both literally and metaphorically gross and yet small enough to be slipped into a coat pocket. The very name Heart of the Ocean suggests not only the *Titanic* itself but also the reversibility and conflation of our sense of the broad and the deep, of the epic and the intimate, of the depth of the heart and the expanse of the ocean. Indeed, in this context, the lines of Rilke's poem that serve as epigraph to this essay (translated as "The world is large, but in us / It is deep as the sea") resonate.[19] While, on the one hand, they uncomfortably evoke the bathetic melodrama of Rose Bukater and Jack Dawson's romance (as well as Celine Dion singing "My Heart Will Go On"), on the other, they evoke the powerful poetic images of "intimate immensity" glossed by Bachelard, images that allow us to "sense the concordance of world immensity with intimate depth of being."[20]

Certainly, there is no doubt of a bathetic descent from Rilke to Dion in the deflation of "intimate immensity" to "*Romeo and Juliet* aboard the *Titanic*" (the "high concept" that Cameron pitched to Fox).[21] Yet in the context of the past decade's male-oriented, effects-laden, action blockbusters that foreground immense and overwhelming explosions at the expense of intimacy, depth, and being, much has been made of *Titanic*'s romantic emphasis on "the intimate depth of being" in the midst of grand historical narrative and technological spectacle. In this regard, Cameron seems to follow Bachelard, who tells us that "*inner immensity . . .* gives their real meaning to certain expressions concerning the visible world," and that "the exterior spectacle helps intimate grandeur unfold."[22]

Such "transactions between two kinds of grandeur" have been noted not just by Bachelard.[23] They have also been discussed by contemporary critics discussing *Titanic*. Arroyo tells us, "By focusing on a single relationship, in the context of some earth-shattering event, it's clear that Cameron and crew strove to make this movie an *intimate epic*."[24] A critic for *Cahiers du cinéma* is reported as writing that "Mr. Cameron . . . raised the great Hollywood spectacular from the ocean floor by presenting the century's most traumatic accident as a love story."[25] And Cameron himself has spoken of his long-standing desire to make a historical epic in the romantic mode of *Doctor Zhivago* (1965) as well as of his pleasure in using the vastness of the ship and complicated special effects technology to serve the smallest and most delicate details of human emotion.[26]

Nonetheless, intimate romance against the backdrop of an immense historical spectacle is hardly novel—as indicated not only by the reference to *Doctor*

Zhivago but also by the many descriptions of *Titanic* as a "return" to "old-fashioned" Hollywood filmmaking. Indeed, as David Thomson ironically but accurately noted long ago in a reference to *Gone With the Wind* (1939)—although he could well have been talking about *Birth of a Nation* (1915), *Cleopatra* (1963), *Reds* (1981), or *Titanic*—the Hollywood epic as it entails history has always been grounded in "Hollywood's faith that historical events rise to the occasion of exceptional human romance."[27] Which is to say, Hollywood epic filmmaking has always availed itself of some tear-diluted and bathetic version of Bachelard's poesis of "intimate immensity."

What is exceptional about *Titanic*, then, is not its generic combination of intimate romance and immense spectacle. Although necessary, it is not sufficient to explain the film's extraordinary appeal to the emotional and historical consciousness of its popular audience. Rather, I would argue, *Titanic* is exceptional in its particular mobilization of an extensive and poetically transposable imagery of vast and deep, large and small, public and private that goes beyond and, indeed, encompasses the romance and spectacle. This imagery evokes in those who felt the film deeply a sense of "intimate immensity" that elevates the bathetic characters to a depth certainly grounded neither in their histrionic passion, nor in their physical stamina, nor in what the *Los Angeles Times* film critic, Kenneth Turan, calls "dialogue that has the self-parodying ring of Young Romance comics."[28] These are all superficial, if necessary, trappings of generic American epic narrative, but their real depth is grounded in another medium: the ocean.

Sea World

According to Bachelard, for the poetic imagination "immensity is a philosophical category of daydream" that "flees the object nearby and right away is far off . . . in the space of *elsewhere*." Furthermore, "when this *elsewhere* is in *natural* surroundings," it produces in the daydreamer a "consciousness of enlargement." This poetic sense of the world's enlargement creates as well an expansion of the world *within ourselves* and so is experienced both as "immensity" and as the "intensity of our intimate being." Thus, Bachelard tells us, "In the presence of such obvious immensity as the immensity of night, a poet can point the way to intimate depth of being."[29] Another such poetic fundament of intimate immensity is, of course, the ocean—not only in its horizonal vastness but also in its depth as an absolute "elsewhere."

Focusing extensively on the writings of adventurer Phillipe Diolé (a deep-sea diver and desert traveler), Bachelard is worth quoting at length insofar as he points to the "intimate immensity" of the ocean in passages that seem particularly relevant to *Titanic* and the fundamental imagistic source of the frame story's poetic power. He writes of Diolé:

> At a little over 125 feet under the surface of the water, he discovered "absolute depth," depth that is beyond measuring, and would give no greater powers of dream and thought if it were doubled or even tripled. By means,

then, of his diving experiences, Diolé *really entered the volume of the water*. And when we have . . . shared with him his conquest of the intimacy of water, we come . . . to recognize in this space-substance . . . a one-dimensional space. One substance, one dimension. And we are so remote from . . . life on earth, that this dimension of water bears the mark of limitlessness . . . in a world . . . unified by its substance.

    Diolé tells us . . . "that . . . deep water . . . allows the diver to loosen the ordinary ties of time and space and make life resemble an obscure, inner poem. . . . to go down into the water . . . is to change space," and by changing space, by leaving the space of one's usual sensibilities, one enters into communication with a space that is psychically innovating.[30]

In another passage, memories of being in the depths of the ocean are awakened in Diolé, and he speaks of his sense of "translucent density," of the solitude of "silence and slow progress." And, in uncanny and yet unsurprising relation to one of *Titanic*'s central metaphors, he speaks of being immersed "in the *heart of a fluid*," a "luminous, beneficent, dense matter, which was sea water."[31]

As I would suggest Cameron does through *Titanic*'s literal and metaphoric bathyspheric descent into the depths of the sea and the past, Bachelard remarks how Diolé gives us

a psychological technique which permits us to be elsewhere, in an absolute elsewhere that bars the way to the forces that hold us imprisoned in the "here." This is not merely an escape into a space that is open to adventure on every side. . . . Diolé transports us to the elsewhere of another world. . . . Here both time and space are under the domination of the image. Elsewhere and formerly are stronger than *hic et nunc*. The *being-here* is maintained by a being from elsewhere.[32]

It is *Titanic*'s frame story that takes us to this "being-here" in an "absolute elsewhere" that we could not get to without it: namely, the deep solitude and silence of the ocean, one of those "fundamental, material images" Bachelard sees as the basis of all imagination.[33] While the busy teleological drama of the great ship goes on primarily at the surface, it is the frame story that takes us where we really want to go—to the deep space and stopped time of reverie and nostalgic longing found here at the bottom of the sea.

Cameron, as well as his audience, gets caught up in this space of nostalgic longing, but since he is a male in our culture, his emotional "desire to desire" is displaced onto the technological and scientific. It is no less a desire to arrive at an "absolute elsewhere." We are told that seeing footage of the actual *Titanic* not only "helped inspire Cameron's 1989 movie, *The Abyss*, giving him the idea of shooting deep ocean as if it were outer space," but also led him to write the *Titanic* screenplay. We are also told it was critical for the director "to dive down through two and half miles of ocean to see the wreck itself," and that "he ended up going down twelve times" (devising a special crush-proof camera in the process).[34] "Going down to the wreck inspired haunting images of drowned grandeur" (while also giving him "schematics"). "Being" on the real ship (this "being there" mediated, of course, by technology) not only instantiated (twelve times) the search for an irrecoverable originary past that leads to excessive acts of repetition, but also clearly generated in the director an excessive (and nostalgic) desire for authenticity. Thus Cameron wanted "to get it right" and went to "considerable extremes" to get "his lifeboat davits and carpets made by the same companies, from the same plans, that made the *Titanic* originals."[35]

Antiquarian in the Aquarium, or Re-Collecting the Past

This nostalgic desire to locate the origins of the present in some "pure context of experience" and to "re-collect" it in the recovery of "lost" and "authentic" material objects that will supposedly resolve the disjunctive gap between past and present informs more than Cameron's own sensibility. This nostalgic desire also drives *Titanic*'s frame story—and thus in-forms the film's overarching and repetitive narrative movement: that is, in the "absolute space" of the ocean, the recovery and loss again and again of both the ship and the necklace (and, at the more banal and surface level of relationship and action, of both Jack and Rose). But these acts of re-collection and loss speak deeply as well to the overarching sensibility of our contemporary culture. Thus it is not surprising that they have been further reenacted by the film's audience, who, extraordinarily moved, have attempted to re-collect their "pure context of experience" in the movie theater in the material replications of gravestone rubbings, paste necklaces, and "hard data" accumulated on both the historical catastrophe and the film's reproduction of it. Again relevant here, Stewart writes:

> Within the development of culture under an *exchange economy*, the search for *authentic experience* and, correlatively, the search for the *authentic object* become critical. As experience is increasingly mediated and abstracted, the lived relation of the body to the phenomenological world is replaced by a nostalgic myth of contact and presence. "Authentic" experience becomes both elusive and allusive as it is placed beyond the horizon of present lived experience, the beyond in which the antique, the pastoral, the exotic and other fictive domains are articulated. In this process of distancing, the memory of the body is replaced by the memory of the object, a memory standing outside the self and thus presenting both a surplus and lack of significance.[36]

What this passage suggests—and *Titanic* and its effects concretely dramatize—is the way in which the alienated subject locates experience in things rather than in social relations.

Of particular interest here is when this replacement of "original" and "authentic" experience by the material things that bear its "trace" involves an attempt at re-collecting not only the personal past but also the historical past. In this instance, "historic" objects are valued personally, and "historical" objectives become confused in the subjective sensibility of the *antiquarian*. Stewart tells us, "In antiquarianism we see a theory of history informed by an aesthetics of the souvenir. Antiquarianism always displays a functional ambivalence; we find either the nostalgic desire for *romanticism* or the political desire of *authentication* at its base." This "functional ambivalence" is essential to *Titanic*, playing itself out along both *genre* and *gender* lines. Thus, in terms of genre, it appears as an ambivalence between *epic romance* and authentic *historical re-creation* and, in terms of gender, as psychological cathexis on commodified objects, which take dual and ambivalent form as "evidence": on the "female side," in the subjective personal *souvenir* and, on the "male side," in the objective *collection* of "historic" material that stands as "factual data" of past experience. In this regard, glossing the notion of nostalgic "longing," Stewart notes "the capacity of narrative to generate significant material objects" or "belongings." These "function within the economy of the bourgeois subject" as a "supplementarity that in consumer culture replaces its generating subject" and *objectifies desire* in two devices: the *souvenir* and the *collection*.[37]

The privatized souvenir "seeks distance (the exotic in time and space) . . . in order to transform and collapse distance into proximity to, or approximation with, the self." The souvenir therefore "plays in the distance between the present and the imagined, prelapsarian experience, experience as it might be 'directly lived'"; in this, it "contracts the world in order to expand the personal"; and yet, as a nostalgic and antiquarian construction, the souvenir "is by definition always incomplete"; it is "metonymic to the scene of its original appropriation," and by only pointing toward an originary moment, it "generates a narrative which reaches only 'behind,' spiraling in a continually inward movement rather than outward toward the future." Thus, in *Titanic*, and for Cameron and his audience alike, both the lost fictional jewel and the irrecoverable (if documented) wreck of the ship itself function as personal souvenirs. And, as Stewart notes, "The only proper context for the souvenir is the displacement of reverie." That is, "the souvenir, so long as it remains 'uncollected,' is 'lost,' removed from any context of origin and use value in such a way as to 'surprise' and capture its viewer into reverie."[38] It is no wonder, then, that the Heart of the Ocean must be thrown into the sea, and the real *Titanic* can never be raised.

The more public collection further objectifies "this process of commodification by which [the] narrative of the personal operates within contemporary consumer society." The collection, according to Stewart, "marks the . . . place where history is transformed into space, into property." Seeking a "form of self-enclosure," it, too, is antiquarian; indeed, it ahistoricizes history and "represents the total aestheticization of use value." That is:

> The collection does not displace attention to the past; rather, the past is at the service of the collection, for whereas the souvenir lends authenticity to the past, the past lends authenticity to the collection. . . . The collection replaces history with classification, with order beyond the realm of temporality. In the collection, time is not something to be restored to an origin; rather, all time is made simultaneous or synchronous within the collection's world.[39]

It is precisely the past that is put at the service of *Titanic*'s nostalgic and antiquarian impulse to substitute and classify material detail for an understanding of relational historical causation. Where the principle of the souvenir operates in the film's frame story, the principle of the collection operates in the narrative it encloses. Back in the past, on the surface of the ocean, we meet Rose's wealthy fiancé, Cal Hockley, who is explicitly dramatized and openly called by Rose a heartless "collector" of objects and people—the Heart of the Ocean and Rose herself being his two most prized examples. However, explicit contempt for Cal's accumulative aspirations notwithstanding, the *Titanic* itself serves a similar desire for collection—and of a much grander scope than Cal's. That is, the ship functions for both Cameron and his audience as a giant museum or vitrine: Cameron's *Titanic*, itself re-collected, is filled with historical objects and people hermetically gathered and sealed in one place, and it, like the antiquarian, makes historical time "simultaneous or synchronous" with both its literal and metaphoric collective capacity.

Thus we can understand as well as see the effects of Cameron's own collector's impulse: his willingness to spare no expense, his meticulous attention to both the cataloging of material details and their grand display, his aesthetic desire to "get" and to show every "thing" just "right." Here Arroyo is "on the money" when he remarks on *Titanic*'s "gorgeously glamorous" lighting and look, points to "the liner's sumptuousness, and the finery of its passengers," the way "table-settings shine, fireplaces glow, *art-nouveau* hairclips glitter," and suggests "'richness' is an important story element."[40] All the "material evidence" in this aesthete's collection is ultimately "authenticated" by an irrevocably "lost" past whose decayed presence its present display busily covers over and up as if it were a decaying corpse (or a decaying wreck of a ship on the ocean floor).

It is fitting, then, that Arroyo also notes how the film, attempting always "significant and grandiose" spectacle and display, "ossifies" everything.[41] And that another critic, Kent Jones, describes how the poetic power of "the dead clothed bodies floating in the water under an icy blue mid-Atlantic light" makes the film come "alive" and is linked to Cameron's "longing" for what we might here characterize as "authentic experience." Indeed, Jones suggests, Cameron "can only imagine people fully when they are either dead or dying."[42] This desire to collect, ossify, and display, however, is not merely characteristic of Cameron in particular (or filmmakers in general). This desire is also cultural—and precisely characteristic of the antiquarian (whether the collector or the collection's spectator). Thus Stewart might well be speaking not only of the nostalgic obsessions of *Titanic*'s filmmaker, but also of the complementary nostalgic pleasures displayed in the film and felt in the fullness of bourgeois sentiment by its mass audience, when she writes:

> In contrast to the historian, who looks for design and causality, the antiquarian searches for material evidence of the past. Yet at the same time, the antiquarian searches for an internal relation between the past and present which is made possible by their absolute disruption. Hence his or

her search is primarily an aesthetic one, an attempt to erase the actual past in order to create an imagined past which is available for consumption. *In order to awaken the dead, the antiquarian must first manage to kill them.*[43]

That Sinking Feeling, or Drowning by Numbers

In this essay, I have argued that *Titanic*'s extraordinary poetic power and mass appeal are essentially tied to and emergent from its framing narrative, which "rounds" off and fills in the loss of a past disaster. Discussing the "phenomenology of roundness," Bachelard prefigures Stewart (whom he inspired) when he writes: "Images of roundness help us to *collect* ourselves, permit us to confer an initial constitution on ourselves, and to confirm our being intimately, inside."[44] Furthermore, the bathyspheric nature of the framing narrative constructs the whole film temporally and spatially as ahistorical, as a hermetic ball closed off in space and isolated from time. Much like those small glass globes filled with snow or water and tiny figures and objects that can be violently shaken up while remaining utterly contained, *Titanic* isolates and seals its objects of desire within its own framing, and, as Bachelard notes, "when a thing become isolated, it becomes round, [and] assumes a figure of being that is concentrated upon itself."[45] History, as it is framed here, is of no real consequence.

Nonetheless, I have also tried to explicate the extraordinary poetic power of *Titanic* as a *historical* form of poesis that is emergent from and tied to a bourgeois culture caught up in escalating processes and increasing layers of mediation and economic exchange. This excessive mediation and exchange generate alienation—as well as the repetitive desire to reconnect with "authentic experience" (even if it is only of a movie) and an ongoing obsession and self-displacement in "things." Here, as a whole and at once, *Titanic* provides its mass audience with both a miniaturized and intimate souvenir and a gigantic and public collection.

Finally, throughout this essay, I have moved—quite ambivalently—between, on the one hand, appreciating *Titanic* as a film that significantly touches and plumbs the depths of contemporary culture and, on the other, criticizing it as a bathetic drama that anticlimaxes in a sea of tears and false historical consciousness. As a related aside, I cannot refrain from quoting Cameron, who has said: "I hope we make people feel like they've just had a good time. . . . Not a good time in the sense they've seen a Batman movie, but a good time in the sense that they've had their emotions kind of checked. The plumbing still works."[46] As a member of my culture, there seems no way for me to resolve this ambivalence. I can only recognize it—hence the bathetic play of my section headings and the punning that deflates high seriousness. Both undercut as well as affirm my serious discussion of the film's effects on viewers, who seem to have drowned by the numbers in its seductive waters. This is to say, historically conscious as I am, I was appalled by *Titanic*; but bourgeois subject that I am (and against my intellectual will and to my shame), I also shed into its collective cinematic bucket a big, wet, nostalgic, and antiquarian tear or two.

Notes

1. Kristen Baldwin, "Dawson's Crypt," *Entertainment Weekly*, 24 April 1998, 13.
2. KFWB Radio News, Los Angeles, 23 June 1998.
3. Peter S. Greenberg, "Something's Afloat," *Avenues* (July–August 1998), 34.
4. Ibid., 34.
5. David Lipsky, "The Unsinkable Kate Winslet," *Rolling Stone*, 5 March 1998, 78.
6. For discussion of the notion of "emplotment" and its various modes (romantic, tragic, comic, satirical, and possibly epic), particularly as it defines historical styles, see the "Introduction" to Hayden White, *Metahistory: The Historical Imagination in Nineteenth-Century Europe* (Baltimore: Johns Hopkins University Press, 1973), 1–42.
7. Susan Stewart, *On Longing: Narratives of the Miniature, the Gigantic, the Souvenir, the Collection* (Baltimore: Johns Hopkins University Press, 1984), 23. Emphasis added.
8. Ibid., 23.
9. José Arroyo, "Massive Attack," *Sight and Sound*, February 1998, 17.
10. Ibid., 17–18.
11. Ibid., 18.
12. Stewart, *On Longing*, 24.
13. Ibid.
14. Gaston Bachelard, *The Poetics of Space*, trans. Maria Jolas (Boston: Beacon Press, 1964), 224.
15. Ibid., 169–170.
16. Stewart, *On Longing*, xii, 65–66, 86, 44.
17. Ibid., xii, 71.
18. Ibid., 86, 70, 102.
19. Quoted in Bachelard as an epigraph without citation, *The Poetics of Space*, 183.
20. Bachelard, *The Poetics of Space*, 189.
21. Arroyo, "Massive Attack," 17.
22. Bachelard, *The Poetics of Space*, 185, 192.
23. Ibid., 193.
24. Arroyo, "Massive Attack," 18. Emphasis added.
25. Alan Riding, quoting Jean-Marc Lalanne of *Cahiers du cinéma* in "Why *Titanic* Conquered the World," *New York Times*, 26 April 1998, 29.
26. See John H. Richardson, "Magnificent Obsession," *Premiere*, December 1997, 130–131, 143.
27. David Thomson, *Warren Beatty and Desert Eyes: A Life and a Story* (New York: Doubleday, 1987), 409. For more on this issue, see my own "'Surge and Splendor': A Phenomenology of the Hollywood Historical Epic," *Representations* 29 (winter 1990), 24–49.
28. Kenneth Turan, "*Titanic* Sinks Again—Spectacularly," *Los Angeles Times*, 19 December 1997, n.p.
29. Bachelard, *The Poetics of Space*, 183–184, 193, 189.
30. Ibid, 205–206.
31. Ibid., 207. Emphasis added.
32. Ibid., 207–208
33. Ibid., 207.
34. Richardson, "Magnificent Obsession," 126.
35. Ibid., 129–130.
36. Stewart, *On Longing*, 133. Emphasis added.
37. Ibid., 140, xi–xii. Emphasis added.

38. Ibid., 140, xii, 137, 135, 151.
39. Ibid., xii, 151.
40. Arroyo, "Massive Attack," 18.
41. Ibid., 19.
42. Kent Jones, "Critic's Heart Is an Ocean of Longing," *Film Comment*, March–April 1998, 23.
43. Stewart, *On Longing*, 143. Emphasis added.
44. Ibid., 234. Emphasis added.
45. Bachelard, *The Poetics of Space*, 239.
46. Quoted in Richardson, "Magnificent Obsession," 129.

"The China Had Never Been Used!"

On the Patina of Perfect Images
in *Titanic*

Julian Stringer

*I*t appears as if nothing on earth can come between *Titanic* and its fans. From Beijing to New York, Moscow to Tokyo, the appeal of James Cameron's epic to global audiences has been truly out-of-this-world. And as scores of observers have already pointed out, between Kate Winslet's radiant beauty and Leonardo DiCaprio's swimming-pool eyes lie a range of other factors that need to be taken into account in any understanding of the reasons for the film's startling international success. One reason why *Titanic* has managed to attract huge numbers of enthusiastic moviegoers is that it stages events from the past in a manner that resonates imaginatively with the widespread contemporary cultural fusion of nostalgia and consumerism.

Cameron's dramatization of this cultural fusion represents a shift in the aesthetics and ambition of the postclassical Hollywood blockbuster. In his invaluable book on the unique form such blockbusters often take, high-concept cinema, Justin Wyatt shows how recent movies as diverse as *Flashdance* (1983), *Top Gun* (1986), and *Batman* (1989) present "perfect images" so as to better exploit the commercial potential opened up by advertising and merchandising tie-ins. Emphasizing the importance of style to the "look" of such titles, Wyatt describes how, at the level of formal composition, they are "linked by a set of production techniques composed of extreme back-lighting, a minimal (often almost black-and-white) color scheme, a pre-dominance of reflected images, and a tendency toward settings of high technology and industrial design."[1] With these films, as well as with *The Hunger* (1983), *Beverly Hills Cop* (1984), *Flatliners* (1990), and many others, perfect visual images work to promote a sense of the contemporary, of newness, so as to promote and market high-profile, multimedia concepts on the basis of their immediacy and relevance.

Titanic is also immediate and relevant, but it displays a different set of perfect images all the same. This high-concept blockbuster is cast in a different light. The film's glamorous "look" does not merely embody a veneer of expensive high-tech industrial design—giving Cameron's technicians ample opportunity to show off their latest gizmos—it also projects very compelling images of the past, circa 1912. That is to say, the movie's visual presentation of a distant era is more properly associated with what critics often refer to as the European, and more particularly the British "heritage film." A style of popular filmmaking obsessed with looking back and re-creating the past in all its glory and nostalgic perfection, rather than depicting the present and all its impossible contradictions, heritage films are very familiar to today's audiences through the stunning art and production designs of many big box office hits. A loose variant of the costume drama, historical epic, and period drama, the genre has a lineage that can be traced most obviously through the Merchant-Ivory cycle of international coproductions usually appropriated on the part of the British film industry (*A Room with a View*, 1985; *Howards End*, 1992; *The Remains of the Day*, 1993; et al.). However, heritage cinema's more immediate relationship to *Titanic* is suggested, through intertextual references via the casting of DiCaprio, Winslet, Billy Zane—in the roles of Jack Dawson, the young Rose Bukater, and Cal Hockley, respectively—and others, to such recent revisionist titles as *Orlando* (1992), *William Shakespeare's Romeo + Juliet* (1996), and *Sense and Sensibility* (1996). Moreover, the impression that Cameron's movie is only one entry in the roll call of Hollywood's new investment in its own substrand of heritage is given by the almost simultaneous release of *Amistad* (1997), *Mrs. Dalloway* (1997), *The Wings of the Dove* (1998), and *Washington Square* (1998), not to mention the earlier *Age of Innocence* (1993), *Little Women* (1994), and *The English Patient* (1996).

Why is Hollywood utilizing a heritage discourse in some of its contemporary movies? Inculcating nostalgia in the form of heritage would appear to be a major component of the American film industry's current global marketing strategies, adding another string to the bow of the 1990s blockbuster by commodifying an appeal to bygone lifestyles and landscapes. True, as the heritage film is implicated in the freezing of national differences—the exhibition of a different set of perfect images—its cultural distinctions can be marketed on the basis of their "retro" glossiness just as easily as present-day dramas can be sold on the basis of their fashionable newness. But *Titanic*'s international success is, in part, the result of a more ambitious undertaking. Combining the wizardry of technological spectacle with pristine heritage visuals, the film looks back to the early twentieth century in a manner that speaks to the uses to which the past is put in all modern capitalist and consumer societies.

In exploring how and why *Titanic* has been so popular in so many distinct cultural arenas, I shall be treating it as more than just another example of Anglo-American hegemony on the prowl. (Having said that, I doubt the phrase "mid-Atlantic culture" has ever been more literally dramatized.) While my understanding

The British heritage film: Anthony Hopkins in *Howards End*

of the heritage film is drawn largely from the work of British critics, and while it is certainly the memory of British-themed films that *Titanic* plays on, I want to offer a reading of the reception of Cameron's movie that goes beyond any solely national identification with the genre. There is no essential reason why this invocation of a bygone era should only be understandable in terms of British or Anglo-American "traditions." As an example of Anglo-American cultural politics, *Titanic* represents a synthesis of two distinct filmmaking styles, high concept and heritage

(I am almost tempted to call the result "high heritage"). As a global phenomenon, however, *Titanic* demands to be read more expansively.

To sketch in some of the local characteristics of the heritage genre, let us consider the views of three British writers. First, in "To Hell with Heritage," a capsule review of *Titanic* together with other period dramas like *The Wings of the Dove* written for the *Times Educational Supplement*, Robin Buss identifies "some of the supposed characteristics" of the form. These characteristics include "conspicuous consumption, a fetishistic approach to objects," nostalgia, and an emphasis on female central characters.[2]

Second, in an auto-critique of his own prior work on the subject, film historian Andrew Higson outlines several elements common to such movies as *Chariots of Fire* (1981), *Howards End*, and *Where Angels Fear to Tread* (1991). For Higson, these films are primarily middle-class "quality" products, key pleasures of which lie in the "artful and spectacular projection of an elite, conservative vision of the national past." More than that, as "intimate epics of national identity played out in a historical context," they embody an "almost pervasive sense of loss, of nostalgia." Often adapted from canonical literary and theatrical texts (Shakespeare, Dickens, Forster), such films also focus on properties of visual display by utilizing the museum imagination—the films aspire to "showcase these various heritage attractions, to display them in all their supposed authenticity." Higson then goes on to discuss the ambivalent pleasures he takes in films like *Howards End* by questioning the whole concept of genre. Arguing both that the films are implicated in the construction of a "distinctive national cinema drawing on indigenous cultural traditions," and that examples of the genre can also be found in the United States as well as continental Europe, Higson points to their open-ended, polysemic qualities. Citing their appeal to diverse audiences, particularly women, he draws attention to the vagaries of historical reception: "The national heritage is a rich, and richly hybrid, set of expectations and should not be reduced to the apparently singular experiences of elite, conservative patriotism." Indeed, the genre offers its own political efficacy. "Nostalgia is always in effect a critique of the present, which is seen as lacking something desirable situated out of reach in the past. Nostalgia always implies that there is something wrong with the present, but it does not necessarily speak from the point of view of right-wing conservatism."[3]

Third, in an interesting article on the emotional appeals of another quintessential mid-Atlantic weepie, *Shadowlands* (1993), Richard Dyer considers the specifically "English" feel of the heritage cycle. Exploring how emotional restraint is codified across its national cinema, Dyer argues that as "the first industrialising, trading middle class and the leading nation of bourgeois imperialism, England led the world in the establishment of certain norms of middle class culture;" that is why, when a certain form of understatement finds expression in cinema, "wherever it is found, it may get labelled 'English.'"[4] Yet when extended further into the heritage genre, this observation leads to a marked instability. On the one hand, Dyer recognizes how common the form is in other national film industries, not only from Europe (*Babette's Feast*, 1987) but also from such countries as New Zealand (*The Piano*, 1993) and India (*The Chess Players*, 1977). On the other hand, one needs to question Dyer's rather sweeping rhetorical statement: "Isn't this kind of emotionality indeed only white and middle class?" by pointing to a string of recent heritage titles produced and consumed avidly in other parts of the world. Such nonwhite (middle-class?) east Asian films as *Farewell My Concubine* (China, 1993), *The Ballad of Narayama* (Japan, 1983), and *Sopyonje* (South Korea, 1993), for example, have drawn on the perception of "indigenous" emotionality and projected the results widely on the international film festival and globalized art-house cinema circuits.

The logic of this is clear. Heritage cinema's local meanings make most sense when unspooled within transnational cultural spaces. The genre's markings of cultural distinction and national difference need international exhibition sites for activation. *Titanic* is very adept at using the heritage aesthetic in ways that are infinitely open to global reception practices, and it does this not just by injecting generic iconography with perfect images of spectacular death and destruction, but through an approach to the past that can jettison its mid-Atlantic associations whatever the immediate viewing context.

It might be suggested that the theme of a luxury cruise taken with people from diverse ethnic, cultural, and religious backgrounds is itself perfectly in keeping with this aspiration. Also, the film's diegetic location in cold, dark sea water is not calculated to offend anyone on the lookout for signs of geographic exactness. Ruth Vasey has provided some historical explanation of why the Hollywood movie industry so often utilizes indistinct and imaginary locations by showing how vague topographies attract global viewers by sidestepping all references to actual existing countries. Interestingly, Vasey recounts the story of how producer David Selznick attempted to bring Alfred Hitchcock to the United States in 1938 to direct a love story centered on the sinking of the *Titanic*. When the British Chamber of Shipping objected to the idea, Arthur Houghton of the Production Code Administration wrote to his boss, Will Hays.

> I am positive that they are unable to see a picture as we see it, probably running for six and a half reels of love story and the incidents in people's lives and the last reel and a half being devoted to the tragedy at sea, and their reactions to it. Also the possible building up at the finish of the fact that the benefits and improvements resulting from the *Titanic* disaster are the very things that stand out as making sea travel on all ships so perfectly safe today.[5]

If you ignore that last sentence, this can stand as a fair-enough description of Cameron's goal—pitch the film as a chick-flick/disaster epic, a combination of romance and action. However, the introduction of heritage elements adds something new. The success of *Titanic* shows how culturally and historically specific images of nostalgia can be marketed anywhere in the world when mixed into the right recipe for success. As a consequence, the emotional resonances on offer do not then have to be experienced solely as middle class, as "English," or as "mid-Atlantic."

In short, coming to terms with the global success of *Titanic* as a high-concept movie that also resembles a heritage film necessitates an understanding of how its reception has transcended national boundaries. How does the movie circulate, and create meaning, within global spaces? In our consideration of this question, the concept of "patina"—a word long used in discussions of art and antique maintenance and restoration but given renewed emphasis recently by Grant McCracken's studies on the symbolic qualities of nostalgia and consumerism—is of particular relevance. Just as the perfect images of high concept suggest a sheen of contemporary newness, the perfect images of heritage present meanings situated out of reach in the past. Yet these meanings can be made immediate and relevant through the intermediary presence of patina.

As is only to be expected when the heritage and museum imaginations are involved, patina refers to that characteristic of goods and objects whereby their age comes to signify cultural status. The longer an object exists in the material world, the more its surface accumulates physical evidence of time's passage. The more evidence accumulated on an object's physical surface, the greater its chances of being endowed with properties highly valued by society. However, this ritual needs constant policing. The mere appearance of age is never enough. To remain culturally valued, objects must also show evidence of being maintained with care and the right technical instruments. As Arjun Appadurai puts it, "while in many cases wear is a sign of the right sort of duration in the social life of things, sheer disrepair or decrepitude is not."[6] Consequently, for the museum owner, private collector, or keeper of the family treasure, the ability to treat "malignant patina" necessitates possession of a further social skill—being able to assemble the right kinds of goods at the right time. The ability to control not just the ashes of time but also its rhythms is crucial to the workings of the patina system.

In his stimulating book, *Culture and Consumption: New Approaches to the Symbolic Character of Consumer Goods and Activities*, McCracken provides a full explanation of patina's cultural properties, For example, he suggests how the patina system legitimates existing status claims. "Its function is not to claim status but to authenticate it. Patina serves as a kind of visual proof of status."[7] McCracken adds, "Patina permits the inference: The greater the patina on certain objects, the longer the owner has enjoyed certain status. It allows the observer to read the duration of a family's status from the amount of the patina on its possessions."[8]

Titanic is clearly about these very problems of verifying authenticity, legitimizing status claims, and visually establishing the symbolic nature of family possessions. From the first few seconds of the voice-over narration spoken by the elderly Rose, the film nostalgically evokes the beauty of perfect bygone images. "It's been eighty-four years, and I can still smell the fresh paint," she recounts. "The china had never been used! The sheets had never been slept in!" The film's narrative will then go on to map out the story, not just of how 1,500 people lost their lives on 15 April 1912, but also the tragedy of all those precious objects and material goods left lying about on the ocean floor. While a final reunion scene magically resuscitates all the doomed passengers for a feel-good ending, Cal Hockley's spying henchman Spicer Lovejoy is not included. The entire narrative trajectory is driven by the parallel desire to resurrect objects previously riddled with the hideous incrustations of malignant patina. How can objects exposed to such disrepair and decrepitude be renewed and made expressive of social status and value?

Titanic's use of a double diegesis is highly significant in this respect. It is rare for such a popular example of the heritage genre to oscillate between two temporal frameworks. After all, such flexibility in terms of how a story can be told might undermine the perceived authenticity of the past being so perfectly recreated. More usually, heritage filmmakers immerse the viewer in a complete, because unified and single-layered, nostalgic illusion. Although Cameron does not do this, his double diegesis cannot exactly be said to constitute a rupture, either. Hollywood's 1997 version of events on the *Titanic* nowhere explores historical contradiction, nowhere provides analytic comparison. Yet this flaw in terms of ideological critique has the effect of opening up the film's reception possibilities a little more. Paradoxically, by drawing such clear distinctions between the old and the new, between the pristine and the decrepit, *Titanic* passes over historical contradictions but heightens emotional investment.

On the other hand, what Cameron's use of a double temporal framework does recognize is patina's function as a system of mediation. Relations between the past and the present, between then and now, the living and the dead, are filtered through the symbolic cultural properties associated with old physical objects. Material culture acts as a "bridge" to the feelings and sentiments we choose to unload on the past. Crucially, as Higson has pointed out, the artful and spectacular projection of various heritage attractions provides an opportunity to discuss issues of inheritance. (Who is to inherit England? as Forster's *Howards End* puts it.) In the case of *Titanic*, it is important to consider just who gets to inherit those once-beautiful, now-decrepit cultural objects. More than that, what symbolic properties do we inherit from those objects, what cultural values do we now invest in them, and who are "we" anyway? In the world of transnational capital and commerce, portrayals of elites, as well as conservative visions of a vague and ambivalently signaled national past, are helped along by the patina system. For whenever elite lifestyles are threatened, new social claims will need to be verified, new questions of inheritance and social status will require legitimation.

Occurring as it did on the eve of World War I, the poignant symbolism of the *Titanic* disaster is easy enough to appreciate. As in Renoir's classic *The Rules of the Game* (1939), the great and the good are doomed from the start, and the poor so-and-sos don't even know it yet. But what does *Titanic* say about the position of elites at the end of the 1990s? It is one of the peculiarities of Cameron's film that this question is displaced onto the terms of gender. If the spectacular destruction of pristine material objects provides a tragic "bridge" to the past, a way of forming emotional connections between the living and the dead, it is unusual for a woman to be allowed to experience and articulate those connections quite so vividly.

In tandem with the supposed characteristics of the heritage cycle, the female central character—Rose Bukater—is the one imbued with a sense of emotional expressivity. No one knew what old Rose really felt in her heart. As a result, the

film's tone is indeed not reducible to the singular experiences of a patriarchal social elite. *Titanic*'s narrative explores such subjects as the performative nature of
class distinctions, family status, inheritance, and the cultural politics of "old" versus "new" money. And, in turn, the symbolic meanings invested in material objects carry most force when directly associated with the character Rose.

First seen making pottery—that is, producing artifacts that will themselves
eventually accumulate patina—Rose is linked, both visually and through spoken
dialogue, with such objects as a porcelain doll, a valuable diamond, a hairpin, a
mirror, a cupid statue, and paintings by Monet, Picasso, and Manet (the quoting
of the latter's *Olympia* in the scene where she poses nude for Jack Dawson on the
couch). Along with Jack's erotic portrait of her, such objects provide both Rose
and the viewer with a "bridge" back into the diegetic past. Moreover, these objects are associated with the patina system because they have been collected at
just the right moment. The ship is about to sink: Rose's fiancé, Cal Hockley, has
already remarked that Jack's artwork might increase in value after his death; Rose
herself knows a thing or two about timing.

It is Rose, then, who initiates the symbolic workings of patina. She imbues
objects from the past with contemporary meanings and uses them to further our
emotional understanding. Consider how the film introduces her through a television report about the salvage operation being undertaken in the Atlantic. The results of this operation—old objects dredged up from the ocen floor smothered in
malignant incrustations—are being sent to museums for cataloging and preserva-
tion. Yet from the moment when team leader Brock Lovett first opens his mouth,
we learn he has no emotional investment in these ghostly relics. Brock has built
no "bridges" to the past; he takes no more than a professional interest in the objects he brings to the surface. Once Rose starts to narrate events, however, the cultural and emotional meanings of all those old objects can be reactivated.

In *Titanic*, then, our contemporary fantasies of love and death are mediated
through the emotional and symbolic properties of material objects. This strategy
represents a significant point of departure for the postclassical Hollywood blockbuster, but one that signals more than just the "Americanization" of the heritage
film. High-concept cinema is now investing in fantasy objects from the past. Promoted through advertising and merchandising tie-ins, these perfect nostalgic images resonate with the patina system as understood by contemporary filmgoers
all over the world. The mobilization of fantasy through the symbolic properties of
old material objects connects diverse audiences with the emotional lives of both
the living and the dead. In turn, such fantasies penetrate actual national boundaries and speak within a variety of distinct cultural arenas.

In his book *A Night to Remember*, Walter Lord provides a memorable description of the juxtaposition of old and new objects on the *Titanic*.

> There has never been a mixture like it—29 boilers . . . the jewelled copy
> of the Rubaiyat . . . 800 cases of shelled walnuts . . . 15,000 bottles of ale
> and stout . . . huge anchor chains (each link weighed 175 pounds) . . . 30
> cases of golf clubs and tennis rackets for Spalding . . . Eleanor Widener's

trousseau . . . tons of coal . . . Major Peuchen's tin box . . . 30,000 fresh
eggs . . . dozens of potted palms . . . 5 grand pianos . . . a little mantel clock
in B 38 . . . the massive silver duck press.[9]

This short extract from a much longer list makes for curious reading. At the end
of the twentieth century, who truly feels emotionally connected to any of these
things? Take this question one step farther, and a new hypothesis is reached.
Titanic's global success may have something to do with the fact that its nostalgia
does not evoke sentiments to which consumers who have genuinely lost something
might react. Or, to put it differently, the main difference between this Hollywood
blockbuster and the European or British heritage cinema it references is that the
film teaches viewers to miss the things they have never actually been denied. Such
instances of what Appadurai terms "armchair nostalgia," or "imagined nostalgia,"
invert consumer fantasy's usual temporal logic. Instead of expecting viewers to
supply lived memories, they are now encouraged to bring nostalgia to an image
that will supply the memory of a loss never suffered. As such, *Titanic* represents
nostalgia without lived experience or collective historical memory.[10] Connecting
these threads, we might say that this is all perfectly in keeping with the theme of
a transatlantic luxury cruise. Nostalgia and consumerism are combined in ways
that help fantasy travel far out into the modern capitalist world.

The promotion of "armchair nostalgia" in contemporary Hollywood cinema
begs other questions: What happens to the patina system when it is opened up for
mass consumption? How can status claims be verified for vast, culturally and nationally distinct audiences? Artifacts from the original *Titanic* have always been
keenly sought, but a veritable feeding frenzy now engulfs the props and gizmos
first built for Cameron's film and then discarded. Both the "original" objects and
their commercial "reproductions" are subject to the fetishizations of popular sentiment. Since the props used in *Titanic* have entered into public circulation, they
have accrued nostalgia for a patina that does not actually exist as yet.

It is tempting to talk about this phenomenon in the language of postmodernism. *Titanic* has generated material simulacras—copies of originals, not the
real things—in a manner similar to the way Tim Hays, an employee of the Coffee
Beanery in Miami, Florida, who happens to physically resemble *Titanic's* principal male star, generated local fame after being discovered and dubbed Leonardo
DiCappucino.[11] However, one weakness with the postmodern notion of simulacra
is its general inability to take into account the very real emotions invested in secondhand objects. In his article on the supposed "Englishness" of heritage films,
Dyer recalls watching the filmic adaption of a representative "British" heritage
novel (actually written by British-Japanese author Kazuo Ishiguro): "The first thing
I wondered about the first shot of Miss Kenton in *The Remains of the Day* was
where she—or the props person—had got her teacup."[12] Fans of *Titanic* can go
this one better. After spending good money on *Titanic*-related purchases from the
Fox Studios memorabilia catalog, one high-placed consumer was agog with the
thrill of a new kind of cultural status: "When company president Arnie Cohen went
to see *Titanic*," write two reporters for *Newsweek*, "he got choked up for a different

Armchair nostalgia: the patina of porcelain

reason than most viewers." The article suggests the potential emotional power of consumption. Cohen, the viewer/consumer, is reported as saying: "I turned to my wife and three sons and said, 'I have that cup.'"[13]

It is one thing to be moved by the romantic sadness of Cameron's film and another to buy tie-in products and paraphernalia; but it is yet another to be "choked up" by having the ability to possess a cup held briefly in one scene by the hand of an actor. At the same time, while traveling shows scour the United States exhibiting objects *actually used in the movie*, tourists can choose to commemorate the *Titanic* disaster in Nova Scotia by visiting the graves of actual *Titanic* victims in Fairview Cemetery.[14] How can these extreme examples of media-induced conspicuous consumption be separated out? The stories just go on. RMS *Titanic* Inc., a public company in New York, sells "authentic" lumps of coal from the ship's furnace; Easter strollers on the same city's Fifth Avenue walk around in retro fashions inspired by the film; the Classic Leather company begins making reproduction furniture in spring 1998.[15] Riding the wave of the film's success, *Titanic* memorabilia offers armchair nostalgia as well as a kind of instant patina. But what kinds of status claims are now being sought and verified? What currently threatened lifestyles are being reasserted? It is likely that *Titanic*'s apocalyptic moments, its premonition of the end of civilization as we know it, works to support this orgy of purchasing. Now it really is possible to manage the temporal rhythms of rampant consumerism. The time is right.

Certainly, it is hardly surprising that, even without reassurance from Cameron and his crew that today's safety measures are better than ever, luxury cruises have grown in popularity since the release of *Titanic*. Who goes on these cruises? What claims to status, what verifications of their own lives are they trying to make? Do these cruises represent a case of "old" money reasserting itself, or is "new" money once again on the rise? Such touristic practices link up very neatly with the whole theme of travel in Cameron's film. Moreover, they once again suggest the kind of vague, transnational spaces habitually mapped out by Hollywood movies.

Such fetishization of both authentic and reproduced cultural objects generates new symbolic properties and status verifications. Indeed, the forward march of transnational capital has only accelerated the tempo of global consumption. All over the planet, we watch the same film, yet the emotional responses we bring to the patina of perfect images in *Titanic* are, in each case, unique. In this sense, the astonishing success of Cameron's film represents one more manifestation of the forces of cultural homogeneity interacting with the forces of cultural heterogeneity. On the one hand, globalization has inculcated in us all an intense desire to build "bridges" back into the past, which we do through the physical properties of material life. On the other hand, these emotional connections operate in distinct cultural arenas through the process known as indiginization.

To illustrate this point, it is worth considering why *Titanic* had its world premiere at the Tokyo International Film Festival. This event inspired much comment from American news sources. For a start, Tokyo is not generally regarded as one of the prime global festivals; it is not on par with a Berlin, Cannes, or Venice, for example. Furthermore, the latest high-concept blockbusters from the United States rarely showcase at festivals before their domestic theatrical release. (Although the decision to unspool Cameron's film at Tokyo only confirms the suspicion that the international film festival circuit now acts as a key preview audience for commercial movies.) Other factors are also worth bearing in mind. The Tokyo festival has a reputation for playing it safe in part because the event is backed by elite conservative business interests. Japanese critics were perceived by *Titanic*'s makers as the most likely to give politely approving reviews. Finally, being in Japan, where DiCaprio is a huge star, opened up yet more opportunities for commercial exploitation—as the actor signed a contract to endorse the Suzuki Company's Wagon R Wide miniwagon vehicle.[16]

Yet these commercial and practical considerations do not completely exhaust the symbolic meanings that circulate around this particular film festival preview. Showcasing *Titanic* in Tokyo may well have been part of an attempt to inject the film with an air of authority, craftsmanship, cultural significance, and historical

Come Aboard the Titanic

and recover your own piece of history!

Click the piece of coal below to find out how!!!

NEW!

The RMS Titanic is now boarding.....All passengers please report to the boarding area immediately.

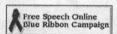

© 1996 CompuClub / Titanic Image © R.M.S. Titanic

[Home] [Ship of Dreams] [Product] [Order] [Remember]

Global consumption on the Internet: *Titanic* coal and chocolate bars

worthiness, announcing to the world that this is more than just your average block-buster. Just as Rose takes an interest in the patina of objects within the film, Cameron's film accumulates social legitimation through its placement at a certain exhibition site. The fact that the world's most expensive movie to date was premiered at an international film festival signals a truly emotional investment in the symbolic properties of contemporary cinema.[17]

Beyond this, though, it is interesting to ask whether the premiere of *Taitanikku* in Tokyo initiated a new emotional investment, not only in Winslet's radiant beauty and DiCaprio's swimming-pool eyes, but in local understandings of the past. In Japan, the verification of status claims can imbue objects with cultural value through the process known as "Japanization," and according to the *New York Times*, the reception of Cameron's film in Tokyo provoked a reconsideration of the concept of "gamen" (*sic*—the correct transliteration is *gaman*) as a means of explaining its appeal. As the writer explains, "many of the characters in the film exhibited a great deal of what the Japanese call "gamen," which can be translated as having a stiff upper lip or, more formally, perseverance in the face of extreme adversity. The mother singing a lullaby to her children as the water swirled up around them, the elderly couple hugging each other on their bed as they faced certain death, the musicians playing on the deck as the boat went down—those scenes could have been tailor-made for Japanese audiences."[18] Tellingly, in light of Dyer's work on the British heritage film, this indiginization of *gaman* (translation: patience) through the stereotype of the British "stiff upper lip" represents an "Americanization" of an already secondhand national sentiment.

A vivid illustration of this sense of *gaman*, of perseverance, and apparent emotional understatement, was provided in Japan through the real-life story of Masabumi Hosono. The only Japanese passenger on the *Titanic* the night it sank, Hosono survived the carnage but was later hounded from pillar to post in nationalistic Japan for the shame of his very survival; a man invested with the true samurai spirit would not have come home alive. In 1998, *People* magazine reported that Hosono's grandson, Haruomi, a musician with the famous techno-pop group Yellow Magic Orchestra (YMO), felt the time was right to speak out and try and resurrect the family name. In other words, with Cameron's film opening in his hometown, Haruomi could make new status claims and so secure a new inheritance for his family through the symbolic objects that circulated around the movie at the moment of its original promotion.

Four photographs accompany the *People* article. The first two are old family snapshots of Masabumi Hosono. The third, a recently discovered letter he wrote to his wife in Japan on 10 April 1912, on authentic *Titanic* stationery, bears all the hallmarks of patina. Worn, torn, and hideously decrepit, this tatty historical relic is now invested with new cultural meaning. The discovery of this letter enables Haruomi to build a "bridge" back to his father's emotional life, and so reverse years of social disgrace, through the symbolic properties encrusted in its patina. The fourth photograph is of the grandson sitting in front of a model replica of the *Titanic*. "My grandfather's spirit is inside me," Haruomi is quoted as saying, "I feel a tremendous responsibility." Elsewhere he continues, "I am extremely relieved.

Honor has been restored to the Hosonos."[19] Clearly, Hosono's utilization of the symbolic possibiltites opened up by Cameron's film has nothing to do with feelings specific only to the United Kingdom or the United States.

Elsewhere in east Asia, the reception of *Titanic* throws up similarly imaginative stories. First, given the fact that Cameron's film has been as successful in South Korea as anywhere else, American media reports may have constructed a false representation of how it was received there. If you go by some sources, for example, the movie seems to have been widely boycotted by Koreans despondent over the worsening economic situation in their country and sick and tired of American imperialist encroachments.

Second, what about *Titanic*'s reception in an emerging modern consumer society like China's? The mainland communist government approved the widespread exhibition of the movie, finding in it compelling evidence of destructive Anglo-American capitalism on the prowl. But desire has also been well and truly stoked in Beijing consumers of *Titanic* paraphernalia, most of whom, like fans the world over, are building bridges to a past never directly experienced. More significant still is the fact that the film has then been viewed as a gateway to a more properly indigenous culture. At the very time the Disney studios' own reworking of a "traditional" Chinese tale, *Mulan* (1998), was opening in the United States, the government of the People's Republic of China announced it would invest $3 million in an effort to technologically upgrade China's major film studios. Emily Parker further notes how, "not to be outdone, studio bosses also weighed in, pledging to marry the new technology with stories culled from China's 5,000 years of history, to produce China's own big-budget disaster flick."[20]

These very brief examples of the global reception of *Titanic* should be enough to suggest something of the film's adaptability. Between the pristine condition of all that new china, all those new sheets, and the ravages of malignant patina lie a myriad possible imaginative uses of such material objects. The film may look at times like a Anglo-American heritage film, it may feature actors familiar from other British-themed heritage titles, but this does not mean it can only produce meaning on this level. Through indiginization, and through the symbolic properties invested in its material objects, new meanings are produced.

In sum, the global success of Cameron's film tells us something about our desire to make status claims in the present based on our appropriations of the past. The patina of objects depicted though nostalgic images provides the medium for this. Taking a more historical perspective, *Titanic* may be seen as having consolidated the union of high concept and heritage. In capitalist and consumer societies, if old objects are to remain culturally valued, if they are to act as bridges between the past and the present, the living and the dead, they have to be maintained with care and the right technical instruments. By resurrecting the ghosts of the mid-Atlantic through a colossal budget and high-tech industrial designs, *Titanic* mimics this aspect of the museum imagination.

Notes

1. Justin Wyatt, *High Concept: Movies and Marketing in Hollywood* (Austin: University of Texas Press, 1994), 28.
2. Robin Buss, "To Hell with Heritage," *Times Educational Supplement*, 6 March 1998, 15.
3. Andrew Higson, "The Heritage Film and British Cinema," in *Dissolving Views: Key Writings on British Cinema*, ed. Andrew Higson (London: Cassell, 1996), 233, 237, 235, 238. Higson is here responding to his earlier piece, "Re-Presenting the National Past: Nostalgia and Pastiche in the Heritage Film," in *British Cinema and Thatcherism: Fires Were Started*, ed. Lester Friedman (London: University College London Press, 1993), 109–129.
4. Richard Dyer, "Feeling English," *Sight and Sound* 4, no. 3 (March 1994): 18.
5. Ruth Vasey, *The World According to Hollywood, 1918–1939* (Madison: University of Wisconsin Press, 1997), 198–199.
6. Arjun Appadurai, *Modernity at Large: Cultural Dimensions of Globalization* (Minneapolis, University of Minnesota Press, 1996), 75.
7. Grant McCracken, *Culture and Consumption: New Approaches to the Symbolic Character of Consumer Goods and Activities* (Bloomington, Indiana University Press, 1990), 32.
8. Ibid., 35–36.
9. Walter Lord, *A Night to Remember* (New York, Bantam Books, 1956), 79.
10. I am here paraphrasing some of Appadurai's ideas. See *Modernity at Large*, 75–85.
11. Gregg Cebrynski, "Box-Office Look-Alike Becomes a Big Star at Coffee Beanery," *Nation's Restaurant News*, 16 March 1998, 120–122.
12. Dyer, "Feeling English," 18.
13. Anne Underwood and Sarah Van Boven, "Honk If You're a Titaniac," *Newsweek*, 23 February 1998, 64.
14. Frank DeCaro, "See the Movie, Covet the Souvenir," *New York Times*, 4 January 1998, 3; Brian Bergman, "Titanic Tourism," *Maclean's*, 1 June 1998, 70–71.
15. Lee Berton, "History for Sale," *Wall Street Journal*, 30 December 1997, B1; "On the Street: *Titanic* Bonnets," *New York Times*, 19 April 1998, sec. 9, p. 5; Underwood and Boven, "Honk If You're a Titaniac," 64.
16. James B. Treece, "Corolla May Get a Sinking Feeling from DiCaprio's *Titanic* Star Power," *Automative News*, 18 May 1998, 24.
17. More generally, the exhibition of new Hollywood releases at international film festivals is a subject worth further investigation. How do commercial blockbusters fit into the globalized art-cinema economy? For one relevant report on this subject written after the Tokyo premiere of Cameron's film, see Stephanie Strom, "Harrison Ford's Not in *Titanic*? Well, No Matter!" *New York Times*, 4 November 1997, E2.
18. Alan Riding, Celestine Bohlen, et al., "Why *Titanic* Conquered the World," *New York Times*, 26 April 1998, sec. 2, p. 28.
19. Sophfronia Scott Gregory and Peter McKillop, "Second Opinion," *People*, 20 April 1998, 75–76.
20. Emily Parker, "Chinese Give Politically Correct *Titanic* Two Billion Thumbs Up," *Wall Street Journal*, 15 April 1998, B1; See also, "*Titanic*'s Socialist Values," *Dollars and Sense*, July–August 1998, 4; and Kevin Platt, "*Titanic* Cultural Invasion Hits China," *Christian Science Monitor*, 20 April 1998, 1.

Titanic, *Survivalism,*
and the Millennial Myth

DIANE NEGRA

*T*he unprecedented success of *Titanic* re-
flects new stakes in popular premillennial visions of catastrophe and recovery. In
conjunction with the numerous fictions of annihilation or near annihilation and
survival that have recently proliferated in film (*Waterworld*, 1995; *Independence
Day*, 1996; *Volcano*, 1997; *Deep Impact*, 1998), television (*Crash Landing: The
Rescue of Flight 232*, 1992; *Avalanche*, 1994; *Meteorites*, 1998), and popular literature (best-selling novels such as Jon Krakauer's *Into Thin Air* and Sebastian
Junger's *The Perfect Storm*), *Titanic* presents itself as a disaster narrative highly
aware of the millennial myth that we are living at the end of human history.

Independence Day and *Deep Impact* are films openly committed to the contemplation of a postdisaster United States. *Titanic* might at first appear to be un-
related to these films, but it shares with them important ideological features about
present-day disaster. As an example of the new survivalist narrative, it assumes a
condition of imminent threat and a fear of nature and technology characteristic of
many other recent disaster-centered blockbusters. Widespread fascination with the
meaning of the 1912 disaster parallels our current obsession with technological
and environmental breakdown. Moreover, American culture in the 1990s seems to
share a sense of unease and uncertainty about American national identity evident
in the early twentieth century. James Cameron's retelling of the disaster displaces
the concerns of our present moment and demonstrates their relevance to an earlier phase of U.S. history. *Titanic* sets itself in an analogous turn-of-the-century
historical moment as an oblique means of interrogating current perceptions of economic, national, and technological fragility, and it suggests that our century began (as it might end) with disasters brought on by overly expansive human visions
of technology in relation to creation. While many have argued that the film's success is a function of its ability to revive old-fashioned storytelling and unite it with

bombastic special effects technology, such explanations may lead us to forget that the film is, in fact, extremely timely in the nature and in the scope of its concerns about environmental threat, human frailty, and survival.

Titanic's extraordinary popularity can be understood to be a response to the popularization of millennialism and the mainstreaming of survivalist ideology. Like numerous other contemporary disaster narratives, *Titanic* distills the rhetoric of imminent threat and survivalism associated with the margins of our culture and makes it a central part of narrative logic. While fringe millennialism holds that a long-prophesied "end time" awaits us and necessitates our preparation, Hollywood films can use elements of that millennialist mind-set to cultivate an expectant relationship toward disaster that infuses it with additional meanings. In *Titanic*, the celebration of survival is so elaborated it becomes a celebration of survivalism. *Titanic's* numerous intertexts are also millennialist and survivalist in orientation, including published accounts of the film's production, a broadcast of *The Oprah Winfrey Show* (entitled "Secrets of *Titanic*") featuring appearances by Cameron and *Titanic* stars Kate Winslet and Billy Zane, who played the parts of Rose Bukater and her fiancé, Cal Hockley, and the proliferation of television programs that highlight disaster preparedness such as the Learning Channel's *Survivor Science*. Viewed alongside these intertexts, the narrative structure of *Titanic* is consistent with the millennial myth that forecasts disaster and the ability to survive it through self-reliance and personal empowerment.

The meanings of the *Titanic* disaster have always been culturally and temporally flexible, as Steven Biel forcefully demonstrates in his cultural history of that event.[1] In 1912, accounts of heroism displayed among the first-cabin males reinforced prevailing understandings of gender and class and indirectly worked to restore an image of heroic masculinity that might put to rest fears of the feminizing effects of modernity. In the 1950s, Walter Lord's best-selling novel and the films *Titanic* (1953) and *A Night to Remember* (1958) slowed down the pace of the disaster in a way that seemed to counteract Cold War fears of a nuclear attack that would give victims no awareness or time to come to terms with death. Similarly, Robert Ballard's discovery of the ship's wreckage in 1985 was consistent with a Reagan-era desire to "fix" history, and the dive to the site unfolded, as Biel puts it, as "a triumphalist story from Reagan's America."[2] In the 1990s, *Titanic's* extraordinary success is in concordance with a preexisting climate that privileges issues of millennial-oriented survivalism. Because of its status as a reconstruction of a real event, *Titanic* forcefully "answers" a number of interconnected millennial concerns by crafting a vision of the twentieth century as an experience in survival, and by reassuring us that survivalism as a prime directive is no new thing.

Survivalism and Premillennial Apocalypticism in American Culture

Popular stereotypes of the apocalyptic are extensively discussed by Daniel Wojcik in *The End of the World as We Know It: Faith, Fatalism, and Apocalypse in America*. Wojcik notes that such views are often associated with cult behavior

Ad for *Escape!* miniseries on PBS's *Nova*

and defined as nonnormative.[3] Yet he also cites data to suggest that, in fact, apocalyptic beliefs are ubiquitous among late-twentieth-century Americans, who seem to readily call upon them in strikingly substantial numbers to make sense of events like the Persian Gulf War, the AIDS pandemic, and the El Niño weather pattern. It seems clear that whether they employ such beliefs in fully-fledged form or not, Americans who entertain apocalyptic projections will respond to disaster-oriented fictions differently than those who assume the continuity of history.

Apocalyptic beliefs have either a secular or religious base. They also form the ideological cornerstone of survivalism, which differs from apocalypticism in the sense that it anticipates crisis as the catalyst for the emergence of a renewed new world. Philip Lamy characterizes survivalism as "a loosely structured yet pervasive belief system and set of practices focusing on disaster preparedness."[4] Yet there are a number of variables that go unacknowledged by such a definition. In a general sense, survivalism stresses a mistrust of government and authority, a logic of self-sufficiency and self-reliance, the expectation of catastrophe, and the desire for preparedness. Survivalism teaches its adherents that with the proper planning they can survive even under the most unfavorable conditions such as nuclear war or large-scale environmental disaster. Perhaps most strikingly, survivalists are characterized by a fervent sense of independence that may lead them to profess fears of a one-world government, to resist taxation, or to implement home schooling for their children. Many contemporary survivalists identify with the political rhetoric of the American Revolution, believing that the present-day U.S. government has moved away from the original goals of the democracy. In the Fort Cosmos Survival Section, a Web site devoted to issues of survivalism, the authors write:

> It is self-sufficiency which fulfills the great promise of freedom, a concept which hardly applies to today's society as it has developed. We are encouraged at every turn to place our responsibilities with others, to let others decide what is "safe" or "necessary" to do or have. People are actually beginning to believe that they are too stupid to make decisions such as these for themselves. Your life is the only thing that is truly yours, but people have no problem letting others tell them what to do with it.[5]

While pure survivalist rhetoric no doubt remains apart from the everyday experience of most Americans, mainstream publications such as *Newsweek*, *Time*, and *Popular Mechanics* have increasingly taken up themes of apocalyptic and survivalist ideology.[6] News accounts have recently highlighted the activities of Doomsday cults like the Branch Davidians in Waco, the Order of the Solar Temple in Switzerland and Canada, and the Aum Shinrikyo cult in Japan which perpetrated gas attacks in the Tokyo subway system. Extensive merchandising of the beliefs of Michel de Nostradamus and Edgar Cayce takes place alongside the dispersion of survivalist rhetoric emphasizing (among other things) the championing of states rights and the suspicion that the U.S. government has become antagonistic to individual freedoms.

All of these developments are chronicled by Damian Thompson in his recent

Imagery and text from the "Perilous Times" Web site

The End of Time: Faith and Fear in the Shadow of the Millennium. Thompson writes:

> There are, however, many less extreme varieties of End-time beliefs which are accessible to large numbers of people; indeed their appeal seems to be growing. . . . No secular ideology is capable of restoring the status quo or guaranteeing stable growth; even the laws of physics are no longer immutable. Never before have people been confronted by such choices or such uncertainty; never before have the uneducated been at such a disadvantage. Yet the technology which has unraveled the social fabric, is, paradoxically, enabling many people to take refuge in apocalyptic fantasies.[7]

Thompson's allusion to cyberspace as a vehicle for the circulation of apocalyptic and survivalist rhetoric is quickly substantiated by a tour of the Internet. For those interested in disaster preparedness and survivalism, the Internet furnishes an increasing number of resources. Web sites such as Eye on the World: Our Violent Planet, Disaster Central Archives, and Perilous Times dedicate themselves to disseminating information about catastrophic events in a culture that seems obsessed with its own survival.[8] Such Web sites often stress the applicability of this information to everyday life, yoking together quotidian concerns such as privacy and crime with earthquakes, floods, and tornadoes.

The dispersion of knowledge about survivalist and premillenialist ideologies has helped shape a significant interpretive framework for films such as *Titanic* that depict survivable disasters. Wojcik points out that "filmic visions of a post-apocalyptic world often are similar to the scenarios imagined by some survivalist and militia groups that anticipate the collapse of society through a series of catastrophes, such as nuclear war, worldwide economic disaster, or race riots."[9] While *Titanic* does not strictly conform to this definition, its concern with the destruction of a ship that served as a floating reproduction of society lends it important metaphoric resonances. Moreover, *Titanic* directly and indirectly substantiates many of the tenets of survivalism in its discrediting of the authoritative confidence that the ship reflects, its assumption of catastrophe, its insistence on the self-sufficiency of the protagonists, and its presentation of a postdisaster "new world" for the film's heroine.

Titanic's Survivalist Text

Titanic presupposes the inevitability of disaster, and it stipulates that there is no epistemological framework that can be called upon to avoid such occurrence. The technological certitude of J. Bruce Ismay (managing director of the White Star Line) and Thomas Andrews (*Titanic*'s designer), the hubris of the White Star Line and its backers, the religion invoked by the minister on the sinking ship as a bulwark against catastrophe, and even instinct and intuition (referenced by the film in the form of the lookout who claims that he "can smell an iceberg") all prove inadequate.

Titanic surpasses other recent disaster fictions such as *Twister* (1996) and *Volcano* by uniting the categories of natural and man-made disaster. In its representation of the collision with the iceberg, the film suggests both a perilous planet (in the form of the iceberg) and an insufficiently wary, overly technology-reliant culture (in the form of the ship). In keeping with the codes of the disaster genre as a whole, the film's most important textual feature is its emphasis on human vulnerability in contrast to the potency of nature and the inadequacy of technology (even at its most grandiose). In view of this, the film rationalizes, we must cultivate a survivalist mind-set. In fact, the film reframes Rose Bukater's life experience as itself a survivalist narrative. Upon this ideological base, *Titanic* unfolds as a long lesson given by Jack Dawson to Rose on the nature of survival. This lesson is embedded within a frame narrative that centralizes the meanings of the *Titanic* wreckage site and argues for the necessity of a conversion in logic from mercenary motivations to emotionalism.[10] The characters of the frame narrative model the position we are expected to take up, acquiring a solemn appreciation of survivalist history that displaces, overwhelms, and trivializes the profit motive.

In the course of the narrative, the film introduces a number of definitions of crisis and survival, which it then goes on to trump in the spectacular disaster sequence. While Ruth Bukater speaks of "a disaster" with the stationers over her daughter Rose's wedding invitations, and Rose's fiancé, Cal Hockley, identifies the theft of the Heart of the Ocean necklace as an "emergency," the film signals us to contrast these skewed terms with the scope of the imminent catastrophe. From the earliest moments of the film, in the frame story that focuses on the exploration of the wreckage, our attention is drawn to the issue of precarious survival. We learn that "if the windows blow, it's gonna be sayonara in two milliseconds." As we enter the flashback portion of the narrative, the first crisis is precipitated and resolved in terms of survival, with Rose threatening suicide and being urged back by Jack, who cues her to take responsibility for her own survival, saying, "Now pull yourself up." In a film that is preoccupied with the symbolic meanings of ascent and descent, such language is noteworthy. This is the first of many instances where Rose will literally and figuratively pull herself up to ensure her survival.

Again and again throughout the film, Jack characterizes himself in relation to his survival skills. While Rose complains of "the inertia of [my] life," Jack defines himself on the basis of a resilient energy: "You could just call me a tumbleweed blowing in the wind." His enterprising individualism at first contrasts with nearly everyone in the film. But in the crucial bow scene whose imagery was used to advertise the film, Jack sings "Come Josephine in My Flying Machine" to urge Rose to substitute faith in technology for faith in herself. (After the sinking, Rose exhaustedly sings the same song to rouse the energy to save herself.) Later, when rewarded for assisting Rose, with a dinner in first class, Jack demonstrates his flexibility and resiliency by smoothly fitting in to this new social environment. At dinner he articulates his survivalist credo to a group that includes an admiring Rose: "I've got everything I need right with me. . . . I figure you'll never know what hand you'll get dealt next." The terms of the lesson to be learned are made clear when Rose asks, "Why can't I be like you, Jack?"

Jack's survivalist energies endow him with a joie de vivre that is well displayed in the steerage scene. In contrast to the stuffy proprieties of first class, Rose experiences the ethnic vitality belowdecks. The "real party" referred to by Jack seems to cement Rose's desire to live her life on new terms. At Jack's prompting, Rose learns to master her fears—"I can't do this," she says of the intricate dance steps. "Just go with it. Don't think," advises Jack—and shows herself to be an astonishingly quick study. Meanwhile, Ruth focuses on the economic survival of herself and her daughter. Alarmed at Rose's behavior and its threat to her engagement, Ruth cautions her daughter: "Our survival is precarious. It is a fine match with Hockley. It will ensure our survival." In response to this coercion, Rose briefly rededicates herself to her engagement, yet she is dissuaded by Jack, who calls upon a more profound definition of survival than the economic one alluded to by Ruth. He speaks eloquently of the survival of Rose's spirit, and when she replies, "It's not up to you to save me, Jack," he answers, "You're right. Only you can do that."

As the disaster unfolds, Jack and Rose meet on increasingly equal terms as survivalists. Unable to find help to release Jack when he is handcuffed on E Deck, Rose has the fortitude and perseverance to rescue him unaided. Her sense of self-reliance and trust in her own perception grows. When Jack asks her how she knew he was innocent of the theft of the necklace, she tells him, "I realized I already knew." When he sends her into a lifeboat, saying, "I'll be fine, I'm a survivor," Rose demonstrates an equivalent sense of agency in her jump back to the ship. From this point forward, the couple's ability to save anyone but themselves is revealed to be limited as they attempt to go back for a child whose father angrily retrieves him, then runs in the wrong direction and drowns. Later, as Jack and Rose cling to the sinking stern of the boat, Rose shares a significant glance with another first-class female passenger, a glance that seems to speak to their mutual recognition that any social guarantees for their safety and security have been utterly stripped away.

This moment of recognition exemplifies Cameron's account of the *Titanic* disaster as it highlights the individualist ideology at the heart of survivalism. While earlier versions of the *Titanic* disaster emphasized the noble self-sacrifice of victims, this film seems to reflect the breakdown of a consensus value system and stable moral hierarchies in the way that it displaces self-sacrifice by an ethic of urgent survivalism. The centrality of this perspective in Cameron's vision is suggested by an anecdote in Paula Parisi's book on the making of *Titanic*. Parisi relays a moment when Cameron stopped filming to rebuke a member of the cast: "'Martin, stop helping people,' he admonishes a minor character. 'I hate that. It's every man for himself.'"[11]

Throughout the sequence, we are given signs that the film not only puts the emphasis on survival but also is thematically engaged with many of the core tenets of survivalism. The stakes for survival are raised through the careful introduction to the design and amenities of the ship. The ensuing meticulous destruction of the mise-en-scène carries a particular force that facilitates our intense identification with the protagonist couple. While survival may take place in a context of social support and is frequently characterized by perseverance, survivalism prioritizes independence, adaptation, and preparation. The film's ability to effectively render the social chaos during the last minutes of the sinking establishes a forceful contrast between the survivalist behavior of the protagonists and the other panicked passengers.

Our identification with the survivalist couple is enhanced compositionally as the mise-en-scène around them becomes chaotic and we visually rely on their familiarity. Increasingly confined to smaller and smaller segments of the ship, Jack and Rose adapt to a variety of environments, making skillful use of tools such as keys and axes. While other passengers look for guidance from authority figures such as the ship's captain and a minister, the protagonists are entirely self-reliant. They understand exactly what is happening and make whatever preparations they are capable of up to the very moment of the sinking of the stern, when Jack instructs Rose on how to prepare for the immersion underwater. The film gives us to understand that their enterprising and nonpanicked response serves them well in the moments when the final passengers are thrown into the water. *Titanic* never casts any doubt on the couple's agency under circumstances in which they can be self-reliant; it is only when all resources are depleted and they can only wait for rescue from others that Jack dies.[12]

In this way, the film disguises the actual restraints placed on the development of Rose's individualism. Significantly compromising any understanding of this film as a quasi-feminist tale of Rose's empowerment is the fact that her accomplished life is presented as the fulfillment of her contract with Jack, a contract that is discursively figured as a marriage. As the two face death together in the water, Jack predicts that "[you're] gonna go on. . . . And you're gonna die an old, old lady warm in her bed. . . . You must do me this honor. You must promise me that you'll survive. Promise me now. And never let go of that promise." Although Rose learns the necessity and value of survival, her spiritual survival is founded on Jack's death (he is only brought to life again as she tells her tale) and Rose's symbolic death. Implicitly reborn as a nonaristocrat, Rose begins her life in a moment of visual contemplation of the Statue of Liberty. With her head covered in a plaid blanket, calling herself Rose Dawson, and sitting among the third-class survivors, Rose's quest is coded as that of the archetypal immigrant. Although she is returning to her own country, she approaches it as if for the first time, a moment of symbolic rebirth that is carried through in old Rose's dream, a postmillennial moment of recovery and harmony in which the old is made new again. As Rose returns to her youthful self in this dream, the ship sparkles as it did on its maiden voyage, and the camera pans up and out of the white domed windows above the ship's grand staircase in a resonant gesture of ascension. As I shall discuss shortly, this kind of concluding gesture, indicative of the cleansing renewal of the past at the conclusion of the survivor's journey, stands at the heart of millennial cinematic fictions, from *Independence Day* to *Deep Impact*.

Before moving on to discuss how discourses of survivalism circulated through promotional coverage of the film's production, and *Titanic*'s important similarities to other survivalist/millennialist texts, I want to briefly return (as does the film) to the frame story. The prologue is significant for reasons far too numerous to be detailed here, but among its functions is the suspicion it draws from us about the uses of technology. The delight taken by the team in their vicarious exploration of the recesses of this ship feels suspect, and our apprehension of such technophiliac endeavors mounts when the computer-projected sinking is vividly narrated to Rose. There is something of a storytelling contest engaged in here, with the brief, mechanical narrative proposed by a crew member entirely displaced by Rose's lengthy, detailed, and emotionally attuned account. For the team, *Titanic* remains a site of failed earlier technology that can be exploited through updated technological means; whereas for Rose, the ship's meanings lie elsewhere, in its status as the "ship of dreams."

Such debate is necessary in part because the site serves as what Kenneth E. Foote terms "a remedial landscape"; that is, a location that cannot easily be accessed and therefore leaves few visible signs available for commemoration. A remedial landscape produces change elsewhere. The actual *Titanic* disaster, for example, along with other early-twentieth-century shipwrecks, served to bring about new maritime safety regulations.[13] This contest over the meanings of the *Titanic* wreckage also indicates something of the film's central project of memorialization—a key strategy in current initiatives to mark out a traumatic landscape. Recent debates over how best to memorializes sites such as the Branch Davidian compound in Waco and the Alfred P. Murrah Building in Oklahoma City attest to our investment in validating survivalist concerns by mapping the landscape with signifiers of peril. There are obvious economic incentives to such projects as "disaster tourism" proliferates, yet a broader, more generalized outcome of such endeavors is the visual proof that we live in hazardous times. While the activities of the *Titanic* profit seekers offend us, their ultimate conversion and Rose's private ritual of sanctification (dropping the diamond necklace into the sea) restore the site of the wreckage to a solemn, noncommercialized invisibility we deem appropriate. The invisibility and inaccessibility of the wreckage site itself leaves a blank space, which is filled by the film and its various signifiers (the faces and bodies of its stars, the lyrics of its theme song, the clout of its director, its staggering box office take, etc).

Thus, while references to the snoopvision trademark and to tabloid tactics in the prologue make it apparent that the team has inappropriately violated a sacred site, Rose's long narrative of survival reorients the meanings of the ship for the team. At the conclusion, team leader Brock Lovett professes, "[I] never got it. I never let it in." In this way, the film validates new emotional terms for the consumption of disaster and cues us that the *Titanic* disaster is worthy of our remembrance because it catalyzed an exemplary experience of survival. Yet despite Lovett's conversion from the narrative of technology and profit to the narrative of emotions, the film of course cannily employs both versions. Cameron's *Titanic* is very much implicated in these issues, for the frame narrative, and particularly the emotional trajectory of Lovett, rationalize Cameron's approach to his historical subject matter. The director indirectly presents himself as a chastened former profit seeker, transformed by the magnitude of *Titanic*'s survivalist narrative.

Surviving *Titanic*: Discourses on Blockbuster Film Production

In attempting to assess *Titanic*'s place with respect to the forms and functions of contemporary cultural storytelling, I think it is important to acknowledge that an "event" movie of this kind sets extremely wide discursive parameters. Thus *Titanic*'s survivalist text resonates beyond the film itself to significantly encompass such features as discourse on the film's production history. In *Titanic*'s promotion, the scope, length, and magnitude of the film shoot itself became framed in a narrative of survival and endurance for the sake of art. Such understandings were firmly in place, for instance, in the aforementioned broadcast of *The Oprah Winfrey Show*, which featured numerous films clips and behind-the-scenes production footage, in addition to the appearances of Cameron, Winslet, and Zane. The broadcast heavily emphasized the rigors of the film shoot, with the actors discussing their laborious experiences in general and particularly their survival of the shooting conditions in icy-cold water. At one point Winfrey asked rhetorically of her audience: "Can you believe what it took to make this movie?"

While allowing for the difficult conditions of production, this promotional event carefully anchored these difficulties to the execution of an authorial agenda. And while the actors were called upon to recount their endurance of a difficult shoot, Cameron's personal and professional fortitude was also stressed, as we heard him chronicle his five-year devotion to the project of *Titanic*. The tendency to celebrate the triumph of Cameron's authorial vision was very much in evidence in Winfrey's effusive, breathless welcoming speech to the director:

But I tell you what's exciting about it and I know you all are feeling the same thing that I am, is that when you see somebody with this much going on, when you just dare to follow your dream, you just keep at it, when everybody says, "Oh, it's overbudget," and "It's not gonna do this," and you just keep at it, we see that part of ourselves, the part that would dare to be what you are.

The widespread celebration of James Cameron as the film's master craftsman is not merely a function of our tedious cultural habit of assigning male authorship in any and all creative endeavors; it is also a functional ideological element in the film's promotional narrative. In the case of *Titanic*, the celebration of Cameron as a technical wizard knits together fears activated by the subject matter of the film with *Titanic*'s extradiegetic narrative of production and consumption. Celebrations of the director's virtuosity become compensatory for our fears that technology threatens to overtake us or will fail to be insufficiently protective against a battery of natural hazards. In this way, the creative narrative of *Titanic* reassuringly answers concerns at the heart of the filmic narrative, by emphasizing Cameron's ability to restage and control the performance of disaster.

Undergirding our appreciation of the actors' endurance and the director's commitment is the special validation attached to such endeavors in the context of *The Oprah Winfrey Show*. In other words, the talk show's generic commitment to discourses of personal empowerment and its vision of everyday life as an experience of survival lend a particular forcefulness to this account of *Titanic* as the artistic end result of a taxing emotional/creative/professional "journey." As Jane Shattuc observes,

> Organic intellectuals dismiss the simplistic discourse of self-help or rugged individualism that predominates on daytime talk shows. As a commercial medium, the shows emphasize a "can-do" (or "can-consume") solution to or a spiritual transcendence of social issues. In fact, *Oprah* is the most well known for this logic; it is marked by its affirmation of individual will and spirituality as represented by Oprah's battle with weight and references to a higher power.[14]

The Oprah Winfrey Show's particular stress on recovery and self-empowerment, and the star persona of Winfrey herself as the proponent and incarnation of a survival-oriented individualism, were fused to an emergent narrative of the film's development and production process as an exercise in survival and the culminating rewards of dedication to a worthy artistic cause.

Parisi pays similar tribute to Cameron in her obsequious book on *Titanic*'s production. Parisi's account installs Cameron as a superheroic adventurer, even a kind of "discoverer" of the *Titanic* through his early dives to the wreckage site. She also presents the director as a survivor of the production process, linking him to the survivors of the sinking. After concluding the shooting at the wreckage site, the director is described as joining "the club of those whose lives the event irrevocably altered."[15] At the end of the editing process, Cameron and his team were "dazed and exhausted, having spent the past two years swimming for their lives, it appeared they were finally being dragged into a lifeboat."[16]

Titanic and the Imagination of Disaster

In "The Imagination of Disaster," Susan Sontag considers the aesthetics and thematics of destruction in cinematic science fiction as a distinct category of film.[17] Yet it would not be difficult to construct the argument that much of American cinema has, from its very inception, been devoted to chronicling disaster. Early trick films, short narrative films such as Edwin S. Porter's *The Life of an American Fireman* (1902), and the historical epics of Cecil B. DeMille all explored the possibilities and potentialities of disaster. During the economic hardships and social strains of the 1930s, American moviegoers could witness scenes of more catastrophic disaster than the collapse of the stock market in films such as *San Francisco* (1936), *The Hurricane* (1937), and *In Old Chicago* (1938). From Paramount's *World in Flames*, a 1938 newsreel catalog of human destruction, to the nuclear doomsday films of the 1960s such as *The Day the Earth Caught Fire* (1961) and *Doctor Strangelove* (1964), to the disaster subgenre cycle of the 1970s—exemplified by films that highlighted the dangers of the natural environment (*Earthquake*, 1974) and the fallibility of man-made structures (*The Poseidon Adventure*, 1972; *Juggernaut*, 1974; *The Towering Inferno*, 1974; *The Hindenburg*, 1975)—the spectacle of disaster has been central to our cinema.

What is the function of the spectacle of disaster in the American ethos? It may be that a nation with such a dynamic vision of its own construction and development frequently needs to visualize the alternatives. And it may be that disaster narratives lend themselves well to the fundamental ideological task of American commercial cinema—the reappreciation of our culture and the values we perceive it to hold. But as we become less and less sure of our own survival, the near-hysterical frequency and hyperbolic scope of new disaster narratives warrants our attention. Popular films seem to repeatedly demonstrate an awareness of an imminent shift into a new millennium in which survival is always precarious and no assumptions are made about structures of support. Clearly, at the close of cinema's first full century, new stakes are emerging that bear some scrutiny. It is difficult to identify another era in which eschatological fantasies were as abundant as they appear to be now.

It is by now a commonplace to observe that post–Cold War American cinema has sought to fill a representational vacuum left behind after decades of direct and oblique depiction of communist threat. There are, of course, a variety of ways in which Hollywood blockbusters have filled that gap with new images of our national enemies: technologically inept post–Gulf War Arabs (Cameron's *True Lies*, 1994), disgruntled white workers whose "American Dream" has sputtered (*Speed*, 1994), and aliens (*Men in Black*, 1997). All of these strategies attest to the way in which the collapse of communism seems to have precipitated a national crisis of identity. There is, however, another increasingly common catalyst that increasingly precipitates crisis and supplies narrative energy to the action-adventure genre: the natural disaster.

An all-consuming emphasis on the visual in television news coverage has certainly heightened our sense of susceptibility to such telegenic forms of natural catastrophe as flood, fire, earthquake, and volcanic eruptions. Whether or not we are directly affected by such events, they are now constructed for us within the terms of the national community defined by television. Through spectatorship, we feel an immediacy to these events, which approximates the position of disaster victim. As disasters are increasingly narrativized and specularized through film and television fictions and through entertainment journalism, we move toward a consensus position predicated on the understanding that disaster and disaster survival are cornerstones of our contemporary experience. Such fictions offer social explanations for a constant state of disaster preparedness and imminent crisis.

Television series and specials focusing upon themes of precarious survival have proliferated in the mid-1990s and routinized our consumption of disaster. A recent two-part PBS series, *Savage Earth*, devoted itself to chronicling the destruction of earthquakes, volcanoes, and tsunamis. A concluding voice-over in the series's second segment observed that "the more we understand our earth the more dangerous a place it seems to be," a sentiment that might be identified as the foundational mantra in a number of programs focusing upon disaster and disaster preparedness.[18] Some of those series and specials include the Learning Channel's *Raging Planet*, *Without Warning*, *Wonders of Weather*, and *Survivor Science*, as well as Discovery Channel's *Storm Warning* and a variety of other specials and made-for-TV movies on Fox and other networks. ABC has broadcast *I Survived a Disaster*. NBC's *Dateline* now incorporates a regular segment entitled "Survivor Story," while PBS broadcast *Escape!*, a program devoted to the premise that life is dangerous and that one must cultivate preparedness strategies. Other offerings in the genre (*Savage Earth*, for example) punctuate their coverage of a speculative future by linking it to the documented past, invoking historical disasters like Pompeii to underscore the constancy and centrality of disaster in the human experience. In such a climate, *Titanic* plays a crucial role in its ability to historicize and personalize disaster.

Catastrophic possibility and quotidian reality intersect most clearly in weather coverage, which has, of course, taken an increasingly disaster-oriented stance in the 1990s. The Weather Channel, the top-rated cable network for morning viewing among adults, has increasingly marketed itself as an outlet for weather as entertainment, garnering its highest ratings during hurricanes and other calamitous events. In the past year, the network has won acclaim for a new ad campaign that features characters in an imaginary sports-style bar called "The Front." Substituting weather for sports, the bar's patrons are intense weather fans, identifying themselves with warm and cold fronts (and painting their faces accordingly), placing bets on weather outcomes, and bragging about old injuries that would prevent them from displaying the weather maps used by the network's meteorologists. The Weather Channel also plans to incorporate into the campaign a new tag line that will further raise the stakes in dramatizing and personalizing its viewers' relationship to the weather environment: "If hell freezes over, you'll hear it here first."[19]

Thus *Titanic* was released into a discursive climate in which themes of disaster and disaster readiness were prevalent on many cultural (not weather) fronts. Late 1997 and early 1998 had seen the emergence of two reality-based best-sellers chronicling the experience of natural disaster in minute detail in a hurricane (*The Perfect Storm*) and in violent snowstorms on Mount Everest (*Into Thin Air*). National weather coverage was in the process of normalizing a constant position of crisis readiness through the popularization of the El Niño weather pattern as an all-purpose hazard that produced a variety of natural disasters from snowstorms to floods.

In contrast to such developments, which cause us to look ahead with great trepidation, many recent films depict the social disruption caused by disaster as essentially positive. *Independence Day* and *Deep Impact* both conclude with the image of a purified United States undergoing reconstruction. In addition, new narrative strategies showcased in the contemporary action-adventure genre forecast the recovery from disaster as the reclamation of an inherent sense of American family values. In so doing, many of the films rely heavily on survival-oriented families and quasi-familial teams and partnerships whose members display a new self-consciousness about the precarious terms of survival in the late twentieth century. Such fictions often present us with an image of the new family. Thus in *Dante's Peak* (1997), *Deep Impact*, and *Armageddon* (1998), older parents sacrifice themselves for the good of a newly convened or shortly-to-be-convened young family, and in *Independence Day*, the heroic exploits of the pilots, Captain Steven Hiller (Will Smith) and David Levinson (Jeff Goldblum), are linked to the rebuilding of coupling relationships. Such priorities are perhaps demonstrated most forcefully in *Armageddon*, where Harry Stamper (Bruce Willis) sacrificially substitutes himself for his daughter's fiance, A. J. Frost (Ben Affleck), to ensure the continuity of his family.

Stamper also heads a drilling team composed of intensely individualistic mavericks whose status as mainstreamed survivalists is confirmed in their request never to pay taxes again when they agree to take on the mission of saving the earth from a gigantic asteroid. A highly conservative text, *Armageddon* is able to make important gestures of acknowledgment toward dissatisfaction with big government, as when Stamper and his team, betrayed by the president and his advisers, decisively overturn their predicament and indict the workings of government. When, in a discursive inversion of conventional terms of power, Stamper radios back to NASA, saying, "Houston, you've got a problem down there," cheers ring out in the control room. In this way, *Armageddon* takes part in a general discrediting of governmental and media authority on display in other 1998 films such as *The X-Files* and *The Truman Show*.

It is apparent that in the "post-*Titanic*" summer blockbuster season of 1998, many of the highest-grossing films replicated and extended *Titanic*'s survivalist interests. Additional recent summer blockbusters point up the ubiquity of concerns about imminent disaster in the form of remakes of classic monster films (*Godzilla*, 1998; and *Mighty Joe Young*, 1998). *Godzilla* sets itself in a New York that is incessantly raining, and where residents' anxieties about the weather are indirectly linked to the spectacular reemergence of the radiation-induced superreptile. Meanwhile, even light romantic comedies such as the recent *Six Days, Seven Nights* (1998) turn surprisingly serious when it comes to issues of survival. Foregrounding the issue of survivalist teamwork central to *Titanic*, the film focuses on pilot Quinn Harris (Harrison Ford) and magazine editor Robin Monroe (Anne Heche), who are stranded on an abandoned island near Tahiti. Their relationship culminates not with sexual intimacy but with survivalist behavior in a sequence marked by the use of eroticizing camerawork in which the pair use their combined ingenuity to repair their damaged plane and thwart a pirate attack.[20]

The perception of a hazardous environment is always linked to mitigation strategies, and in the mid-1990s the most popular of these appears to be family formation and the cultivation of a domestic fortress mentality not unlike that of the 1950s. In this sense we can see how gestures of community based on collective trauma and survival are fundamentally more exclusive than inclusive. As survivalist spectatorship becomes more prevalent in American films, it is worth bearing in mind the points Kai Erikson raises about the psychological and social dimensions of the survival experience. Erickson characterizes a survivalist ethos as follows.

> That new ethos can involve a feeling that the persons and institutions in charge of complex technologies cannot be relied upon, that the technologies themselves are based on theories and calculations of no merit, and that the environment in which all this takes place—both social and natural—has proved to be brittle and full of caprice. It is a view of life born of the sense that the universe is regulated not by order and continuity but by chance and a kind of natural malice that lurks everywhere. It is a new and special truth.[21]

Michael Barkun argues that "the categories of disaster and millennium collapse into each other. The former not only prepares for the latter, disaster is the millennium."[22] Crisis in the current wave of disaster films serves the function of transition in the terms that Frank Kermode uses to characterize the nature of millennial transformation. Kermode notes "the triple nature of the phenomenon: transition with decadence on one side of it and renovation or renaissance on the other."[23] In a film such as *Titanic* where endings and beginnings are constantly conflated—from the opening scenes of the ship's departure on its doomed maiden voyage to old Rose's death and joyful reconstitution in the scene of spectacular recovery and unity that closes the film—a spirit of technological overconfidence hints at decadence, while apocalypse prefigures the installation of utopia. According to such narrative paradigms, cultural exhaustion gives way to a triumphant new era marked by the imagery of paradise regained. *Titanic* and other similar fictions correct for the prevailing sense of fragmentation and alienation in contemporary culture in line with what Eric Hobsbawm and Terence Ranger term "the invention of tradition."[24] That is, the film produces a powerful historically based account of survival that displaces awareness of the contemporary loss of social bonds. We fantasize consensus based on our identification with survivor figures of the past, who serve as touchstones for the present and the future.

Thus I think it is reasonable to claim that the proliferation of disaster-based fictions and reenactments in the mid-1990s says something about our cultural awareness of the upcoming millennial transition. While we could map a history of American cinema as it intersects with the awareness of national threat—science fiction films in the Cold War 1950s, disaster films that fault corporate malfeasance as the consumer and antinuclear movements gathered strength in the 1970s, and so forth—we could also note that there are specific social variables that shed light on the meanings of our current disaster narratives and the specific kinds of fears and pleasures they activate.[25]

The Pleasures of Survival

Contrary to claims that *Titanic* represents a reversion to a set of old-fashioned norms and values, it is far from an anachronistic text. Indeed, the film displays a number of up-to-the minute concerns characteristic of a broad range of texts in late-twentieth-century popular culture. The success of *Titanic* can only be adequately contextualized when we note that the film has been produced and consumed in a cultural climate that increasingly prioritizes taking responsibility for one's own survival. The proliferation of survivor narratives is one sign of the way in which the more extreme rhetoric of survivalism is currently undergoing "cultural processing." Other signs include the emergence and wide circulation of an expert discourse of security and self-protection in the realms of popular print fiction as well as film and television. For instance, security expert Gavin de Becker's best-selling *The Gift of Fear* promulgates the value of self-defense awareness in everyday life.[26] In his numerous appearances on talk shows and news programs, de Becker argues that societal development has stifled our instincts for self-protection, and that we need to reestablish our connection to such fundamental instincts to effectively negotiate the dangers of everyday life in the modern world. Coupled with the tropes of threatening nature and fallible technology, such a discourse of self-protection carries a powerful charge. These discourses are also the cornerstones of an emergent narrative paradigm that has taken powerful hold in the national imaginary, a formula which stages the near-miraculous endurance of a small, privileged group of survivors in the face of catastrophic disaster. In the final analysis, *Titanic*'s spectacular popularity may be attributed in large part to its status as a seminal example of the new survivalist text.

Not only does the circulation of survivalist issues offer a level of intertextual enhancement to *Titanic* (making a historically based film "feel" timely), it also tends to deflect more broad-based critical questioning about the nature and direction of contemporary culture. The new survivalist narrative is also highly responsive to fears of the loss of personal empowerment and agency, and by making endurance itself heroic, this film restores a sense of autonomy and agency that is largely disabled in the experience of everyday life in the late twentieth century. The success of *Titanic* is intimately bound up with the ways that disaster has emerged as an important part of our contemporary (and, by extension, historical) consciousness. Disaster narratives, whether their setting is historical or present-day, reassure us that our reliance on technology is still rational by employing new effects technologies to display disaster and by emphasizing its survivability. Further work is needed to assess how and why epistemologies of disaster are increasingly conjoined with the spectatorial pleasures of film and television, yet it is clear that a film like *Titanic* can be seen to be compensatory for a widely shared sense of anomie. In this way, we should not lose sight of the fundamentally conservative character of survivalist texts, for they are designed to camouflage and assuage the insufficiencies of a highly technologized, bureaucratic, and dehumanized culture, offering up the pleasures of survival only as a last resort.

Notes

1. Steven Biel, *Down with the Old Canoe: A Cultural History of the Titanic Disaster* (New York: Norton, 1996).
2. Ibid., 208.
3. Daniel Wojcik, *The End of the World as We Know It: Faith, Fatalism, and Apocalypse in America* (New York: New York University Press, 1997). See also Paul S. Boyer, *When Time Shall Be No More: Prophecy Belief in Modern American Culture* (Cambridge, Mass.: Harvard University Press, 1992) and Neil Schlager, ed., *When Technology Fails: Significant Technological Disasters, Accidents, and Failures of the Twentieth Century* (Detroit: Gale Research, 1994).
4. Philip Lamy, *Millennium Rage: Survivalists, White Supremacists, and the Doomsday Prophecy* (New York: Plenum Press, 1996), 14.
5. http://www.fortcosmos.com/survivalold.html
6. See, for instance, Peter Klebinikov, "Time of Troubles," *Newsweek*, 7 April 1997, 48; Mark Alpter, "Killing Asteroids," *Popular Mechanics*, April 1997, 40–43; and "1001–2000: The World as It Was and the Events That Changed It," *Life* special issue, fall 1997.
7. Damian Thompson, *The End of Time: Faith and Fear in the Shadow of the Millennium* (Hanover, N.H.: University Press of New England), 330–331.
8. Eye on the World: Our Violent Planet (http://www.iwaynet.net/~kwroejr/violent.html); Disaster Central Archives (http://www.promit.com/d-central/discent.html); Perilous Times (http://www.teleport.com/~jstar/index.html).
9. Wojcik, *The End of the World*, 10.
10. This tension between the appropriate meanings of *Titanic* (whether it should be exploited as a massive source of untapped profit or revered as a shrine) has also been evident in Cameron's statements about the film. Cameron (echoing Jack Dawson) has made such hyperbolic pronouncements as "I'm the King of the World!" and "Bigger Is Better,"

yet he has also lapsed into moments of emotional remembrance for the victims of the disaster, calling for a moment of silence at the Oscar ceremonies.

11. Paula Parisi, *Titanic and the Making of James Cameron* (New York: Newmarket Press, 1998), 145.

12. It is worth pointing out that similar emphasis on themes of individualist survivalism can be found in the film's intertexts. For instance, the logic of survivalism is appended to the romance narrative in Celine Dion's performance of the film's theme song, "My Heart Will Go On." The song's opening lines, "Every night in my dreams, I see you. I feel you. That is how I know you go on," seem to posit a female-centered logic of survivalist romance, in which the death of a partner becomes a lesson in perseverance and resilience. A popular radio remix of Dion's song sampled a variety of dialogue lines from the film, most prominently Brock Lovett's invitation to Rose, "Are you ready to go back to *Titanic?*" as a blatant appeal for repeat consumption of the film. The remix also indirectly positioned listeners as "survivors" of the *Titanic* viewing experience, calling upon perceptions of empathetic identification with Rose, and furthering understanding of the film as a "survivor's journey" on a number of levels.

Indeed, it appears that *Titanic's* text is so saturated with themes of endurance and survivalism that those themes can easily be transplanted into other contexts. In July 1998, the film's thematic connections to survivalism were activated and extended in news accounts of Chinese gymnast Sang Lan, a competitor at the Goodwill Games in New York, who fell on a practice vault, damaging her spinal cord and becoming paralyzed. *Titanic* star Leonardo DiCaprio paid a visit to the girl, seeming to serve, in this instance, as a spokesperson for the spirit of survival. See "Actor DiCaprio Visits Injured Chinese Gymnast," *Reuters News Service*, 31 July 1998. Public discourse about the visit tended to highlight intertextual connections to *Titanic*. On an E broadcast of *The Gossip Show* on 8 August 1998, a columnist reported that DiCaprio "gave a *Titanic* lift to the paralyzed Chinese gymnast," while Fox's *Fox Files* commended the actor in its broadcast of 6 August 1998, noting, "For that show of goodwill, he's a *Titanic* hero."

13. See Kenneth E. Foote, *Shadowed Ground: America's Landscapes of Violence and Tragedy* (Austin: University of Texas Press, 1994) for an astute analysis of the functions of disaster in cultural memory.

14. Jane Shattuc, *The Talking Cure: TV Talk Shows and Women* (New York: Routledge, 1997), 107.

15. Parisi, *Titanic and the Making of James Cameron*, 57.

16. Ibid., 202.

17. Susan Sontag, "The Imagination of Disaster," in *Against Interpretation: And Other Essays* (New York: Farrar, Straus & Giroux, 1965), 209–225.

18. Charles Strum, "Moments of Frailty and Appalling Majesty," *New York Times Television* 13 (19–25 July 1998): 3, 22, 23.

19. Diane Werts, "If Hell Freezes Over, You'll Hear It Here First: An Acclaimed New Ad Campaign Positions the Weather Channel as Something Cool," *Newsday*, 4 July 1998, D20.

20. Indeed, Todd McCarthy in his *Variety* review of the film, on 8 June 1998, noted Quinn was a "resourceful survivalist."

21. Kai Erikson, *A New Species of Trouble: Explorations in Disaster, Trauma, and Community* (New York: Norton, 1994), 240–241.

22. Michael Barkun, *Disaster and the Millennium* (New Haven: Yale University Press, 1974), 210.

23. Frank Kermode, "Waiting for the End," in *Apocalypse Theory and the Ends of the World*, ed. Malcolm Bull (Oxford: Blackwell Press, 1995), 258.

24. Eric Hobsbawm and Terence Ranger, *The Invention of Tradition* (Cambridge, England: Cambridge University Press, 1983).

25. Maurice Yacowar, "The Bug in the Rug: Notes on the Disaster Genre," in *Film Genre Reader II*, ed. Barry Keith Grant (Austin: University of Texas Press, 1986), 261–279.

26. Gavin de Becker, *The Gift of Fear: Survival Signals That Protect Us from Violence* (Boston: Little, Brown, 1997).

"It Was True! How Can You Laugh?"

HISTORY AND MEMORY IN THE RECEPTION OF *TITANIC* IN BRITAIN AND SOUTHAMPTON

ANNE MASSEY AND MIKE HAMMOND

All these Southampton women were proud that their men had entered into service on the greatest vessel ever built by man. They prattled of the *Titanic* with a sort of suggestion of proprietorship. . . . Rumours and legends and tales of her glories and luxuries and powers were bandied about in every street in Southampton . . . in the phrase of the people she was "the last word."—*Daily Graphic* (1912)

The *Titanic* sailed from Southampton, England, on 10 April 1912, with a considerable number of Southampton's residents on board as employees of the White Star Line. The ensuing disaster made an impact on the people of Southampton that is rivaled only by the human and material cost of the two world wars.[1] Over five hundred households within a radius of a few miles lost a family member in the sinking of *Titanic*, known locally as "The Big 'Un."[2] At Northam School, in a working-class area near the docks, one hundred twenty-five of the two hundred fifty students lost a parent in the *Titanic* disaster. Most of these children were the sons and daughters of the stokers and firemen who tended the ship's massive boilers. For these children, and their children, and their children's children, the memory of the *Titanic* was personal, and the history of the sinking was something more than local lore. Certainly, it was not just a passing national concern or the source of a controversy ultimately relegated to the distant past.[3]

When James Cameron's *Titanic* was screened in Southampton, it enjoyed record attendance. Why was *Titanic* popular in Southampton? Did it speak differently to Southampton residents than to other audiences? We can assume that

Reproduction of a 1912 illustration from the *Daily Echo*—
Southampton's newspaper—marking the sinking of the *Titanic*

local history as well as evocations of personal memory were revived by the film's appearance, but the apparent connection between popular cinema and the history and memory of Southampton is not as straightforward a phenomenon as it might appear. *Titanic* was extremely popular throughout Great Britain, and at first glance, there seems little point in forcing connections where there may be none. In terms of local affect, Southampton's role in the *Titanic* story has been overlaid with the palimpsest of subsequent historical forces. The social and demographic shifts in the city's population that have occurred across the eighty-seven years since the disaster have seen living memory fade into history. Only one of the survivors who stayed in the community is alive. The number of people working in the liner trade has been greatly reduced, and Southampton now has a significant student population, much like any of the midsize urban communities in Britain.

Nevertheless, Southampton's connection with the *Titanic* tragedy was important enough for Twentieth Century Fox's London office to include it in plans for the national premiere. There was to be a simultaneous release in the three cities that had direct *Titanic* links: Belfast, Liverpool, and Southampton. Although these plans changed and the premiere was held in London, the historical links with Southampton were asserted in the local and national press throughout the first few weeks of the film's British release. In spite of the fact that references to the history of the *Titanic* as a disaster connected to Southampton are almost nonexistent within the film, the stories and the memories, collective and personal, that circulated through the national and local media provided access to the film for British citizens and Southampton residents beyond the narrative hook provided by the love story of Jack Dawson and Rose Bukater.

In Britain, the Southampton connection to *Titanic* became fodder for the film as media event that lasted the better part of the months of January and February 1998. For example, on 28 January 1998, the British tabloid newspaper the *Mirror* ran a story entitled "Port's Icy Welcome for *Titanic*'s Launch." The gist of the article was that Southampton audiences were reluctant to see *Titanic* because "the action was a little too close to home for folk in Southampton."[4] It appears that the authoring journalist had ascertained that the film was not doing the business in Southampton that it had enjoyed elsewhere in the country. Actually, the film was experiencing the same kind of interest level and audience numbers as in the rest of Britain and, indeed, was the biggest-grossing film for all of Southampton's cinemas for the first part of 1998.

What is notable about the article is not its lack of accuracy but the impulse behind its assertions. Its references to the "folk of Southampton" resonate with what Eric Hobsbawm calls the "twilight zone between history and memory."[5] The implication is that the story of the *Titanic* is a *British* story that has been given the Hollywood (read, "American") treatment steeped in fantasy. That fantasy treatment, this view implies, collides dangerously with the memory and actual history of the real event, which the people of Southampton possess, on the one hand, and represent, on the other.

Tabloid journalism often trades in rhetoric that activates the stories that the nation tells itself and also those that "tell the nation." In this case, the article in the *Mirror* refers to the history of Southampton's involvement with the *Titanic* disaster and uses it to create a picture of Southampton filled with the mourning relatives and descendants of the real victims of the *Titanic*. This ostensibly works to claim the real event for Britain through the real-life sacrifice of the good "folk" of Southampton. To reinforce the "Britishness" of the story of the *Titanic*, the *Mirror* ran a picture of British star Kate Winslet with the caption "Star: Kate Winslet." Leading man and acknowledged heartthrob Leonardo DiCaprio was reduced to functioning as a structuring absence.

Seen in this light, Southampton presents itself as a "natural" link between the local and the national reception of Cameron's film in Britain. Through an analysis of film reception in Southampton as being dependent on intertexts beyond the film text itself, it is possible to account for the almost unprecedented attendance figures across a broad range of age groups. This connection also allows space to construct a critical perspective on the fact that various age groups paid to see the film for different reasons: some for the "global address" (i.e., DiCaprio) and some for the opportunity to satisfy historical interests that have been sparked by the *Titanic* sinking since 1912. Other viewers may have paid to see the film to investigate the local connection with the catastrophe, thus providing another rationale for considering this specific local area in analyzing the film's reception. In forging a critical perspective on these various responses, this investigation relies on selected interviews, a sampling of critical commentary in the national press, and the consideration of memorials and other representations of public memory in the city of Southampton.

Titanic is a blockbuster, and blockbusters, of course, require large audiences in order to recoup their high production costs. To appeal to a wide range of viewers, they typically construct references that allow multiple ways into the film. These references are in the film text and in the surrounding "paratexts" associated with the film. The various forms of address created through multiple references engage an imagined viewer in what Barbara Klinger calls "cinematic detours" or digressions. Klinger provides a useful model for thinking about how viewers may "digress" from a film's narrative through the diversity of access to mainstream film texts provided by mass media intertexts. She suggests that the "economy of the classic text within its mass cultural situation obliges that it be extended beyond itself." She refers not only to the practices of the marketing and advertising of the film but also to the subsidiary forms of circulation where the stories generated around the film appear in order "to produce multiple avenues to the text that will make the film resonate as extensively as possible in the social sphere in order to maximize its audience." Klinger builds a model of heterogeneous reception that takes into account the dynamic between the film as a text and mass cultural forms of intertextuality in order to account for how viewers might "construct economies of viewing that fragment rather than assemble the text, truly 'manhandling' and 'interrupting it.'"[6]

Klinger proposes a model for digressions in film viewing that identifies the mass entertainment industries' production, distribution, and advertising mechanisms as the primary generators of intertexts. This necessary set of limitations permits reception to be theorized as variable but avoids the chaos of infinitely possible readings. The criteria for relevant intertexts are based on their ability to place the film's narrative elements (i.e., the star, the special effects, the director) within readable (for the researcher) frameworks for digressions within the viewing experience. These digressions are limited by the mass media intertexts, however, and the spectator produced by this model is an idealized, global, albeit historical one. The by-product of centering the focus of the reception of popular Hollywood film on the production/advertising part of the industry is that the spectator/viewer, which this element produces through its own address, is, by and large, North American.

A case study of the reception of *Titanic* in a specific local area such as Southampton paradoxically serves to illustrate this point and emphasize the importance of considering the *site* of reception. The *Mirror*'s reference to Southampton's particular experience draws attention to the blurring of the boundaries between the "top down" industry-produced, "North American" spectator/viewer model and the wider range of probable readings available within a specific area or community of viewers. The "digressing" viewer(s) from the local exhibition site benefit from a combination of the relative certainty of the global address offered by the industry and mass media intertexts and the specific and more uncertain address by local media and exhibition practices aimed at local audiences. This makes it possible to account for a range of responses to *Titanic*, from a fourteen-year-old girl's emotional investment in star DiCaprio to a forty-five-year-old man's scrutiny of the film for historical accuracy because he is an enthusiast of the ship. While we hasten to add that the range of infinite possible readings does not diminish in response to such a study, the digression model could be extended to include other forms of address and other intertexts that are not feasibly included when articulating a model for global reception.

The Reception in the National Press

The reception of *Titanic* in Britain must be framed within the complex history of British reactions to American culture during the twentieth century. There are significant differences within this national framework in audience reactions to the film, which correspond to social class, gender, and generation differences and also map onto a unique discourse around the issue of Americanization. On the one hand, the *Titanic* represents the idealized notion of the American Dream, a dream which motivated mass migration on board the transatlantic ships. It also provides an important space for daydream and fantasy—a fantasy shared by, predominately, working-class Britons. But just as the United States was regarded as the land of opportunity by most throughout the twentieth century, so it was regarded with equal disdain by a significant minority, including many British cultural critics. The latter view epitomizes the hate-hate relationship that the cultural elite of one nation have enjoyed with American culture throughout the twentieth century.

This British reaction to American popular culture has its historic roots in the 1920s in the literary tradition associated with Cambridge don F. R. Leavis. It was also a common thread in the writings of novelist Evelyn Waugh and George Orwell. For left and right alike, as Dick Hebdige convincingly argues, the "*spectre of Americanisation*" fueled debates about elite and popular culture in Britain from the 1930s onward: "America was seen by many of these writers as the prime mover in (a) terrifying process, as *the* homogenising agent. . . . the United States (and its productive processes and scale of consumption) began to serve as the image of industrial barbarism; a country with no past and therefore no real culture, a country ruled by competition, profit and the drive to acquire."[7]

In the 1950s, Lawrence Alloway of the Independent Group was one of the few cultural commentators in Britain who wrote positively about American mass culture. In December 1954, Alloway wrote: "There is a tendency to regard cinema as a great art form which has been ruined by popularity and commercialism. . . . It is proposed to arrange a series of meetings on cinema which does not treat the film as an art form manqué but as a modern popular art. These meetings will deal with the currency of the movies, not with hypothetical absolutes."[8] In practice, a challenge to the orthodox attitude of British Americanophobia was mounted through various projects of the Independent Group, including the bringing of popular American cinema into film programs at the Institute of Contemporary Arts (ICA) in London.

This rejection of aesthetic absolutes drawn in accordance with British-American differences was concomitant with the shift in focus in literary studies from investment in the immanent meaning of the literary text to a concern with cultural context, or, more precisely, "ordinary culture." This shift was represented in the work of Raymond Williams and Richard Hoggart. British cultural studies was established during the late 1950s and early 1960s through foundational texts by Williams (*Culture and Society*) and Hoggart (*The Uses of Literacy*), the *New Left Review*, as well as through the setting up of the Birmingham Centre for Contemporary Cultural Studies in 1963. One of the consequences of this shift was that the concern with Americanization became the crux of debates around consumption and its role as either passive or active.[9] By 1980, Hebdige was able to argue that consumption was often an act of appropriation, and in 1986, Cora Kaplan suggested that "in Britain the genres and narratives of American popular culture acted as a kind of wedge, forcing into the open, through a contrast and a wild dissonance, the class-bound complacency of the Great Tradition of British Culture."[10] However, as Duncan Webster points out, "It is important to realize that this insight goes against the grain of a long and influential tradition which sees American popular culture as homogenous and as something which invades or 'colonizes' British culture."[11]

The subsequent influence of these debates on the British critical establishment is reflected in the reviews of *Titanic* in the national press and in cinema-specific publications. Writing in the venerable British film magazine, *Sight and Sound*, Laura Miller comments, "That everything about *Titanic*—from its stereotyped characters to its bright, even lighting—feels ersatz and obvious may only trouble the kind of people who dislike the immaculate, synthetic recreations of real places in Disney theme parks." Miller describes the film as "crude," "simple-minded," and "vulgar."[12] Laura Miller's review recalls the "long tradition" that resonates back through the century and is predicated upon distinctly upper- and middle-class, commonsense notions of the world. In such accounts, British prejudices about American wealth, American lack of authenticity, American lack of history or real understanding of "high culture" are perennial issues.

And yet *Sight and Sound* is a magazine that, more than most, implicitly reflects contemporary intellectual currents as they apply to film. In the same aforementioned issue, José Arroyo's review of *Titanic* performs an exquisite balancing act, calling the film "impressive and depressing in about equal measure": impressive being the spectacular action counteracted by a depressing lack of development of character and story line. Arroyo's critique of the film arises out of the "long tradition" only in terms of the demands of a qualitative review. What is more in evidence here is the awareness of the discourse of Americanization and the clarity with which Arroyo speaks to that while evaluating the film. He closes the article, "If the film's lacks seem to be those of contemporary Hollywood in general, its attributes are uniquely its own."[13] The critique of contemporary Hollywood films is separate from the "uniqueness" of Cameron's "peerless direction of action." This mode of film criticism is informed by the debates that have shaped film studies since the 1980s and takes as a given that popular culture, and Hollywood cinema, are subjects worthy of serious consideration.

Sight and Sound is read by a minority of the moviegoing public in Britain, and more relevant, perhaps, as a possible influence on British reception, the mainstream press reviews of *Titanic* showed a remarkable regression to the "long tradition." British prejudice about American wealth echoed throughout the reviews. Almost every piece of writing headlined the fact that this was the most expensive film ever made: "The budget started to climb and climb and climb," wrote David Eimer, "until *Titanic* became the most expensive film ever and the latest symbol of Hollywood excess."[14] The British monthly periodical linked with satellite broadcasting, *Sky Magazine*, even featured "Other Stuff You Can Get for $200 Million," including 14 radio stations, 52 percent of a new luxury cruise liner, 5,000 Audi TT convertibles, 10,416,666 visits to the cinema (including the price of snacks), or even 8,250 trips to the moon.[15] Such an approach reinforces stereotyped perceptions—of Americans as having more money than they know what to do with—which have existed in Britain at least since the 1940s.[16] These privileged earlier images also equated excess with American culture through exemplary icons such as World War II GIs who were commonly referred to as "oversexed, overpaid and over here." The GIs find their equivalent throughout subsequent decades in other American cultural symbols, and as Hebdige points out, these are the material of subcultural appropriation as well as cultural critique. Yet these myths of the United States' intrusion into British life also resonate with the historical dominance of Hollywood cinema on British screens. Many measures were adopted over the years to compete with Hollywood, including the 1927 Film Act (also known as the "Quota Act") and schemes to lend state support for the British film industry, the most recent being the use of Lottery money to fund film projects. These measures, however, have not met with notable success.

Against this background, *Titanic* was often criticized in Great Britain as not being of high quality, despite its budgetary extravagance. For example, in *Time Out*, Geoff Andrews lamented: "Unlike its namesake, this glossy, bombastic, overweening juggernaut will not sink; everyone will see it anyway, and so they should, if only to ponder the future of mainstream cinema. With this kind of budget, you'd think we could expect something less hackneyed and manipulative, more complex and genuinely moving; sadly, such hopes seem to be quite forlorn."[17] Such regrets over the film's likely success were frequently juxtaposed with a nostalgic comparison of *Titanic* to the British-made, black-and-white account of the sinking, *A Night to Remember* (1958). The invocation of the Roy Ward Baker–directed film suggests an endorsement of the "Britishness" of the *Titanic* tragedy as presented in that film. Significantly, *A Night to Remember* was screened on BBC2 during the Christmas holidays, a time when television programming on all five terrestrial stations is virtually given over to feature films for family viewing. Marc Lee commented that "*Titanic* is steaming towards what promises to be an Oscar night to remember. However, if it went head-to-head with Roy Baker's film of the tragedy, made in black and white in 1958 for less than one hundredth of Cameron's budget, it would be sunk."[18] After *Titanic* won eleven Oscars, John Lyttle lamented in the quality daily broadsheet the *Independent*: "Cameron is being congratulated—not to mention rewarded—for singularly failing to deliver what *A Night to Remember* and *Titanic Mark One*[19] casually took for granted: the human story, the warmth to melt the iceberg. Perhaps punters were smarter back then."[20]

If *A Night to Remember* was too old a film to suffice as the most immediately relevant evidence of British superiority in cultural and cinematic terms, then the British-made comedy *The Full Monty* (1997) stood in its place. The contrast between *Titanic* as an icon of American cultural domination and *The Full Monty* as a symbol of honest and thrifty British filmmaking was made even more poignant by the failure of the latter, the most successful British film ever made, to win but one Oscar (for the soundtrack) despite being nominated for four, while *Titanic* swept the board. According to the headline in the *Independent*, "The Oscars [Were a] Night When *Titanic*, Not Britannia, Ruled the Waves: Tim Cornwall Reports from Los Angeles on a Disappointing Night for Britain."[21] David Gritten acidly commented, "You could produce 57 *Full Montys* for the money it cost to make *Titanic*."[22] Other points of comparison included the even more low-budget, British fine art short *Diary* (1998). Geoff Brown noted: "In a week engulfed by *Titanic* it is healthy to remember there are other kinds of cinema. Go one weekend to the Artists' Studios and Gallery at 155 Vauxhall Street, London SE11, and you will currently find exhibited *Diary*, a haunting short film by Peter Todd, crafter of poetic ruminations about ordinary life. Cameron employed some 1,100 people; Todd used three crew members, plus four actors. . . . Todd's own bill was £2,000."[23]

While the fact that Cameron was given almost unlimited financial resources to make *Titanic* was unpalatable to most British critics, the film's huge profit seemed even more unbearable. Describing the "thoroughly loopy new film *Titanic*,"[24] the *Daily Telegraph* observed:

> *Titanic* is the first film ever to gross a billion dollars, and its success alone has ensured a great year for Twentieth Century Fox and Paramount, the studios that co-financed it. Thousands of well-paid Hollywood denizens (many of them Academy voters) are grateful for, and relieved by, its success. The town is awash with money; their opulent lifestyles are secure for a while. . . . Hollywood has reasserted itself, with *Titanic* proving a perfect rallying point.[25]

Beyond the astronomical costs and unbelievable profits of *Titanic*, further insult to the British sense of ownership of the *Titanic* story was created by Cameron's appearance at the Oscar ceremony itself, which was blasted by British critics as overemotional, and crassly emblematic of the cultural divide between the United States and the United Kingdom. Imogen Edwards-Jones was out "On the Prowl" for the *Times* and observed, "James Cameron's 'I'm the king of the world' speech and special moment of silence were suitably American."[26] For British journalists the phrase "King of the World" resonated with George Bush's New World Order or American Live Aid's title song "We Are the World"—images which make transparent American cultural imperialism and "cocacolonization." The "moment of silence" signaled American emotional overindulgence and exhibitionism in marked contrast to the "ordinary," understated quality of the English national character.[27] These are common terms in the public vocabulary concerning Americanization that reinforce Webster's observation that "the discourse of americanisation is shadowed and generated by an unquestioned ideology of Englishness."[28]

Flinching from "in your face" emotion also runs through British commentary on the film. Paul Goodman squirms in his seat and complains: "If emotional restraint can drive a life on to the rocks, cannot emotional indulgence, too? 'They don't make them like that any more,' we sigh, as we watch those pre-war films in which real people grapple with the complexities of life. Indeed they don't. They make them like this."[29] The memory of the prewar films Goodman refers to is misplaced. His example of good filmmaking applies more easily to the wartime British film. Writing on the criticisms of British cinema by the likes of Satyajit Ray and François Truffaut, Charles Barr eloquently argues:

> British Cinema came into its own in World War Two. In these years . . . the life of a community *is* at stake, inescapably and dramatically, and the classic feature films of this period (*In Which We Serve*, *Millions Like Us*, *Fires Were Started*, *The Way to the Stars*, *San Demetrio London*) do "put the personals in their proper place." . . . Audience pleasure comes from the maintenance of group effort. . . . Choking back, or snapping out of, grief for the death of a loved one becomes—in all five of the films named . . . a central and very moving motif.[30]

This characteristic of depicting community *and* restraint also marks *A Night to Remember*, where the issues of class and national character hinge on the stoic heroism of the mostly British crew and particularly on Kenneth Moore as Second Officer Charles Lightoller.

Titanic works in an entirely different direction, centering not on the crew or even on isolated representatives of the Britishness of that crew like Lightoller, but on the story of two young Americans (Rose and Jack) and sacrifice for individual gain (Rose's freedom) rather than for community. The depiction of British national character as equivocal in the case of Ewen Stewart's First Officer William Murdoch or David Warner's evil Spicer Lovejoy, henchman of Cal Hockley, raised the ire of the broadsheet critics. Christopher Tookey of the *Daily Mail* objected to "sentimental schlock and brainless Brit-bashing" and in his byline complained: "Cameron's thesis . . . is that the upper classes, and especially the English, are to blame. In common with virtually every Hollywood movie of the Nineties, *Titanic* bashes the British—as usual, we're cold, cowardly, conceited and cruel while bathing the loveable lower orders, multiethnic and overwhelmingly Irish, in golden light."[31] The belief that the film bashes Brits is frequently interlinked with observations about the poor treatment of the upper classes by Cameron. Auberon Waugh, son of eminent British author Evelyn Waugh, objected to the general tendency in contemporary Britain to blame the upper classes for everything: "In the worlds of politics and entertainment, this hatred of toffs is more or less obligatory. A new film about the sinking of the *Titanic* devotes itself to the untrue proposition that first-class passengers behaved badly."[32] Both Tookey and Waugh assume the position that Britishness is equivalent to the upper or middle class, a sentiment that was certainly recognizable in the aftermath of the disaster in 1912.

Waugh's reference to historical accuracy is indicative of a major point of controversy in the British reception of *Titanic*. The letters pages of newspapers like the *Daily Telegraph* were filled with earnest debates about whether details of the ship's fate as depicted in the film were historically accurate. One debate centered on the question of whether, when the ship is shown heading toward the iceberg and the senior officer shouts "Hard to starboard," this would be an accurate rendition of what happened. While this debate was not taken up in the U.S. newspapers, more populist newspapers in Britain also commented on such anachronisms in the film as its use of halogen lamps; the hymn sung during the religious service, which was not written until 1937; and Jack's claim that he comes from Lake Wissota, a town not established until 1917. Much of the debate was focused on the film's depiction of First Officer Murdoch as shooting a passenger and then himself in the final moments before the ship's sinking. Murdoch is celebrated as a local hero in his Scottish hometown for getting off warning shots and saving passengers' lives while going down with the ship himself.[33] A catalog of Cameron's failure to authentically replicate the social mores of the different social classes on board the *Titanic* also runs through the published written criticism.

The strength of the concern for historical accuracy in the British press indicates the issues of national identity inherent in the contested nature of the *Titanic* story. For these critics and letter writers, Cameron's film spectacularly claims the story as an *American* narrative resplendent in its ideology of transformation and ignorant of the virtues of a sense of community and self-sacrifice, that is, *British* virtues. Through these examples of British responses to the film, we can see that the *Titanic* story mobilized a discourse of Britishness that worked as an important intertext for the film in Britain. This, in turn, raised interest levels among a wide range of social groups indicated by the readership of the broadsheets and the tabloids. The criticism and controversy also informed talk, or word of mouth, which contributed to the runaway success of the film in terms of audience attendance throughout the country. In this respect, the reception of the film in the city of Southampton was no exception, and yet the city was singled out by the national press as exceptional because of its history, thus almost willing the film to fail there as a triumph of national history over American cultural imperialism.

Southampton, a City in Mourning: Local Memory and History

In Southampton there are two multiplex cinemas and one independent cinema. All are located in the refurbished dock area. They have been the subject of rebuilding and development from the early 1980s and are the focus of the city's economic regeneration at the end of the twentieth century. The Virgin Cinema, under its previous ownership by MGM, was the first of the multiplexes in the area. The Odeon cinema opened in August 1997, as the centerpiece in the Odeon Leisure World Complex, which includes theme restaurants, tenpin bowling, arcade and video games, and themed nightclubs. The Harbour Lights Cinema, opened in 1996, is the first purposely built independent cinema in the United Kingdom since the late 1960s and is funded by grants from the Southampton City Council, the Regional Arts Board, Southern Arts, and the British Film Institute. Harbour Lights has two screens and, in line with the regional film theater tradition, has a programming policy that aims to screen a wide range of films beyond the mainstream commercial products.

The distribution offices of Twentieth Century Fox were aware of the uniqueness of Southampton to Cameron's film, and discussions took place with the cinema managers and directors beginning in the summer before the film's premiere there on Friday, 23 January 1998. The aim was to release the film across eight screens in Southampton with press and preview screenings at Harbour Lights and Odeon. Harbour Lights had set up in its gallery an exhibition of *Titanic* artifacts supplied by the Southampton City Council's Heritage Department. The local press, although not part of the national media campaign, were quick to pick up on the local connection with the film.[34] The news reports ranged from calling attention to the heightened profile for the city that the film and publicity provided, to noting the connection of the film's story with the survivors and relatives of the victims still living in the area.

The sensitive nature of *Titanic* to survivors of the sinking and their living relatives became apparent early on. Special screenings were to feature the appearance of Millvina Dean, a living survivor of the *Titanic* disaster. Dean had been a subject of interest to the international campaign for the film, but she had refused invitations to the New York and Hamburg premieres of the film. (She did, however, have a telephone interview with television talk show host Larry King in the United States.) Local Southampton press articles ran the story of Millvina, who was nine weeks old when she, her mother, and her brother, were put onto lifeboats while her father, adhering to the "women and children only" directive, was left behind to perish in the sinking. Dean agreed to attend the opening ceremonies in Southampton but said she would not be watching the film. She was quoted as saying: "The reviews say it is extremely good and it will recoup its massive outlay. It's a love story and I could have happily seen the first half but no more. . . . At the end there is panic, shouting and screaming. What if he [my father] is one of those people who jumps overboard or is one of the bodies in the water? I couldn't stand to see that. It would cause too much anguish."[35] The publicity value of her statement is obvious, but it also emphasizes the problem facing

The Harbour Lights Cinema, Southampton, 1998

Twentieth Century Fox, which was anxious not to jeopardize the film's release in any way.

By drawing attention to a public memory of bereavement in Southampton, the *Mirror* article "Port's Icy Welcome for *Titanic* Launch," previously cited, caused some consternation with the studio's London office and a nervous anticipation that this could be negative publicity that would result in poor audiences.[36] The presumption that Southampton was particularly sensitive to the film's representation of a tragic event was repeated in the trade press journal *Screen International*: "While cinemas in London sold out and movie-goers flocked to see the £200m-plus ice cube on its opening weekend, reaction in the port from where the ship first sailed all those years ago has been altogether different. The film has weathered a cool reception in Southampton where tickets for this particular pleasure cruise were selling slowly."[37] The studio, in the end, had little to worry about. *Titanic* took in £63,000 for the first week. Out of a city population of approximately 240,000, and at an average ticket price of £3.00, that figure represents an audience made up of 10 percent of the population of Southampton. The film broke records for attendance at the Odeon and Harbour Lights and was the largest-grossing film at the Virgin since *Independence Day* (1996).

The story of a mourning Southampton provided the British national press and the trade press with a counter to the primarily positive blockbuster business stories that accompanied the film in its first weeks of release. Although Twentieth Century Fox's London office did contact the director of Harbour Lights expressing some concern over the story and its effect on attendance figures, there is also an advertising value in any story that promotes "talk" about the film and works to invoke or support the crucial word of mouth needed for a blockbuster success.[38] In addition, the story of a city in mourning converges with Raphael Samuel's notion of unofficial histories. Samuel calls for a history that encompasses "unofficial knowledges," the collection of legends, mythical heroic figures, and factual histories that combine to form popular memory. He calls for an attempt to follow the "imaginative dislocations which take place when historical knowledge is transferred from one learning circuit to another—as, say, in screenplay adaptations of the literary classics where the written word is translated into imagery; or in comic-strip versions of grand narrative."[39] The connection between the film and the history of the city made by the national and local press highlights such "unofficial knowledges" that contribute to the variety of ways that viewers frame their responses to a film. Thus the explanation for viewer response to *Titanic* cannot be found in the (film) text alone. Intertexts must also be examined.

The local intertexts and their sources are varied. Knowledge of the impact of the *Titanic* tragedy on the city can be acquired in the local history section of Southampton Public Library and in the oral history work of the Southampton City Council Heritage Department. Stories in the local press reported that the researchers for the film had used the Heritage Department's archive and that Cameron had relied on the book *Titanic Voices* (compiled and written by the oral historians of the Southampton City Council Heritage Department) on the set of the film to maintain historical accuracy. The subject of a recent local news story, The Grapes pub was where a number of the crew supposedly enjoyed a last libation before joining the *Titanic*. The Grapes still stands on Oxford Street in a historic area untouched by the bombing of World War II. Although there were actually no pubs as close to the docks as the film depicts, The Grapes was one of the closest and is the possible inspiration for the pub where Jack and Fabrizio win their ticket of passage. The news item claimed that the manager of The Grapes pub had discovered from some visiting Americans the story of the Slade brothers, crew members of the *Titanic*, who missed the boat because they had lingered too long over their drinks in her pub. The Americans had read this in *Titanic Voices*.[40]

However, for local inhabitants, seeing memorials for the *Titanic* and places like The Grapes is not always, if at all, the trigger of local memory. These may often go unnoticed or unremarked, only surfacing, perhaps, when a local notices a stranger reading the inscriptions. But, like the proverbial "loud American tourist," *Titanic* regenerated these memories. Southampton's signs of public memory linked to the *Titanic* became more visible, fueled by the local and national press coverage of the film as an event and, in turn, by the popularity of the film itself.

The impact of the original disaster is visible through the numerous monuments dispersed throughout Southampton. If you walk from the top of the high street to any of the three cinemas located at or near the docks, you will encounter at least three. The largest is the monument to the ship's engineers, which stands just across from the cenotaph (the Great War memorial). There is also a replica of the musicians' memorial plaque, which was replaced in 1990, fifty years after being

The Grapes pub

destroyed along with the library during the Blitz. The crew memorial at Holyrood Church now stands in the ruins of the church, bombed during World War II. These memorials provide visible evidence of local lore that must inevitably intersect in the imagination with fictional cinematic reproductions of the event. And yet there is a complexity to these encrustations of memory, to the stories that attach themselves to "official history," and to the history of these stories.

Southampton Public Library has kept a record of inquiries concerning the *Titanic* disaster and reported a dramatic increase since the release of *Titanic* in Britain in January 1998. The majority of the inquirers were looking for possible family members who were on the *Titanic*. Here, popular and personal memory combine across this particular local site. After the release of Cameron's film, the Home James Company, a local coach tour operator, initiated a one-and-a-half-hour tour on an "executive coach" to "help you create the part Southampton played in the story. . . . the old city echoes with memories of both the survivors and those lost at sea." "The *Titanic* Experience; A Legend Remembered," as the tour was called, ceased business after the interest in the film subsided in May.

Personal Accounts

Across the country *Titanic* attracted a significant percentage of audience members over the age of twenty-five.[41] In an interview, one member of this group, Claire M., spoke over the phone and recounted her experience of viewing the film. The background to Claire M.'s response is her particularly vivid family memory of the disaster. Her grandmother was one of the students at Northam School. Claire

The memorial to the engineers of the *Titanic*

M. remembers her father recalling how his mother told him that after the sinking, many children were off from school and how "the kids [were] crying for a week." Her father refused to see the film, and he felt it should never have been made. For her family, the memory of the *Titanic* disaster was "like Remembrance Sunday." Her response to the film was one of anger. While she had enjoyed the film's spectacle of nostalgia, she felt the film was "too happy and way off beam." She kept thinking about "the crew" and did not like the American treatment of the British and the Irish. Here is an echo of Christopher Tookey's objection to the depiction of "brit-bashing," perhaps, but Claire M. did not share Tookey's disparaging response to the film's "loveable, predominately Irish, lower orders." Claire M.'s reaction to *Titanic* demonstrates the force field of local, family history even as it shares characteristics evidenced in British critical reaction to the film's treatment of what was perceived by British nationals as British history.

These collisions between family history/memory and mass media/entertainment/history underscore the "imaginative dislocations" that can occur across experiential realms. The association of melodramatic spectacle with a "vulgar" American mass entertainment is evident in British viewer response to *Titanic*, as is the sense of frustration with the focus of the film being away from what has been called "the real story" (of which there are many; the bravery of the crew or the outrageous victimization of the steerage passengers as a metonym for the atrocities of the class system). Claire M.'s repeated use of the phrase "I kept thinking . . ." refers to her account of her own personal memory, which was elicited as a counter-response to the film's depiction of history.

Claire M.'s response while watching the film could be presumed to draw on

A close-up of "the engineer"

her knowledge of the *Titanic* disaster, and although it is important to treat such consciously recounted stories of viewing with caution, this does suggest that experiential digressions in the cinema work outside of, or even against, industry-centered intention. Cameron has been cited in the documentary *Titanic: Breaking New Ground* as having intentionally placed real "historical" people in the background of the scenes throughout the film, and this squares with Klinger's idea of the industry building multiple entries or appeals into the film text. By building historical references into the film and by then advertising claims for meticulous authenticity, Cameron was able to appeal to those enthusiasts who possessed a historical awareness and at the same time pique the interest of those uninformed about the *Titanic* disaster. However, the particularity of Claire M.'s response as a viewer, and of her father's refusal to be a viewer, shows that the same avenues can also be barriers to the pleasurable consumption of the text or even, in her father's case, to consuming the text at all.

Other viewer accounts focused more squarely on the historical accuracy of the film's depicted events. One such account was that of Bob J., who is related to a *Titanic* survivor represented in the movie:

I went to see the film with my wife, and having visited the exhibition of "Titanic" artifacts at the National Maritime Museum in Greenwich several years ago and also having read a variety of literature on the vessel's tragic loss, I was very impressed with the technical accuracy of the film's mock-ups and computer simulations. The representation of the ship was

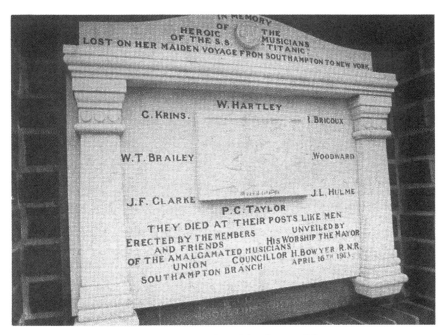

The reconstructed musicians' memorial

incredibly realistic and obviously very well researched, as was the background and appearance of many of the named characters. However, I was surprised by the "artistic license" that was applied to the actions and character of several of the ship's officers, particularly that of Richard [sic] Murdoch, the first officer, who was shown shooting a passenger and then committing suicide. This was a sad slur on an officer who was last seen trying to launch extra boats as the ship was sinking. Leaving the romantic plot aside, this was such a contrast to the accuracy of the rest of the film that it left me rather angry and disillusioned with the film makers.

Bob J.'s account provides a sense of the specific intertexts that helped to inform his experience of the film: the visit to the museum, his expertise in maritime technology, and his concern for the family of Officer William Murdoch. Without being fully aware of its implications, Bob. J. recognizes the impact of popular forms on popular memory and points us to *Titanic*'s "post-modern hubris," a phenomenon that has been discussed in a scholarly context by Thomas Elsaesser. In an essay on Steven Spielberg's *Schindler's List* (1993), Elsaesser notes that "once one concedes that one cannot get very close to *Schindler's List* by arguing whether Spielberg was right in showing 1,000 Jews rescued where six million perished, it is possible to recognise in his films a typically post-modern hubris, namely the faith that the cinema can redeem the past, rescue the real, and even rescue that which was never real."[42] *Titanic* demonstrates this same faith in the cinema's ability to redeem the past, the real, and "that which was never real."

The Home James Company's "*Titanic* Experience" brochure

Cameron's narrative emphasis on the fictional story of Rose and Jack—the "never real"—effects a way into the text and functions as a framing device to allow other stories to be shown—*shown* because these visual references that occupy the periphery of the frame are there to provide an ambiguous hint that there are other stories. Implying as much is an homage to Roy Ward Baker that echoes the reverse camera angle of the scene in *A Night to Remember* where Thomas Andrews, the designer of the *Titanic*, standing at the fireplace of the first-class lounge, speaks to a young couple. This strategy not only allows multiple avenues of access but justifies the use of the love story through the spectacular portrayal of catastrophe. The critiques in the national press that seemed to hinge on praise for the spectacle/effects and condemnation of the romantic story are inflected differently in these personal viewer accounts. In the latter, the peripheral stories of actual historical figures are the ornate frame around a silly central narrative.

For Claire F., this frame's relation to local memory provides an experience beyond the intentions or skill of the director: "The film was a positive blend of fiction and fact—a true story seen through the medium of a fictional romance. But the power and lasting impact of the film is a result of the knowledge that such suffering really occurred, on such a great scale, and so unnecessarily. It's haunting." Here we have cinema re-creating the affect of the moment, the affect of history, addressing those desires of the audience to have been *there*—at the original scene of the depicted event. The ideological work within a rhetorical documentary may seem transparent through the obvious didactic address; by way of contrast, in *Titanic* as a fictional/historical text, the transparency of the ideological work may come and go for the viewer. Claire F. wrote: "I thought the characters, some of the actors, and in particular the script were awful and hence the film was one of the worst I have ever seen, and yet at the same time I was totally absorbed and whole-heartedly moved by the second, tragic half of the film and for that reason it is the best film I have ever seen." Tears may be evoked from the mass address of spectacle or from the personal empathetic recognition of representations of family and doomed loved ones played out in the various tableaus of tragedy: the old couple clinging to each other in their stateroom bed as the water rises around them, the mother reading to her frightened children, and, finally, Jack disappearing into the deep. Claire F. wrote of her own emotional response to the film: "I have never felt so affected by a film as I was by *Titanic*. I was moved by the film, but not in a sentimental way. I think I was feeling grief. For weeks after seeing the movie I dreamt about it, or I would feel a wave of emotion upon hearing the theme tune on the radio. I felt down in my spirit."

The shifting digressions for Claire F. as she reported them included the impression of local memory: "I was aware at points during the film of the connection with Southampton, and I do think that any connection with a place or people we know does have an impact. We relate to it more closely. I was talking about this to a colleague whose great-grandfather had been a surviving crew member of the *Titanic*. He had chosen not to go to the film (which surprised me) on the grounds of his perception that it was so inaccurate." Inaccuracies and disrespect to the memory of the dead are often cited in these accounts from the local residents

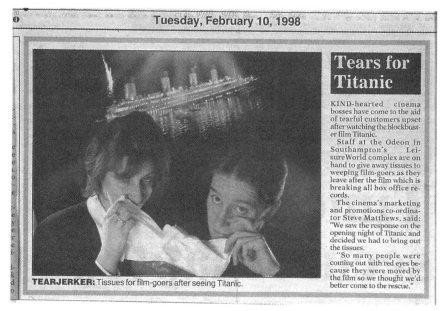

Tuesday, February 10, 1998

Tears for Titanic

KIND-hearted cinema bosses have come to the aid of tearful customers upset after watching the blockbuster film Titanic.

Staff at the Odeon in Southampton's LeisureWorld complex are on hand to give away tissues to weeping film-goers as they leave after the film which is breaking all box office records.

The cinema's marketing and promotions co-ordinator Steve Matthews, said: "We saw the response on the opening night of Titanic and decided we had to bring out the tissues.

"So many people were coming out with red eyes because they were moved by the film so we thought we'd better come to the rescue."

TEARJERKER: Tissues for film-goers after seeing Titanic.

A story from the *Daily Echo* about staff from Odeon Leisure World
passing out tissues to the outgoing patrons

we contacted. They lend some perspective on the way in which *Titanic*, and, by inference, its status as an American narrative/product, was engaged by viewers nationally and locally in Britain and Southampton.

By allowing memory a visual expression that transcends the inadequacies of the sentimental tendencies of Hollywood filmmaking, the *Titanic* disaster becomes (or remains) a British story and, moreover, a Southampton story. For the respondents, the film acts as a catalyst for those (public/popular/personal) memories and elicits a sense of ownership through the local and national identities that the romantic fictionalized story appears to suppress. In addition, the narration that emerges from Rose's memory provides a textual reference. Like them, she corrects inaccuracies and imparts a history and identity to the characters involved. She provides the evidence "that such suffering occurred" in place of the "forensic analysis" of Brock Lovett, the salvage crew leader, and one of the crew members. She takes up the role of guardian of the memory, the real history, against Brock's motivations to use the *Titanic* for financial gain. Thus the presence of Rose in *Titanic* may be read as an unintended metaphor for the invasion of a Hollywood blockbuster on the memory of a local tragedy.

Gender, Generation, and the Local

In her book *Melodrama and Meaning*, Barbara Klinger offers a rationale for concentrating on the national ad campaigns of the Douglas Sirk melodramas of the 1950s rather than on the local exhibitors' campaigns. Sirk's home studio, Universal, had developed a centralized preselling approach in order to reach audiences who were no longer going to the movies but watching television.[43] By extending Klinger's model to include local popular memory as a source of intertexts, we have so far concentrated mainly on viewers over the age of twenty-five. Although aware of the local history of the *Titanic* disaster, these viewers are not necessarily consistent moviegoers, and they are also less attuned to the kind of intertexts associated with contemporary mainstream Hollywood, such as star interviews, popular magazine stories, and the national and global film advertising campaigns.

The viewers who are more likely to be plugged into the intertexts of mainstream Hollywood, and in the case of *Titanic*, those who are drawing on the star persona of Leonardo DiCaprio, are under twenty-five. In our attempt to gauge the range of intertexts and probable nature of the kind of digressions available to *Titanic* viewers, we conducted semistructured interviews with fifteen girls between the ages of nine and fourteen.[44] All came from the Southampton area. Most had seen the film more than once; the average attendance was 2.6. The questions we used to spark response came primarily from comments made in the national press.

The fact that this was the most expensive film ever made presented no problems for the girls. When asked, "What do you think about the fact it cost $200 million to make?" they expressed opinions suggesting they were well aware of the stories about the huge expense. For them, this was part of the attraction of the film. The overwhelming response was summed up by Laura (age fourteen): "I think it was worth it." That the film made a huge profit was also not a problem. Chloe (also fourteen) expressed the typical point of view: "They took a risk and it has paid off." As if to anticipate our own argument, they equated blockbusters with Hollywood and understood their need to appeal to more than one aspect of the market: "American films are open to a much wider audience and they have much more money"(Kate, age fourteen). Hollywood excess and spectacle were positive attributes, while the British film industry was described as "a bunch of losers" (Laura, age fourteen) who could not make films to the American standard.

The interview group tended to agree with the British press on the crassness of Cameron's performance at the Academy Awards ceremony, but they became animated when discussing the press's charges regarding the sentimentality of the film. When asked, "What about the criticism of the film being overemotional?" Laura replied: "Well, the subject is emotional. What are you going to say? If people are dying and you're hanging off a ship with your feet in the air, are you going to say? 'Oh, I'm really not happy about it. Oh dear, I've got a tear in my dress.' The fact that it was true, how can you laugh?" Conversely, the charge of lack of historical accuracy did not present a problem for the girls, although it did for their history teacher, who announced she would never go and see the film. The girls realized that "it's a blockbuster. They have to twist the story to get people interested"(Lizzie, age fourteen).

There is a sense here that "real" history and the demands of blockbuster cinema are not the same thing. Moreover, the level of reflection hints at viewers who are aware of the narrative requirements for entertainment while simultaneously maintaining a suspension of disbelief. The history teacher's refusal to see the film represents, perhaps, a missed educational opportunity in tapping into such viewer practices, given that the significant realization that history is *narrative* is at the forefront of the girl's stated reasons for liking the film. This kind of opportunity was not usually missed by English teachers in the area as they had organized student trips to Harbour Lights Cinema to see *William Shakespeare's Romeo + Juliet* (1996) the previous year.

The girls' sources of information on the film—their chief intertexts—did not seem to include broadsheets, tabloids, or *Sight and Sound*, but did include television shows such as *The Big Breakfast*, magazines such as *Empire*, and the talk among their friends at school. When prompted, the interviewees did not share the criticisms of the British press. When asked, "The British press didn't like the film, is that one of the reasons you like it?" The response was a definite "No. Do you mean, like being rebellious? No. We really don't care what people think" (Laura). So why did they like the film and return to see it again when they generally do not see other films more than once, despite going to the movies at least once a fortnight, on average? When we asked, "Why do you go and watch it?" the stock answer was "Because Leonardo DiCaprio is in it and it's a really good film" (Amy, age nine). Other, lesser reasons included "Because everyone else has seen it" (Lizzie) and response to the general hype surrounding the film. The interviewees were initially drawn by the starring role of DiCaprio, as they had been to his roles in *William Shakespeare's Romeo + Juliet* before it and *The Man in the Iron Mask* (1998) after it. However, after the first viewing they realized what a good film it was and returned to see it again. "It's a new experience, nobody had ever seen it like that before . . . and you think, it really happened, and you think about it" (Lizzie).

The poignancy of seeing the film in Southampton, home to so many who died in the *Titanic* sinking, was not lost on the young interviewees. One had been to see it at the newly built Leisure World, right by the dock from where the actual *Titanic* embarked: "I saw it in Southampton on the anniversary—you walked out of the cinema on to the dock, didn't you? It makes a difference seeing it in Southampton" (Laura). Here "the difference" is the "being there." The actual place and the word "difference" speak for a feeling that has its parallel in the swell of music and the gasp the elderly Rose makes as she drops the Heart of the Ocean necklace into the sea at the actual spot where the ship sank. The act of standing on the dock can allow a stepping into the narrative via the real, just as the function of Rose's memory-driven story in the film is to provide the promise of adventure while offering the possibility of the safety of an undying and yet impossible (i.e., lost) love.

The blurring of the factual and the fictional also informs the girls' infatuation with DiCaprio. "I think most of the girls fall in love with his character in *Titanic*, he's an ideal man" (Chloe). When asked if she did not prefer a more masculine sort of man, Louise (age fourteen) responded: "No, I think they're really disgusting. The tough working woman doesn't want a hard, action figure." This is a perspective on DiCaprio that also has appeared in the British press. In the *Daily Mail* Vicky Ward and Jonathan Margolis commented: "There is what some call his [DiCaprio's] 'dumb blond' quality . . . his lack of a girlfriend. . . . He is a loving, dutiful son."[45] During the star's visit to London for the premiere of *The Man in the Iron Mask*, Suzanne Moore wrote in the *Independent*, "The combination of gentleness, ability to form good friendships with women and yet never to have a permanent girlfriend is the perfect way to get a young girl's heart for it implies a sexual passivity in the midst of a sexually aggressive culture."[46] The *Independent* hails him as "top banana for millions of teenage girls,"[47] but the more conventional critics find him anathema to the acting profession. Geoff Brown complained in the *Times* that "there is only so much cocksure grinning one movie can stand, especially if there is nothing much in the script to back up the dental display."[48]

The girls we interviewed about the film contradicted much of what the critics from the national press said, and offered their own, perhaps surprising reasons for responding in the way they did to the film. The special effects, the viewing of the film in Southampton, the blurring of fact and fiction, the mix of history and fantasy all played a part—particularly in their adulation of DiCaprio, whom they idolize because he is like the boy next door. The intertexts available to these girls seem to have been incorporated with the historical significance of their locale in a way that is virtually the converse of the older viewers' experience. For the former, the romantic story of Jack and Rose was a reason to see the film rather than a focus of criticism, and the elements of history within the film were secondary points of interest as they unfolded through repeated viewings. Accordingly, there was no sense of indignation at the Americanization of the story arising from any sense of British national identity; in fact the Americanized shaping of the story was cited as one of the film's appealing qualities. In addition, there was no real evidence of resistant appropriation in terms of speaking out against the critical establishment. There was little sense of any awareness of this critical discussion. What does seem to come through, however, is a sense of camaraderie, of belonging, forged through publicly expressed taste preferences.

While a fuller ethnographic analysis would situate these preferences and responses within the wider context of consumption, our primary purpose here has been to explore the sources of cinematic digressions. Although based on a small sample of interviews, these digressions suggest that while the global mainstream media industry provides the sources for intertexts relevant to the young girls' interpretations of *Titanic*, those are augmented by other factors, such as a parodic self-awareness and a burgeoning sense of local identity, the latter instigated by the film. These negotiations shed some light on the reason why, in spite of its historical associations with the *Titanic* disaster (or perhaps because of them), *Titanic* was still immensely popular in Southampton.

Conclusion

Titanic's reception in Britain and Southampton generally provides a rich ground for exploring issues of national identity, personal and public memory, and the significance that "intertextual" media events have for the study of popular film and transnational reception. The hegemonic domination the Hollywood film industry holds over movie screens in Britain does not necessarily translate into a wholesale endorsement of Hollywood mainstream cinema, nor does it produce "radically resistant" viewers. Nevertheless, memories, both public and private, and a number of nonglobal intertexts work to shape and inform viewers' potential "man-handling" of texts.

The conclusions we draw here illuminate the ways in which the film was received "over here"—our own sense of address "naturally" aims across the Atlantic—through the national press reviews, local press coverage, and interviews with local residents. These conclusions relate specifically to *Titanic* but might be used to suggest more broadly that the reception of American films in Britain is, as would be expected, informed by discussions and representations of taste that position American mainstream cinema as vulgar and invasive. Yet British reception is also informed by the following: the serious national identity issues with which the story of the *Titanic* is linked, the playful and inventive ways in which adolescent girls drew on a wide set of media intertexts in their accounts of their response to the film, and *Titanic*'s resonance with and elicitation of local and personal memory in Southampton. The model for cinematic digressions provided by Klinger and reworked here opens up a space for considering local sites of reception. The important intertexts of public memory are to an extent identifiable and appear to be activated in the responses of the group of viewers over the age of twenty-five, while those impacting young girls seem to come more from the global address of the mainstream media.

What is clear is that neither set of intertexts is "pure." By expanding the digressions model to include intertexts specific to a national and local identity other than to a North American viewer, we can identify different "avenues of access" beyond the intentions of the filmmaker or the industry. These avenues may be different, but they worked enormously well in attracting large audiences to *Titanic* in Britain and Southampton.

Notes

1. Southampton suffered a great deal of bombing damage from the Luftwaffe raids over England during World War II.
2. Donald Hyslop, Alastair Forsyth, and Sheila Jemima, *Titanic Voices: Memories from the Fateful Voyage* (New York: St. Martin's Press, [1994] 1997), 82.
3. The hearings that took place in the U.S. Senate immediately after the *Titanic* disaster and, subsequently, by the British Board of Trade (responsible for Britain's maritime regulations) focused on who as well as what was really responsible for the sinking. There was considerable controversy over the roles played by certain figures such as J. Bruce Ismay, managing director of the White Star Line, on board as a first-class passenger, and Stanley Lord, captain of the SS *Californian,* a ship in the area of the sinking that failed to come to the *Titanic*'s rescue despite observing distress signals. After the hearings, if nothing else was settled, there was agreement by the British Board of Trade that requiring enough lifeboats to give all passengers and crew a seat would help prevent future loss of life at sea: *Titanic*'s lifeboats had a maximum capacity of 1,178 people (and, in the sinking, were loaded with fewer than 800), in contrast to the 3,547 passengers and crew the ship was designed to carry.
4. "Port's Icy Welcome for *Titanic*'s Launch," *Mirror*, 28 January 1998.

5. Eric Hobsbawm, *The Age of Empire* (London: Weidenfield and Nicholson, 1987). The full quote is, "For all of us there is a twilight zone between history and memory; between the past as a generalised record which is open to relatively dispassionate inspection and the past as a remembered part of, or background to, one's own life."

6. Barbara Klinger, "Digressions at the Cinema: Reception and Mass Culture," *Cinema Journal* 28, no. 4 (summer 1989): 4, 9, 10.

7. Dick Hebdige, "Towards a Cartography of Taste 1935–62," *Hiding in the Light: On Images and Things* (London: Routledge, 1988), 52.

8. Anne Massey, *The Independent Group: Modernism and Mass Culture in Britain, 1945–59* (Manchester, England: Manchester University Press, 1996), 78.

9. For a comprehensive account of the intellectual foundations and history of British cultural studies, see Patrick Brantlinger, "Cultural Studies in Britain," in *Crusoe's Footprints: Cultural Studies in Britain and America* (London: Routledge, 1990). For a concise and thought-provoking account of the role that fears of Americanization played in British intellectual debate, see Duncan Webster, "The Long Reaction: Americanisation and Cultural Criticism," in *Looka Yonder: The Imaginary America of Populist Culture* (London: Routledge, 1988), 174–208.

10. Webster, *Looka Yonder*, 178.

11. Ibid., 179.

12. Laura Miller, "*Titanic*," *Sight and Sound*, February 1998, 52.

13. José Arroyo, "Massive Attack," *Sight and Sound*, February 1998, 19.

14. David Eimer, "That Sinking Feeling," *Time Out* (London), 31 December 1997–7 January 1998, 17.

15. James Anderson, "Other Stuff You Can Get for $200 Million," *Sky Magazine*, February 1998, 94.

16. See Hebdige, *Hiding in the Light*, 42–43.

17. Geoff Andrews, "*Titanic*," *Time Out* (London), 31 December 1997–7 January 1998, 18.

18. Marc Lee, "Films: Ocean Emotion," *Daily Telegraph* (London), 21 February 1998, A10.

19. *Titanic Mark One* is journalese for *Titanic*, the 1953 film directed by Jean Negulesco.

20. John Lyttle, "*Titanic*: Is It Really the Sail of the Century?: Is It Possible for a Film to be the Biggest Box-Office Success Ever . . . and Still Be a Turkey? John Lyttle Says Yes," *Independent* (London), 27 March 1998, 5.

21. Tim Cornwall, "The Oscars: Night When *Titanic* Not Britannia, Ruled the Waves: Tim Cornwall Reports from Los Angeles on a Disappointing Night for Britain," *Independent* (London), 25 March 1998, 18.

22. David Gritten, "Can *Titanic* Be Sunk?: *Titanic* May Have Equalled the Record for Oscar Nominations, says David Gritten, But Watch Out for *The Full Monty*," *Daily Telegraph* (London), 11 February 1998, Arts sec., 19.

23. Geoff Brown, "Tragedy Replayed as Epic Spectacle," *Times* (London), 22 January 1998, 33.

24. Ryan Gilbey, "I've Got That Sinking Feeling: The Big Picture," *Independent* (London), 23 January 1998, 8.

25. David Gritten, "Oscars: *Titanic* Proves Unsinkable after All: Hollywood Breathes a Sigh of Relief as James Cameron's Blockbuster Collects 11 Academy Awards," *Daily Telegraph* (London), 25 March 1998, 20.

26. Imogen Edwards-Jones, "Arty Animal: Imogen Edwards-Jones Out on the Prowl," *Times* (London), 28 March 1998, 3.

27. We use the term "English" here to illustrate a characteristic of the discourse of national identity in Britain that often supplants "English" for "British."

28. Webster, *Looka Yonder*, 195.

29. Paul Goodman, "The *Titanic*'s Second Sinking," *Daily Telegraph* (London), 28 January 1998, 22.

30. Charles Barr, "Introduction: Amnesia and Schizophrenia," in *All Our Yesterdays: 90 Years of British Cinema*, ed. Charles Barr (London: British Film Institute, 1986), 2.

31. Christopher Tookey, "A Fright to Remember," *Daily Mail* (London), 23 January 1998, 44.

32. Auberon Waugh, "Way of the World: Kill the Toffs," *Daily Telegraph* (London), 11 March 1998, 25.

33. It was reported in the press that First Officer Murdoch's family, insulted by the film's portrayal of him, demanded and received a written apology from Twentieth Century Fox and Paramount.

34. We do not wish to give the impression that the film *Titanic* "awoke" the press to the value of the real event in the city's history. References to the city's link with the liner and the sinking can be found throughout the local press archives since the time of the disaster.

35. "*Titanic* Survivor Set to Boycott New Film," *Daily Echo* (Southampton, England), 13 January 1998, 10.

36. "Port's Icy Welcome for *Titanic* Launch." This article apparently originated with reports solicited from staff at the box office of Harbour Lights and Odeon Leisure World that it was possible to find empty seats during showings of the film in its first week's run. After discussing this article with people at Twentieth Century Fox, Rod Varley, the director of Harbour Lights, wrote to David Lee, the *Mirror*'s news editor, on 27 January for an explanation and retraction as it was clearly misinformed. Lee wrote back on 29 January explaining that they had acquired the story from the Press Association News Agency, which stood by the story.

37. "*Titanic* Town," *Screen International*, 30 January–5 February 1998, 28.

38. This information comes from an interview with the director of Harbour Lights, Rod Varley.

39. Raphael Samuel, *Theatres of Memory* (London: Verso, 1994), 8.

40. "The Luckiest Escape of All," *Daily Echo* (Southampton, England), 16 January 1998, 27.

41. The Cinema Advertising Association, CAA/Caviar. The fieldwork carried out by CAA showed that the percentage of people over the age of twenty-five who viewed the film in the first month of release was 61 percent, with those over the age of forty-five comprising 25 percent of the overall attendance.

42. Thomas Elsaesser, "Subject Positions, Speaking Positions; From Holocaust, Our Hitler, and Heimat to *Shoah* and *Schindler's List*," in *The Persistence of History, Cinema Television, and the Modern Event*, ed. Vivian Sobchack (New York: Routledge, 1996), 166.

43. Barbara Klinger, *Melodrama and Meaning; History, Culture, and the Films of Douglas Sirk* (Bloomington: Indiana University Press, 1994), 170.

44. This film was rated as a "12" in Britain; that is, the minimum age of entry was twelve years old. However, four of the girls were only nine and had lied about their age at the cinema.

45. Vicky Ward and Jonathan Margolis, "The Great Leonardo Debate," *Daily Mail* (London), 20 March 1998, 40.

46. Suzanne Moore, "Getting to Grips with Leo," *Independent* (London), 21 March 1998, 19.

47. *Independent* (London), 16 March 1998, 17.

48. Geoff Brown, "Tragedy Replayed as Epic Spectacle," *Times* (London), 22 January 1998, 33.

Notes on Contributors

Matthew Bernstein teaches film studies at Emory University. He is the author of *Walter Wanger: Hollywood Independent* (University of California Press, 1994; to be published in paperback by the University of Minnesota Press in 2000) and co-editor with Gaylyn Studlar, of *Visions of the East: Orientalism in Film* (Rutgers University Press, 1997). His essays have appeared in *Film Criticism*, *Film Quarterly*, *Griffithiana*, the *Velvet Light Trap*, and *Wide Angle*. He is currently co-editing anthologies on John Ford westerns and movie censorship, as well as co-authoring a history of movie culture in Atlanta, Georgia, which is supported by a National Endowment for the Humanities research grant.

Mike Hammond lectures in film studies in the English Department at the University of Southampton. He is presently working on a study of the reception of cinema in Britain during the First World War.

Susan Hunt is a faculty associate at Glendale College. She was a film columnist for the *Phoenix Gazette* and is currently writing a book on masculinity and the representation of the mind/body split in film and popular culture. Her most recent publication is an article on the changing representations of the male body in 1970s and 1990s films in the spring 1999 issue of *Framework*.

Alexandra Keller has a Ph.D. in cinema studies from New York University. Her essays have appeared in the *Drama Review* and the anthology *Cinema and the Invention of Modern Life* (University of California Press, 1995). She currently teaches at Vassar College.

Peter Krämer is a lecturer in film studies at the University of East Anglia (UK). His essays on aspects of American film history have been published in *Theatre History Studies*, the *Velvet Light Trap*, *Screen*, and a number of edited collections. He is currently working on a collection of essays on film acting, jointly edited with Alan Lovell, and on a study of contemporary Hollywood cinema.

Martti Lahti holds a tenured lectureship at the University of Lapland, Finland, and is currently finishing his dissertation, entitled "White Disease: Whiteness, Masculinity, and the Cinematic Body," at the University of Iowa. He has edited several books and published numerous articles. His latest publications include an edited collection of essays on new technologies and an article on Tom of Finland and masculinity.

Peter Lehman is a professor in the Interdisciplinary Humanities Program and the Hispanic Research Center at Arizona State University. He is the author of numerous books, including *Running Scared: Masculinity and the Representation of the Male Body* (Temple University Press, 1993), and editor of *Defining Cinema* (Rutgers University Press, 1997). He is a former president of the Society for Cinema Studies.

Anne Massey is a professor of design history and dean of the media arts faculty at Southampton Institute. She has published widely on the relationship between high culture, modernism, and popular culture, including *The Independent Group: Modernism and Mass Culture in Britain, 1945–59* (Manchester University Press, 1995) and *Romancing Hollywood: The Reception of Glamour* (Millais Gallery, 1997).

Adrienne Munich, professor of English and women's studies at the State University of New York at Stony Brook, is the author of *Andromeda's Chains* (Columbia University Press, 1989) and *Queen Victoria's Secrets* (Columbia University Press, 1996) and co-editor of collections on women and war, on Queen Victoria, and on Robert Browning. She co-edits the journal *Victorian Literature and Culture*. She is currently working on a project on the cultural uses of diamonds in the nineteenth and twentieth centuries.

Melanie Nash, a Ph.D. candidate in film studies at the University of Iowa, is finishing her dissertation on cultural femininity and three female MGM stars (Joan Crawford, Greta Garbo, and Norma Shearer) during the transition to the sound period. Her recent projects include an article on the gendered reception and Internet fandom of Beavis and Butt-head in the spring 1999 issue of the *Velvet Light Trap*.

Diane Negra is an assistant professor and graduate adviser in the Department of Radio, TV, and Film at the University of North Texas, where she teaches courses in critical and cultural studies of film and television. Her work has appeared in a number of anthologies and journals. She is author of *Off-White Hollywood: American Culture and Ethnic Female Stardom* (Routledge, forthcoming), a study of the dynamics of white ethnicity, assimilation, and celebrity from the silent era to the present.

Laurie Ouellette is an assistant professor in the Department of Journalism and

Mass Media at Rutgers University, where she teaches courses in media studies. She received her doctorate in communication from the University of Massachusetts, Amherst, with a concentration in media and cultural studies. Her work focuses on cultural theory, media representations, and the social construction of class and gender identities. She has published articles in the *Velvet Light Trap, Cultural Studies*, and *Afterimage*, and in several anthologies, including *Transmission: Toward a Post-Television Culture* (Sage, 1995) and *In The Eye of the Beholder: Critical Perspectives in Popular Film and Television* (Bowling Green, 1997). She has an article forthcoming in *Media, Culture, and Society*.

Kevin S. Sandler is the editor of *Reading the Rabbit: Explorations in Warner Bros. Animation* (Rutgers University Press, 1997) and author of articles that have appeared in *Hitchcock Annual* and *Animation Journal*. He is a graduate of the University of Michigan and recently completed his dissertation on British and U.S. technologies of film censorship at Sheffield Hallam University in England.

Jeff Smith is an assistant professor of film studies in the Performing Arts Department of Washington University and the author of *The Sounds of Commerce: Marketing Popular Film Music* (Columbia University Press, 1998). He has also published essays in the *Velvet Light Trap, Cinema Journal, Film Quarterly*, and in several forthcoming anthologies.

Vivian Sobchack is associate dean and professor of film and television studies at the UCLA School of Theater, Film, and Television. Her work focuses on film and cultural theory and its intersections with philosophy and historiography, and her books include *Screening Space: The American Science Fiction Film* (Rutgers University Press, 1997), *The Address of the Eye: A Phenomenology of Film Experience* (Princeton University Press, 1993), and an edited anthology, *The Persistence of History: Cinema, Television, and the Modern Event* (Routledge, 1996). She is currently completing a collection of her own essays, entitled *Carnal Thoughts: Bodies, Texts, Scenes, and Screens*.

Maura Spiegel teaches literature and film at Columbia University and Barnard College. She recently published with Richard Tristman *The Grim Reader: Writings on Death, Dying, and Living On* (Anchor Doubleday, 1997).

Julian Stringer has degrees in film studies from the University of North London (B.A.) and Indiana University-Bloomington (M.A.), and is currently writing a Ph.D. dissertation on the cultural politics of film festivals at Indiana University. His articles appear in *Asian Cinema, Cineaction, Film Quarterly, Millennium Film Journal, Popular Music*, and *Screen*, as well as the anthologies *Asian American Screen Cultures* (Temple University Press, 1999), *Encyclopedia of Chinese Film* (Routledge, 1998), *Mythologies of Violence in Postmodern Media* (Wayne State University Press, 1999), *The Road Movie Book* (Routledge, 1997), and *Jack Nicholson: Movie Top Ten* (Creation, forthcoming).

Gaylyn Studlar is the director of the Program in Film and Video Studies and professor of film and English language and literature at the University of Michigan, Ann Arbor. She is the author of *This Mad Masquerade: Stardom and Masculinity in the Jazz Age* (Columbia University Press, 1996) and *In the Realm of Pleasure: Von Sternberg, Dietrich, and the Masochistic Aesthetic* (University of Illinois Press, 1988), and co-editor of three anthologies, with one forthcoming on John Ford's westerns. She is currently working on a social history of American women and Hollywood cinema.

Katherine Vlesmas completed her master's degree in the Department of Media Arts at the University of Arizona. Her areas of concentration were political economy and gender studies. She is currently working in the media industry in New York City.

Justin Wyatt is an associate professor of media studies at the University of Arizona. His work on media economics and history has been published in *Sight and Sound*, *Wide Angle*, the *Velvet Light Trap*, *Cinema Journal*, and various anthologies. He is the author of *High Concept: Movies and Marketing in Hollywood* (University of Texas Press, 1994) and *Poison* (Flicks Books, 1998). He is series editor for "Commerce and Mass Culture" at the University of Minnesota Press and a member of the executive council of the Society for Cinema Studies.

NOTES

Farewell My Concubine (1993), 209
Fat Man and Little Boy (1989), 44*n*52
Fatal Attraction (1987), 62*n*19
Fifth Element, The (1997), 153*n*16
Flashdance (1983), 205
Flatliners (1990), 205
Foolish Wives (1922), 30, 43*n*2
Foote, Kenneth E., 228
Ford, John, 143
Forrest Gump (1994), 124, 130*n*55, 149
Four Weddings and a Funeral (1994), 137
Friedkin, William, 43*n*11
Full Monty, The (1997), 137, 246

Gable, Clark, 21, 103
Garber, Victor, 20
Ghost (1990), 124, 130*n*55
Godfather, The (1972), 139
Godzilla (1998), 140, 141, 233
Goldberg, Danny, 49
Goldfinger (1964), 125
Gone With the Wind (1939), 15, 23, 24,
    26*n*7, 30, 60, 64, 72, 109, 125, 133,
    140, 197
Good Will Hunting (1997), 137, 174
Goodman, Ellen, 102–104
Goodman, Paul, 247
Graduate, The (1967), 49
Gramsci, Antonio, 186*n*5
Grant, Cary, 91, 103
Grapes, The (pub), 251, *252*
Grease (1978), 43*n*10, 49
Great Expectations (1998), 174
Gremlins (1984), 62*n*19
Griffith, D. W., 24, 64
Growing Pains (TV series), 67–68
Guggenheim, Benjamin, 98

Halloween (1978), 128*n*24
Hamilton, Linda, 99, 100, 129*n*35, 145,
    154*n*33
Hammond, Mike, 12
Harris, Ed, 149
Hays, Will, 209
Heaven's Gate (1980), 31, *33,* 35, 37,
    43*n*11, 133, 139
Hebdige, Dick, 243
Henreid, Paul, 103
heritage cycle. *See* British heritage films

High Noon (1952), 48, 61*n*12
Higson, Andrew, 208, 219*n*3
Hindenburg, The (1975), 231
His Girl Friday (1940), 113
History Is Made at Night (1937), 13*n*2
Hitchcock, Alfred, 143, 209
Hobsbawm, Eric, 234, 241, 263*n*5
Hoggart, Richard, 244
Home Alone (1990), 62*n*19, 124
Hope Diamond, 158–159, 164, 167*n*3
Hope Floats (1998), 141
Horner, James, and musical score of
    Titanic, 8, 46, 50, 51, 55, 56, 59, 60
Hosono, Masabumi, 217–218
Howards End (1992), 206, *207,* 208, 211
Hunger, The (1983), 209
Hunt, Susan, 8–9, 13
Hurd, Gale Anne, 110, 127*n*13, 129*n*33
Hurricane, The (1937), 231

I Survived a Disaster (TV special), 232
In Nacht und Eis (1943), 13*n*2
In Old Chicago (1938), 231
Independence Day (1996), 47, 136; box
    office, 62*n*19, 83*n*5, 113, 123, 124,
    130*n*55, 250; and survival motif, 220,
    228, 233
Indiana Jones and the Last Crusade
    (1989), 44*n*52, 130*n*55
Ismay, Bruce J., 98, 102, 105, 177, 225,
    262*n*3

J. Peterman Company, *157,* 164
Jaws (1975), 36, 43*n*10, 83*n*5, 110, 124,
    140
Jegeus, Tomas, 36
Jennings, Will, 8
Jerry McGuire (1996), 54
JFK (1991), 147, 148
Juggernaut (1974), 231
Jurassic Park (1993), 38, 39, 47, 62*n*19,
    83*n*5, 109, 124, 130*n*55, 136

Kaplan, Cora, 244
Kauffmann, Stanley, 10, 27*n*9
Keller, Alexandra, 9, 10
Kermode, Frank, 234
King, Larry, 249
Klein, Michael, 1, 13*n*1

Titanic